Man & Music

ANTIQUITY
AND THE
MIDDLE AGES

Man & Music

ANTIQUITY
AND THE
MIDDLE AGES

From Ancient Greece to the 15th century

EDITED BY JAMES McKINNON

M

First published in the United Kingdom 1990 by
The Macmillan Press Limited
Houndmills, Basingstoke, Hampshire RG21 2XS
and London

Associated companies in Auckland, Delhi, Dublin, Gaborone,
Hamburg, Harare, Hong Kong, Johannesburg, Kuala Lumpur,
Lagos, Manzini, Melbourne, Mexico City, Nairobi, New York,
Singapore and Tokyo.

ISBN 0-333-51040-2 (hardback)
ISBN 0-333-53004-7 (paperback)

British Library Cataloguing in Publication Data
Man and music. – (A social history)
    Vol. 1, Ancient and medieval.
    1. Music to 1985
    I. McKinnon, Jim II. Series
    780′.9

Typeset by Glyn Davies, Cambridge
Printed in Hong Kong

Contents

Illustration
Acknowledgments

The publishers would like to thank the following institutions and individuals who have kindly provided material for use in this book.

Mansell Collection, London/Alinari, Florence: 1, 3, 23, 25, 75, 81; Rheinisches Landesmuseum, Trier: 2; Musée Condéé, Chantilly (65/1284, ff.71v, 1v, 158r)/Giraudon, Paris: 5, 11, 12; Bibliothèque Nationale, Paris: 6 (lat.1, f.215v), 13 (fonds.fr.12574, f.181v), 29, 33 (lat.1141, f.3r), 43 (lat.7211, f.9v), 57 (Ancien Gaignières 2896, fr.22297, no.31), 64 (fr.146, f.34r), 66 (fr.1586, f.30v), 67 (fr.9221, f.16r), 68 (fr.1584, f.D), 70 (fr.159, f.277v), 71 (fr.616, f.13r), 78 (Chantilly 1047, f.11v), 84 (fr.12476, f.98r); photo Ann Münchow, Aachen: 7; photo James Austin, Cambridge: 8, 9; Courtauld Institute of Art, London: 10, 55; Staatliche Museen Preussischer Kulturbesitz, West Berlin: 14 (Kupferstichkabinett, 78.D.5, f.59r), 21 (Antikenmuseum); Archaeological Museum, Heraklion/Deutsches Archäologisches Institut, Athens: 15; Trustees of the British Museum, London: 16, 19; Museum of Fine Arts, Boston (John Michael Rodocanachi Fund): 17; Museo Nazionale (Villa Giulia), Rome/Mansell Collection, London/ Alinari, Florence: 18; Antikenmuseum, Basle (Sammlung Ludwig): 20; National Archaeological Museum, Athens: 22; photo Antonello Perissinotto, Padua: 24; Staatsbibliothek, Bamberg: 26 (Msc.class.5, f.9v), 37 (Msc.lit.6, f.7r); Biblioteca Apostolica Vaticana, Rome (Reg.lat.316, f.4r): 27; Stiftsbibliothek, St Gall (359, f.27r): 28; Oxford Illustrators: 30, 41, 56, 59, 62, 69; photo Josephine Powell, Rome: 31; Fitzwilliam Museum, Cambridge: 32; Gabinetto Comunale delle Stampe, Rome: 34; Musée du Louvre/Réunion des Musées Nationaux, Paris: 35; Bodleian Library, Oxford: 36 (lat.liturg.f.5, ff.3v, 4v), 80 (Douce 195, f.150v); British Library, London: 38 (Cotton Caligula A.XIV, ff.3v–4r), 39 (Egerton 2615, f.50v), 42 (Additional 36881, ff.13v–14r), 52 (Egerton 1151, f.47r), 53 (Egerton 3307, f.72v), 54 (Cotton Domit.A.XVII, f.122v), 72 (Additional 12228, f.222v), 82 (Harley 4425, f.12v); Musée Nicéphore Niepce, Challon-sur-Saône/photo Combier: 40; Herzog August Bibliothek, Wolfenbüttel (Cod.Gud.lat.8.334); Bibliothèque Municipale, Chartres: 45; Verlag Peter Lang AG, Berne, from Paléographie Musicale, 1st ser., xvii (1958): 46; Bildarchiv Foto Marburg: 47; Bibliothèque Interuniversitaire, Montpellier (H.196, f.350r): 48; Pierpont Morgan Library, New York: 49 (M.521r), 61 (M.638, f.17r); President and Fellows of Corpus Christi College, Oxford (CCC.489, f.9iv): 50; Governing Body, Christ Church, Oxford (92, f.43r): 51; photo Jean Dieuzaide, Toulouse: 58; photo Christian Fourcade, Aix-en-Provence: 63; Musée des Arts Décoratifs, Paris: 65; Biblioteca Medicea Laurenziana, Florence (87, ff.25v, 121v): 73, 77; Landesbibliothek, Fulda (D.23, f.302r): 74; Rosgarten Museum, Konstanz: 79; Musée de Versailles/ Réunion des Musées Nationaux: 83; Universitätsbibliothek, Innsbruck (B.1432): 85; National Széchényi Library, Budapest (cod.lat.424, f.41r); 86; National Gallery of Art, Washington, DC (Samuel H. Kress Collection): 87.

Abbreviations

AcM	*Acta musicologica*
AMw	*Archiv für Musikwissenschaft*
AMP	Antiquitates musicae in Polonia
AnnM	*Annales musicologiques*
CMM	Corpus mensurabilis musicae
CS	E. de Coussemaker: *Scriptorum de musica medii aevi nova series* (Paris, 1864–76/*R*1963)
CSM	Corpus scriptorum de musica
DTÖ	Denkmäler der Tonkunst in Österreich
EDM	Das Erbe deutscher Musik
EECM	Early English Church Music
EM	*Early Music*
EMH	*Early Music History*
Grove 6	*The New Grove Dictionary of Music and Musicians*
JAMS	*Journal of the American Musicological Society*
JM	*Journal of Musicology*
JMT	*Journal of Music Theory*
JPMMS	*Journal of the Plainsong and Medieval Music Society*
JRME	*Journal of Research in Music Education*
KJb	*Kirchenmusikalisches Jahrbuch*
MB	Musica britannica
MD	*Musica disciplina*
Mf	*Die Musikforschung*
ML	*Music and Letters*
MMA	*Miscellanea musicologica*
MQ	*Musical Quarterly*
MSD	Musicological Studies and Documents, ed. A. Carapetyan (Rome, 1951–)
NOHM	*The New Oxford History of Music*, ed. E. Wellesz, J. A. Westrup and G. Abraham (London, 1954–)
NRMI	*Nuova rivista musicale italiana*
PalMus	Paléographie musicale (Solesmes, 1889–)
PMFC	Polyphonic Music of the Fourteenth Century
PRMA	*Proceedings of the Royal Musical Association*
RIM	*Rivista italiana di musicologia*
RISM	*Répertoire international des sources musicales*
RMS	Renaissance Manuscript Studies
SMM	Summa musicae medii aevi
TVNM	*Tijdschrift van de Vereniging voor Nederlandse muziekgeschiedenis*

Preface

The *Man and Music* series of books – eight in number, chronologically organized – were originally conceived in conjunction with the television programmes of the same name, of which the first was shown by Channel 4 in 1986 and distributed worldwide by Granada Television International. These programmes were designed to examine the development of music in particular places during particular periods in the history of Western civilization.

The books have the same objective. Each is designed to cover a segment of Western musical history; the breaks between them are planned to correspond with significant historical junctures. Since historical junctures, or indeed junctures in stylistic change, rarely happen with the neat simultaneity that the historian's or the editor's orderly mind might wish for, most volumes have 'ragged' ends and beginnings: for example, the Renaissance volume terminates, in Italy, in the 1570s and 80s, but continues well into the 17th century in parts of northern Europe.

These books do not, however make up a history of music in the traditional sense. The reader will not find technical, stylistic discussion in them; anyone wanting to trace the detailed development of the texture of the madrigal or the rise and fall of sonata form should look elsewhere. Rather, it is the intention in these volumes to show in what context, and as a result of what forces – social, cultural, intellectual – the madrigal or sonata form came into being and took its particular shape. The intention is to view musical history not a series of developments in some hermetic world of its own but rather as a series of responses to social, economic and political circumstances and to religious and intellectual stimuli. We want to explain not simply *what* happened, but *why* it happened, and why it happened when and where it did.

We have chosen to follow what might be called a geographical, or perhaps a topographical, approach: to focus, in each chapter, on a particular place and to examine its music in the light of its particular situation. Thus, in most of these volumes, the chapters – once past the introductory one, contributed by the volume editor – are each devoted to a city or a region. This system has inevitably needed some modification when dealing with very early or very recent times, for reasons (opposite ones, of course) to do with communication and cultural spread.

These books do not attempt to treat musical history comprehensively. Their editors have chosen for discussion the musical centres that they see as the most significant and the most interesting; many lesser ones inevitably escape individual discussion, though the patterns of their musical life may be discernible by analogy with others or may be separately referred to in the opening, editorial chapter. We hope, however, that a new kind of picture of musical history may begin to emerge from these volumes, and that this picture may be more accessible to the general reader, responsive to music but untrained in its techniques, than others arising from more traditional approaches. In spite of the large number of lovers of music, musical histories have never enjoyed the appeal to a broad, intelligent general readership in the way that histories of art, architecture or literature have done: these books represent an attempt to reach such a readership and explain music in terms that may quicken their interest.

The television programmes and books were initially planned in close collaboration with Sir Denis Forman, then Chairman of Granada Television International. The approach was worked out in more detail with several of the volume editors, among whom I am particularly grateful to Iain Fenlon for the time he has generously given to discussion of the problems raised by this approach to musical history, and also to Alexander Ringer and James McKinnon for their valuable advice and support. Discussion with Bamber Gascoigne and Tony Cash, in the course of the making of the initial television programmes, also proved of value. I am grateful to Celia Thomson for drafting the chronologies that appear in each volume and to Elisabeth Agate for her invaluable work as picture editor in bringing the volumes to visual life.

London, 1990   STANLEY SADIE

Chapter I

Early Western Civilization

JAMES McKINNON

THE HEBRAIC AND HELLENIC HERITAGE, 750 BC TO AD 410

If pressed to date the beginnings of Western civilization, one could do worse than to suggest 750 BC; very close to that year the shepherd Amos of Tekoa, first of the recorded Old Testament prophets, denounced the ruling classes of Israel with inspired eloquence. He proclaimed a new ideal of social justice and a new conception of God; the latter was not yet the pure monotheism of Deutero-Isaiah, but already it portrayed a Jehovah who exercised power beyond national boundaries and who was more concerned with righteousness than tribal honour. These are clearly themes of the most basic importance to the ethical and religious thinking of the West; what relevance they or any other aspect of Amos's teaching might have to music will be considered later, after we turn to Greece in search of some figure to share with Amos the role of Western civilization's honorary founder.

If the capacity for abstract thought is the most singular Hellenic contribution to Western civilization, then we need look no further than Thales, the 'father of philosophy', who flourished in the prosperous Ionian city of Miletus during the earlier part of the sixth century BC. He held that the primary stuff of all things was water, a dubious notion to be sure, and one that his younger fellow-citizen Anaximander pointedly refuted. 'It is neither water nor any other of the so-called elements', he maintained, 'but a nature different from them and infinite, from which arise all the heavens and the worlds.' But what Thales and Anaximander had in common was more important than their differences. They were the first to grapple with the most basic of all philosophical questions, that of the One and the Many; they sought generalized laws or principles to explain in a rational way the confusing diversity of nature and of human experience. The relevance of this to music is more direct and obvious than that of the ideas of the Hebrew prophets; the Greek penchant for abstract thought gave rise eventually to music theory, a discipline that exerts a profound influence upon Western music, at times positive and at times negative. It was at its most negative,

1

1. The Theatre of Dionysus, Athens (342–26 BC), the site of annual festivals at which classical dramas were performed

perhaps, during the later centuries of classical antiquity. Although to speak of a negative influence upon music at this time does not mean that it exercised a direct influence upon music, somehow rendering it less good in itself; rather it diverted attention from real music to intellectual constructs with musical subject matter, depriving real music of cultural respectability in the process. But there is much more to the problematical status of music in late antiquity than this, and to gain some insight into the factors that affected it, one should turn to music at Athens in the time of Plato, who lived from about 428 to 347 BC, nearly two centuries later than Thales.

Greek music in the centuries before Plato was not inhibited by musical theory or any other intellectualist considerations, as Andrew Barker in Chapter II makes clear. It had a rich history that culminated in the century of Plato's birth, the so-called 'classical period', the 'golden age' of Pericles, the great Athenian statesman who died within months of Plato's birth. For much of this century Athens was the dominant commercial and political force in the Mediterranean basin. Alongside its temporary ally Sparta it had repulsed the Persian threat, and in the ensuing years its citizenry under enlightened leadership engaged in an outpouring of artistic and literary creation seldom if ever to be equalled in Western civilization. The Acropolis was topped with buildings like the Parthenon, the Propylaea and the Erechtheum, while the adjoining courts were adorned with statuary by sculptors such as

Phidias. Philosophy continued its advance beyond the primitivism of Thales with Anaxagoras' theory of the *nous* and the pragmatism of the Sophists. In literature there were the choral odes of Pindar and Bacchylides and above all the three sublime tragedians, Aeschylus, Sophocles and Euripides and the comedian Aristophanes. Their plays were performed at the great annual religious festivals in the theatre of Dionysus, carved from the south slope of the Acropolis.

Music cannot be considered a lesser art at this time; indeed poetry, drama and music are by and large coterminous. The Greek word 'mousike' embraces not only the tonal phenomenon but also the text that is set and even the accompanying dance. The odes of Pindar and Bacchylides were sung and danced by Athenian choruses, and the drama itself was choral in origin with individual spoken parts added at a later stage; it was thought of as a musical genre still in the time of Plato's younger contemporary Aristophanes (?*c*450–385). His comedy *The Frogs*, written in 405, just one year after the death of Euripides, centres on a musical contest between Euripides and the earlier Aeschylus (*d* 456). Aristophanes portrays the god Dionysus, dissatisfied with post-Euripidean musical efforts, journeying to Hades to arrange the competition between the two dramatists which Aeschylus wins with his solemn traditional choruses over the more fashionable lyrical complexities of Euripides.

It is important to note that the Athenian chorus was made up of the citizenry, not professionals. Athenian freemen were given formal education in music so that they could serve both as chorus members and as a discriminating audience for the frequent dramatic presentations. The theatre, however, was by no means the only form of Athenian musical activity. There were competitions at the festivals involving solo lyrics accompanied by kithara and solo aulos music that strove for programmatic effect; at the same contests gymnasts were accompanied by the aulos. Music was regularly employed at meals, whether it be the aulos-girl accompanying singers of *skolia* at the symposium or schoolboys showing off snatches of Homer they had learnt at school. And certainly there must have been numerous other occasions of informal music-making in a population that was so carefully schooled in music and so frequently exposed to musical entertainment and edification.

Aristophanes' preference for the song of Aeschylus over that of Euripides marks him as a conservative in a time of musical innovation. His conservatism is generally considered to be typical of one with agrarian roots and not particularly ideological in character. Plato's more intense conservatism, on the other hand, had a complex social, political and philosophical background. He was himself a consummate artist in prose and clearly a critic of singular musical sensitivity, but his views on music and art, once stripped of their beguiling expression, strike the modern observer as crudely reactionary. They are expounded

3

throughout his many dialogues, but most especially in the passages concerning education from his two utopian prescriptions, the earlier *Republic* and the later *Laws*. Indeed, it might be said that it is in the *Republic* where he is beguiling and in the *Laws* where he is crude.

Plato was an impressionable youth at a time when the glories of Periclean Athens were a recent memory; in fact, much that was splendid was still in progress. He heard Sophocles, Euripides and Aristophanes in the flesh, and witnessed the building of the Erechtheum. But at the same time Athens was at war with Sparta, a ruinous struggle that ended in ignominious defeat in 404, when Plato was about 25 years old. Athens recovered to a considerable extent from the catastrophe, enjoying several decades of relative prosperity and cultural vitality during the time of Aristotle, but Plato did not. His bitter disappointment clouded his political and social views for the rest of his life. Like other members of the aristocratic party, he tended to blame Athens's problems on its democratic institutions and conversely to admire the authoritarian nature of Spartan society. Again it could be said that the *Republic* is a portrait of Sparta disguised, and the *Laws* of Sparta unveiled.

It is in any case the traditional Homeric aristocratic educational ideal that Plato advocates for his utopian state. A youth acquires basic literacy, to be sure, but the emphasis is upon the twin skills of gymnastics and music; he must be strong and brave in war yet not uncouth – he should be able to sing passably while accompanying himself in simple fashion upon the lyre. Complicated instruments like the aulos and the kithara have their place in the cult and ceremonial music of the state, but they are to be played by professionals, not by the well-born amateur who confines his efforts to the more refined lyre. One sees in this aristocratic bias against professionalism the same disdain that Plato has Socrates express towards the Sophists, who accepted fees to teach students marketable forensic skills. Indeed, it is historically legitimate to see in this antithesis the roots of that existing between the ideal of a liberal arts college and a business school, between a gentleman and a tradesman. The liberal arts are those pursued by a man who is free (*liber*), while the mechanical and commercial arts are pursued by one constrained by vocational exigencies. The idea is expressed even more explicitly by Plato's student Aristotle in his own utopian document, the *Politics*: 'No man can practise virtue who is living the life of a mechanic or labourer'. The liberal arts were not yet categorized in the time of Plato as they would be in late antiquity, when they come to be grouped into a set of three language arts (grammar, rhetoric and dialectic) and a set of four mathematical arts (arithmetic, geometry, astronomy and music); but if they had been, music might very well have been looked upon as something closer to language than to mathematics. This shift in the intellectual's conception of music from an artistic activity to a numerical science is allied to the baleful influence of musical theory referred to above.

Plato was also particular about the character of the music to which the youth of his ideal society would be exposed. They ought to learn the Dorian strain ('harmonia' is his term) and the Phrygian, the former imparting courage and the latter thoughtfulness, but must not be exposed to the enervating and lugubrious Lydian and Ionian modes. We have here the classic statement of the so-called 'ethos' doctrine, the belief that different kinds of music have a direct working upon the character of the listener. It is a doctrine that, while never entirely absent from the musical thought of Western civilization, has its most pronounced effect in late antiquity. It took the exaggerated form then of a belief that a musical scale, by the very arrangement of its pitches, had an effect upon human behaviour that the modern observer would have to classify as magical. Still, the authentic Platonic notion of musical ethos is strong enough by our standards. For the Greeks all art was to a great extent mimetic, and for Plato music in particular bore within itself images of virtue and vice that 'find their way to the inmost soul and take strong hold upon it'.

For all the influence that Plato's educational and ethical ideas about music have had upon subsequent musical thought, an even greater influence was wrought by an aspect of his philosophy that was only indirectly related to music. This is the most basic of all Platonic positions, his famous doctrine of ideas. For him reality was not that which we observe with our senses, but rather ideas existing external and immutable, of which natural objects are but faint reflections. The doctrine is best understood by what seems a *reductio ad absurdum*, but is Plato's own example: the beds we see and feel are but imperfect copies of the ideal bed 'existing in nature, which is made by God'. In this way of thinking, art, in particular visual art, occupies a low place in the hierarchy of value; a picture of some object exists at two removes from reality. It is an imitation of an imitation. This denial of reality, which moderns can only view as a rejection of the healthy Greek naturalism that characterized much of the sixth and fifth centuries, had a profound effect upon every aspect of thought and culture. In music it is that which underlies the contempt for musical practice and the fixation upon musical theory that characterizes late antiquity. Plato, of course, is not solely responsible for it. There were other movements before and after his time, such as Orphism, Pythagoreanism and dualistic Eastern religions, that fostered a retreat from reality, but it was Plato's beguiling idealism that had the most direct effect upon the intellectuals of subsequent centuries.

Still, we must distinguish between Plato's influence and his own everyday concerns. Unlike the thinkers of late antiquity he was responding directly to the music of his time, which, it is true, he did not

2. *Hydraulic organ and cornu (horn), probably at a circus: detail of a Roman mosaic (AD 230–40) at Nennig-bei-Trier*

much care for. He complained especially about the contemporary tendency to mix musical styles and genres: dirges with hymns, paeans with dithyrambs, and the imitation of the versatile aulos by a kithara with an expanded number of strings. He was disturbed by the popularity of contemporary musicians like Timotheus and Philoxenus; to him the appeal of their virtuosity was demagogic: they entertained rather than edified. To us, could we hear what was happening, it might have sounded rather more like inevitable progress; Barker (p.63) refers to Plato's pronouncements as 'pious twaddle', pointing out that change, innovation and competition were long since part of the Greek musical tradition. And it is true that Plato's strictures fell by and large upon deaf ears in his time; the compositions of Timotheus and Philoxenus became Greek classics, and Aristotle was considerably less restrictive than his former mentor in his attitudes towards what was musically acceptable. Yet Plato's views are at least symptomatic of a growing pessimism about everyday musical culture that eventually would come to characterize the educated observer of later Hellenistic and Roman times.

Their views aside, what are we ourselves to think of the music of late antiquity? To make the question just slightly less unmanageable, we might focus upon Roman music, leaving out of consideration the even more complex case of Hellenistic music. Until very recent times musical historians have tended to dismiss Roman music as unworthy of serious study; they took their cue from the general academic prejudice in favour of classical Greece and the corollary attitude that everything coming after it must be looked upon as decadent. If nothing else, they spared themselves an immense scholarly task. In his *Musica romana*, Günther Wille quotes no fewer than 4000 passages from ancient sources that describe contemporary Roman music. Wille is perhaps the foremost among a small group of historians who seek to rehabilitate Roman music. They may not yet have achieved a satisfactory chronology of the subject, but certainly they have done much to establish the proposition that music was a rich and constant presence in Roman life.

As in Greek musical life, the theatre was a venue of central importance. The comedies of Plautus (*d* 184 BC) and Terence (*d* 159 BC) featured tibia preludes and interludes (the tibia was the Roman equivalent of the aulos) and instrumentally accompanied songs and dances. In the pantomime professional actors and musicians presented a series of scenes on traditional and mythological themes that regularly employed solo and choral singing, instrumental music and dance. These performers, referred to collectively as *pantomimi*, had their more popular counterparts in the *mimi*, ancestors of the medieval *jongleurs*, who eschewed the paraphernalia of classical theatre like masks, and staged humorous and sentimental scenes from everyday life or borrowed from comedies, generally with music playing a prominent part. In addition to theatrical music there is evidence that at least some of the lyric poetry of figures like Virgil, Catullus and Horace was set to music. At the same time there is abundant testimony to song in everyday life – rowing, reaping and weaving songs, table songs, songs of mourning, lullabies, wedding songs, love songs and even satirical songs.

Then there is of course Roman military music, with its systematic usage of an interesting variety of brass instruments, some of which date back to the Etruscans. Not only military instruments, incidentally, but instruments of every sort enjoyed an impressive technical development at Rome. To cite just one, the Alexandrian hydraulis, or water organ (fig.2), functioned both as a powerful instigator of the crowd at the circus and a delicate chamber instrument, like that recovered at Aquicum (present-day Budapest), with a keyboard action not equalled again in its efficiency until the late Middle Ages. Cult music was regularly present in Roman life also, ranging from elaborate festival performances to the obligatory tibia that accompanied every sacrificial act, whether it involved the slaughtering of an animal (fig.3) or a simple incense offering. Roman cult musicians were organized into guilds (as were their theatrical counterparts), and at an important annual ceremony, the *tubilustrium*, the sacral trumpets were solemnly blessed.

The anecdotal evidence for Roman musical practice is virtually inexhaustible; suffice it to mention soft music being played during an evening meal at Pliny's villa; loud trumpet playing at a party given by Trimalchio; instances of extravagant fees for popular musicians; and of course the musical exploits of emperors, among whom Nero is only the best known. The case has been made, I believe, that the Romans were not unmusical; on the contrary, music-making appears to have been more pervasive in Roman society than in that of many other advanced cultures. But the question remains: what are we to think of it from the aspect of musical worth? The answer is bound to be disappointing; not having been present, and not possessing Roman ears with which to hear it if we had been, we can never know. Indeed, we are deprived of even the graphic representation of it that some regularly employed system of musical notation would grant us. We can only say on the one hand, that while it seems anachronistic for the revisionist partisans of Roman music to propose analogies with the European classical music of recent centuries (claiming, for example, as one historian has, that accompanied Roman lyrics are the aesthetic equivalent of Schubert lieder), it seems equally fatuous on the other hand to maintain that all Roman music was vulgar and meretricious. It defies common sense that among so many individuals, devoting their lives to music in such varied circumstances over so long a period of time, there would not have been many of great talent, even genius, and that they would not have afforded sensitive listeners moments of the most refined musical pleasure – even if in environments generally less conducive to an elevated response than, say, the eighteenth-century court or the nineteenth-century concert hall.

Still, we are left guessing about the real nature of the Roman musical experience, and this is especially the case because of the jaundiced views of contemporaries. Moralizing pagan philosophers like Seneca,

3. *Tibia player at the sacrifice of a bull: detail of a relief on a Roman sarcophagus (mid-2nd century AD)*

Juvenal and Tacitus – let alone their Christian counterparts – chose to emphasize what was tawdry in Roman musical life, while academicians, dealing with music as one of the liberal arts, totally ignored the music of their time and fashioned instead tonal and rhythmic constructs that existed for their own sake. But it is this very theoretical impulse, it will be claimed in the third chapter of this volume, that is the most enduring contribution of Greco-Roman musical culture. Whatever its music was in reality, then, what it bequeathed to us is the habit of musical theory, a trait that will have an immense influence upon the character of later Western music.

★

There is at the same time another equally important, and quite sharply contrasting, heritage of the music of antiquity; to define it we must return to Amos of Tekoa, the eighth-century BC Hebrew prophet. To start with, one makes a rather obvious point about music in connection with his activity. He was not the first prophet, but the first of the 'literary prophets', that is, of those whose teachings were recorded in the Bible; before them there existed a guild-like class of prophets who plied their trade while under the influence of music. Samuel tells Saul 'as you approach the town you will meet a band of seers coming down from the high place with harp, drum, pipe and lyre playing before them while they prophesy' (1 *Samuel* x.5); and Elisha upon one occasion, reluctant to exercise his powers, relented finally and said, '"Bring me a minstrel", for whenever a minstrel played, he fell into a trance from the Eternal' (2 *Kings* iii.15).

Students of ancient religion will readily recognize this phenomenon of musically inspired prophecy as one that was common enough in antiquity to leave etymological traces in several languages; to cite only the Latin, 'praecinere' means both to prophesy and to play the aulos, and 'carmen' means both a magical charm and a song. Again, students of religion see in Amos's type of prophecy the manifestation of a higher form of religious activity, one where prophecy manifests itself through the instrumentality of human reason rather than musically induced hysteria. There is present here at least a hint of a much broader hypothesis – that all the musical accoutrements of ancient religion have no place in the higher religions like Judaism, Christianity and Islam. In addition to musically inspired prophecy, one must cite the even more widespread phenomenon of orgiastic dance, in the most extreme manifestations of which the participants were driven by the music of pipe and drum to acts of self-mutilation or the dismemberment of a live creature. And there is of course the most common of all such cultic activity, animal sacrifice, which appears always to have been accompanied by instrumental music in the various religions of the Mediterranean basin. The function of this music is difficult to define, no doubt

9

because it was perceived differently as sacrifice itself took on different meanings throughout the centuries, ranging from the feeding of some fearsome demigod to the act of praise and thanksgiving performed in the Temple of Jerusalem. This music has in any case been thought at various times to summon wanted deities, to frighten off unwanted deities and to give pleasure to others as they consumed their symbolic meal.

To spell out the hypothesis further, such primitive musical manifestations have no place in a religion of 'the word' or 'the book', which centres about a canon of sacred writings like the Bible. Such a religion – and here one engages in hyperbole to make the point clear – must first purge itself of music in order to develop eventually a music appropriate to its nature. In the case of Judaism the psalmody that accompanied sacrifice in the late Temple was music in the fullest sense, but the psalms recited in the synagogues, and in the early Christian gatherings as well, were more scripture than song. They were no doubt recited with some sort of cantillation, but so was all scripture; it would take several centuries in each of the religions before psalmody became music in a selfconscious sense.

But before pursuing this hypothesis, there are other more modest musical points to cite in connection with the teaching of Amos. 'Woe to those who lie upon beds of ivory', he exclaimed, 'who sing idle songs to the sound of the harp' (*Amos* vi.45), a pronouncement echoed a generation or two later by Isaiah, who makes the same connection between ill-gotten wealth and musical indulgence: 'Woe to those who join house to house, who add field to field . . . They have lyre and harp, timbrel and pipe and wine at their feasts; but they do not regard the deeds of the Lord' (*Isaiah* v.8–12). This element of prophetic indignation over social justice, while by no means the major element in later Christian musical puritanism, is nevertheless a recognizable strain in Western musical thought.

Of closer relevance to our hypothesis are seeming denunciations of sacrifice, one of which makes explicit reference to music:

> I hate, I despise your feasts
>   and I take no delight in your solemn assemblies.
> Even though you offer me your burnt offerings and cereal
>   offerings, I will not accept them,
> and the peace offerings of your fatted beasts
>   I will not look upon.
> Take away from me the noise of your songs;
>   to the melody of your harps I will not listen,
> But let justice roll down like waters, and righteousness
>   like an ever flowing stream.

> [*Amos* v.21–4]

The apparent condemnation of sacrifice becomes a frequently repeated theme in prophetic writings, even if the accompanying music is usually not mentioned: 'I desire steadfast love and not sacrifice', says Amos's younger contemporary Hosea, 'the knowledge of God, rather than burnt offerings' (*Hosea* vi.6). It is generally agreed that these prophets were not calling for an outright end to the practice of sacrifice, but rather were stressing the priority of the devotee's interior disposition over mere ritual – again a theme of profound importance in Western religious thought, and one that was never expressed with remotely the same clarity and force in the Greco-Roman tradition. Subsequent religious reforms in Israel, in any case, all of which owe much to the prophetic movement, serve not to abandon sacrifice but to refine it. The Deuteronomic reform of the century following Amos and Hosea sought to root out unregulated sacrifice in the countryside and confine it to the Temple at Jerusalem, thus elevating its status, one might argue. It is not known when the elaborate instrumentally accompanied psalmody that was performed during the act of sacrifice as described in the Book of Chronicles and in the Talmud came into existence, but one can assume that music in some form was present from the time of Solomon and probably renewed in splendour during the Deuteronomic period.

The Pharisaic movement of the last centuries before the Christian era in many ways echoed the prophetic movement, particularly in its stress upon ethical concerns, and while it tended to centre about the local synagogues, placing increased emphasis upon the reading and interpretation of the Scriptures, and leaving the Temple and its cult in the hands of the Sadducees, there is no evidence that it bore any antagonism towards the Temple and the sacrificial rites practised there. Indeed, Judaism as a whole was piteously stricken by the Roman destruction of the Temple in AD 70, and to this day has not formally renounced its sacrificial cult.

It might be said that in the destruction of the Temple, historical events gave a nudge to the hypothesis under consideration here. During the centuries immediately following the destruction Judaism was slow to develop ritual music in its synagogues, and when it did so in the early Middle Ages the music had nothing in common with the cult music practices of antiquity. The Book of Psalms came to be chanted and sacred poetry was composed, but in each case text preceded song – the book and the word, rather than cultic or magical act, gave birth to music.

In the case of Christianity, the destruction of the Temple took place at too late a date to have much bearing on its early musical history. That history was nevertheless roughly parallel to that of Judaism, even if developments were, for various reasons, considerably accelerated. Original poetry and, perhaps to a lesser extent, biblical psalms were sung at common evening meals during the first three centuries, no doubt in a modest fashion corresponding to the modest circumstances enjoyed by the faithful. But in the fourth century, as described in chapter III below, there was an unprecedented flourishing of psalmody, a movement in the course of which not only did the frequency of psalmody increase, but the very conception of it changed. It existed in the Eucharist of the earliest centuries as a form of scriptural reading, and among the first Christian monks as an aid to meditation, but by the late fourth century it had become ecclesiastical song. By the end of the Middle Ages, of course, it will have become something far more elaborate, surpassing in splendour the psalmody of the Temple or any other cult music of antiquity, and it will also have become, along with other ecclesiastical extravagances, the object of prophetic scorn on the part of the more radical Protestant reformers.

But the psalmody of the late fourth century was still a relatively chaste musical phenomenon, one that was acceptable, even if after a measure of soul-searching, to a man as scrupulous as St Augustine. And it was, we can be sure, a music that was utterly remote from the secular music of the time – the instrumentally accompanied song of theatre, circus and banquet, so vividly depicted in the condemnations of the Church Fathers. It shared this remoteness, ironically, with Greco-Roman music theory, and, as a matter of fact, this alliance of circumstance became one of intention when the church, while continuing to renounce pagan musical practice, adopted musical theory along with pagan learning as a whole. At the end of antiquity, then, the Christian Church, soon to become the principal vehicle of Western culture, enjoyed a dual musical endowment: the Hebraic inheritance of psalmody and the Hellenic inheritance of musical theory. They were maintained at first in the most radical isolation from each other, but the Carolingian period would see the two come together, as the first medieval musical theorists sought to explain ecclesiastical chant. Eventually this effort resulted in the complexities of Western polyphonic music, with its mathematically based rhythmic measure, its mathematically based harmony and its tendency towards architectonic formal design.

THE DARK AGES AND GREGORIAN CHANT, 410–800

That interim period of three to four centuries, between the fall of the Roman empire and the birth of medieval Europe under the Carolingians, is frequently referred to as the Dark Ages. It was a time characterized by barbarian incursions, the deterioration of the physical infrastructure, the loss of governmental services and the decline of learning; not surprisingly, such conditions have resulted in a paucity of contemporary historical documentation, obscuring events for historians and contributing to the aptness of the metaphorical invocation of darkness. Actually, there may be more than metaphor to the designation, since climatologists speak of a trend towards increased cold and rain during the fifth to seventh centuries. Be that as it may, Gregorian chant appeared in full bloom at the end of the period, like some peculiar plant requiring shelter from the sun for its nurture. Indeed, most of the important dialects of Western chant, not just the so-called Gregorian, but the Gallican, the Ambrosian and the Beneventan – with the Mozarabic forced into a somewhat different timetable by the Moors – seem to have reached a peak of development just as the supposed period of darkness was drawing to a close. At first glance, the normal processes of cultural history appear to be reversed. We expect singular artistic and literary achievement to take place, for the most part, in a context like that of classical-period Athens, one characterized by self-confidence, prosperity and outreach. We expect also that singular musical achievement be accompanied by analogous achievement in literature and the visual arts. But here, again at first glance, it seems that a musical development of monumental scope and significance took place in a hostile environment of political chaos and economic desperation, and that it took place at a time when the production of literature, architecture, painting and sculpture was at its most pitiful in the entire history of Western civilization.

It will be suggested here, on the contrary, that our normal expectation – the common sense of cultural history, so to speak – is not contradicted in this case, but rather that the fortunes of Western ecclesiastical chant go hand in hand with those of contemporary political and cultural existence.

First, one must ask if the Dark Ages were in reality all that dark. There is a tendency on the part of recent experts in the period to refute what they refer to as the popular conception of unmitigated chaos brought about by the unremitting savagery of the invading barbarians. Certainly they are right in doing so; this is a period of several centuries with considerable variation in circumstances from year to year and from region to region. Still, to the general observer, it is a time when Western civilization appears to have been at its lowest ebb.

When did it begin? Clearly with the fall of the Roman empire, but this is, of course, an answer that merely begs the question, because the chronological precision of that event itself is another of those perennially unsolved historical conundrums. Some might wish to centre their speculations on a key date such as 476, when the last Western emperor, the boy Romulus Augustus, was deposed by the Visigoth Odoacer; while some might wish to emphasize the long-range process of deterioration, both internal and external, and the alternating attempts to shore up the empire that characterized its last centuries. Here, for want of a better alternative, the date 410 is cited, the year that the Visigothic leader Alaric sacked Rome; the event must have had damaging psychological effects that went far beyond its immediate consequences.

Of even greater significance, perhaps, is what had happened a few years earlier, in 406, when the Roman imperial general Stilicho, in an attempt to halt Alaric's drift southwards through Italy, ordered his troops home from the Rhine frontier. Since the time of Julius Caesar, the migrating German tribes had been confined to the east bank of the Rhine, but now they began a great push westwards, a movement that was as much migration as invasion. The Vandals progressed southwest through Spain to northern Africa and by 430 were besieging Hippo as St Augustine lay on his deathbed; they were a particularly savage people and their mode of conquest best matches the popular conception of unrestrained barbarism. The Burgundians, a more peaceable nation (and the source of the *Niebelungenlied*), settled at first in the middle Rhineland, but were forced at mid-century by the Roman general Aetius, using largely Hunnic troops, to resettle in the region between Lyons and Geneva, the medieval Burgundy. The Franks, a people equally adept at war and agriculture, who would eventually emerge dominant from all this movement, occupied the northern Rhineland, while the Visigoths remained in control of northern Italy. Meanwhile, the Roman legions abandoned Britain in the 420s and joined the sporadic efforts at resistance offered by Roman troops on the Continent. The last Roman military victory was achieved under Aetius in 451, when he defeated the Huns with an army comprised largely of Visigoths, Burgundians and Franks.

A period of comparative stability followed, even though Roman power was effectively ended with the assassination of Aetius by the emperor Valentinian III in 454, and the assassination soon after of Valentinian by loyal followers of Aetius. Valentinian was the last descendant of Theodosius, and the so-called emperors who succeeded him were mere puppets in the struggles of the various German generals and chieftains vying for control in Italy. Finally, in 476, Odoacar emerged victorious, deposed Romulus Augustus, and named himself King of the Germans in Italy. Later in the century his kingdom also collapsed under the weight of an invasion by Theodoric's Ostrogoths, and the Visigoths retreated westwards towards the south of France, establishing a capital at Toulouse. While Theodoric was asserting himself in Italy, Clovis, a leader of equal competence (and considerably less civility), was active in the north, consolidating the gains made for the Franks by his father Childeric (*d* 481), the first Merovingian. Clovis was baptized a Catholic in 496, an event of obvious long-range significance, which in the short term enabled him to win the support of the Gallo-Roman clergy and to lay claim to the lands held by other German tribes, most of whom were Arians. He easily subdued the Burgundians, and in 507 conquered the Visigoths at Toulouse, forcing them to withdraw to Spain where they established a kingdom that survived until the coming of the Moors in 711. There existed thus, after a century of

Germanic incursion, two particularly strong kingdoms: the Ostrogoths in Italy and the Franks in the north.

Just what was it like in those times? Was it a century of unmitigated darkness? It was of course a mixed picture, difficult to characterize in a single generalization, unless one is satisfied with the proposition that the disruption grew progressively worse as one moved north from Italy. Some appeared actually to welcome the barbarians after centuries of Roman taxation and police-state methods, although conditions must have been difficult in areas directly subject to invasion and resistance. Urban life in northern Gaul was devastated and the Gallo-Roman population fled south. Atrocities were not uncommon, especially in Vandal-occupied Africa, while occasional efforts at resistance in Gaul, by patriotic Romans realizing their empire was at risk, were ruthlessly suppressed. Many Gallo-Roman aristocrats, ostrich-like, retreated to the security of their estates. The case of Sidonius Appolinaris (*d* 480) is instructive in this respect. The last Roman belletrist, he expressed at one time in his exaggeratedly literary letters admiration for an intelligent Visigothic king who played backgammon, and in another passage voiced impatience with the voracious louts billeted on his land who smeared butter in their hair. He displayed a different side of his character, however, after assuming the bishopric of Clermont in 469; by this time ecclesiastical officials were increasingly moving to fill the vacuum in political leadership created by the breakdown of Roman government, and he led his city in resistance to a series of Gothic sieges. When it fell in 475, he was imprisoned, but within a year permitted to return to his estate and live out his days editing his letters and poems. In summary, it might be fair to say that the century after 406 was as much a century of decline as of devastation, but rapid decline, certainly, with Roman government having virtually disappeared by about 500, and with Roman society and culture barely surviving in most regions. Worse was yet to come.

But first there was a sort of Roman twilight in Theodoric's Italy during the early decades of the sixth century. Educated, as a child hostage, in Constantinople, Theodoric had a sincere respect for Roman institutions and allowed his Italian subjects to live under Roman law. He undertook public works and put a stop to brigandage; Roman citizens were by and large satisfied with his reign even if they were made uneasy by his Arianism and inconvenienced by the expropriation of a third of their land for Gothic colonization. Cassiodorus, an official at Theodoric's court in Ravenna, wrote lavish praise for the king in his elaborate letters, and Boethius, another official, wrote his digests of classical knowledge and his masterpiece *The Consolation of Philosophy*. That work was written in prison before his execution in about 524, a turn of events indicating that the good times of the Ostrogothic kingdom were at an end. Boethius and other members of the nobility were

4. *The octagonal basilica of S Vitale, Ravenna, commissioned during Theodoric's reign and completed (540–47) under Justinian's rule (note the Byzantine-style apse with cathedra, or throne, and semi-circular synthronon for the seating of clergy)*

suspected of participating in a Byzantine plot to overthrow Theodoric. Theodoric had already begun to form alliances with other German nations in an apparent bid to establish a united German kingdom. Since 476 Byzantium had looked upon itself as *de jure* inheritor of the Western empire and considered Theodoric a client ruler. But it was not until the arrival of the dynamic young Justinian that direct action was contemplated; he found Theodoric's ambitions intolerable and was resolved to reconquer the West. It was he already, as adviser to his uncle the emperor Justin, who had enlisted the sympathy of Theodoric's Roman officials by espousing their orthodox Catholic theological positions (and thereby eventually creating disaffection among Byzantium's Monophysite Eastern allies); and finally in 530, three years after his accession to the crown, and four years after the death of Theodoric, he struck, dispatching the brilliant general

Belisarius westwards by way of Africa.

Vandal North Africa was subdued with surprising ease, and by 533 Belisarius had already begun his Italian campaign. Here, however, resistance was fierce and protracted; it took nearly three decades to subdue the Ostrogoths. At the end of the struggle, known to historians as the Gothic War, Italy lay in devastation, a condition from which it would take centuries to recover. 'There is nothing left but for the people to die', was the anguished reaction of a contemporary. In its weakened state it was easy prey for still another invasion; the Lombards swept southwards, rapidly subduing the entire peninsula save for the area around Ravenna and Rome, and a narrow band of territory linking the two. By the end of the century Italy was not much better off than Gaul.

There, after a second century of decline, Western society was in the worst state of its entire history. The cities had all but ceased to exist; Arles, the former capital of southern Gaul, had withdrawn within its amphitheatre, while the remaining population of the Adriatic city of Split moved into Diocletian's palace, leaving the rest of the city's fabric to crumble and erode with the passing years. There was no central government to speak of, and the countryside was dominated by illiterate warring chieftains, the forerunners of the feudal aristocracy. The peasants were little better off than beasts of the fields; they bred, toiled and died. There were no parish churches as yet, and the people's religion was a hotch-potch of saints, relics and pagan superstition. It was only marginally better in the towns where the cathedral clergy were themselves scarcely literate. Virtually no education took place outside the monasteries, and even there it was a primitive affair, enough to recite the Office and read the Bible. Individuals became monks at this time to escape the world and save their souls; they had no thought of instructing the population, let alone preserving Western culture.

This bleak picture remains substantially valid for much of the seventh century; indeed, there will be only the most gradual amelioration of conditions for the majority of the population, high and low, with as many setbacks as advances, until the more general recovery of the later eleventh century. The various achievements of the period – the educational accomplishments of seventh- and eighth-century Irish and English monks, their missionary efforts on the Continent, the eighth-century Roman assertion of independence from Byzantium, the Carolingian *renovatio* and its Ottoman continuation – are in a sense exceptional rather than characteristic; their long-range significance is undeniable, but they had a relatively limited immediate effect upon the general tenor of life beyond their rather narrow sphere of influence.

If the Dark Ages are indeed dark, then, what of the special case of ecclesiastical chant? Rome, of which we know far more than any other Western centre, offers the best opportunity to consider the question. By the time of Gregory I's reign (590–604), the city was in a sorry state. Its

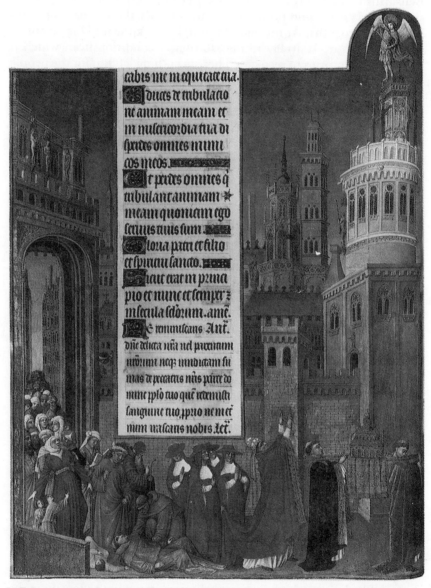

5. *Fifteenth-century depiction of Gregory I leading the litany to seek relief from the plague in sixth-century Rome: miniature (1413–16) by the Limbourg brothers from the 'Trés Riches Heures' of Jean, Duke of Berry*

population, estimated to have been about 800,000 when sacked by Alaric in 410, had been reduced to some 30,000 by the time the Byzantine general Narses recaptured it in 552, although it swelled significantly during the ensuing years with the influx of refugees from Lombard spoliation. Plague, famine, flood and chronic siege were the city's lot for most of the sixth century. The shrunken population confined itself to the vicinity of Tiber Island, the so-called *abitato*, while most of the city's area within its great walls, the *disabitato*, was given to ruins and open spaces. Gregory's achievement was to wrest some semblance of order from the chaos. He saw to it that food arrived more regularly from the church's estates in the south, that widows and orphans were cared for from the income of these estates, that the sick were nursed and that the water supply was restored. In the absence of any effective local government he furnished both a civic and an ecclesiastical bureaucracy, and even took responsibility for defensive measures against the ever-threatening Lombards – all this while being bedridden as often as not. It would seem that he had little time or energy left for church music, and it is true that no music historian today would uphold the extravagant claims for his musical involvement that were made by the Solesmes monks who dominated chant scholarship during the first half of the twentieth century.

Still, most do maintain a more or less substantial role for Gregory, even if it is confined more to liturgical organization in general than to matters of chant in particular. Chapter IV in this volume, however, takes the extreme position that Gregory had virtually nothing to do with either liturgy or chant. It is true that legends generally have some basis in fact, some dimly remembered grain of truth that blossoms in the imagination of subsequent generations; however, the early medieval legend that Gregory composed the chant under the inspiration of the Holy Spirit appears to be not pious exaggeration but an outright mistake, brought about by, among other things, a confusion of various popes bearing the name Gregory. It is possible to go still further and claim that among all popes of the era Gregory was singular in his lack of interest in liturgy. His voluminous ascetic and pastoral writings, and his hundreds of preserved letters, are remarkable for their near-total silence on the subject. On one occasion he was prodded into denying that he had introduced Byzantine liturgical practices and on another he forbade deacons to sing in church; that is more or less the extent of what he had to say.

If the view expressed here is correct, it would tend to justify the hypothesis suggested at the beginning of this reflection on the Dark Ages – that we should not expect significant development in ecclesiastical chant when civilization is at so low an ebb. There is evidence in Chapter IV that during the chaos of the sixth century the modest psalmodic practice of the late patristic period was in peril of its very survival. Then, in the time of Gregory, he and his clergy were too absorbed in more basic pursuits to pay much attention to the development of an elaborate liturgical music. But in the century and a half after Gregory Rome experienced a significant revival. Its population increased, it benefited economically from the growing influx of pilgrims, and its country estates flourished during long periods of stalemate with the Lombards, who themselves showed signs of maturation as a society, converting to Catholicism and adopting Roman customs.

Most essentially, Rome emerged independent of Constantinople in the first quarter of the eighth century. In Gregory's time Rome still felt allegiance to the Eastern capital, to which it was united both by deep-seated juridical ties and by the reliance upon its troops for protection from the Lombards. In the course of the seventh century, however, theological differences increasingly polarized the two, while at the same time the imperial military became steadily more Italianized in its sympathies. The critical incident came during the reign of Gregory II (715–31), who in 723 refused to pay taxes any longer to Constantinople on the papal estates. Shortly after, in 727, Gregory again defied the emperor, Leo III, this time refusing to sanction his newly announced policy of iconoclasm. In each case threats of military action by the emperor were thwarted by the loyalty of the Italian soldiery, and one might say that the Papal States had in effect come into existence – Rome was once again the capital of a temporal realm. It was, incidentally, this same Gregory II who manifested Rome's new self-confidence and outward-looking policies when he sent Petronax in 717 to rebuild Monte Cassino (sacked by the Lombards in 577) and when he commissioned St Boniface in 719 to carry on his momentous missionary effort among the Franks. He was truly a great pope, and surely it was he, not Gregory I, whom late eighth-century Italians had in mind when they first attributed the composition of an antiphoner to an unspecified Pope Gregory.

In any case, it is argued in Chapter IV that it was during this period of pride and accomplishment in Rome, the later seventh century and earlier eighth, that the musical and liturgical developments traditionally attributed to Gregory I were carried out. It was the period of the splendid Stational liturgy, with its imperial overtones, and the heyday of the Schola Cantorum. It was also a time of significant artistic revival in Rome; several contemporary popes, most notably John VII (705–7), Gregory III (731–41) and Zacharias (741–52), were outstanding patrons of the arts, responsible for the building of impressive basilicas adorned with splendid mosaics. Curiously, however, it was not a period of conspicuous literary activity, and here one must add a qualification to the hypothesis in question. While it may be that musical achievement will frequently go hand in hand with general prosperity and achievement in architecture and art, literature is often excluded from the equation. To cite just one more example, without attempting to explain it, Cluniac monasticism, which represents the pinnacle of medieval monastic wealth and influence, and of monastic liturgical music, architecture and the decorative arts, was singularly unproductive of humanistically inspired writing.

Before undertaking the most cursory application of our hypothesis to the other Western liturgical dialects, it is necessary to emphasize the unique circumstances existing at Rome. Chapter IV attempts to explain how the Roman liturgical and musical developments of the time could have been produced only by a body like the Schola Cantorum, where, over a period of a generation or more, an annual cycle of feasts was firmly established, text formularies specific to each feast were determined and musical settings for each formulary were either adapted from existing material or freshly composed, with much of the prodigious repertory being committed to memory. This was an enormous enterprise that required the single-minded dedication of a closely-knit community of talented individuals, enjoying support and stability during a significant period of time. One might wish to make an analogy with fifteenth-century music, where an elaborate programme of polyphonic music was practical only in those exceptional cathedrals and courts that boasted the apparatus of a well-endowed *cappella* of professionally trained singers.

A group roughly comparable to the Schola Cantorum might very well have existed in contemporary Constantinople, but one must be sceptical about the Western centres; or, to state the proposition more positively, one ought to anticipate the existence of an organized liturgy and chant more or less to the extent that Roman circumstances were duplicated. For centres occupied by the Lombards, Milan in the north and Benevento in the south, we should not expect this to happen before the eighth century, probably somewhat later than in Rome and then not genuinely comparable in scope. For Gallican chant there is, in addition to this factor of cultural and social maturity, the question of geographical definition. In speaking of Gallican chant, ought we to think of, say, Pseudo-Germanus's Autun or Merovingian St Denis? What was it that Pepin suppressed in favour of the *cantus romanus* – can we seriously claim that it was a fully articulated liturgical year, with assigned texts and chants, sung uniformly through the Merovingian realm? Perhaps the place that comes closest to the conditions proposed here is Toledo, the capital of pre-Moorish Spain, where the Catholic Visigoths and Iberian-Romans lived together with a fair measure of cooperation for a century or more, but even here one hesitates to claim that circumstances were truly comparable to those at Rome.

All this, of course, is the most informal sort of speculation; its purpose is simply to suggest that claims for the maturity of some branch of Western chant must be judged in a broad historical context. It seems only reasonable to assume that favourable conditions are necessary for the nurture of a sophisticated and stable ecclesiastical music, and as a corollary one must also question the notion of a chant developing gradually during several centuries of chaos and disruption. A comparatively rapid development, one requiring decades rather than centuries, is perhaps more likely.

IMPERIAL, ROMANESQUE, GOTHIC, 800–1270

A number of music history texts label their chapters on medieval music 'Music of the Romanesque' and 'Music of the Gothic'. The use of these terms, not without problems in their original contexts of art history, is particularly puzzling in a musical context because the authors make little or no attempt to explain what they mean. Certainly to do so would be no easy task; it appears on the face of it that medieval music in its various stages, whether monophonic or polyphonic, is plainly and simply lacking in qualities that one would specify as Romanesque or Gothic. Take the most obvious candidate for finding such a relationship: the *organum purum* of Léonin. A canon of Notre Dame Cathedral, Léonin was composing this music during the very years that the Gothic choir of the building was under construction, yet most fail to perceive anything particularly Gothic about it. If anything, with the protracted stasis of its lower voice and the rhapsodic windings of its upper voice, it reminds one of twentieth-century minimalism.

This is not to deny the existence of such relationships at other times and places in the history of music. The grandeur and the kaleidoscopic orchestral colour of Johann Sebastian Bach's overtures for orchestra, to choose just one example from his works, find a striking aesthetic resonance in Balthasar Neumann's great staircase and hall at Würzburg. One senses similar qualities in those monumental ceilings of Tiepolo where heaven merges with earth, and in an operatic culture that portrays mostly gods, emperors and heroes. That these affinities are by no means coincidental is brought home by the sharp contrast to follow: opera on subject matter like *La serva padrona*, paintings entitled 'The Washerwoman' or 'Pipe and Jug', the harmonic and instrumental simplicity of early Classical music and the chaste symmetry of neo-Palladian architecture.

If one fails to perceive this immediate sort of aesthetic kinship between medieval music and the other arts of the time, is it illegitimate to inquire about any other sort of significant relationship, something beyond the mere coincidence of contemporaneity? Surely not. If there is an obvious fatuousness in speaking of Romanesque or Gothic music without attempting to define it, there is a corresponding mindlessness in refusing to consider whether the medieval music, art and architecture which were sponsored by the same agency might reveal certain

6. King David in a classical context surrounded by musicians, guards and personifications of the imperial virtues: miniature from the 'First Bible of Charles the Bald', Tours, 843–51

genuine affinities if subjected to serious examination. Again, this is not the appropriate forum to pursue such an examination with any degree of thoroughness; the best that can be expected is to outline an approach that might reward future study. The key element in this approach was just hinted at in speaking of medieval music, art and architecture which are sponsored by the same agency; it may be that the most significant factor uniting the arts at any time throughout the Middle Ages is their common auspices – the monasticism, for example, that is largely responsible for Romanesque architecture as well as the music, sculpture and painting of the period. It is just possible that by working from this broad starting-point one might be able to specify certain traits of the music or musical culture of one period that would be inappropriate to any other – even if one does not go nearly so far as to produce a definition of Romanesque or Gothic music.

First it is necessary to improve, ever so slightly, the periodization of the Middle Ages that confines itself to the Romanesque and Gothic. One text extends the musical Romanesque backwards to include not only the Carolingians but Gregory I and St Ambrose. The primitive

7. *The Palatine chapel at Aachen (792–805); built for Charlemagne as his shrine, this octagonal building was modelled after S Vitale, Ravenna (fig.4) and is an example of the Carolingian classicizing tendency*

historiography displayed here has an amusing correspondence with the origins of the term 'Romanesque', which was adopted in the nineteenth century to cover the architecture of the period between antiquity and the rise of Gothic. Here we will speak of imperial, Romanesque and Gothic. The notion 'imperial', borrowed from the contemporary French cultural historian Georges Duby, is used to cover both the Carolingian period and the ensuing Ottonian, extending from the later eighth to the earlier eleventh century. It carries with it the connotation of reviving the Western Roman empire; certainly this was the intention of Pope Leo III when he crowned Charlemagne 'Carolus Augustus' in that famous event at St Peter's on Christmas in the year 800. Charlemagne, for his part, displayed a measure of ambivalence towards the title; with his reluctance to offend Constantinople, and his strong sense of German kingship, he preferred the title of 'Emperor, King of the Lombards and Franks' to 'Emperor of the Romans'. His advisers like Alcuin, on the other hand, thought of his court in terms of *renovatio*, and his son Louis the Pious (813–40) and grandson Charles the Bald (843–76) embraced the papal antiquarian notion; while the Saxon Ottonians, chief among them Otto I (936–73) and Otto II (973–

83), although lacking a dynastic link to the Carolingians, thought of themselves as perpetuators of both the Carolingian and the ancient Roman empires.

King or emperor, in any case, the art of the time was a regal art. Certain monastic and ecclesiastical centres were prominent in the production of manuscript illumination – especially Metz, Rheims and Tours during Carolingian years, Reichenau, Fulda and Trier during the next century – but a strong link to the court was always present. As often as not their more splendid books were commissioned by the emperor, who was always on the move, celebrating the principal ecclesiastical feasts in one or other of his favourite religious establishments. And just as the art of the time enjoyed some imperial connection, it tended to echo some antiquarian theme. Constantine and Theodosius were the Romans most frequently invoked, Christian and classical antiquity were not distinguished, David and later Charlemagne himself were the principal hero-kings. Stylistically, the large-scale portraits that are the most prominent subject matter of manuscript illumination take the figures of Byzantine painting as their starting-point but manage to inform them with a measure of genuine classical naturalism. Large initials in the Celto-Germanic linear mode remain common, but the ornamental borders of the pages displaying human figures generally utilize some classically inspired device like architectural columns surmounted by an arch. In architecture itself, Charlemagne's Palatine chapel (fig.7) recalls Justinian's S Vitale of Ravenna (fig.4 above), while the early Christian basilica, as exemplified in St Peter's, is revived at St Denis and Fulda. Possibly the most extreme antiquarian gesture was Bishop Bernward of Hildesheim's bronze column, decorated with scenes from the life of Christ but modelled after the Columns of Trajan and Marcus Aurelius he had admired when visiting Rome.

The Romanesque, primarily an architectural phenomenon, was not regal in its auspices but monastic, nor was it selfconsciously antiquarian in spite of its employment of the rounded Roman arch. And although it spread over most of Europe eventually, its geographical base stood in similarly sharp contrast to that of imperial art. The latter flourished in precisely those areas where Carolingian influence was concentrated, the Rhineland and the river valleys of northern France, while the Romanesque developed most characteristically in the territory least affected by the empire, France south of the Loire – Burgundy and Aquitaine, the home (it is no coincidence) of Cluniac monasticism. Romanesque architecture was the house architecture of that most splendid period in the annals of Western monasticism, extending from the later tenth to the mid-twelfth century, when Western civilization was plainly and simply a monastic culture, and when Cluny was only the most prominent of a number of great monastic alliances. The resurgence of monasticism went hand in hand with a general awakening in Europe. The abbeys had for centuries been the focus of life in an essentially rural society, and freed now from the marauding of Viking and Saracen, they introduced improvements in agriculture that fostered population growth in a chronically hungry Europe. Education too, albeit a more practical than humanistic education, spread with the dramatic increase in new monastic foundations. They were exempt from allegiance to local bishops, answering only to Rome, making their influence all the more powerful at a time when the particularism of feudalism had greatly weakened the centres of monarchy. Less tangible, but no less important, was their moral stature; the monks were holy men and diocesan clergy were not, at a time when the Christian faith was experiencing a general resurgence of its own.

The newly prospering monastic communities required an architecture commensurate with their status; they found it in the importation of stone masons from Lombardy, who were able to erect towering stone vaults upon the basis of a sturdy Ottonian understructure. At the east end the aisles were extended in a loop round the basilican apse, enclosing the choir on the inside and giving access on the outside to numerous small chapels (fig.8), where the monk-priests said their private Masses and where relics were displayed for the veneration of the pilgrims that thronged these churches, many of which were on the various pilgrimage routes to Santiago de Compostela. Monumental sculpture flourished for the first time in the Middle Ages, adorning the churches' west portals with fearsome scenes of the Last Judgment (fig.9). Manuscript illumination was characterized by a curious interval between classically inspired naturalism of the imperial and the Gothic periods; large initials predominated, decorated with a renewed Celto-Germanic linear ornamentation and vivified with struggling monsters and contorted human figures. The central art of the period, however, was the liturgy, and all else was subordinated to it. Choir monks spent about eight hours on an ordinary day, and more than that on principal feasts, chanting a Mass and Office that had swelled to breaking-point with every conceivable variety of expansion and addition.

Gothic architecture was born in a monastery, Abbot Suger's St Denis in the 1140s, but this was a royal monastery. Charles Martel lay buried there as well as Pepin the Short and the early Capetians, and Suger's famous renovations were intended to produce a building worthy of kings. Indeed, as the new style, the *opus francigenum*, spread rapidly through the north, it did so precisely in that area where the newly revived French monarchy had subjugated the restive forces of feudalism. At the same time the focus of medieval life was shifting from the countryside to the rapidly developing cities which, with their fairs and markets, now reaped the commercial fruit of agricultural progress. Paris, needless to say, home of the Capetian monarchy, was easily the

8. East end of the Romanesque church of Fontgombault (1091–1141) showing the radiating apsidal chapels

foremost of these cities. The revival went far beyond economics; its social, intellectual and artistic dimensions were equally revolutionary. The Cluniac reform was a spent moral force, and the contemporary Cistercian revolution would soon go the same way. In an age that appeared weary of dispersion and seemed to welcome centralization of any sort, the papacy emerged as a dominant religious power and formed a strong alliance with the French monarchy that reached its climax in the reign of Louis IX (1226–70), canonized a saint not long after his death.

This was the time of one of the great intellectual movements of European history: scholasticism. The educational pabulum of the monastic schools was obsolete; leadership had passed to cathedral schools like Chartres and Laon, and eventually Paris, where the school in the cloister of Notre Dame outgrew itself and expanded to the left bank of the river Seine, there to form one of the earliest universities. In these institutions the liberal art of dialectic came to occupy the privileged position once enjoyed by grammar. Everything was questioned, analysed, distinguished and broken down into its smallest logical parts; yet at the same time all came together in a grand unity that was subject to a commonly held faith. Just as this was a time that favoured central government, both secular and ecclesiastical, it was a

9. *Last Judgment scene (c1135) carved on the tympanum over the west door of the Romanesque church of Ste-Foy, Conques*

time that favoured centralized knowledge; it was the age of the encyclopedia, of Thomas Aquinas's *Summa theologica* and Vincent of Beauvais's
universal history.

The outstanding artistic achievement of the time was of course the
Gothic cathedral; indeed, it stands out as one of the wonders of all
Western civilization. The various impulses of the period are manifested
in it. It retains Suger's theology of light, derived from Dionysius the
Areopagite's *Celestial Hierarchy*, with its walls that are reduced to a
framework for multi-coloured glass; its soaring height expresses the
faith of the time, but also the competitive spirit of the prosperous towns,
with each newly planned building surpassing those of its neighbours;
and as Erwin Panofsky has shown in his classic essay, *Gothic Architecture
and Scholasticism*, it reflects the thought of the age, with its multiplicity of
clearly articulated parts coming together in a unified whole. Georges
Duby makes the related point that a Gothic cathedral was planned on
paper, using mathematical instruments, whereas previous buildings
employed a more intuitive approach to their construction. Similar
traits are manifested in the other arts. Sculpture produces figures that
are naturalistic but idealized and arranged moreover in programmes
that are at once complex and clear in their organization. The pages of a
contemporary illuminated manuscript display the same figures, and
the same clear organization, enclosed, usually within the frame of a
Gothic architectural border. It was an age of remarkable homogeneity,
characterized by self-confidence, prosperity, intellectual and artistic
achievement, with all directed efficiently (disturbingly some might say)
towards common religious and political goals.

★

If the artistic production of the three periods described here is illuminated by reflection upon their auspices – monarchy for the imperial,
monasticism for the Romanesque and a combination of centralized
church and crown for the Gothic – is there anything to be gained by a
consideration of music in the same context? It was suggested at the outset that the area of musical style itself might not be very promising, but
there are other possibilities. It is already a commonplace that the
Carolingian urge to unify and the related hankering after authenticity
played a role in the stabilization of liturgy and chant; and it can be
added now that the Romanization which was a central theme in that
process is related, apparently, to the antiquarian strain in the other
arts. If the chant could not be traced to the time of Constantine, it could
be traced at least to Rome in the time of Pope Gregory I.

Music theory, however, might provide the most convincing example
of overt antiquarianism. Just as manuscript illumination began with a
basically Byzantine human figure and enlivened it with classical
naturalism, music theory adopted the broad notion of its central

theoretical construct, the eight ecclesiastical modes, from the Byzantine octoechos, and over a period of two centuries supplied the details with elements from classical theory as provided by Boethius. These elements include the Hellenic tetrachordal system, the basic consonances as demonstrated on the monochord, the designation of pitches by Greek instrumental fingerings, the application of scale types or octave species and even the misunderstood nomenclature of the ancient *harmoniae* – the Dorian, Phrygian, Lydian and the like. However, what is truly striking about the development of modal theory from the present point of view is that in its final phase, in the early eleventh-century work of Guido of Arezzo and that of the pseudo-Odonian author of the *Dialogus de musica*, it shed much of its Boethian baggage in favour of a clearly intelligible pragmatism, adopting among other things the modern pitch names of the gamut. (On one occasion Guido said of Boethius's revered treatise, with just a hint of disapproval, that it was of no use to singers, but only to philosophers.) The auspices of the earlier theory, even its geographical location, had been precisely those of imperial art; indeed, Hucbald may have been a relative of Louis the Pious. The new pragmatic theory of the eleventh century, however, came from outside this sphere. It would make the parallel with the other arts altogether too neat if the Pseudo-Odo of Cluny actually had been Cluniac, but while a monk like Guido, and a monk at the time of the general monastic reform alluded to above, he was, like Guido, an Italian. Still, the larger truth corresponds well enough with the line of thought under consideration.

The entire period of monastic and Romanesque ascendancy was not a particularly productive one in the area of music theory after Guido and Pseudo-Odo. From Burgundy and Aquitaine virtually nothing was achieved in this field, so that the climax of medieval monastic polyphony, the music of what was formerly designated the St Martial or Limoges school, goes without an explanation of its rhythmic conventions. Monastic theorists of the so-called Liège school, most notably the able Johannes Afflighemensis, were content to rework the doctrine of Guido; while in eleventh-century Germany, where imperial pretensions were being kept alive, figures like Berno, Hermann and Aribo formed a curious theoretical backwater, tinkering still with the Boethian apparatus (to the despair of students today).

Theory had an impressive revival in the thirteenth century, when a series of writers provided explanations of the rapidly evolving rhythmic systems of Parisian polyphonic music. It has been claimed, with some justification, that medieval musical theory enjoyed two especially productive periods: the Carolingian, when it met the need of explaining the chant, and the thirteenth century, when it responded to the similar challenge provided by Notre Dame school polyphony. But this pragmatic explanation is not sufficient; for one thing, it fails to account for the theoretical hiatus of Cluny, and, more importantly, it ignores the intellectual context of Carolingian and thirteenth-century theory. Carolingian theory is difficult to imagine without the antiquarian impulse of the time, and thirteenth-century theory, with its orderly presentation of every smallest detail within a clearly comprehensible whole, and its Aristotelian echoes, can be properly understood only within the milieu of scholasticism. This latter point is surely one that would repay fuller study.

Theory is one consideration; the textual subject matter of ecclesiastical polyphony is another. Marion Gushee makes the point in Chapter VI that Aquitanian polyphony sets not the texts of the liturgical mainstream, but the same sort of original sacred poetry observed in the para-liturgical genres that characterize the region. Notre Dame polyphony, however, reverts sharply to the Carolingian core repertory; Léonin's *Magnus liber* sets the most central of liturgical chants, the graduals, alleluias and Office responsories of the principal feast days. It is by no means fanciful to detect in this a sense of thirteenth-century orthodoxy, a sense of adherence to the values of the centralized church. Moreover, Pérotin accomplished the precise musical analogy of the encyclopedia or *summa*: he provided not selected settings but a systematic collection covering the entire annual cycle, an enterprise that is inconceivable in twelfth-century Aquitaine and for that matter nearly as unlikely in any region during the fourteenth century.

The secular monophony of the time provides another area for reflection, but here there is an element that fails to synchronize with the broad periodization under consideration. It is true that the song of the troubadours developed in the region one might have assumed it would, the south of France, where the ideal of chivalry flourished in a milieu far removed from the influence of centralized monarchy and church. What is amiss, however, is the element of chronology; one might have expected the art of the troubadours to have flourished in the heyday of the Romanesque, the peak period of Aquitanian ecclesiastical poetry, but instead the most outstanding practitioners of the genre were contemporaries of Léonin and Pérotin, as was their most renowned patron, the fascinating Eleanor of Aquitaine. The explanation for this is simple enough: the centuries-old cultural characteristics of southern France persisted long after the triumph of king, church and Gothic in the north. Even Romanesque architecture was slow in giving way to the new style, while in the sphere of religion the south struck back with heresy, of which Albigensianism is only the most famous example. Within the fold of the church this resistance had its own manifestation in what might be called a theology of love. St Bernard, himself a son of the Burgundian nobility, championed the affective religion of St Augustine against the aridity of scholasticism. St Francis never completely abandoned the chivalrous ideals of his youth and styled himself a minstrel of God. Long after Pope Innocent III ordered the members of Francis's brotherhood to attend the University of Paris (to become learned shock troops against heresy, like the Dominicans), St Bonaventure, the 'Seraphic Doctor', would uphold the superiority of mystical illumination over rationalistic theology.

Yet this largely southern strain is barely discernible in the Gothic context of thirteenth-century Paris, and as a final reflection, again merely a suggestion for further study, it can be argued that as the century progresses it is increasingly possible to make closer analogies between music and the general cultural milieu, closer analogies than ever before in the history of music and perhaps than for some time afterwards. This is not to say that one should expect anything with the aesthetic immediacy of the eighteenth-century examples cited above, but still something beyond the broad considerations suggested up to this point, even venturing, perhaps, however hesitantly, into the area of musical style. It should not surprise us to find that there is a measure of similarity in the compositional process of the time and the rational manner of constructing a building or designing the page of an illuminated manuscript. Contrast the orderliness of a folio from the Bamberg or Montpellier codices with one of Aquitanian polyphony, and, more to the point, note the carefully maintained hierarchy in the voice parts of a three-voice thirteenth-century motet. It might be a mistake to make much of its resemblance to the three-tiered layering of a Gothic wall – aisle level, triforium and clerestory – but the utter clarity of its horizontal articulation is a legitimate consideration. The motet adds vertical to horizontal articulation with repeated rhythmic patterns in the tenor, a trait that culminates in the early fourteenth-century isorhythmic motet. Again one must resist the temptation to make simplistic comparison with the bays of a Gothic nave, separated as they are by vertical shafts; Romanesque buildings already enjoyed both a three-tiered horizontal articulation and a vertical division into bays by way of their columns. Yet this membrification is utterly more complex and selfconscious in a Gothic building, and there may be a legitimate comparison between the impulse underlying that trait and the general compositional tendency towards clear articulation in a motet. One notes, however, that the musical manifestation is not only considerably simpler but considerably later than that of architecture; this last point raises questions of cultural comparisons too vexed for even the most preliminary sort of consideration here.

THE LATE MIDDLE AGES, 1270–1474

Until recently there was a tendency in the writing of music history to treat the period beginning with the close of the thirteenth century as one of decline and decadence. This is curious in a discipline that appeared on the other hand to maintain a rather uncritically positive position on the significance of the Renaissance. One had to forgive students their confusion over the apparent contradiction, and it was not enough simply to distinguish between an Italian Renaissance and a northern 'waning of the Middle Ages' (to borrow the English-language title of Johan Huizinga's classic work on the subject). Even if one concentrates exclusively upon the north, there are serious difficulties with looking upon the fourteenth and fifteenth centuries simply as a time of 'waning'. It is possible to produce evidence of both decline and fresh initiatives, of depression and prosperity, of despair and happiness, of death and burgeoning life. Indeed, the more one reflects upon these contradictions, the clearer it becomes that this is the central point of the period: it is peculiarly recalcitrant to the sort of unitary explanation that renders history comforting. It suffers from comparison in this respect especially with the immediately preceding period, where one witnesses a rare unity of church and state, intellectual life and culture in Western Europe – at least in the Île de France. By a sort of historiographic reflex one tends to view the breakup of this unity as disintegration, while it might be just as legitimate to see it as the manifestation of variety and abundance.

Still, if one isolates the fourteenth from the fifteenth century, it can be said with considerable objectivity that it was a particularly troubled time in the history of Europe. In the closing decades of the thirteenth century agriculture was already showing itself incapable of feeding the greatly increased population. Exhausted soil in the valleys along with a climatic shift that rendered the uplands too cold for cultivation brought about disastrous famines in 1315–17, 1332 and 1345–8. The population was already in sharp decline when the terrible catastrophe of the Black Death struck down possibly a third of Europe's inhabitants in 1347–8. Eventually the resulting labour shortage would mean better wages and an end to serfdom, but attempts by the peasants to ameliorate their lot – such as the Jacquerie of northern France in 1358 and the English Peasants' Revolt of 1381 – were brutally suppressed by the landed gentry. It was a time of incessant warfare; the protracted struggle known as the Hundred Years War, conventionally dated from 1337 to 1453, might be said to have started already in 1294 when war broke out between England and France after nearly a century of peace. Paradoxically, during the extended period of chronic hostility that followed, ordinary people suffered even more when active fighting was at a standstill; these intervals frequently were the result of exhausted treasuries, forcing mercenary troops to ravage the countryside for their support. The papacy was heavily involved in much of this conflict, thus sacrificing the moral authority it had enjoyed in the earlier thirteenth century. When the Sicilian population rose up against their Angevin rulers in the bloody rebellion of 1282 known as the Sicilian Vespers, and subsequently pledged their loyalty to the house of Aragon, the French

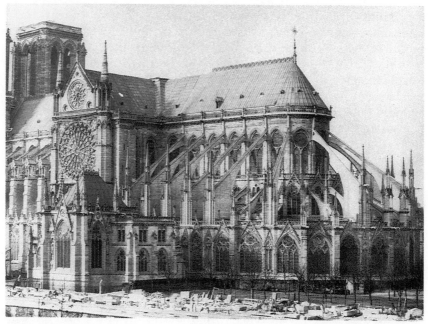

10. *East end of the Gothic cathedral of Notre Dame, Paris (mid-fourteenth century)*

pope sided with his countrymen, threw his financial support behind them and shamelessly declared the Angevin invasion of Catholic Aragon to be a crusade. When the invasion failed, however, the first Capetian defeat in over a century, the French turned on the pope, blaming him for inadequate support. This was the first step in a bitter dispute between France and the papacy that was resolved only by the virtual appropriation of the papacy from 1305 to 1378, the so-called Babylonian Captivity, when a series of French popes reigned at Avignon. Matters became only worse in 1378 when the Italian Urban VI settled in Rome; a rival French pope was elected, and the scandalous situation of anti-popes was maintained until resolved by the election of Martin V at the Council of Constance in 1417.

The unity of the church was also threatened by heresy of the most serious sort arising from the views of the Oxford philosopher and theologian John Wycliff. He declared that the Bible was the sole religious authority, and went on to demonstrate that neither the pope nor the religious orders were sanctioned by Scripture (he found the friars particularly obnoxious). What ultimately earned his condemnation by ecclesiastical authorities at Oxford in 1381, however, was his attack on the Eucharistic doctrine of transubstantiation. His views found relatively little political support in England, but his Bohemian follower Jan Hus had the backing of his country's patriotic aristocrats, who associated his opposition to ecclesiastical hierarchy with their own complaints against the German domination of the local church. In 1415 Hus was burnt at the stake by order of the Council of Constance; he displayed great fortitude during his ordeal and became a national hero, inspiring a strong strain of Bohemian proto-Protestantism.

If the religious unity of Europe was threatened in the later fourteenth century, its intellectual unity was all but shattered earlier in the century by the notorious doctrine of two truths proclaimed by the Oxford Franciscan William of Occam (*d* 1347). The Dominican St Thomas Aquinas had striven mightily to achieve a synthesis of faith and reason, but the philosophers of subsequent generations, particularly the rival Franciscans, had difficulty in reconciling the two. Finally, William taught explicitly that God, with his omnipotence and omniscience, was not subject to rational analysis but could be apprehended only by faith. The things of this world, on the other hand, were to be subjected to ever more penetrating scrutiny, that viewed them as singular objects rather than representatives of universal categories. The theological side of Occam's thought can be associated with the tendency towards mysticism in the fourteenth and fifteenth centuries – that is, the impulse to attain direct contact with God without the intermediary of ecclesiastical apparatus – while his stress upon the significance of singulars over universals is allied to inductive reasoning and the beginnings of scientific method.

One sees already in this last point that Occam's thought, however destructive of the medieval consensus, was not necessarily a symptom of decline when viewed from a broader historical perspective. Certainly there is not much to be said for the famine, plague and violence that characterized much of the fourteenth century, but Occam's views represent for many the beginnings of modern philosophy. Similarly, Wycliff's theology is altogether closer than that of the thirteenth-century church to most contemporary thinking on religious issues. And the artistic production of the century, while no doubt set back in times and places actually experiencing the disaster of plague or war, is impressive in its diversity and innovation. Paris, pre-eminent in the first half of the century, saw the manuscript illumination of Jean Pucelle, creator of the *Hours of Jeanne d'Evreux* and an artist unsurpassed in the genre at any time and place. And surely the mid-fourteenth-century east end of Notre Dame provides one of the most satisfying architectural exteriors in existence today (fig.10). It is, moreover, just one of numerous contemporary Gothic masterpieces ranging from the great cathedral of Prague, itself an important artistic centre in the second half of the century, to the spectacular choir, east window and fan-vaulted cloister of Gloucester. An entirely new art was created at the time, tapestry weaving, providing elegant and warming coverings for the walls of home and castle. In literature the century saw the flourishing of vernacular writing in several languages. To cite only the two most obvious examples, there was Dante earlier in the century (an Italian, but more a medieval than a Renaissance figure) and Chaucer later. In each case the author was all but personally responsible for making his native tongue a literary language.

Music was no less important than the other arts. The technical innovation of the so-called four prolations, allowing a flexible range of duple, triple and compound metres, changed music as fundamentally and as suddenly as any other such development in its history, as Daniel Leech-Wilkinson points out in Chapter IX. It made possible the Ars Nova of early fourteenth-century music, and it is interesting to note that Occam's contemporary philosophy is similarly referred to as the *via moderna*. Its chief beneficiary was Guillaume de Machaut (*d* 1377), a truly great composer, perhaps the first whose music has an immediate and deep appeal to twentieth-century listeners. His biography tells us something about the period. He was a cleric, devout enough for all we know, yet very much a man of the world. During the earlier part of his career he served as secretary to the King of Bohemia, and although he settled as a canon at Rheims Cathedral in about 1340, he continued to enjoy noble patronage, such as that of Jean de Berry, and it was during these later years that he conducted his famous love correspondence with the young Péronne d'Armentières. His output, both poetic and musical, was primarily secular, and in his unrivalled polyphonic chansons the Western polyphonic mainstream failed for the first time in its history to rely upon a liturgical tenor as its compositional starting-point. Machaut's secularism is characteristic of the entire period. We witness it in every facet of fourteenth- and fifteenth-century life, and, again, while it may suggest decline from the limited viewpoint of the thirteenth-century medieval consensus, it can hardly be construed as such from a broader historical perspective.

The musical climax of the century comes in the refined chanson composition of the Avignon school, the so-called Ars Subtilior, that emulated and ultimately far exceeded the rhythmic complexity represented in some of Machaut's later works. This has been referred to as a decadent, *fin-de-siècle* art, but surely there is a measure of prejudice in the view. It is true that it was an art of the connoisseur, one in which insiders competed with each other to produce the most difficult notational conundrums possible, but (as Leech-Wilkinson explains) the results always made musical sense and one can only admire the consummate skill that brought this about.

Much of the fifteenth century, particularly the first half, witnessed the continued spectacle of chronic warfare, but the period enjoyed none the less a broad and sustained general revival that saw the population restored to its thirteenth-century level. It was, moreover, an entirely different sort of population with a good portion of the peasantry replaced by city-dwellers, many of them prosperous members of the

11. Jean, Duke of Berry (seated right) dining with the Bishop of ?Chartres, surrounded by members of his family and retinue (the tapestry behind is a representation of the Trojan War as imagined in medieval France): miniature (1413–16) by the Limbourg brothers from the 'Trés Riches Heures'

newly emerged middle class. One observes this in northern Italy, of course, but – more to present purposes – in even more remarkable fashion in the commercial centres of the Low Countries and northern Germany. On the docks of a city like Bruges, for example, and in her step-gabled warehouses, there were furs from Russia, salt herring from Scandinavia, metallic ores from Germany, and above all wool from England, feeding the looms of Flanders. The dominant political power for much of the century was the Duchy of Burgundy. In 1363 John the Good of France had given the duchy to his youngest son Philip, but the truly decisive event was the marriage of Philip in 1369 to Margaret,

12. *Celebration of Christmas Mass (Jean, Duke of Berry is behind the curtain): miniature (1485)
by Jean Colombe from the 'Trés Riches Heures'*

daughter of the count of Flanders and Artois. When the count died in 1384 Philip inherited the immense wealth of the Low Countries, enjoying access to credit in the banking houses and a prodigious income from taxes and tolls on trade, river traffic, the textile industry, maritime commerce and the like. Under a series of dukes, most notably the long-reigning Philip the Good (1418–64), Burgundy came to eclipse Paris as a political centre; indeed, Burgundy sided with England for much of that phase of the Hundred Years War when England was in the ascendancy and occupying Paris.

Meanwhile, the artistic centre of gravity shifted from Paris to the north-east. Jean de Berry (*d* 1416) spent much of his time in Paris as did the outstanding manuscript illuminators that he patronized like the Boucicaut Master and the Limbourg brothers (figs.5 and 11). But Philip the Good, himself an enthusiastic patron of the arts, favoured his client cities in the Low Countries, where, remarkably, many of the Paris-based artists of the Jean de Berry era had been born. Panel painting now came to surpass manuscript illumination as the genre where the most significant developments were taking place in the work of towering figures like Jan van Eyck and Robert Campin, but the later decades of the century saw a splendid resurgence of Flemish manuscript illumination initiated in the work of the Master of Mary of Burgundy.

To describe the contemporary achievements in music as momentous would be an understatement. The central event in this frequently told story (presented with a fresh perspective by Peter Lefferts in Chapter VII and Reinhard Strohm in Chapter XI) was the transference to the Continent of certain developments by English composers such as John Dunstable and Lionel Power, possibly by their presence in France at the courts of occupying British magnates like John of Bedford. These developments were taken up, along with native Flemish elements and possibly Italian influences as well, into the magnificent synthesis of Guillaume Dufay's music, which by the time of his death in 1474 had gone far towards achieving what is referred to, even if dubiously, as the Renaissance musical style. The present reflection, however, is concerned less with inherent greatness than it is with the notion of cultural variety, and it might best close with a review of the remarkably diverse musical institutions of the Burgundian era.

The cathedral retained something of its thirteenth-century importance. Late medieval cathedrals were generally well endowed from centuries-old land holdings that had greatly appreciated in value, and from this an extensive staff could be supported. There was the bishop of course, and those in immediate attendance upon him, but the core of the cathedral establishment was made up of a group of senior clergy called 'canons'. The term means, literally, 'rule', and it was adopted earlier in the Middle Ages, during the peak period of monastic influence, when it was thought essential that cathedral clergy follow a regulated life similar to that of monks. The central activity of monastic life was of course the singing of the Office, and this in turn was at first the chief duty of cathedral canons. With the passing of time, however, they found themselves increasingly involved in the administration of the diocese and frequently in civic administration as well. It was necessary, then, to appoint a cadre of lesser clergy, choral vicars, who would take their place in choir.

At Dufay's Cambrai the situation was somewhat more complex. Aside from the canons, there were nine 'greater' vicars (three priests, three deacons and three sub-deacons), who were chiefly responsible for carrying the plainsong that still formed the musical backbone of Mass and Office. A rich admixture of polyphonic music was added by the 'lesser vicars', about fifteen generally younger clerics, who were engaged primarily on the strength of their musical ability. In addition there were six choirboys in year-round residence; as the fifteenth century progressed, the boys added an increasing amount of polyphonic singing to their regular singing of chant. The entire cathedral personnel gathered in the enclosed choir for the more solemn liturgical events such as Mass on Sunday and major feast days; symmetrical groupings of vicars and boys faced each other in the choir stalls, while canons occupied *prie-dieus* in the open presbytery between choir stalls and high altar, to the north of which the bishop sat on his throne. Much polyphony was heard on these occasions, and a complex schedule of polyphonic music was performed throughout the week, sometimes involving all the lesser vicars and boys in choir, but more often involving smaller groups at various altars and chapels throughout the great building. Frequently the singers' stipends for these activities were paid from a special endowment established by some pious individual.

Perhaps of even greater significance to the music of the time were the organizations at the courts of music-loving rulers. The principal association here was the 'chapel' (*chapelle, cappella, Kapelle*), made up of a number of accomplished musicians. They were still mostly clergymen in the fifteenth century, and the name of their group derived from the fact that they sang religious services in their lord's private chapel (one notes that, in the fifteenth century, a choir is more often a place, and a chapel a group of people), but their duties involved secular entertainment as well. It was chiefly they – literate musicians as they were – who sang and played the refined chanson repertory of the time, while a cadre of lesser social standing, the lay *ménestrels* or minstrels, played in a great variety of circumstances. They would appear at the same formal suppers as the members of the chapel, playing lighter, improvised music, monophonic and polyphonic; they accompanied dancing, provided music at outdoor festivities, signalled the coming and going of their master, provided military music and much else. While not men of

13. Wedding feast accompanied by musicians playing two shawms and a sackbut: miniature from 'L'Histoire de Olivier de Castile et Artus d'Algarbe', written and illuminated for Philip the Good, Duke of Burgundy (fifteenth century)

learning, they must have been impressively skilled musicians, since a position at court was the ultimate goal of a late medieval instrumentalist.

The pay records of Philip the Good's court for 1443 show sixteen chaplains, including Dufay's eminent contemporary Gilles Binchois, and a comparable number of *ménestrels*; the latter are given descriptive designations such as 'trompette de guerre', 'harpeur' and 'joueur de vielle'. Philip recognized no one location as his capital, but moved his court about with him from place to place; he favoured especially his northern cities, like Bruges, Ghent and Lille, and when sojourning there the travelling portion of his court would join resident courtiers and the musicians of other local organizations to celebrate both ecclesiastical and secular occasions. Perhaps the principal such centre was Bruges. The most prominent of the city's musical organizations was that of the great collegiate church, St Donatian. Bruges, along

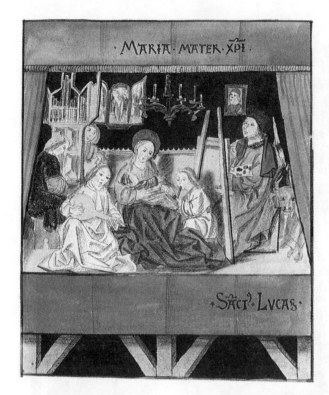

· MARIA· MATER· XPI ·

+ SÃCT? · LVCAS ·

14. Tableau vivant representing the Virgin and Child and St Luke, with musicians playing organ, pipe and lute: miniature from a Flemish manuscript describing the wedding ceremonies of Philip the Fair and Joanna of Castile (1496)

with several other important commercial centres of the Low Countries, was founded too late in the Middle Ages to be named a diocese. The wealthy town fathers, however, not to be outdone by episcopal sees, had cathedral-like churches built and endowed them with the income to support a similar clerical establishment, lacking only the bishop, of course – hence the term 'collegiate church'. St Donatian boasted a complement of canons, vicars and choirboys that was if anything larger than that of the cathedral at Cambrai, and it supported a correspondingly complex programme of polyphonic music. (One recognizes in the collegiate church, incidentally, which was essentially a lay-sponsored institution, still another example of the rise of late medieval secular influence.)

Cathedral, court and collegiate church represent the dominating musical organizations of the fifteenth century, but it is one of the chief virtues of Strohm's work to show that there was much more to the urban musical life of the time. While monasteries and the stricter priories did not allow polyphonic music, some religious institutions, like the Carmelite priory, were hospitable to numerous organizations that maintained musical programmes. The 'Merchant Adventurers', an association of English wool merchants, was only one of several foreign trade groups so involved; they built a chapel in the Carmelite priory after 1344, where, in addition to burials, christenings and the like, a polyphonic mass was sung each week. Craft guilds, like those of the sailors, brewers, chandlers and lace makers, sponsored similar activities, as did numerous religious confraternities, the most famous of which, the 'Chambre du Rhétorique du St Espirit', was more than incidentally musical. Its members functioned somewhat like their contemporaries, the Meistersinger, composing vernacular poetry and song and performing mystery plays.

All these organizations, including the court, the major churches and the town trumpeters, joined together in the great outdoor processions that marked the principal annual festivals; among some twenty of these the foremost perhaps was the procession on 3 May of the Holy Blood coinciding with the May Fair. As bells sounded from every church tower, literally hundreds of musicians sang and played while the people joined in the singing of their favourite chants. Mystery plays were staged along with colourful *tableaux vivants* (fig.14), static representations of scenes like the Nativity, the Resurrection and the Tree of Jesse – they were static, except for the playing of angelic and Davidic instrumentalists, familiar to us from the painting of the period.

Bruges at this time can be taken as a microcosm of late medieval musical life, and clearly it suggests not a time of decline but a time of diversity, a diversity so rich that it poses difficulty to the historian trying to encompass it within some unitary explanation. But there is one assertion that can be made with a degree of confidence: it all appears to have little to do with the Renaissance. Some might wish to argue this point, but they will find no northern Petrarch, Boccaccio or Lorenzo Valla to share their argument and to claim that they were participating in a rebirth of antiquity. Least of all would they find an Antonio Filarete or Antonio Manetti to extol the virtues of Brunelleschi's purported revival of Roman architecture and to express disgust (*odio*) with the Gothic as did Filarete. Indeed, there is little in the entire northern visual world to suggest the Renaissance. It is a thoroughly Gothic world and those Italianisms that one witnesses in Loire Valley illuminators like Fouquet, for example, strike one immediately with their foreignness. Perhaps the ultimate visual confirmation comes further north in Reginald Ely's incomparable chapel of King's College, Cambridge, built at the turn of the century; it is a thoroughly medieval building and nothing could bring this into sharper focus than the Renaissance choir screen donated by Henry VIII in the 1530s. Two generations after the death of Dufay, the Renaissance was finally tangibly present in the north. At what point would one wish to describe the music as Renaissance?

Antiquity and the Middle Ages

BIBLIOGRAPHICAL NOTE

The Hebraic and Hellenic heritage, 750 BC to AD 410

H. Banford Parkes's *God and Men: the Origins of Western Culture* (New York, 1959) has for many years influenced my thinking on early Western civilization; the reference to Amos of Tekoa that opens the present essay is borrowed from that work. On Greek music the best overview remains I. Henderson's 'Ancient Greek Music', *NOHM*, i (1957). On the relationship of temple, synagogue and early Christian music see J. McKinnon, 'On the Question of Psalmody in the Ancient Synagogue', *EMH*, vi (1986), 159–92. W. Wiora's *The Four Ages of Music* (New York, 1965) is a rich and original reflection on the place of music in Western civilization. A work that does something similar for architecture and that had a direct influence on my essay is S. Kostof's *A History of Architecture: Settings and Rituals* (London, 1985).

The Dark Ages and Gregorian chant, 410–800

Of the many texts on general medieval history I find the most cogent and compelling narrative in N. F. Cantor's *Medieval History: the Life and Death of a Civilization* (New York and London, 1969). D. Knowles is probably our most outstanding historian of Western monasticism; there is an eloquent distillation of his oeuvre in the popular *Christian Monasticism* (New York, 1969). Among the works cited in the bibliographical note to Chapter IV below, those of Noble and Krautheimer were particularly helpful in the preparation of this essay.

Imperial, Romanesque, Gothic, 800–1270

G. Duby's *The Age of the Cathedrals: Art and Society, 980–1420* (London, 1981) is superb cultural history, overflowing with insight on every page; it greatly influenced this portion of my introduction. I. Panofsky's *Gothic Architecture and Scholasticism* (New York, 1951) is a generally successful attempt to explore the comparison implied in its title; it should be read by all those attempting similar comparisons. I. Chartier has provided a useful overview of medieval musical theory in 'Musical Treatises', *American Council of Learned Societies Dictionary of the Middle Ages*, viii (1987), 636–49.

The late Middle Ages, 1270–1474

The reader will find in the fourth portion of this introduction echoes of two general studies: M. Vale, 'The Civilization of Courts and Cities in the North, 1200–1500', in *The Oxford Illustrated History of Medieval Europe* (Oxford, 1988), and W. Swaam, *The Late Middle Ages: Art and Architecture from 1350 to the Advent of the Renaissance* (Ithaca, NY, 1977); the latter work is superbly illustrated. For a colourful portrait of music during the period, see R. Strohm's *Music in Late Medieval Bruges* (Oxford, 1985) and more particularly C. Wright, 'Performance Practices at the Cathedral of Cambrai 1475–1550', *MQ*, lxiv (1978), 295–328. For the significance of the Renaissance in Western civilization one turns again to the greatest of our cultural historians, E. Panofsky, and his *Renaissance and Renascences in Western Art* (New York, 1960).

Chapter II

Public Music as 'Fine Art' in Archaic Greece

ANDREW BARKER

The Greeks had no expression for 'fine art' as distinct from 'craft', and no sharp differentiation between aesthetic values and ones rooted in social, ethical or religious function. It is sometimes argued that at least in pre-classical times they recognized no division between 'popular' and 'refined' manifestations of culture. But the lyrics of Sappho and Alcaeus are not folksongs; and the Greeks saw in the works of their best musicians a touch of genius that set them apart from the commonplace musical fodder of religious ritual. Classical tragedy was in our terms 'art' of the highest excellence, and the point was not lost on the Greeks: Aristophanes in his *Frogs*, for instance, shows one tragedian sneering at another for deriving his melodies from unsuitably humble sources – drinking songs, party pieces, dirges and so on – rather than from the noble tradition of the kitharodes. But if artistic snobbery was perfectly possible in the fifth century, the distinctions underpinning it had their origins in the extraordinary social and artistic ferment of the seventh and sixth. What did these distinctions amount to, and how did they arise?

These questions are difficult, not least because of the state of the evidence that bears on them. The data include poems from the archaic period itself, mostly fragmentary;[1] comments about the past by writers of the classical era (the fifth and fourth centuries), not always unprejudiced or well directed; the essays and encyclopedias of scholars in later antiquity, whose sources cannot always be identified, or trusted where they are known, and whose judgment is as fallible as any historian's must be;[2] and finally we must make what we can of the mute evidence presented by archaeologists, especially their priceless treasury of painted pottery. Of the melodies of this period we have not so much as a phrase. It is obvious that we must reorganize the evidence and sometimes go beyond it if we are to understand it: some degree of speculation is unavoidable.

For some centuries after the collapse of the Bronze Age kingdoms, Greece was in no condition to generate sophisticated art of any sort. For one thing, very few people lived there. Those that did lived in scattered hamlets, probably associated on a tribal basis but without clear political focus. The economy, such as it was, was predominantly pastoral. Writing was unknown and foreign contacts were few. Those aspects of religious ceremony that can provide a breeding-ground for the arts seem to have remained as primitive as this general picture would lead us to expect.

In the space of a few generations during the eighth century, the picture altered dramatically. Suddenly, for whatever reason, the population soared, and political and social changes followed fast.[3] In place after place, neighbouring villages joined forces to create what were called *poleis*, unified and notionally independent political entities. These little states were conceived from the start as corporate enterprises, not the property of a monarch or an aristocracy. Even where gross inequalities of power and wealth existed, this feeling for the *polis* as a communal undertaking was never wholly lost.

The *poleis* flourished and grew, allowing space for those aspects of human culture that depend on leisure from the mere struggle for survival. Foreign contacts gave glimpses of more sophisticated ways of life, and awakened in craftsmen an intense feeling for beauty and imagery. About 750 BC, for the first time in perhaps four and a half centuries, the art of writing reappeared in Greece. Probably it came initially as an adjunct to trade; but scholars have argued that the form acquired by the alphabet in Greek hands was the direct result of its use as a notation for poetry.[4] Certainly it played a crucial role in the development of the poetic arts and in the breakdown of local artistic isolation. The whole complex of mainland and Aegean *poleis* became linked in a network of cross-fertilizing cultural ventures.

But it is not the fact that it was written that distinguished 'artistic' poetry and music from folksong and ritual. One eminent modern author, in discussing the early growth of certain musical genres, repeatedly counterpoises the 'traditional' forms of the remotest past with the 'literary compositions' of the more advanced culture we are studying.[5] This approach to the contrast is misleading. 'Literary composition' is a category that later Greeks would have recognized, but it was not as literature that the archaic poet-composer's work was valued. His written text was at most a partial blueprint for something that confronted the senses more directly, not a poem to be read, but a performance. The poet was a 'maker', not a writer, a craftsman in living sights and sounds. If his product was a solo song, his task was to execute it with voice, instrument and gesture. Where it was a piece for chorus, he did not just write words and compose music and choreography, but produced the work, training his singers and dancers, instructing and directing their accompanist on aulos or kithara (whom the poet also paid, as a master-builder might pay his masons), or even playing the accompanist's role himself. When Pindar sent poetic manuscripts to distant patrons, he also sent clear instructions about the manner of performance and the style of the music, and even a proxy director, carefully rehearsed in advance by Pindar himself. In distinguishing the 'fine art' of the poet-musician from other cultural phenomena, the notion of 'literature' will give little help.[6]

It is plain that a sense of corporate unity was crucial to the well-being of the early *polis*. This unity was underpinned from the start by religion and cult, by the dedication of a sacred place to a presiding deity, and the performance of regular rituals in which the citizens expressed and cemented their common bond. There was no attempt to suppress the multifarious cults that had proliferated previously in favour of an 'official' religion; many minor local ceremonies survived. What mattered was that certain cults should be common to all members of the new community, and that these should be recognized as peculiarly significant. The worship of the gods had always used music and dance. In the development and aggrandizement of cults focal to the *polis*, such practices had to be refurbished and enlarged and equipped with a specially compelling magnetism of their own. We are bound to envisage their establishment in these times as an act of deliberate political decision and planning, quite distinct from the organic continuation and growth of ancient ritual in its original setting.

If the archaic Greeks had been content merely to construct musical ceremonies appropriate to their ritual and civic functions, designed solely to unite the citizens in invoking and propitiating the guardian divinities, little more might have been heard of their products, except where they could be disinterred as anthropological curiosities. What made the crucial difference was the association with ritual of another order of activity, one dear to the Greeks throughout their history and always close to the fringes of religious observance, but never quite intrinsic to it. This critical ingredient was competition.

We do not really know how early the competitive mode became integrated into Greek musical institutions, but there are traces of it in Homer, and traces also of a distinction in kind between competition and ritual. Homer mentions music-making of several different sorts.[7] Some are quite informal; some are clearly elements in religious rituals or essential social institutions. Other cases suggest no special social or religious function and treat music and dance simply as forms of enjoyment and relaxation. These descriptions regularly express profound admiration for the performers' skill and the language of competition is always close to the surface, though the performances are not formally competitive in the style of Homer's athletic contests. They are entertainments in kings' courts. But this fact locates them in a world quite different from Homer's own. His performances required a different setting, and one passage gives a hint of the form it would take. It presents

15. Bronze statuette of a 'Homeric' minstrel singing to his phorminx (late eighth century BC) from Crete

the legendary musician Thamyris as a travelling virtuoso in *kitharōdia*, the art of singing to the accompaniment of a kithara or phorminx, plucked by the singer himself. He is described as taking on all comers in competition. He boasted, indeed, that he would be the winner even if the Muses themselves sang against him, and he was struck blind and deprived of his skills in punishment for his blasphemous arrogance.

This little story points unequivocally to the context in which musical excellence, as contrasted with simple enjoyment or the performance of religious function, was recognized and pursued in its own right, and *kitharōdia* was certainly among the earliest genres to be established as a focus for competition. The oldest historical instance of which we have explicit record is from about 700 BC, when Hesiod, as he tells us himself, won the prize for song at a king's funeral games at Chalkis, across the sea from his Boeotian homeland. Hesiod's words suggest nothing of participation in a religious ceremony; they express his own delight in his victory and convey a suggestion of the lustre added to the dead king and his family by their patronage of the event.[8]

Roughly contemporary with Hesiod is the 'Homeric' hymn to *kitharōdia* for the Delian festival, and it gives precious information about that institution in early times. It included contests in boxing, dancing and song. To it there came great gatherings of 'Ionian' Greeks in their ships, dressed in trailing robes, escorting their wives and children. They came from far and wide, for we are told that when the Delian maidens sing, 'they can imitate the voices of all people and their clattering: everyone would say that their utterances were his own, so well is their beautiful song joined together'. This means that they can sing in whatever accent or dialect the piece they perform requires: the 'clattering', it has been well conjectured, is the percussive articulation of rhythm, and the poet's words draw attention to differences of rhythmic type characteristic of different regions.[9]

The hymn itself cannot have been choral.[10] It was solo *kitharōdia*, whose metre was the epic hexameter which remained the norm in this genre to the fifth century: it is of the type attributed by later sources to Terpander (who will be discussed below). But it clearly refers to choral competition in song and dance and compliments the maidens of Delos on their outstanding skills. It has the intriguing implication that though the compositions were brought from other places, in a variety of dialects and rhythms, the performers were home-grown. We may guess that the poet-composers came in advance of the festival to train the choruses; their prowess lay, as we have seen, as much in the field of musical and choreographic direction as in that of composition. Similar procedures were often adopted elsewhere in later years, but at Delos the system changed: all later references to the Delian choral contests, and many describing events in other centres, imply quite clearly that the chorus itself was transported to the festival along with the song.[11]

Such occasions must have given great impetus to the musical arts, not only through the stimulus of competition but by the exchange and cross-fertilization of styles, ideas and techniques and by creating an awareness of a continuous 'song-culture' extending from mainland Greece through the islands to the Asiatic coast. But the Greeks, with good reason, never saw themselves as racially homogeneous, and the major racial groups may at this time have been culturally isolated from one another, to some degree. Delos was an 'Ionian' festival and its adherents came mainly from Attica and the islands of the central Aegean. For the Dorian Greeks, the major cultural centre in early archaic times was Sparta.

Before trying to trace some steps in its musical history, let us look at a specimen of its wares, a fascinating Spartan composition that probably dates from the mid-seventh century. Sparta was then at peace, and growing fast in political and cultural importance. It was a merry place, revelling in dance and song and in the delight of intricate craft-work, wholly different from the grim bastion of arid militarism that it notoriously became. Though the papyrus that contains the piece, a *partheneion* or 'maiden-song' by Alcman, is badly damaged at the beginning, what remains is not only wonderful poetry but also splendidly informative.[12]

It is a song of a little over a hundred lines, designed to be performed with dancing by a choir of ten girls. Other fragments indicate that it will have been accompanied by a kitharist, perhaps by Alcman himself. ('All the girls among us praise the kitharist', says one fragment; and in another, with some charming imagery, the aging Alcman regrets that he can no longer whirl around with maidens in the dance.) Its opening recounted a myth, the tale of the killing of the sons of Hippocoön, and was followed by some brief moralizing comment. But the longest and best-preserved section makes a surprising shift. The ten singer-dancers turn from mythical narration to sing of themselves, giving their names, evoking the beauty of their leader, detailing some of the functions they perform, uttering comments of suitable modesty about their prowess as singers, and referring unambiguously, in my view (though the matter is much discussed), to a rival choir with whom they compete.

We have here an admirable opportunity to investigate the relation between ritual and competition. Certainly the occasion of the piece had ritual significance. Probably it belonged to the rites of the goddess Ortheia, whose sphere was that of fertility, birth and growth. We can assume, too, that the myth was felt as being religious in content and tone; but it is not immediately clear what its scenes of battle and bloodshed have to do with the Ortheian cult and the dances of the maidens. It seems less relevant to the cult than to the legendary history of the Spartan state. In Alcman's version of the tale, the sons of Hippocoön, King of Sparta, were apparently killed by Castor and Pollux, demigods of great importance in Spartan legend, whose father, Tyndareus (Hippocoön's brother), then succeeded to the throne. In the usual form of the story, it was Heracles who did the killing; the condition of the text does not allow us to discern whether Alcman's adaptation included him or not. But we do have evidence that Alcman modified the tale in another way, by making Hippocoön's sons rivals of Castor and Pollux in love. This novel variation is significant. It makes sense of the moralizing theme of the sequel, which is that mortals should not aspire to marry goddesses; and the topics of love and marriage link naturally enough with the occasion of the song. Thus themes of femininity and marriage, appropriate to the ritual, have been grafted on to a legend whose principal focus is the Spartan *polis* itself. The celebrating community is not womankind (as perhaps in earlier forms of the cult) but the city: the rites of passing maidenhood are placed within the framework of the whole community.

When we turn to the later part of the poem, with its references to skill and competition, it is at once obvious that the contest was not one of ritual correctness or service to the goddess, conceived simply as such. The criteria implied are, in a broad sense, aesthetic, and they are of wide scope: personal beauty, nimbleness of foot, splendour of costume, sweetness of singing – all these are elements that contribute to good performance. Success for the maidens is victory in the competition, which will be judged on these and similar grounds, and Alcman's words make it virtually certain that the petition which the chorus leader is described as offering was not a ritual supplication for fertility but a prayer that her chorus should win.

What we see here is a stage in a process whereby certain musical performances produced for religious occasions became detached, in content and function, from the ritual context in which they were set. Behind this detachment lie two major factors: first, the decision to add new political status to some of the old, non-civic religious festivals; and secondly, the introduction of competition, where the excellence of performance would lie in its beauty, melodiousness, agility and so forth, not primarily in its accommodation to a religious role. Later, as we shall see, ritual performance and 'artistic' performance came, in certain contexts, to be completely distinct; and in these cases the latter were invariably competitive. Out of these competitions there emerged a canon of values that may quite properly be called specifically 'musical' or 'aesthetic'.[13]

Later sources agree that Sparta was an outstanding centre for music in early archaic times.[14] We find references to two phases of the 'establishment' of music there, linked to names that allow us to date the periods with moderate confidence. The first, associated with Terpander of Lesbos, must be placed around the beginning of the seventh century, and the second, involving Xenocritus (from Locri Epizephyrii in Italy), Thaletas (from Crete), Sacadas (from Argos) and several others, belongs to a time not far from the year 600. In political terms, these dates make good sense. Sparta had emerged as a political unit by about 740, and in the latter years of the eighth century had set out to secure itself a wider territory by annexing Messenia, to the north. The struggle was long-drawn, but successful, and the likely date of Terpander follows hard on its completion, when the new Sparta was settling down to a period of prosperity and peace and developing the rich culture in which Alcman found his niche. In about 640 the subject Messenians revolted, and it was twenty years before their rebellion was finally suppressed – the Spartans being inspired to courage and endurance, so it was said, by the bracing songs of Tyrtaeus. Thus the second 'establishment' of music marks the hopeful beginning of a new peace and the healing of social wounds inflicted by protracted war. Greek writers link Thaletas, in particular, with the efforts of statesmen to re-establish Spartan society on a sound footing; they credit him with curing a 'plague' there by musical means. It is probable that 'plague' is a metaphor and that the disease which music charmed away was not a medical condition but an affliction of the body politic.

Some Greek historians state that it was these musicians who instituted the two greatest Spartan festivals, the Carneia and the Gymnopaidiai. That is certainly untrue, since both are much older, but it was indeed in the seventh century that musical contests were grafted on to the ancient rituals.[15] Kitharodic competitions at the Carneia seem to date from about the 670s: Terpander is said to have been the first victor. The Gymnopaidiai included choral contests from the later seventh century, and it is for choral works that most of the composers of the second 'establishment' were best known. All our evidence points in the same direction. The instigation of musical competitions on the occasion of traditional festivals was the product of conscious political decision with clear aims, one of which involved the attraction of artists from abroad. Of all the musicians linked by our authorities with these changes, not one was a native Spartan.

Our attempt to piece together a picture of the music of these times and its social setting must take account of the judgments made by writers of the classical period. In authors from the late fifth century onwards, most strikingly in Plato,[16] we find a series of bitter polemics against the social, moral and aesthetic evils of 'modern' music, as compared with the nobility and decorum of earlier days. Along with complaints against senseless elaboration, unintelligible complexity, virtuosity pursued without artistic warrant and a general degradation of taste for the sake of popular appeal, we find two criticisms of special interest. First, the modern fad is for dramatic *mimēsis*, 'imitation', and the arousal of emotion by vivid musical representations of action and passion. Secondly, modern music is undisciplined, in that it fuses together styles that had once belonged to rigorously distinguished genres, whose subject matter, rhythmic structure and melodic basis had been clearly determined by unbreakable rules. Aristophanes, Plato and their successors (notably Aristoxenus and the later scholars who drew on his voluminous works) thought of this older and nobler musical tradition as culminating in a 'golden age' during the first decades of the fifth century, the time of Pindar and Aeschylus. Its decline is laid to the account of a string of composers who worked through the subsequent 80 years or so, especially Phrynis, Melanippides, Philoxenus, Cinesias and Timotheus and the tragedians Euripides and Agathon. This period of rapid musical change lies beyond the scope of this essay,[17] but we need to inquire how accurate the later conceptions of pre-Pindaric music really were and how likely it is that the alleged 'golden age' displayed such features as the polemicists praise. Are their nostalgic comments to be treated as history, or merely as the projection of disappointed ideals into an imagined past?

Let us consider first the question of 'rules', formulated to govern the styles and structures proper to works of each genre. In music designed purely to satisfy the needs of ritual – paeans, hymns, processionals and the rest – traditional forms undoubtedly persisted, and the scholars of late antiquity had little difficulty in tabulating them. Something similar

16. Barbiton and aulos at a symposium: detail of a kylix (red-figure style, early fifth century BC) from Vulci

is true of various semi-public forms of entertainment, such as the songs sung at symposia and on other convivial occasions. Sympotic music became very diverse in the fifth century, drawing in pieces from the repertory of lyric love-song and incorporating professional entertainments that a modern night-club would be happy to present. But it had a staple diet whose lines had been fixed in Dorian communities more than two centuries earlier, consisting of songs in elegiac couplets accompanied by the aulos.

For reasons that cannot be pursued here, the main characteristics of this genre were outstandingly well suited to its social function, and the persistence of the form can be explained without reference to explicitly imposed 'rules'.[18] The same is not obviously true, however, of the great competition pieces, where artistic inventiveness was at a premium and the original ritual context imposed few restraints. But the conditions of competition themselves naturally presuppose some norms defining the type of piece to be judged. Further, given the political ambience of the contests, it seems likely that the practice of codifying and inscribing civic laws, which spread rapidly from the seventh century, may have extended to the regulations of the festivals: these were, indeed, an integral part of a state's political institutions.[19] Later commentators insist that in this musical sphere as much as in any other, the genres were carefully distinguished, and the structures and styles appropriate to each were rigorously fixed.

It is notable, however, that in this connection our sources focus most attention on one genre in particular, that of *kitharōdia*. Terpander, who was prominent in the early history of kitharodic contests both at Sparta and at Delphi, is credited with the invention of a canon of seven types of piece, each with its own name and formally defined structure. The lists of types given by the historians do not inspire much confidence and we know little about the rules that are alleged to have been imposed and from which, so it was said, the pieces acquired their generic name, 'nomoi'; 'nomos', in other contexts, means 'law' or 'customary usage'. But there is evidence that kitharodic competition music was indeed resistant to change. Thus Terpander's *nomoi* are said to have been in epic hexameters, in the tradition of Homer and Hesiod and of pieces like the Delian hymn; indeed, Terpander apparently sang passages from Homer as *nomoi*, as well as his own verses. Some 250 years later, Timotheus, the great musical iconoclast, is reported to have written his first *nomoi* in the same metre, and his *nomos* called *Persians*, much of which survives, begins (though it does not continue) with hexameters of epic purity.[20] Similarly Euripides, in Aristophanes' *Frogs*, makes fun of Aeschylus for deriving the rhythms of his tragic lyrics from the hexameters of *kitharōdia*, which must mean that the epic metre was still standard in kitharodic performance when *Frogs* was produced, late in the fifth century.

A string of well-known anecdotes supports a similar conclusion. They concern fifth-century kitharodic performers who incurred official penalties for breaches of competition rules, especially in connection with new-fangled modifications to their instruments. Most of the stories, admittedly, are set in Sparta, which was by then notorious for

17. Solo competitive performance by a kitharode: detail of an amphora (red-figure style, c480 BC) from Attica

its conservatism; in Athens, at least, the rules were less constrictive. What is clear is that the rules were formal and institutional, not just projections of the judges' taste. The criteria breached were not those used in deciding who should win, but those determining which performances counted as legitimate entrants. It seems likely, moreover, that the stories reflect resistance not only to changes in the structure of instruments but also to the jumbling of melodic forms and the modulation between different modes of attunement (*harmoniai*) of which Plato often complains; for these structural alterations (especially the addition of extra strings) were adopted precisely to make such modulations possible.

Kitharōdia, however, is arguably a special case. The sixth century was a time of unprecedented political vitality, self-confidence and experiment and it witnessed musical innovations that were equally extraordinary. Some, like the intimate lyrics of Sappho, Alcaeus and others, made little immediate impact on public music-making, though their time was coming. Of those that did, most were connected with the competitions, and almost all involved the music of the aulos. This double-reed pipe had existed in the Greek world for centuries, yet it was consistently spoken of as something foreign (usually, as originating in Phrygia). It was mysterious and exciting, almost magical in its emotional power and range: it was an essential ingredient in the frenzied and ecstatic cults of Dionysus.[21]

Before the end of the seventh century there is no sign of its adoption into the competitive festivals. It was pervasive in demotic cult, particularly in rites connected with fertility. It was much used in symposia and in martial music and in all sorts of informal merry-making. According to Aristotle, Spartan citizens routinely learnt to play it, in early times, and used it in their dances. (This he states as something rather surprising, since in his day it was thought of as an instrument for professionals and hirelings; its performance distorted both physical dignity and moral character, though listening to its sounds, in an appropriate context, had the useful psychological effect of purging and discharging dangerous emotions. Musical education for citizens was restricted to singing and playing the lyre. Plato, characteristically, banned the aulos altogether from his ideal republic.)

It is possible that the Spartans were the first to introduce aulos music into public contests; but the earliest case for which we have reliable evidence is the adoption of *aulōdia* (solo song with aulos accompaniment) and *aulētikē* (solo aulos playing) into the Pythian festival at Delphi during the 580s. By the end of the century two other musical forms that depended on the aulos had become important items in the competitive repertory: the choral genres of dithyramb and tragedy. Not long afterwards we begin to hear protests, of a kind that later became commonplace, at the aulos's increasing domination of the musical scene.

18. Aulete on the battle-field: detail of an amphora (early Corinthian style, c640 BC)

What is this hubbub? What are these dances? What loud-clattering arrogance has come upon the Dionysian altar? . . . It is song that the Muse made queen: let the aulos dance after it, since it is a servant. . . . Batter the one with the mottled toad's breath! Burn that spittle-wasting reed with its deep-chattering mouth and its step that wrecks tune and rhythm, a menial whose body is formed with a drill!

[Pratinas, frag.1]

Once the aulos had passed, through the competitions, into the hands of professionals who were prepared to refine its structure and their own techniques, and to explore its expressive possibilities, it became an instrument through which, for the first time, pure wordless sound could be transformed into a vividly dramatic vehicle for emotional representation and evocation. Some idea of its scope can be gained from the following passage. Its author is a late lexicographer, but the piece he describes belongs to the sixth century, and his sources may well be reliable.

The auletic *Pythikos nomos* has five parts, called *peira, katakeleusmos, iambikon, spondeion* and *katachoreusis*. The *nomos* is a representation of the battle of Apollo against the serpent. In the *peira* ['test' or 'trial'] he surveys the ground to see if it is suitable for the contest. In the *katakeleusmos* ['challenge'] he calls up the serpent, and in the *iambikon* [a reference to its rhythm] he fights: the *iambikon* also includes sounds like those of the trumpet and gnashings like those of the serpent as it grinds its teeth after being pierced with arrows. The *spondeion* ['libation song', in spondaic rhythm] represents the victory of the god; and in

the *katachoreusis* ['triumphal dance'] the god performs a dance of
victory. [Pollux, *Onomastikon*, IV.84]

Another source gives a slightly different account, with variant titles
for the piece's 'movements'; a particularly striking touch occurs in what
he says of the section called 'syringes', where he explains that the player
'imitated the death of the monster as it expired with its final whistlings
[*syrigmoi*]' (Strabo, *Geography*, IX.3.10).
This spectacularly mimetic music for solo aulos is something that
the plucked strings of the kitharist could hardly hope to rival. Solo
kitharistikē, without singing, must always have been 'rather thin fare', as
a modern writer has remarked. But this apparently obvious fact seems
not to have stopped the kitharists from trying. Strabo's account of the
Pythikos nomos states that it was sometimes performed on the solo kithara
instead of the aulos; a passage from the historian Philochorus gives
some hints about the way this formidable task might have been
approached:

> Lysander, the kitharist of Sicyon, was the first to alter the character of
> solo *kitharistikē*, stretching the strings at great tension and giving bulk
> to the sound, and presenting an aulos-like performance on the
> kithara. . . . He overthrew the thin style usual among solo kitharists,
> and was the first to play the kithara with colourful shadings, playing
> *iamboi* and the *magadis* – the *syrigmos*, as it is called.
> (quoted by Athenaeus, *Deipnosophistai*, 637f–638a)

'Iamboi' and 'magadis' or 'syrigmos' seem here to be the names of
unusual musical 'effects' generated by specially contrived instrumental
techniques and clearly related to those mentioned in similar terms
in our descriptions of the *Pythikos nomos*. The reference to 'aulos-like
performance' is to be understood as indicating dramatically varied,
flexible and expressive playing of the sort that auletes had so remarkably developed. Commentators on later music confirm, time and again,
that efforts by composers and performers to improve the melodic ver-
satility and extend the emotional range of music for strings were inspired by an ambition to emulate the achievement of the aulos.
The accounts we have of the *Pythikos nomos* and other such pieces
suggest that they may have observed certain formalities: in particular,
the series of movements into which this *nomos* was divided may have
been more or less fixed in number and character, in conformity with the
outlines of the story represented. But such rules were clearly not such as
to discourage inventiveness. Auletes were pursuing with special
enthusiasm just that uninhibited musical *mimēsis* to which Plato
objected in performances of his own time. Despite the long-standing
existence of the mimetic choral dancing,[22] this kind of dramatic representation through pure sound depended crucially on technical
ingenuity and expertise; in classical Greece it was considered a

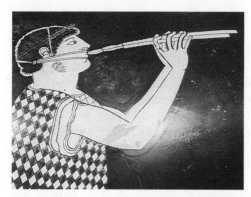

19. Solo competitive performance by an aulete wearing a phorbeia to support his cheeks: detail of an amphora (red-figure style, c480 BC) from Attica

preserve of professional soloists. The same was true of singing: choral performance, by citizen-amateurs, tended to retain simpler, less mimetic and more formalized patterns (as in the rhythmic correspondence of strophe and antistrophe, which was probably mirrored in melody too), and to avoid rapid shifts of mood or melodic structure. (See especially Aristotelian *Problems*, bk XIX, 15 and 48.)

Early professional explorations of the more vividly dramatic possibilities of musical sound coincided in date with a striking political novelty, the institution (or anti-institution) which the Greeks called 'tyranny'.[23] The two phenomena may well be related. The break with constitutional, aristocratic government represented by tyranny may sometimes have been inspired by popular discontent. But tyrants were always members of aristocratic families, whose feuds and rivalries played a significant part in the process whereby a single man came to seize power. The tyrants combined the culture of their class with the trappings of a court and were not slow to see how patronage of the arts could enhance their international prestige and could help to focus the pride and civic identity of their *polis* on their own persons. Their quasi-monarchical status, and its disruption of the communal, law-based institutions of the past, encouraged the development of 'art' for its own sake, which could now strike out further beyond the social necessities of its religious and civic occasions. The spectacular and the innovatory could come into their own, as untroubled by breaches of existing 'rules' as were the tyrants themselves by their abandonment of existing constitutional frameworks.

The tyrants' courts attracted artists, including musicians, from all over the Greek world (notably Arion at the court of Periander in Corinth, and later Lasus, Pratinas, Simonides and Alcaeus at that of the Athenian Pisistratids). Some such rulers plainly set out to use the musical festivals as a deliberate instrument of policy. Thus Cleisthenes of Sicyon seems to have waged a form of propaganda warfare against his neighbour, Argos, transferring the patronage of a local choral festival from the Argive hero Adrastus to Dionysus. This was more than mere chauvinism, since Dionysus was no special possession of Sicyon: it symbolized a rejection of a whole scheme of values belonging to the conservative establishment of the Dorian states and embraced an aspect of Greek life much nearer to popular culture, rooted in strange and exciting ritual and nourished by the music of the aulos at its most disturbing and emotive. It is worth recording that for a time under Cleisthenes Sicyon controlled the town of Cleonai, on the Argive borders. During the 570s Argos regained it, and by about 572 was using it as the centre for the Nemean festival – in honour of the hero Adrastus. One can hardly doubt that the Argives intended a direct reply to Cleisthenes' cultural provocation.

In the 590s and 580s, when Cleisthenes was at the height of his fortunes, a powerful alliance of forces (principally from Thessaly) combined in the first 'Sacred War', whose declared aim was to remove from the people of Crissa their control of the religious centre at Delphi, and of the Pythian festival. Cleisthenes and his navy formed an important part of the alliance: its victory was celebrated by a 're-founding' of the Pythian festival in 582, at which Cleisthenes was present in person. It was then that contests involving the aulos were introduced to the festival; the victor on this occasion, and the next two, was Sacadas of Argos, to whom later authorities attribute the invention of the auletic *Pythikos nomos*. No doubt the real motives behind the 'Sacred War' were complex and to some extent straightforwardly political and commercial. But it would be a mistake to underestimate the passion of both individuals and states to be seen to control the great festivals and the religious centres that housed them, and thereby to dispense patronage and to surround themselves with the splendours of artistic achievement.[24]

We have had little occasion so far to mention Athens, which began

20. Chorus singing to Dionysus: detail of a column krater (red-figure style, early fifth century BC) from Attica

to emerge as a major force only during the sixth century; in the fifth, of course, it became a dominating political power and a showcase of Greek culture that was second to none. Enough is known of its musical institutions in late archaic times to give us some idea of the background from which its spectacular successes emerged.[25]

The kind of unrest that led to tyranny in other states was slower to do so in Athens, whose social tensions were defused for a while by the moderate, though scarcely democratic, reforms of Solon, probably in the 590s. But Athenian aristocrats had friendly relations with tyrants elsewhere, notably with Cleisthenes, and this may have helped to inspire in them the ambition to convert Athens, too, from an indistinguished provincial town into a major centre for the arts. It was in the mid-560s that the first of Athens's outstanding festivals, the Great Panathenaia, was inaugurated; its establishment displays features that are by now familiar.

In the first place, it was built on the foundation of an existing festival, the annual (or 'Little') Panathenaia, whose rituals were older than anyone could remember. In this guise the ancient festival continued; but to it was added, every fourth year, an impressive collection of competitive events, both athletic and musical. The latter included contests in *kitharōdia* (fig.17), in the new competitive genres of *aulōdia* and *aulētikē*, instituted less than a generation earlier at Delphi, and in the unusual art of solo *kitharistikē*, for whose development Sicyonian artists were perhaps mainly responsible. In addition, probably from the start, it presented contests between rhapsodes, declaimers of Homeric epic without musical accompaniment, an event unique to the Panathenaia. It cannot be too heavily stressed that this programme was not a gradual growth but a deliberate institution set up, in a particular year, by political decision. Further, though it was certainly an expression of civic pride and self-confidence, it was intended not just to provide a platform for Athenian artists, but to enhance the city's prestige by attracting competitors from all over Greece.

Most of the great solo performers of the competitions were also producers of choral works. It is to be expected that such pieces, whose performers, however well trained, were citizen-amateurs, should be slower to cut loose from their civic and religious roots and from the relatively simple musical forms that they inherited from long tradition. But times were changing, and by the later sixth century, under the influence of professionals whose experience in the solo competitions had revealed to them the enormous expressive power that well-trained and imaginative musicians could exercise, two major additions were made to the Athenian repertory of choral competition. These were dithyramb and tragedy. Both were choral forms (the part of solo 'actors' in tragedy was initially minimal), and to that extent involved citizens' participation: they were organized as contests between choirs

21. *Maenads (one of whom plays an aulos) dancing before an image of Dionysus: detail of a kylix (early fifth century BC) from Attica*

representing different 'tribes' or administrative subdivisions of the Athenian people and they generated intense partisan enthusiasm. For the citizens of the *polis* these events were never mere spectacles to be observed, but parts of life to which they were vigorously committed. Both derived from ancient, mysterious cult practices indigenous to the countryside which had hitherto found no civic role. Their presentation at civic festivals seems to reflect political recognition of the potentially dangerous magnetism of these deep-rooted folk-rituals and a decision to try to relocate their focus in the heart of the political community itself. Intimately allied to the cult of Dionysus, both brought with them the music of the aulos at its most deliriously ecstatic.

The history of these genres has been ably chronicled elsewhere.[26] Dithyramb was a circular dance and song, accompanied by an aulete. Its words were usually narrative and its dancing was mimetic. Though it was introduced on a serious basis at Corinth during the tyranny of Periander, about 600 BC, it did not appear in Athenian competitive festivals until late in the sixth century. Here its artistic character was apparently altered and determined for the future by Lasus of Hermione, one of several famous musicians in the retinue of Hipparchus, son of the tyrant Pisistratus.

Dithyramb remained an important civic focus – Plato speaks of it with approval; but as 'art' it was not a success. Already in the generation after Lasus we find Pindar complaining that its true nature has been emasculated by Lasus' innovations: it has been made elegant and civilized, divested of its dangerous emotional violence and orgiastic vigour (Pindar, frag.61). Perhaps the decision to give it a central role in the civic framework had inspired these efforts to tame it, to absorb it into polite art, to eliminate its uncultured antecedents. The dithyrambs of Pindar's younger contemporary Bacchylides are notably genteel;

and by the later fifth century the dithyramb's traditional wildness found only an artificial echo in the strained and absurdly elaborate diction of such composers as Cinesias. Aristophanes' mockery of these effete warblers seems well deserved.

Tragedy, the greatest achievement of the Greek performing repertory, had its origins in masked mummings whose nature and background are almost wholly obscure. As its masks indicate, it was from the start more directly representational than most musical productions: the performers could visually become the characters of their embryonic drama. But in other respects, early tragedy was just one of a host of evocative dance forms – dithyrambs, *hyporchēmata*, the ritual expressions of maenadism and phallic cult, the performances of the curious padded dancers or 'fat men' centred on Corinth, and many others.[27] It was scarcely a 'play' as we understand such things. It portrayed a mythical episode in mimetic dance and song, mainly choral but admitting snatches of solo for the chorus-leaders, all accompanied by the aulos; spoken dialogue was introduced only gradually.

Competition in tragedy was introduced into the festival of the Dionysia in the mid-530s, during the tyranny of Pisistratus. From a religious point of view the festival was quite unimportant, and remained so. Other Dionysiac celebrations in Athens had far greater significance (particularly the Anthesteria and the Lenaia): the Dionysia itself seems to have been on a par with many equivalent celebrations elsewhere in rural Attica. This fact may have worked to the advantage of the newly adopted musical form. The festival had its rituals, but – perhaps because of their relative unimportance – no attempt seems to have been made to integrate tragedy with them.[28] Tragedy was never part of the ritual, but a free-standing addition, with no ceremonial niche to fill and very little history to constrain it. Its composer-producers were therefore free to invent their own forms, uninhibited by formalized definitions of genre. The developed tragedy of classical times is strikingly eclectic, borrowing and brilliantly redeploying elements whose original homes were in other musical settings – linguistic, poetic and choreographic elements, as well as ones of a strictly 'musical' sort.[29] It is no surprise that Plato singled out tragedy for some of his bitterest attacks: it is the paradigm case of an art that was not only auletic, mimetic and equipped with irresistible powers of emotional persuasion but was constituted by just that multifarious 'jumble' of styles that he found most deeply suspect.

Tragedy, like dithyramb, began as folk art transported, by political fiat, into a new civic setting and established as a field for competitive musical endeavour. Its astonishing successes lie in the fifth century, beyond the scope of the present essay, and they were due to poet-composer-producers whose genius cannot be wholly accounted for by the ruses of social history. But the opportunity seized to such effect by

22. *Comic padded dancers: detail of a skyphos (late sixth century BC) from Attica*

Aeschylus, Sophocles and Euripides can evidently be traced, in part, to the very artificiality of the connection between the musical form and its occasion. Where dithyramb was fixed in a mould that it could only prettify, tragedy was free to invent; and its invention drew on every musical genre and expertise that archaic Greece had developed.

Let us pull together some threads and take stock of the situation at the threshold of the fifth century, the beginning of the brief 'golden age' on which later conservatives cast such longing glances. From their point of view, it marked the summit of political history, at least in Athens, a time of moderate institutions, before the excesses of the radical democracy, when solid citizens of worth and honour, respectful of tradition, led a disciplined and god-fearing state: it was the time of the 'men of Marathon' and their glorious repulse of the Persian menace. Their music's claim to greatness lay, for Plato and his like, in a nobility which reflected that of the community itself and was well accommodated to the emotional training of its citizens' sensibilities, awakening in them a sense of their human and corporate dignity; it was music of high artistry, but its aesthetic aims had not yet detached themselves from its religious, civic and educational purpose.

Our investigations will have suggested that much of this is pious twaddle. Though it is certain that the developments to which Plato objected gathered pace rapidly in the fifth century, their roots were much older. Nevertheless, these unhistorical fancies conceal a grain of truth. The detachment of competitive art from ritual function was an absolutely necessary condition of the growth of musical expertise and invention in the hands of serious professionals. At the same time the deliberate purpose of the competitions, from the outset, was civic and political: the weapon was shrewdly wielded by statesmen throughout archaic times, and again in the classical period and beyond. Plato could only have admired the way in which they helped to forge a sense of communal endeavour and self-esteem and brought honour to the communities responsible for them. But by the end of the sixth century the essential ingredients of this political and musical nexus were poised in an equilibrium as precarious as it was artistically fruitful. Citizens could justly pride themselves on the cultural magnetism of their *polis* and of the festivals it controlled. In some cases they could participate directly as chorus members; there can have been few Athenians who had not been trained in the choral arts. The community was involved at every level and its musical life gave it an inspiring emotional focus. But the aesthetic achievements of the preceding century had been forged by professionals, whose technical prowess far outstripped the capacities of ordinary amateurs. A gap was opening between artist and audience, between the capacity to appreciate and the capacity to participate, especially (but not only) in performance on instruments. The refinement of auletic techniques stimulated the development of dramatic musical *mimēsis* and emotional expression, and these were fuelled further by the absorption into the civic competitions of the wild music of the Dionysiac cults. The influx into prominent *poleis* of distinguished musicians from elsewhere, which had been part of the political point of major competitive institutions, introduced novelties into local styles and led to the growth of an 'international' musical language, undoing further the bonds between the music and the tradition of the community.

In the early fifth century, perhaps, these factors still maintained a balance that could satisfy both the artist and the political moralist. But it is not surprising that in the heady atmosphere of intellectual, social and political radicalism that swept Greece in the years after 450 BC, many composers were seeking to break right away from the conventions of the past and from the formalities that linked music to a more ordered and hierarchical kind of society. Just as philosophers and sophists were advertising the autonomy of the individual's mind and will against socially imposed norms,[30] so composers like Melanippides and Timotheus, the *bêtes noires* of conservatives in the later fifth century, sought to give aesthetic autonomy to music conceived simply as music, and recognized no constraints in tradition. 'I do not sing the old songs', sang Timotheus, 'for my new ones are better. A new Zeus reigns . . . Away with the old Muse!' Despite what his eminent detractors said, we may believe that his elaborate 'songs' were after all pretty good. They were hugely popular in their own time and were remembered for centuries: his longest surviving fragment, the *Persians*, displays a most sophisticated artistry in style and rhythm. We have no more reason to doubt their musical credentials than those of Euripidean tragedy. The change that had come over music was not a decline in aesthetic standards but the culmination of a progressive separation of artistic from social values whose origins we have found more than two centuries earlier. It is a separation that Plato not only deplored but thought strictly impossible. 'Styles of music are nowhere altered without change in the greatest laws of the city', he asserts, quoting the fifth-century theorist Damon. From one point of view he was right. This detachment of aesthetic excellence from social function was not an isolated phenomenon: it was an aspect, perhaps in part a cause, of a wholesale transformation of society. Plato's ideal *polis* was one in which each citizen's aims and ideals coincided completely with the corporate objectives of the community, and where musical values, like all others, were wholly absorbed in social ones. What was socially undesirable was thereby morally and aesthetically ugly. Such a *polis* never existed, but it was certainly closer to reality in late archaic Greece than in classical times. The autonomous freedoms of late fifth-century music reflected to perfection the individualistic, humanistic pluralism of the new democracies.

NOTES

[1] The main Greek texts are collected in D.L. Page, *Poetae melici graeci* (Oxford, 1962); E. Lobel and D.L. Page, *Poetarum Lesbiorum fragmenta* (Oxford, 1955), and M.L. West, *Iambi et elegi Graeci ante Alexandrum cantati* (Oxford, 1971–2). Translations of most of the relevant poems will be found in *Lyra graeca* and *Greek Elegy and Iambus with the Anacreontea*, ed. J. M. Edmonds (Loeb Classical Library).

[2] Some of these writings are collected in A. D. Barker, *Greek Musical Writings*, i: *The Musician and his Art* (Cambridge, 1984).

[3] On the history and culture of the period see A.R. Burn, *The Lyric Age of Greece* (London, 1960), and especially A. Snodgrass, *Archaic Greece* (London, 1980).

[4] The idea appeared first in H. T. Wade-Gery, *The Poet of the Iliad* (Cambridge, 1952).

[5] A. Pickard-Cambridge, *Dithyramb, Tragedy and Comedy*, rev. edn. by T. B. L. Webster (Oxford, 1962); see for instance pp.9–10.

[6] The poet's role as 'producer' is a major theme of J. Herington, *Poetry into Drama* (Berkeley, 1985). The cultural issues are illuminated in E. A. Havelock, *Preface to Plato* (Cambridge, Mass., 1963), particularly in chaps.7–10.

[7] Relevant passages are assembled in Barker, *Greek Musical Writings*, chap.1.

[8] See T. B. L. Webster, *From Mycenae to Homer* (London, 1958), chap.8, section 5.

[9] See T. B. L. Webster, *The Greek Chorus* (London, 1970), 55, and compare his *Greek Art and Literature, 700 to 530 B.C.* (London, 1959), 6–10.

[10] Webster (*The Greek Chorus*, 54) takes a different view, but his grounds are unconvincing.

[11] There is some ancient evidence that the two practices existed side by side at Delos in the eighth century; see Webster, *Greek Art and Literature*, 8–9.

[12] For text, translation and extended discussion see D. L. Page, *Alcman: the Partheneion* (Oxford, 1951). Other useful accounts are in C. M. Bowra, *Greek Lyric Poetry* (Oxford, 2/1961) and Herington, *Poetry into Drama*.

[13] For a different interpretation, emphasizing the pervasive religious element in all major archaic Greek competitions (but with special reference to athletic contests) see K. Adshead, *Politics of the Archaic Peloponnese* (Aldershot, 1986), especially chap.3.

[14] The fullest sources are the Plutarchan *De musica* (translated in Barker, *Greek Musical Writings*), and Plutarch's *Life of Lycurgus*, ed. B. Berrin (Loeb Classical Library).

[15] Ancient evidence about music at festivals throughout Greece is summarized in Herington, *Poetry into Drama*, appx.1.

[16] The most significant passages are in books 3 and 10 of the *Republic*, and books 2 and 7 of the *Laws*; some of them are collected in Barker, *Greek Musical Writings*, chap.10.

[17] For discussions see M. I. Henderson, 'Ancient Greek Music', *NOHM*, i (1957), and W. D. Anderson, *Ethos and Education in Greek Music* (Cambridge, Mass., 1966), chap.2.

[18] See C. M. Bowra, *Early Greek Elegists* (Oxford, 1938), and especially Herington, *Poetry into Drama*, 32–5.

[19] See Snodgrass, *Archaic Greece*, 118ff.

[20] The manner in which this piece was performed is admirably re-created in Herington, *Poetry into Drama*, chap.7.

[21] The classic, though still controversial, account of this instrument is K. Schlesinger, *The Greek Aulos* (London, 1939/*R*1970).

[22] See particularly T. Georgiades, *Greek Music, Verse and Dance* (New York, 1955/*R*1973), and Webster, *The Greek Chorus*.

[23] For a study of this phenomenon see A. Andrewes, *The Greek Tyrants* (London, 1956).

[24] On the political significance of the great festivals see Snodgrass, *Archaic Greece*, chap.3, and Adshead, *Politics of the Archaic Peloponnese*, chap.3.

[25] See especially A. Pickard-Cambridge, *The Dramatic Festivals of Athens*, rev. edn. by J. Gould and D. M. Lewis (Oxford, 1968); H. W. Parke, *Festivals of the Athenians* (Ithaca, NY, 1977); and Herington, *Poetry into Drama*, chap.4.

[26] Notably in Pickard-Cambridge, *Dithyramb, Tragedy and Comedy*, and G. F. Else, *The Origin and Early Form of Greek Tragedy* (Cambridge, Mass., 1965).

[27] Many types are described in Webster, *The Greek Chorus*.

[28] For a summary account of the ritual see Herington, *Poetry into Drama*, 88ff, mainly following the more detailed investigations of Pickard-Cambridge, *The Dramatic Festivals of Athens*.

[29] See Herington, *Poetry into Drama*, chap.5; the best analysis of rhythmic and metrical detail is A. M. Dale, *The Lyric Metres of Greek Drama* (Cambridge, 1968).

[30] These debates are discussed in, for example, W. K. C. Guthrie, *History of Greek Philosophy*, iii (Cambridge, 1969), and G. B. Kerferd, *The Sophistic Movement* (Cambridge, 1981).

BIBLIOGRAPHICAL NOTE

Social, historical and philosophical background

The flavour of the period is well captured in A. R. Burn's *The Lyric Age of Greece* (London, 1960), though some of its details are disputable; an admirable and more recent treatment is A. Snodgrass's *Archaic Greece* (London, 1980). The classic account of the courts of the sixth-century despots is A. Andrewes, *The Greek Tyrants* (London, 1956). Two other useful and provocative studies of social history are J. P. Vernant's *Myth and Society in Ancient Greece* (London, 1980) and K. Adshead's *Politics of the Archaic Peloponnese* (Aldershot, 1986). On the shifting patterns of ideas about man, society and the cosmos see J. P. Vernant, *The Origins of Greek Thought* (London, 1982), and H. Fränkel, *Early Greek Poetry and Philosophy* (Oxford, 1975). Ideas behind the political and social radicalism of the fifth century are well discussed in G. B. Kerferd, *The Sophistic Movement* (Cambridge, 1981); of the many works on early philosophy, the most judicious and inclusive is W. K. C. Guthrie, *A History of Greek Philosophy*, i–iii (Cambridge, 1962–9). A. E. Havelock's, *Preface to Plato* (Cambridge, Mass., 1963) offers an evocation of the specifically poetic and musical mode of consciousness which Platonic 'rationalism' was, in his view, designed to undermine and replace.

Competitive festivals

Much information about these important institutions will be found in A. Pickard-Cambridge, *The Dramatic Festivals of Athens*, rev. edn. by J. Gould and D. M. Lewis (Oxford, 1968), and in H. W. Parke, *Festivals of the Athenians* (Ithaca, NY, 1977). Political aspects are discussed in Adshead's *Politics of the Archaic Peloponnese*; details to do with the production of musical events are splendidly illuminated by J. Herington, *Poetry into Drama* (Berkeley, 1985). Pickard-Cambridge's better-known book, *Dithyramb, Tragedy and Comedy*, rev. edn. by T. B. L. Webster (Oxford, 1962), is still essential reading on the early history of these genres and their place in the festivals, and on the mummings and rituals from which they emerged; see also G. F. Else, *The Origin and Early Form of Greek Tragedy* (Cambridge, Mass., 1965).

Poetry

An enormous amount has been written on early Greek poetry. Much of it is very technical. Good, accessible accounts of the earliest period include T. B. L. Webster's *From Mycenae to Homer* (London, 1958) and two books by G. S. Kirk, *The Songs of Homer* (Cambridge, 1962), and *Homer and the Oral Tradition* (Cambridge, 1978). Poetry of the archaic period is clearly discussed and related to other aspects of culture in T. B. L. Webster's *Greek Art and Literature, 700 to 530 B.C.* (London, 1959), in D. Campbell's *The Golden Lyre* (London, 1983) and in Herington's, *Poetry into Drama*. Though the writings of Sir Maurice Bowra are now a little out of fashion, his *Early Greek Elegists* (Oxford, 1938) and *Greek Lyric Poetry* (Oxford, 2/1961) remain informative and inspiring, despite their idiosyncrasies. Among studies of individual poets, D. L. Page, *Alcman: the Parthene-ion* (Oxford, 1951), and A. P. Burnett, *Three Archaic Poets: Archilochus, Alcaeus, Sappho* (London, 1983), are both, in their quite different styles, impressive fusions of scholarship and imaginative sensitivity. The complex and problematic topics of metre and rhythm are probably best approached through the work of A. M. Dale, especially her *The Lyric Metres of Greek Drama* (Cambridge, 1968).

Music

Greek texts concerned with the practice of music are translated with commentary in A. Barker, *Greek Musical Writings*, i: *The Musician and his Art* (Cambridge, 1984). The most reliable and comprehensible accounts of the growth and character of musical forms and styles, and of technical issues to do with scalar systems and patterns of attunement, are still, I think, those in the second chapter of G. Reese, *Music in the Middle Ages* (New York, 1940), and in M. I. Henderson, 'Ancient Greek Music', *NOHM*, i (1957). On relations between musical conceptions and ideas of an abstract sort see E. A. Lippman, *Musical Thought in Ancient Greece* (New York, 1964), and on the place of music in educational theory and practice see W. D. Anderson, *Ethos and Education in Greek Music* (Cambridge, Mass., 1966). Matters concerning performance and production are well handled in Herington, *Poetry into Drama*; see also Campbell, *The Golden Lyre(?)*.

The most valuable discussions of dance are in T. Georgiades's *Greek Music, Verse and Dance* (New York, 1955) and T. B. L. Webster's *The Greek Chorus* (London, 1970). There is as yet no adequate book in English on the instruments, though there are useful articles in *Grove6*. The account in K. Sachs, *The History of Musical Instruments* (New York, 1940), is brief and unsatisfactory. K. Schlesinger, *The Greek Aulos* (London, 1939), is packed with detail on many aspects of Greek music, as well as on the aulos itself, but its theories are still very controversial. The most important families of string instruments are sensibly treated in H. Roberts, 'The Technique of Playing Greek Instruments of the Lyre Type', in *British Museum Yearbook*, iv. There is a tolerable German survey in *Griechenland*, Musikgeschichte in Bildern, ii/4, ed. M. Wegner (Leipzig, 1963). The more recent French book by D. Paquette, *L'instrument de musique dans la céramique de la Grèce antique* (Paris, 1984), contains material that is well worth studying, but is spoilt by the savagely cut-down illustrations and the hastiness of many of its interpretative conclusions. S. Michaelides, *The Music of Ancient Greece: an Encyclopedia* (London, 1978), is a compendium of short but careful entries on a multitude of Greek musical terms and topics; it is a reference work that every student of the subject will be glad to have at his or her side.

Chapter III

Christian Antiquity

JAMES McKINNON

We know very little about the beginnings of Christian liturgical chant. In the absence of musical notation we are all but totally ignorant of its melodic character, and at the same time the sort of literary sources that provide a fairly clear description of fourth- and fifth-century liturgical chant are by and large wanting for the first years of the church's existence. The New Testament references to music, for example, are imprecise and illusive even if they do create the general impression that sacred song was encouraged.

There is, however, one precise document that goes far towards salvaging an otherwise hopeless situation. Justin Martyr (*d c*165) wrote a remarkably clear description of the Sunday Eucharist at Rome in the middle of the second century.

> And on the day named for the sun there is an assembly in one place for all who live in the towns and in the country; and the memoirs of the Apostles and the writings of the Prophets are read as long as time permits. Then when the reader has finished, he who presides speaks, giving admonishment and exhortation to imitate those noble deeds. Then we all stand together and offer prayers.
>
> And when, as we said above, we are finished with the prayers, bread is brought, and wine and water, and he who presides likewise offers prayers and thanksgiving, according to his ability, and the people give their assent by exclaiming Amen. And there takes place the distribution to each and the partaking of that over which thanksgiving has been said.[1]

One notes immediately the absence of any reference to liturgical song, but before attempting to discuss the implications of this omission it is necessary to explain the positive significance of the passage. Even when considered outside its historical context it creates the impression of a substantially complete description: events are described sequentially, and each is prefaced by some connective – an adverb meaning 'then', or an adverbial clause referring to the completion of the previous item – that precludes the omission of any significant action. Considered in its historical context, the passage depicts a Eucharistic celebration that is essentially the same as that known from the more abundant late fourth-century sources. The first portion, the pre-Eucharistic 'service of the word' or Mass of the Catechumens, is made up of three essential elements: the reading of scripture, a homily or sermon based on it, and congregational prayer. In the second portion, the Eucharist proper or Mass of the Faithful, the Eucharistic elements are brought in, the priest recites the Eucharist prayer over them, the people respond 'Amen' to the prayer, and finally the elements are distributed to all present.

It would appear that the shape of the Eucharist, to borrow Dom Gregory Dix's memorable phrase, was substantially intact by the middle of the second century and that it is well described by Justin. What are we to think, then, of his omission of liturgical music, or to put it more properly, his omission of psalmody? It has been customary in musicological writings to explain away the omission on the grounds that the pre-Eucharistic service of the word was made up not of three elements but of four: reading, homily, prayer and psalmody. Not only is this clear from the fourth-century sources, according to this view, but the pre-Eucharistic service is plainly and simply an adoption of the synagogue service.

Only in the most recent years has this cherished view been called into question.[2] It is true, of course, as both scriptural and talmudic literature vividly demonstrate, that in the great Temple of Jerusalem an elaborate form of instrumentally accompanied psalmody was performed in conjunction with the sacrifice. But a critical review of the evidence reveals nothing analogous for the synagogues. These local institutions were as much secular meeting places as houses of prayer, and while scripture was regularly read and discussed in them at the time of Jesus, it is unlikely that there was already in place a formal service of the word that could be adopted *en bloc* by the first Christians. Such a synagogue service began to take shape only after the destruction of the Temple by the Romans in AD 70, while its psalmodic element was introduced surprisingly late, perhaps not until the eighth century. Interestingly enough, nostalgia for the Temple, and a realization that its psalmody was intimately related to the act of sacrifice, inhibited the establishment of daily synagogue psalmody.

This is not to deny the profound influence of Judaism upon early Christian liturgy. The first Christians were after all a Jewish sect, and whatever the carryover from the parent religion to the other with respect to specific practices, it is axiomatic that there be basic familial similarities. Most important perhaps is that the early church benefited from the synagogue's most revolutionary contribution to the history of religion: the synagogue was a meeting room within which co-religionists assembled, not a temple square in which they witnessed sacrifice. And in their meeting both Jews and Christians heard a canon of sacred books read and discussed. The very notion of a liturgical week, with certain days singled out for special emphasis, as well as an annual cycle

23. Spoils from the Temple at Jerusalem, including the seven-branched candlestick and silver trumpets: relief on the Arch of Titus, Rome, erected (AD 81) in honour of Roman victories in the Judean War which ended with the Sack of Jerusalem (AD 70)

of festivals, was another original aspect of Jewish religion taken for granted in Christianity. And finally Judaism alone possessed a canonical hymnal, the unmatched 150 psalms attributed to David. The simple fact that the two religions came to share the book is significant enough in itself, even if the manner in which each used it differed more than one would like to think.

There is one psalmodic legacy of Judaism that is both specific and greatly important. It involves not the pre-Eucharistic service but rather the Eucharist proper. In the Gospels of both Matthew (xxvi.30) and Mark (xiv.26) there appears a brief passage that provides the kind of precise information lacking in most New Testament references to music. We read that, as the Last Supper came to a close, 'after singing a hymn, they went out to the Mount of Olives'. If the Last Supper took place on the Passover as the three Synoptic Gospels indicate, then the Last Supper was the Passover Seder, and in all probability the 'hymn' sung was the Hallel (Psalms cxiii–cxviii). John, however, appears to place the Last Supper on the preceding day, and many exegetes follow him in this. In any event the meal is a ceremonial Jewish supper at which the participants chanted psalms.

The passage takes on expanded significance when viewed in the context of the post-biblical Christian references to music. It has been indicated here already that literary references to music become abundant in the fourth century but are extremely sparse in the earliest years of the church's existence. An interim period, corresponding roughly to the third century, can also be defined, during which such references are comparatively scarce yet sufficient to discern broad patterns and tendencies in liturgical song. The dominant positive characteristic of the period to emerge is the continued cultivation of liturgical song at communal Christian meals.

These meals can legitimately be viewed as the direct descendants of the Last Supper, even if they are no longer Eucharistic celebrations. In the primitive church the Eucharist had been celebrated at an evening meal. Paul's first Epistle to the Corinthians vividly describes such a celebration as well as the attendant abuses in eating and drinking that were virtually inevitable. Because of these abuses, presumably, the Eucharist was moved to the early morning and joined to an introductory service of instruction and prayer. Evening communal meals remained popular, however, and at their most formal constitute a liturgical genre called the *agape* or love feast. There are several descriptions of these meals in the third-century patristic literature, some to be classified as examples of the *agape* and some not. Psalmody plays a prominent role in most of them, as in this attractive passage from Cyprian of Carthage (*d* 258):

> Now as the sun is sinking towards evening, let us spend what remains of the day in gladness and not let the hour of repast go untouched by heavenly grace. Let a psalm be heard at the sober banquet, and since your memory is sure and your voice pleasant, undertake this task as is your custom. You will better nurture your friends, if you provide a spiritual recital for us and beguile our ears with sweet religious strains.

Thus the general approval of sacred song one senses in the New Testament finds fulfilment in the practice of singing at common meals. What was sung? Can we assume it was the Psalms of David, or might it have been newly composed Christian psalms like the so-called *Odes of Solomon*? A brief digression on this point is essential. First, it must be emphasized that the terms 'psalm' and 'hymn' when used in early Christian literature do not mean necessarily a biblical psalm and a newly composed hymn respectively. The terms are used interchangeably, and while the context of a passage frequently reveals which meaning is intended, just as often it does not. That much of the question is simple; what is an extremely difficult issue is whether the Christian sacred song of the first three centuries was more a matter of biblical psalmody or original hymnody. Aside from whatever light may be thrown on the question in what is to follow here, the present author can only assert that, while there is certainly some evidence for the singing of Davidic psalms in the early church, there seems no reason to dissent from the common view that newly composed Christian hymns were more the norm than biblical psalmody before the fourth century.

Granted that the common meal was the most prominent venue for Christian song in this earlier period, what of the early morning Eucharist? Is there evidence that contradicts the description of Justin Martyr? I have analysed what little evidence there is elsewhere and concluded that it does not.[3] And when one turns to the later sources, those of the later fourth century, there are hints that the psalmody appearing then in the pre-Eucharistic service is an innovation. Moreover there is an indirect indication of this in the circumstance that the clerical office of cantor emerges only at about the same late date. The counterpart of the cantor, the lector or reader who enunciates the scriptural readings during the pre-Eucharistic service, was well established in the literature before the middle of the third century.

To summarize the state of Christian song during the first three centuries, Christians no doubt sang at their religious gatherings from the beginning. The New Testament creates this impression with several warmly positive references to psalmody even if it often fails to make clear the precise circumstances in which it took place. Singing at common evening meals, however, emerges both from the New Testament and from subsequent literature as the principal musical practice of Christianity before the developments of the fourth century. This should come as no surprise when one considers the universal custom in antiquity of musical entertainment at formal meals. But what might surprise is the apparent lack of psalmody in the pre-Eucharistic service. Indeed, this must now be qualified by invoking an important distinction – that between reciting a psalm as an example of scripture reading and singing a psalm as an explicitly musical event. Justin mentioned reading both the 'memoirs of the Apostles and the writings of the Prophets' at the pre-Eucharistic service, and one can safely take the latter to refer to Old Testament books in general, including the Psalter. Surely psalms were read at least occasionally as scripture selections, and it is not improbable that their inherent lyric characteristics might have caused the lector to render them in a somewhat more overtly musical fashion than the other readings. But what the evidence fails to suggest is a discrete liturgical event that would have prompted Justin to single it out and would have necessitated the establishment of a class of clerical officers to perform it. This happens finally in the later fourth century, and in fact one can see reflected in the sources then the change-over from an occasional psalmic reading to a regular musical event. Before witnessing this transformation, however, it is necessary to observe a broad psalmodic development of an entirely different sort.

★

The monastic movement originated in Egypt and Palestine towards the end of the third century for reasons not entirely clear. Certainly a factor in its dramatic success was the laxity within the clergy and general Christian population that followed in the wake of mass conversions. Stalwart souls fled the luxury of the cities to live lives of harsh deprivation in the deserts, hoping to recapture the fervour of pristine Christianity. It has been maintained that these fierce ascetics were overtly hostile to the blandishments of liturgical song, but this view is based on later evidence.[4] There is a wealth of genuine fourth-century literature on desert monasticism, and it shows the original monks engaged in the chanting of psalms as a matter of course. They compensated for the presumed lack of quality in their chanting by quantity, and this is the very point of their contribution. They maintained an ideal of constant praying, and in furtherance of this ideal they adopted the practice of reciting large portions of the Psalter in order, the so-called *cursus psalmorum* or *psalterium currens*. The following anecdote from the *Apophthegmata patrum* illustrates the point and also suggests the peculiar attraction the desert fathers hold for modern readers.

> Once Abba Serapion was passing through a certain Egyptian village and saw a harlot standing in her cell; the old man said to her, 'Expect me later today, I wish to come and spend the night next to you'. She replied, 'Very well, Abba'. And she prepared herself and made ready the bed. When it was evening the old man came to her, went into the cell, and asked her, 'Have you prepared the bed?' She replied, 'Yes Abba'. He closed the door and said to her, 'Wait a moment, since we have a regulation which I must first fulfil'. So the old man commenced with his synaxis: beginning the Psalter he said a prayer after each psalm, beseeching God for her that she repent and be saved. And God heard him. And the woman stood trembling and praying by the old man, and as the old man completed the entire Psalter, the woman fell to the ground. . . . Realizing that he did not come to her to sin but to save her soul, she prostrated herself before him and said, 'Do an act of charity, Abba, and lead me to where I can please God'.

Serapion's recitation of the entire Psalter may have been exceptional, but the recitation of several psalms in order, interspersed with prayer, is characteristic of desert monasticism. In the course of the fourth century one discerns a formalization of monastic Offices, particularly for Lower Egypt, where a sequence of twelve psalms appears to have been the norm for the common Saturday and Sunday Office held twice a day, early in the morning and late in the afternoon.[5] On weekdays the monks performed their Office in solitude, and Palladius recalls a visit to the great monastery on Mt Nitria when, at about the ninth hour, one could hear psalmody issuing forth from cells on every side as the monks wove linen and chanted. Evidently precise ensemble was not a prerequisite of such psalmody, and it may be assumed that the conscious pursuit of musical values had little to do with a manner of chanting that was fundamentally a form of meditation. But the practice has great significance for music history in that it brought the *cursus psalmorum*, the backbone of the medieval Office, into the Christian liturgy.

In the course of the fourth century the monastic movement spread from the deserts to the great urban ecclesiastical centres of the East like Jerusalem, Antioch, Caesarea and Constantinople. There its Office exercised a profound influence on the secular cathedral Office, virtually inundating it with psalmody.[6] The public cathedral Office itself had taken shape in the fourth century after the emancipation of the church under Constantine in 312. Although differing in detail from city to city, it displays a substantially homogeneous shape in the later fourth-century sources. Like the Egyptian monastic Office, it was held twice a day, in the morning and evening, corresponding to the later Lauds and Vespers. The bishop, clergy and people were in attendance, and the ceremonies reflected the time of day in their prayers, gestures and carefully selected psalms and canticles. The Vesper service, for example, included the ceremony of lamp-lighting and the singing of Psalm lxii (lxiii), with its appropriate verse, 'Let my prayer be counted as incense before thee, and the lifting up of my hands as an evening sacrifice'. Under monastic influence the service became a hybrid, opening with a period of continuous psalmody followed by the cathedral service, a form clearly discernible in medieval Vespers with its five psalms and subsequent group of miscellaneous items.

More dramatic, perhaps, was the effect upon the morning Office, although before discussing this mention should be made of the remaining Office Hours. By the sixth century, of course, as best exemplified in the Rule of St Benedict (written *c*530), the Office had stabilized in its classic form of eight services: the nightly vigil later called Matins, the dawn Office of Lauds, the four 'little hours' of Prime, Terce, Sext and None, the sunset Office of Vespers and finally Compline at the close of the day. At least three of these – in addition to the morning and evening Offices – were introduced into the liturgy during the second half of the fourth century under the influence of monasticism. The third, sixth and ninth hours of the day were sanctified in various scriptural references, and pious souls had observed them privately as special hours of prayer during the early centuries of Christianity. As part of the process of increased formalization observable in the fourth-century monastic liturgy these three hours became publicly celebrated and in turn entered the cathedral liturgy as Terce, Sext and None. They were made up apparently of a shorter span of continuous psalmody, corresponding closely to their medieval format. The status of Compline is less certain – it appears in some sources but is absent from most – while the situation with the morning Offices of Matins, Lauds and Prime presents a fearsome tangle, not subject to easy summarization here and better left to the specialized sources.[7]

That issue aside, the description of early morning vigils at

Jerusalem as described by the Spanish nun Egeria (*fl c*400) is instructive. Each morning, except for Sunday, monks and nuns gathered in the
great Constantinian church of the Anastasis:

> Before cockcrow, all the doors of the Anastasis are opened and all the
> *monazontes* and *parthenae*, as they are called here, come down, and not
> only they, but also those lay people, men and women, who wish to
> keep vigil at so early an hour. From that time until it is light, hymns
> are sung and psalms responded to, and likewise antiphons; and with
> every hymn there is a prayer.

The difficult term 'antiphon' must be ignored here in favour of what is
obvious.[8] The classic division of monastic and cathedral contributions
is clearly present in this passage, with the monks and nuns carrying the
continuous psalmody while members of the local clergy officiate for the
alternating prayers. (It is revealing in this respect that the bishop
finally appears at the next service, which represents the traditional
cathedral morning Office.) Of special musical relevance is another
Office, the early Sunday morning vigil that replaces the weekday vigil.
Whereas devout laity simply observed the monastic psalmody during
the week, now they imitate it.

> On the seventh day, that is the Lord's Day, all the people assemble
> before cockcrow, as at Easter, as many as is possible in that place, the
> basilica, which is located next to the Anastasis, yet out of doors, where
> lamps are hung for the occasion. Since they fear they might not arrive
> before cockcrow, they come early and sit there. Hymns are sung and
> antiphons also, and there are prayers with each hymn and antiphon,
> since priests and deacons are always prepared for vigils in that place
> because of the crowd which gathers.

The service appears to be an exact duplicate of the monastic vigil
except that in the singing of psalms the laity take the place of the monks
and nuns. Psalmody at this time, incidentally, was primarily soloistic,
with choral responses or antiphons after each verse. We are not sure
who sang the psalm verses at this service, but, in the absence of monks
and nuns, there is clearly the same degree of participation by the laity in
responses and antiphons as there would be ordinarily by the rank and
file monks and nuns.

This pair of passages from Egeria constitutes only one of the
more explicit manifestations of a great movement in late fourth-century
Christianity – what might be called a psalmodic revolution, sweeping
from East to West. There are a number of patristic passages describing
vigils commencing before daybreak at which psalms are sung hour
upon hour. There are also extended passages of praise for the virtues of
psalmody; the Book of Psalms is credited with summing up within its
pages all that is valuable in the entire Bible, and God is thanked for
making the psalms more accessible than other scripture through the

sweetness of melody. All this culminates in the remarkable pair of sermons by Niceta of Remesiana (*d c*414): *De vigiliis* and *De bono psalmodiae*. We note, incidentally, that what in desert monasticism must have been a simpler sort of chanting has become a more richly melodic song (recall, for example, Augustine's scruple that Milanese psalmody might be better if less musical); but on the broader issue of monasticism's overall musical role it would appear that the late fourth-century wave of enthusiasm for psalmody could not have taken place without the monastic discovery of the Psalter as an aid to meditation.

★

It was probably this development which provided the impetus necessary for the establishment of psalmody in the Eucharist. The medieval liturgy has made us familiar with psalmody at four places in the Mass: there is an entrance psalm called the introit, a complex of psalms related to the readings including especially the gradual and alleluia, a psalm at the offertory and a communion psalm. It has been customary to attribute all five of these items to the liturgy of the early church – indeed, to trace the gradual and alleluia to the synagogue – but only two of them appear in the late fourth-century sources and then only for the first time. These are the communion and the gradual.

The history of the communion psalm is more straightforward than that of the gradual psalm. There are several late fourth-century references to the singing of a psalm during the distribution of Communion, most of them specifying Psalm xxxiii (xxxiv) with its appropriate verse 8: 'O taste and see that the Lord is good'. The psalm was sung in the standard responsorial manner; that is, a soloist would sing the verses and after each verse the people would respond with a refrain selected from the psalm, in this case verse 8. The silence of the sources before the late fourth century does not necessarily preclude the existence of this practice before that time, but the broader history of fourth-century psalmody makes it probable that it was an innovation of the period. The situation is not quite so clear in the West; there are references to Psalm xxxiii there also, and one readily imagines the adoption of so appropriate a custom, but a passage from St Augustine might be taken to suggest a wider selection of communion psalmody at Carthage. This passage is of fundamental importance in the history of early Christian psalmody.

> Meanwhile a certain Hilary, a lay catholic of tribune rank, angered – I know not why – against the ministers of God, as often happens, attacked the custom which had begun then in Carthage . . . of singing at the altar hymns from the Book of Psalms both before the oblation and while what had been offered was distributed to the people.

24. The Good Shepherd with panpipes, the most popular of early Christian subjects with musical significance: detail of the mosaic floor (fourth century AD) in the Christian basilica, Aquileia

The language does not absolutely exclude the possibility of one ordinary communion psalm, but might more plausibly be interpreted to imply the opposite. The point is noted here only because of its potential relevance to the characteristic of Western, especially Roman, liturgy to employ full cycles of psalmody in the Mass, as opposed to the Byzantine trait of greater selectivity.

Actually, the passage is more crucial to the history of the gradual than to that of the communion.[9] It reveals that the singing of psalms in the pre-Eucharistic liturgy was an innovation at Carthage, capable of stirring controversy as late as the end of the fourth century. Another passage from about the same time does not mention controversy, but it does tell us that Pope Celestine I (*c*432) introduced psalmody at Rome into the Fore-Mass where before only Epistles and Gospels had been read: 'He decreed that the 150 psalms of David be sung before the sacrifice, which had not been done before; only the Epistle of Paul the Apostle and the Holy Gospel had been recited – and so were Masses celebrated'.[10]

The passage also suggests a point of basic importance to the history of the gradual when it closely associates the psalms with the scripture readings. This is a comparatively late example of the literally dozens of references to the singing of psalms in the pre-Eucharistic service of the late fourth and early fifth centuries. One who studies these passages systematically is struck by the circumstance that most of them appear in homilies on the psalms, preached at Sunday morning Eucharist by figures like Augustine, Basil, John Chrysostom and Jerome. A typical reference makes it clear that the psalm had been sung previously in the service and that the church father chose to base his homily on the psalm, in many cases on the verse that was sung as a refrain. The subject of the early Christian homily was not chosen arbitrarily, but rather was based on one of the scriptural texts that had been read on the day of its preaching. This circumstance suggests that in its early history the gradual was looked upon as a reading, rather than as a lyric response to a reading as it is usually described. Indeed, the suggestion is made explicit in several patristic passages, as when Augustine says: 'We heard the Apostle, we heard the psalm, we heard the Gospel; all the divine readings sound together'.

That the pre-Eucharistic psalm was initially thought of as a scriptural reading suggests a hypothesis concerning its origins. The psalm that figured occasionally as an Old Testament reading in earlier centuries was transformed into a psalm sung at every Eucharistic service of the later fourth century. This happened because of the great general popularity of psalmody at the time. The psalm, while still anachronistically described as a reading, now functions as a discrete musical event, requiring the skilled offices of a cantor. Thus singled out it attracted the disapproving attention of a minority figure like Hilary, but it was gratefully accepted by the majority, including the most influential ecclesiastical leaders, East and West. Within a comparatively short time it would lose its status as an independent reading and become thematically subordinate to the reading that precedes it; thus we read of the mid-fifth-century priest of Marseilles, Musaeus, who selected 'readings from the Holy Writings appropriate to the feast days of the entire year and responsorial psalms appropriate to the season and to the readings'.

One can no longer argue seriously for the existence of introit and offertory psalms in the liturgy of the early church, but what of that other responsorial psalm of the pre-Eucharistic service, the alleluia psalm? There are various categories of patristic musical reference which are conventionally applied to the alleluia of the Mass. The most noteworthy of these comprises colourful descriptions of the jubilus, a kind of wordless melody of which Augustine says: 'a man delighting in his joy, from some words which cannot be spoken or understood, bursts forth in a certain voice of exultation without words . . . because filled with too much joy, he cannot explain in words that in which he delights'. Virtually all historians of chant identify this jubilus with the rhapsodic vocalization on the concluding syllable of the medieval alleluia, but there is no hint of such an identification in the sources themselves. The descriptions turn up in psalm commentaries on the word 'jubilare', not 'alleluia', and the latter term does not so much as appear in these passages. Moreover, the jubilus is explicitly defined as a type of work song, sung 'either in the harvest, in the vineyard, or in some other arduous occupation', not a liturgical chant of any sort. Descriptions of it make their way into the psalm commentary in the normal manner of allegorical exegesis: an object serves as a symbol of something sacred, in this case the jubilus stands for the attitude of the soul before 'the ineffable God'.

There are, on the other hand, numerous genuine fourth-century references to the singing of alleluia. None of these, however, refers necessarily to a liturgical item that can be singled out as the alleluia of the Mass. For example, when Augustine inquires, 'observe, brethren, whether in these days Amen and Alleluia are said throughout the entire world without cause', the impression is created that the alleluia, like the amen, might be used in various ways as a liturgical acclamation. Yet there are occasions where alleluia appears to have been sung as a refrain to a responsorial psalm in the pre-Eucharistic service. This happens particularly in the case of those psalms for which the word 'alleluia' is superscribed in the Book of Psalms; traditionally these psalms, in both Judaism and Christianity, have used alleluia as their refrain. To interpret such instances properly one must bear in mind that generally only one responsorial psalm was sung in the fourth-century pre-Eucharistic service. Hence in the exceptional cases where alleluia appears as a refrain, one speaks of a gradual psalm with allelulia as its refrain; to call an item *the* alleluia would require the presence of two responsorial psalms at each service, the second of which always used alleluia as its refrain.

This way of thinking is legitimized by the very fact that the dual-psalm pattern does finally appear in an Armenian lectionary thought to reflect the early fifth-century liturgy of Jerusalem.[11] The alleluia thus became a part of the fifth-century Eastern Eucharist, but there is no indication that it spread immediately to the West. This circumstance is significant in itself. It signals the end of the early Christian period of liturgical homogeneity and the beginning of the medieval period of liturgical heterogeneity. The communications system of the Roman Empire had assured that homogeneity, but now, with the crumbling of the Empire, we see the increasing isolation of various regions and the development of disparate liturgies like the Byzantine, Mozarabic, Gallican and Ambrosian.

One might well assume that the actual music of the early Christian period is irretrievably lost, since we have no notated examples of liturgical music before the ninth century. Thanks to an extraordinary study by Kenneth Levy, however, we appear to have a good idea of the music of the fourth-century Mass Ordinary.[12] The familiar Western medieval Mass Ordinary is made up of five choral chants: Kyrie, Gloria, Credo, Sanctus and Agnus Dei. Of these only the Sanctus was present in the fourth century, and it was less a set musical piece than a congregational acclamation, bringing to a conclusion the Preface, that is, the opening

25. *Interior of S Sabina, Rome (422–33); it is one of the better preserved early Christian church interiors, but has also been greatly restored.*

portion of the celebrant's chanted Eucharistic prayer. Actually, the Preface and Sanctus are only one phase of a declaimed dialogue between priest and people that extends from the beginning to the end of fourth-century Eucharist, East and West.

In a wide-ranging study of medieval notated sources it was established that there existed a basic congregational Sanctus melody, and indeed an entire complex of celebrant and congregational Ordinary chants that share a common melodic substance. They are in a sort of E mode, with a typical range of *e* to *c'*, reciting usually on *b* or *c*. The Sanctus melody survives in the familiar Requiem Mass Sanctus, while the conventional Preface and *Pater noster* chants are equally well-known portions of the complex. The material can be firmly established in tenth-century notated sources, but how does one bridge the enormous gap to the fourth century? We start with the knowledge that there is a certain universality about the material; it appears in so many sources, East and West, that a substantial degree of antiquity may be assumed for it, at least as far back as the period of maximum interchange between East and West during Charlemagne's reign (768–814). Bridging the remainder of the gap is a firm literary tradition: precisely the same texts were sung by celebrant and congregation from the fourth century to the early Middle Ages. This being the case there are only two genuinely possible histories the music might have pursued. Either it was passed on from generation to generation substantially intact, or at some point in its history the entire apparatus of chants we know from the medieval sources was imposed by fiat, without benefit of notation, upon clergy and people, who learnt it willingly and allowed the traditional system of chants to pass from the scene unremembered and unregretted. The homogeneity of the material renders implausible the third possibility of a gradual evolution, while of the two under consideration the former certainly seems altogether more likely.

★

During the same years that the liturgical chant of Christian antiquity was beginning to establish itself, another musical development of an entirely different sort was taking place within the church. The intellectual groundwork was being laid for the flowering of music theory in the Western Middle Ages. There is something paradoxical about this because it involved the approval of one facet of pagan musical culture by an institution that appeared generally hostile to it.

The attitude of the church fathers towards the day-to-day manifestations of music in pagan society is well known. 'Where the aulos is, there Christ is not', exclaimed John Chrysostom, and on another occasion he referred to musical instruments, dancing and bawdy songs as 'the devil's rubbish'. His position is typical even if his rhetoric tends to stand out somewhat. Most of the major church fathers of the third and fourth centuries uttered such remarks, condemning the musical practices that were customary at the theatre, the circus, banquets and weddings. Their motivation appears to have been twofold: they were concerned with the obvious idolatrous associations of some of these events like theatrical presentations, but perhaps even more so they were disturbed by the manifestations of sexual licence involved – for example, the common employment of prostitutes as female dancers and musicians. This kind of attitude is not unique to the church fathers, only exceptional in its intensity and the vividness of its expression. Something similar can be observed within ancient Judaism, among certain pagan intellectuals and later in Muslim savants.

In any case the existence of this tradition was acknowledged in the Middle Ages along with the seemingly contradictory acceptance of music as an intellectual discipline. Actually, the latter phenomenon is simply a facet of the general patristic position on classical intellectual culture. That position was not without its ambiguities, but it was ultimately, indeed inevitably, positive. There was, after all, only one intellectual culture available, and the church had to accept it if it wished to express its beliefs systematically, to defend them effectively, and eventually to occupy a central place in society. It is true that there were figures like the irascible Tertullian (*d c*225), who thundered: 'What has Athens to do with Jerusalem? What has the Academy in common with the church?', but the majority saw that they must make use of the pagan intellectual heritage in furtherance of ecclesiastical aims. What this meant in practice for the typical Christian intellectual of the fourth century was a thorough grounding in grammar and rhetoric as a youth, and as an adult ecclesiastic an attempt to avoid enjoying classical literature for its own sake while using its language and concepts in the interpretation of scripture.

The discipline of music occupied a fairly important place in classical intellectual life, and as such was subject to the compromise just described. It had its beginnings as an academic discipline already in Greece during the classical period – in the calculations of the Pythagoreans, in the astral speculations of Plato's *Timaeus*, in the rich social and educational philosophy of his *Republic* and *Laws*, but most formally perhaps in the theoretical writings of Aristotle's pupil Aristoxenus of Tarentum. Aristoxenus wrote on the two principal divisions of Greek music theory, harmonics and rhythmics, although very little of his treatise on the latter survives. 'Harmonics', the subject of greatest interest to theorists, dealt with considerations of pitch such as the mathematical proportions underlying intervals and the way in which intervals combine to form what we would call scales and modes. 'Rhythmics' dealt with the mathematical proportions involved in musical duration; by necessity it tended to overlap with a third division of music theory, 'metrics', which considered the systematization of poetic metres. In the time of Plato and Aristoxenus theorizing about music, while evincing a measure of intellectualism, was in relatively close touch with actual music, but this seems not to have been the case in late antiquity. Music theory flourished in the third and fourth centuries of the Christian era but was generally consistent with the other literary productions of the time. This was, in M. L. W. Laistner's phrase, 'the age of potted knowledge', when writers compiled abstracts of earlier works rather than fresh and original creations. Music theory equalled other subjects in the degree of its retrospection and surpassed them in the extent to which it was removed from everyday reality. Existing thus for its own sake it could, when served by an exceptional author like the great second-century scholar Ptolemy, achieve the status of an admirable intellectual construct, displaying considerable ingenuity and consistency, but it was somewhat less than that in the hands of later figures like Alypius and Aristides Quintilianus.

Augustine breathed a measure of life into the tradition with his *De musica*, six books on rhythmics. The first five books were written not long before his baptism in 387, when he was a neo-Platonist, and the final book a few years later. There is a different mood about the sixth book. It is not just that it is overtly Christian, substituting an Ambrosian hymn for its classical poetic examples; actually, it is more deeply and fervently neo-Platonic, and even neo-Pythagorean with its numerical view of reality. In the first book, the basic theme of the superiority of the spiritual over the material – or at least of the intellectual over the practical – is already announced; thus the typical aulos player is no more a musician in the true sense than a nightingale because he too is ignorant of the science underlying the sounds he produces. (One notes here an anticipation of the medieval *musicus* versus *cantor* topos.) This way of thinking is deepened and enriched in book 6 where Augustine describes a series of hierarchically ordered musical 'numbers'. At the lower end are sensible or corporeal numbers, that is, the musical sounds produced by the player and felt by the auditor. At the upper end are 'judicial numbers' whereby the soul evaluates the equality and harmony of the lesser numbers. These judicial numbers in turn reflect a 'number-liness' (*numerositas*) that pervades creation and which ultimately reflects the eternity and immutability of God. What is special in all of this is not so much the philosophical and theological framework as the vivid descriptiveness and psychological veracity that is unique to Augustine. One is reminded of the *Confessions*, where again he reveals himself to be keenly sensitive to the beauty of music but compelled at the same time both to denigrate his sensible reaction and somehow to justify it.

Augustine, one of the surpassing geniuses of all antiquity, was atypical in style and approach, but his basic positions were altogether conventional. His preference for 'unheard music' was consistent with that of the late classical intellectual establishment, and in his accep-tance of the academic discipline of music he shared the general patristic position. The context in which he stated his views was similarly typical. His *De musica*, six books on rhythmics, was to be complemented by six more 'de melo', that is, on harmonics, constituting altogether a total coverage of music. His work on music, in turn, was to be one of a pro-jected series on the liberal arts. He did not come close to finishing the series, but his north African contemporary Martianus Capella did, in his *De nuptiis Philologiae et Mercurii*. This allegorical work was written in nine books, the first two of which set the scene of the marriage between Philology, who stands for learning, and Mercury, who represents eloquence. It is the seven remaining books that constitute a series of treatises on the liberal arts, each taking the form of a speech delivered by one of the bridesmaids personifying her subject, and thus inspiring the medieval seven (appearing here for the first time as a complete group) even though the general conception of liberal arts, and of many of the individual subjects, appeared already in Plato's *Republic* and Aristotle's *Politics*. The seven are, in their feminine Latin forms, Grammatica, Rhetorica and Dialectica, followed by Arithmetica, Musica, Geometrica and Astronomia. Implicit in their order is the medieval grouping, if not yet made explicit, of the Trivium of language arts, which are propaedeutic to the Quadrivium of mathematical arts. The point behind the favoured position granted to the Quadrivium, of course, is the mathematical view of reality alluded to above.

26. *Musica, Arithmetica, Geometrica, Astrologia: frontispiece to Boethius, 'De institutione arithmetica', c850*

Augustine was prompted to write his *City of God* by the terrible event of Alaric's sack of Rome in 410; he died in 430 as the Vandals held his bishopric of Hippo under siege. We know nothing of Martianus Capella's biography, but assume he must have written the *De nuptiis* before the Vandals' sack of Carthage in 439. The Western Roman Empire had collapsed and was completely overrun by barbarian tribes throughout much of the fifth century. In the late fifth and early sixth centuries, however, Roman civilization enjoyed a twilight period in Italy under the benign Ostrogothic king Theodoric (*d* 527). Two Christian scholars who lived during his reign – indeed, served together in his court – made immensely important contributions to music theory; they are Boethius (*d c*524) and Cassiodorus (*d c*580).

Boethius, the author of the classic *Consolation of Philosophy*, was the stronger scholar of the two. His *De institutione musica* was a youthful work and part of a projected series on the liberal arts, like the one contemplated by Augustine; only it and the *De institutione arithmetica* survive. The first four books are based on Nicomachus and the fifth and final book on Ptolemy. It is derivative, but is none the less a competent synthesis of its sources and provides a coherent treatment of Greek theory. The famous threefold classification of music into *musica mundana*, *musica humana* and *musica instrumentalis* is an innovation of this book. The first involves the harmonious relationship between heavenly bodies – that is to say 'music of the spheres'; the second has to do with the harmonious relationship between body and soul; with the third, however, the logic of the classification seems to break down. Boethius defines *musica instrumentalis* as simply that music 'residing in certain instruments', thus leaving us to speculate on what he had in mind. The conventional interpretation is that he meant music in our sense, that is, actual sounding music, but this seems improbable in view of his tendency not to concern himself with contemporary music. It seems more likely that he had harmonics in mind, that is, the intervals and systems of pitches that 'resided in instruments' and could be demonstrated on them, particularly on the monochord – the portable laboratory, so to speak, of harmonics.

Cassiodorus wrote on music in his *Institutiones divinarum et humanarum litterarum*. The first portion of this work, on 'divine letters', enunciates his theory of Christian scholarship, in essence the conventional view that classical learning is to be cultivated solely as an aid to the interpretation of scripture. The section on 'human letters' comprises short books on each of the seven liberal arts. The book on music is extremely brief and perfunctory, omitting many of the most basic features of Greek theory. It was, however, Cassiodorus's work that was more influential (along with that of Isidore of Seville) during the ninth century, the first century of medieval music theory, while Boethius's work did not come into its own until the tenth. Their respective contributions were of an entirely different sort. Cassiodorus provided the liberal arts framework and helped to establish the basic notion that one should study music theory. The Carolingians, with their great repertory of Gregorian chant, then began to provide a systematic explanation for it. There was little of specific technical usefulness in Cassiodorus's work to develop that explanation, not much more, indeed, than the idea that simple mathematical ratios accounted for the basic musical intervals. But once the process was well under way, the more complex doctrines of Boethius could be assimilated and adapted, and by the end of the tenth century a coherent exposition of music space was possible, best exemplified by the gamut of Guido of Arezzo's *Micrologus*.

There is a fundamental difference between the medieval ecclesiastical writers on music and their forebears in Christian antiquity. The medieval authors took it for granted that they were to apply their theory to the chant they sang every day at Mass and in the Office, while it never occurred to Augustine, Boethius and Cassiodorus that the academic discipline of music had anything to do with the psalmody they heard in church. Yet if the church fathers had not given their blessing to the *ars musica*, it is possible, indeed probable, that Boethius and Cassiodorus would not have made their contributions to the subject, and it is possible in turn that the Carolingians would not have been so inclined to cultivate music theory. One can argue further that without the development of medieval music theory, Western music itself would have followed a different course. With the vertical rationalization of harmony and the horizontal rationalization of metrical schemes it seemed driven to pursue architectonic structure at the expense of the melodic and rhythmic subtleties that characterize other world musics.[13]

The musical bequest of Christian antiquity, then, was twofold. There was of course the establishment of ecclesiastical psalmody that would develop into Gregorian chant and indeed eventually into Western art music, and, less obvious perhaps, there was the theoretical impulse that would help to form the unique character of that music.

NOTES

[1] All passages from early Christian literature either quoted or cited here are to be found in J. McKinnon, *Music in Early Christian Literature* (Cambridge, 1987).

[2] See J. Smith, 'The Ancient Synagogue, the Early Church and Singing', *ML*, lxv (1984), 1–16, and J. McKinnon, 'On the Question of Psalmody in the Ancient Synagogue', *EMH*, vi (1986), 159–91.

[3] 'The Fourth-Century Origin of the Gradual', *EMH*, vii (1987), 95–7.

[4] See *Music in Early Christian Literature*, 51–2.

[5] On the Office of desert monasticism see R. Taft, *The Liturgy of the Hours in East and West* (Collegeville, Minn., 1986), 57–74.

[6] On the cathedral Office see the relevant portions of Taft's work cited immediately above as well as those of P. Bradshaw, *Daily Prayer in the Early Church* (London, 1981). For a particularly cogent exposition of the relationship between monastic and cathedral Offices, see W. J. Grisbrooke, 'The Formative Period – Cathedral and Monastic Offices', in C. Jones and others, *The Study of Liturgy* (London, 1978), 358–69.

[7] One might begin with those cited in *Music in Early Christian Literature*, 150.

[8] There is no completely satisfactory explanation of the origin of antiphonal psalmody; see H. Leeb, *Die Psalmodie bei Ambrosius* (Vienna, 1967), 18–23.

[9] See 'The Fourth-Century Origin of the Gradual', 103–4.

[10] On this passage see P. Jeffery, 'The Introduction of Psalmody into the Roman Mass by Pope Celestine I (422–32)', *Archiv für Liturgiewissenschaft*, xxvi (1984), 147–65.

[11] See A. Renoux, 'Un manuscrit du lectionnaire arménien de Jérusalem', *Muséon*, lxxiv (1961), 361–85, and lxxv (1962), 385–98.

[12] K. Levy, 'The Byzantine Sanctus and its Modal Tradition in East and West', *AnnM*, vi (1958–63), 7–67.

[13] See W. Wiora, *The Four Ages of Music*, trans. M. D. Herter Norton (New York, 1965), 125–30.

BIBLIOGRAPHICAL NOTE

The subject of patristics and music has not been well served in the literature until the most recent years. The pioneering work in the field, H. Abert's *Die Musikanschauung des Mittelalters und ihre Grundlagen* (Halle, 1905), labours under a pro-Hellenic bias that offers no possibility for the objective evaluation of Christian musical attitudes and practices. It is at least an original work, however, unlike T. Gérold's derivative *Les pères de l'église et la musique* (Strasbourg, 1931), which has the virtue, none the less, of correcting certain of Abert's distortions. J. Quasten, *Musik und Gesang in den Kulten der heidnischen Antike und christlichen Frühzeit* (Münster in Westfalia, 1930), is an important book that brings the subject for the first time into the realm of professional patristic studies.

It does, however, neglect the actual history of liturgical song in favour of attitudes towards music, a lack made up for, to some extent, by H. Leib's *Die Psalmodie bei Ambrosius* (Vienna, 1967), an authoritative study that can be faulted only by its limitation of focussing upon a single author. An altogether singular work is E. M. Caglio's *Lo jubilus e le origini della salmodia responsoriale* (Milan, 1977), which displays an impressive acquaintance with the sources and a perceptive interpretation of them, all, however, in the service of the dubious hypothesis that the jubilus described by St Augustine is to be identified with responsorial psalmody. For additional bibliography on music and patristics, including shorter studies, see J. McKinnon's *Music in Early Christian Literature* (Cambridge, 1987).

On the subject of early Christian liturgy, it may be the case now that the groundbreaking classic L. Duchesne, *Origines du culte chrétien,* is no longer required reading, but that later classic, G. Dix, *The Shape of the Liturgy* (London, 1945) still does. Useful also are J. Srawley, *The Early History of the Liturgy* (Cambridge, 1947), J. Jungmann, *The Early Liturgy* (Notre Dame, Ind., 1959), and the collection, *The Study of Liturgy,* ed. C. Jones and others (London, 1978). The standard history of the Mass remains J. Jungmann, *The Mass of the Roman Rite,* trans. F. X. Brunner (New York, 1951–5), while there are two excellent recent works on the early Office: P. Bradshaw, *Daily Prayer in the Early Church* (London, 1981), and R. Taft, *The Liturgy of the Hours East and West* (Collegeville, Minn., 1986). Barely fitting within the category under consideration, but to be highly recommended none the less is, T. Mathews's *The Early Churches of Constantinople: Architecture and Liturgy* (University Park, Pa., 1977).

Books on the general historical and religious background are too numerous to cite even representatively, and instead I include a few titles for which I have special admiration. W. A. Meeks's *The First Urban Christians* (New Haven, 1983) is a model of recent church history. D. Chitty's *The Desert a City* (Oxford, 1966) paints an unforgettable picture of early desert monasticism. E. R. Dodds's *Pagan and Christian in an Age of Anxiety* (Cambridge, 1965) brings to the subject at least a measure of the qualities that made his *The Greeks and the Irrational* a classic. H. B. Parkes's *Gods and Men: the Origins of Western Culture* (New York, 1959) is not a classic, but it ought to be.

Chapter IV

The Emergence of Gregorian Chant in the Carolingian Era

JAMES McKINNON

We are fairly well informed about the state of liturgical chant at the close of Christian antiquity, that is to say, in about AD 450, but there is a sharp decline thereafter in the quantity and quality of the literary sources that provided our knowledge of the earlier period. Most of Christendom endured a protracted period justly referred to as the Dark Ages, a time characterized by barbarian incursions, the breakdown of governance and communication, the deterioration of the physical infrastructure and the decline of education. Liturgy and chant some-how survived all this, indeed seem to have flourished, so that by the ninth century one observes splendid systems of ecclesiastical song in both the East and the West. Our task here is first to describe the chief Western representative of these systems, Gregorian chant, as we know it from the early medieval sources, and then to make some attempt to penetrate the gloom of the intervening centuries.

Gregorian chant exists in the context of the liturgy, the public prayer of the Christian Church. One speaks of a liturgical year and a liturgical day. The liturgical year comprises a great dramatic cycle of feast days that recapitulate each year the earthly life of Jesus Christ. These feast days centre upon two dates, the one fixed, Christmas, falling on 25 December, and the other variable, Easter, falling on the first Sunday after the spring full moon. The two commemorate, respec-tively, the Birth and Resurrection of Christ. The year begins with a four-week period of preparation for Christmas called Advent. Easter is similarly preceded by a preparatory season, Lent, beginning 40 days earlier on Ash Wednesday. The Easter season extends for 50 days, highlighted by Ascension Thursday on the 40th day and concluded by Pentecost Sunday, which celebrates the descent of the Holy Spirit on the Apostles. The year is completed by the Sundays after Pentecost, which number from 23 to 28 depending on the date of Easter. In addi-tion to this annual cycle memorializing the events of Christ's life, many dates of the year are set aside to honour individual saints. In the liturgi-cal books of the Carolingian period these dates are simply interspersed throughout the annual cycle, but eventually they are separated out to form their own calendric cycle. There are thus two concurrently running cycles, a so-called Temporale and Sanctorale. In the case of a conflict of dates, preference is generally given to the feast of the Temporale: its liturgy would be celebrated with the inclusion of brief prayers commemorating the superseded date of the Sanctorale.

The liturgical day consists of Mass and Office. The latter is a series of eight services beginning with Matins (called Vigils in the Middle Ages from its placement in the early hours of the morning before daylight). Lauds, a service of praise, followed; it was timed to begin just as the first rays of the rising sun were visible through the east windows of the choir. There followed the four 'little hours' of the day: Prime, Terce, Sext and None; they were to be sung at the first, third, sixth (noon) and ninth hour of the Roman solar day, although None might be performed immediately after Sext to allow for a longer afternoon work period. Vespers were sung in the early evening followed shortly thereafter by Compline at dusk. The main body of Office texts was provided by the Book of Psalms, which was sung in its entirety in the course of a week. In addition to psalms, each Office included a strophic hymn, short scriptural passages and various short prayers and chants. Included also at each service, other than those of the little hours, was a biblical cantical, while Matins, the most elaborate of the Offices, had an extended series of readings. It is estimated that at the time of St Benedict the entire Office might have required about four hours to recite, but by the ninth or tenth centuries the more elaborate style of chanting would have required possibly twice that time on an ordinary day and considerably longer on important feast days. This is a point of some musical significance. The intellectual élite of Europe was engaged for a goodly part of the day, seven days a week, 365 days a year, from childhood to death, in the singing of Gregorian chant. Surely this has at least some bearing on the existence of a body of music of such stunning beauty and staggering quantity.

The community Mass was generally celebrated after Terce. It was the highlight of the liturgical day, and in a large monastery or cathedral of the ninth or tenth century it was performed with great ceremony at the main altar in the east end of the choir. The various levels of clergy participated in differing ways and used liturgical books containing only those texts appropriate to their function. The celebrating priest was the resident abbot or bishop; his book, called the sacramentary, had only the text of the Canon or Eucharistic prayer which he said silently at every Mass, and the three orations and Preface that varied each day. (The standard liturgical term for an item which varies is a 'Proper' item, and for one which is the same each day an 'Ordinary' item.) The recitation tone the celebrant employed for the orations was a simple one not requiring notation; it consisted of a single pitch with standard

27. *Beginning of the Gelasian Sacramentary (northern France, c750), an important early example of Romanized liturgy in Gaul*

inflections at points of punctuation. The Preface tone was somewhat more elaborate and appears among the earliest examples of notation surviving from the ninth century. Its great antiquity, along with that of the remainder of a dialogue of priestly greeting and congregational response, was discussed in Chapter III. Apparently it all survived intact with the single difference that the main body of the Eucharistic prayer, which had been declaimed aloud in the early church, came to be spoken silently in the Middle Ages.

The scriptural readings of the medieval Fore-Mass, the successor to the early Christian pre-Eucharistic service of the word, were recited from the ambo, a pulpit situated in the sanctuary area. There were two readings, the Epistle and Gospel; their annual cycle of texts appeared in books called lectionaries, or more properly epistolaries and evangeliaries. Their recitation tones were not notated, consisting of a single pitch with a somewhat more elaborate system of inflections at points of punctuation than that used by the celebrant for the orations. In a cathedral a subdeacon sang the Epistle and a deacon the Gospel.

The Mass chants so far alluded to all fall within the general classification of liturgical recitative; the more elaborate chants were sung by the remainder of resident clergy, which served as congregation and choir. There existed by the high Middle Ages a fairly complex hierarchy of singers with a performing practice to match, but for the period in question it will be sufficient to distinguish simply between solo chants and choral chants.

The principal chants of the Mass Ordinary were performed as choral chants during the Carolingian period although they had originally been sung by the congregation. It was seen in Chapter III that only the Sanctus was sung in the early church. *Ordo romanus I*, a document describing the papal liturgy of about 700, shows three more items in place: the Kyrie, Gloria and Agnus Dei, while the fifth and final item, the Credo, did not enter the Western Mass until the eleventh century. Already by the end of the tenth century, the Ordinary chants were sung to a great variety of melodies. They frequently appeared with tropes, that is, with additional texts applied to the more elaborate melodic flourishes of shorter chants like the Kyrie, or with new phrases of both melody and text inserted between the original phrases of a chant with a lengthy text like the Gloria. The Credo, incidentally, was not considered to be an appropriate vehicle for troping, probably because its text possessed more or less the status of a legal document. The circumstance that the earliest notated examples of Ordinary chants appear as elaborate troped melodies has led some scholars to believe that Ordinary chants were originally of this sort, but that is unlikely. In all probability the original Ordinary chants were simple untroped melodies sung by the congregation without the aid of written texts or musical notation. That such melodies appear later in the sources actually speaks for their antiquity. It can be established as a principle of the early written transmission of chant that the most ancient and universally known melodies were frequently the last to be notated because there was no practical need to do so. This is especially true of Byzantine chant, where Ordinary chants were not notated until the thirteenth century, and then in highly elaborated versions, but true also to a lesser extent of Gregorian. In modern times the more popular Gregorian Ordinary chants have come to be assembled in a book called the kyriale, whereas they first appeared in collections of tropes and later as supplements to the gradual, the book containing the Proper chants of the Mass.

★

This broad survey of early medieval liturgy and chant closes with a somewhat more detailed description of the Proper chants of the Mass. And then, with a basic knowledge of this category established, there will be an attempt to deal with its history during that long period intervening between the close of Christian antiquity and the Carolingian era.

We know the early medieval Mass Propers from three principal bodies of evidence. First there are literary sources, such as *Ordo romanus I*, that describe the Roman Mass as it was celebrated in the first half of the eighth century.[1] Then there are several unnotated ninth-century graduals, the earliest of which date from about 800;[2] these establish the texts of the Franco-Roman Mass Propers for that date, while their music appears finally in our third category of evidence, notated graduals, the earliest surviving examples of which date from sometime after 900.[3] It should be added that there are also the liturgical books alluded to above like sacramentaries and lectionaries, the earliest examples of which pre-date the earliest chant books. While lacking chant texts, they provide the musicologist with indispensable information on the history of the liturgical year.

Ordo romanus I is but the earliest in a series of *ordines romani* that describe the papal Stational liturgy and its adaptation to the cathedrals and monasteries of Charlemagne's realm. The Stational liturgy is so called from some 30 Roman stations, that is, venerable churches that were visited by the pope on set days in the course of the year for the solemn celebration of Mass; for example, the great basilica of S Maria Maggiore on the first Sunday of Advent. The pope and his court travelled by procession to the station where they were met by the local clergy; the pope was then led into the secretarium, a sacristy near the entrance of the church, where he prepared for the Mass. *Ordo romanus I* describes this Mass in great detail, and one observes that all the principal Proper chants – the introit, gradual, alleluia, offertory and communion – were already in place whereas only the gradual and communion were present in the Western liturgy at the close of antiquity.

The introit was sung by the Schola Cantorum, the papal choir, from their place before the altar, while the pope and his retinue processed down the centre aisle towards the sanctuary. The introit consisted of a psalm, sung by a cantor, after each verse of which an antiphon (a melodic composition of moderate length) was sung by the Schola. The gradual, called *responsum* in *Ordo romanus I*, was sung by a cantor from the steps of the ambo after the deacon recited the Epistle. He sang this, according to *Ordo romanus I*, from a cantatorium, a chant book containing only the solo chants of the Mass, the gradual and alleluia, as opposed to the choral or Schola chants, the introit, offertory and communion. The early unnotated graduals give the full text of all five items, and it is necessary to turn to these to gain some idea of the structure of *Ordo romanus I*'s *responsum*. One recalls that in the early church a complete psalm was sung with a congregational refrain or response after each verse, but in the Frankish graduals of *c*800 there appears only the response with a single verse. In the notated graduals of the following century this response and verse display highly florid chant in conformity with their solo performance, so that a fundamentally important question is raised: at what point in its history did the gradual change from a complete psalm to a brief text set to elaborate music?

Immediately after the gradual, the cantor sang the alleluia from the steps of the ambo, or if it was a penitential occasion a chant called the tract. (A further complication in the relationship of these chants associated with the readings is that during much of Eastertide the gradual was omitted and two alleluias were sung.) From the early graduals, unnotated and notated, one sees that the alleluia consisted of a single verse of moderately florid music, preceded and followed by the word 'alleluia' sung to a melody of great elaboration. The tract was unique among Mass chants in that it did not use the verse and refrain device, but consisted simply of a series of psalm verses sung to a rather florid formula. It is significant that *Ordo romanus I* speaks of both alleluia and tract as optional; it says that only the gradual is to be sung if there is no time for the alleluia and tract. This would seem to suggest that the alleluia and tract were relatively recent additions to the Roman Mass. There are other indications of this. The most obvious in the case of the alleluia is that those for the Sundays after Pentecost were not assigned to specific feasts until a late date. In the early graduals the four items, introit, gradual, offertory and communion, appear in place at each feast day, while the alleluias are confined to an appendix at the end of the book to be selected at each Mass according to the preferences of individual churches. In the case of tracts, while they are theoretically the substitute for alleluias on penitential occasions such as the week-days of Lent, a large portion of such days are not provided with one. Perhaps the most plausible hypothesis for the appearance of the two chants in the Roman Mass is that the alleluia was adopted under Byzantine influence in the later seventh century – one recalls from the previous chapter that the alleluia was present in the East already in the fifth century – and that the tract, which might have been used earlier in the Roman liturgy on special occasions, was now added to the Mass with some regularity as the penitential analogy of the alleluia, a symmetrical arrangement that was never completely realized.

The offertory was sung by the Schola during a series of ceremonies including the reception and preparation of the gifts and the washing of the celebrant's hands. The early graduals reveal that the offertory con-sisted of a refrain with two or three verses, the music of which approaches the solo chants in its florid character. The final Proper chant, the com-munion, was sung as the Sacrament was distributed to clergy and people. It resembled the introit in that it consisted of a full psalm with antiphon.

To summarize, then, we know from the *ordines romani* that the five principal Proper chants of the Mass were sung at Rome by about 700. We know the texts and format of these chants for the entire liturgical year from unnotated Frankish graduals written about 800, and we

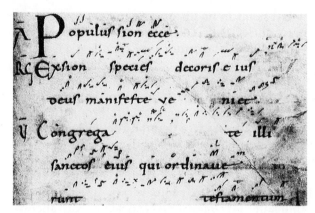

28. *Unheightened neumes (the first two are examples of podatus) in an early tenth-century cantatorium from St Gall*

know their music from notated Frankish graduals written some time after 900. One notes, concerning the last group of sources, that their notation does not provide precise pitches. Rather there is over each syllable of text one or more notational signs called neumes (originally what we call the neume was called a *nota neumarum*, while the *neuma* itself referred to the actual melodic entity, not its notational sign). A neume, consisting of one or more pitches, indicated at this early stage simply the number of pitches and their relative direction within the neume. The *podatus*, for example, indicated two pitches the second of which was higher; it did not indicate how much higher or its relationship to the surrounding neumes (fig.28). Thus chant notated in such neumes, termed unheightened or non-diastematic, is undecipherable if considered in isolation. However, the number and type of neumes of a given chant in the early non-diastematic sources match closely the number and type in later diastematic sources so that we can safely conclude that the melodies are substantially the same and that they existed in their mature form by about 900 at the latest.

Until recently it was widely assumed that these earliest extant notated graduals were indeed the earliest to have been copied and that therefore the chant, passed on from generation to generation by the quasi-improvisational means of oral transmission, failed to stabilize before the end of the ninth century. In 1987, however, Kenneth Levy made the remarkable claim that a fully neumated gradual must have existed during the lifetime of Charlemagne (*d* 814), perhaps as early as the last quarter of the eighth century.[4]

This revolutionary argument is introduced with a reflection on the probabilities of manuscript survival for this period. Only three unnotated graduals survive from about 800, but we know from literary sources that every monastery and church from this period would have had at least one – St Riquier alone had six. This amounts to only three from what must have been hundreds, and three, moreover, that had their chances of survival greatly enhanced because they appear in elegantly prepared composite manuscripts, the chief component of which is the perennially useful sacramentary. It is not surprising on the other hand that no notated gradual exists from before 900 when one considers that notated graduals would not have been particularly numerous to start with, that they tended to be plain practical books lacking in attractive illumination, that they usually did not share manuscripts with other valuable items like sacramentaries and that they would soon be rendered obsolete by the development of diastematic neumes.

The first of Levy's series of positive 'indexes' for his proposition, 'palaeographic common sense', has sufficiently broad implications to merit summary here. The early notated graduals are widely distributed geographically and display distinctly different styles of neumation, yet they present substantially the same melodies with closely analogous neumatic configurations. It is not possible that such a set of circumstances is the result of coincidence; it can be explained only by a considerable previous history of neumated graduals. (One might suggest the not entirely inappropriate analogy of Shakespeare's plays appearing simultaneously in several different languages.) It would seem that at

29. The Benedictine abbey of St Riquier (c790–99), an important centre of liturgy and chant in north-east France: engraving (c1612) after a miniature in the Chronicle of St Riquier (c1088), destroyed by fire in 1719

the very least this history would have had to pre-date the split between East and West Francia that was formalized in the Treaty of Verdun (843). Additions to the chant repertory from after that date, such as sequences, diverge widely from East to West in contrast to the remarkably homogeneous standard repertory.

The final and (in Levy's view) most conclusive of his indexes is highly technical. It has to do with a particular chant, *Factus est repente*, that ceded its status as Pentecostal offertory to *Confirma hoc Deus* in the unnotated graduals from *c*800. It disappears from virtually all northern sources but turns up in a single notated gradual from *c*1000. At the same time it is common in Beneventan graduals as the offertory for Pentecost Thursday, but was recently discovered by Levy to exist as the Pentecost offertory in a Beneventan source in an American library. The northern and Beneventan sources display precisely the same neumation, leading one to speculate on the date of the chant's transmission from north to south. All probability, based both on the changed liturgical status of the chant, as well as general historical circumstances, points to its taking place during the reign of Charlemagne.

Perhaps the most tenuous point in the argument comes finally when Levy attempts to move from the existence of this single neumated offertory in *c*800 to that of an entire gradual. Yet one could argue that common sense is on his side; why should the Carolingians notate a single offertory rather than the entire gradual? And is it not likely, in view of their preoccupation with liturgy and chant and in view of their penchant for preservation and systematization, that they would do the logical thing and complete the task? Levy's proposal is too new and untested for uncritical acceptance; it may very well be that it will not survive the scrutiny of chant scholars entirely unscathed. Yet there is much in its reasoning that is so persuasive, particularly in the earlier stages of the argument, that it will be absorbed in the speculations to follow here. For now, it is enough to suggest that it promises to narrow to at least some extent that gap in our knowledge of Western chant previously defined as extending from about 450 to 900.

★

Turning now to that gap, a musicological no-man's land, there are several major categories of evidence with which to attack it. Among these is the literary evidence, consisting for the most part of numerous brief remarks about music scattered throughout sermons, letters, biblical commentaries, collections of ecclesiastical legislation and various other types of writing. Such material is frequently quoted, but generally selectively, and has never been assembled chronologically and regionally in the hope of revealing as yet undiscovered patterns of musical activity. Similarly, the general historical background is only imperfectly understood, whereas a more thorough knowledge of it might

30. *Map showing the partition of the Carolingian Empire by the Treaty of Verdun in 843, which brought about a divergence of Eastern and Western Gregorian repertories and styles*

conceivably lead to sounder speculation about the interrelation of the major liturgical dialects. That interrelation has not been studied much in recent decades, although it poses obvious questions that should reward investigation. Why, for example, did Spain and Gaul adopt Byzantine chants like the Cheroubikon and Trisaghion while Rome did not; and what are the historical implications of the Roman tendency to use psalmic cycles in the Mass and the converse Byzantine tendency to employ Ordinary chants?

That these categories of evidence have been insufficiently explored is easily understood; each would demand an enormous effort from the scholar with only limited prospects of success. But there is one area, correspondingly difficult but probably offering greater hope for immediate results: the history of the Roman liturgical year, both Temporale and Sanctorale, especially during the seventh and eighth centuries. Later in the present essay there will be some indication of the direction such study might follow.

The final category of evidence is the music itself. It is true that we know it only from sources later than the period in question and that it exists as only the final stage of that history we are seeking to penetrate, yet there is something to be learnt of the earlier stages from an examination of the end product. What chant scholars generally do with the music is, in a word, to compare. Chants number in the thousands and important manuscripts in the hundreds, leaving innumerable possibilities for such comparison, certain instances of which have a direct bearing on the question of Gregorian origins. For example, an intriguing area of comparison is in chants of a different genre with the same text, say, an introit antiphon, offertory and communion with the text 'Ad te levavi'. It is at least a plausible hypothesis that all have descended from an original psalmodic version that might be discernible beneath their more florid final state.[5]

A highly significant type of comparison takes place between chants, or genres of chant, from the different liturgical families. An obvious result of such comparisons is the knowledge that a number of Carolingian chants are direct borrowings from Byzantine chant. There are more difficult tasks remaining in this area such as a comparison of Gregorian and Byzantine alleluia verses in the hope of shedding light on the origins of the Western alleluia. An area of great subtlety is that involving the non-Roman Italian chant dialects such as the Milanese, Beneventan and Ravennese. The sources for these regions are mostly late and subject to strong Gregorian influence, yet they are not without occasional indications of something earlier that tempt one to think of important discoveries in Italian chant before it succumbed to the Carolingian programme to impose Gregorian. Similar hopes remain that more of the Gallican repertory, suppressed already under Charlemagne's father Pepin (*d* 768), will emerge from comparison of the appropriate sources.

Of very special relevance to our subject is the comparison of Gregorian sources with the so-called Old Roman. The Gregorian manuscripts, as indicated above, while retaining their traditional nominal connection with Pope Gregory I, are actually Frankish sources since notation seems to have been a Carolingian innovation. A group of notated Roman manuscripts do finally appear, however, at a substantially later date. There are two antiphoners, that is, books containing chants of the Office, and, more to present purposes, three graduals, the earliest of which was written in 1071. The two repertories provide an ideal opportunity for comparison in that they are obviously related yet quite different. The liturgical texts are virtually identical, indicating a common origin, while the melodies are undeniably related but so

31. St Irene, Constantinople (begun 532), an especially well-preserved example of the standard early Christian sanctuary with semi-circular synthronon (see fig.4 above)

dissimilar in many important respects as to indicate sharply divergent histories during the time of their separation. There are numerous hypotheses concerning the nature of the relationship. To summarize one of the simpler and more plausible – not by way of advocacy but simply to orientate the reader – there was only one *cantus romanus* in the eighth century which split to form the Gregorian and Old Roman. The Gregorian came about with the transmission of the *cantus romanus* to the north, with its adaptation to Frankish taste and with its relatively early stabilization in notation, while the Old Roman resulted from the *cantus romanus* staying at home and enduring three centuries of oral transmission until finally becoming notated.[6] A considerable amount of valuable work has already been accomplished in comparing the two repertories, perhaps more than in any other area of chant scholarship.

Finally, there is a type of musical comparison that has a direct bearing on the argument of the present essay. If one compares the same chants as they appear in a generously representative selection of early notated manuscripts and finds them to be nearly identical, then one must conclude that the chants existed in substantially the same form for a considerable period before the manuscripts were written. This is precisely the conclusion arrived at in a recent study by David Hughes.[7] He finds that the variations existing between different versions of certain

32. Medieval archbishop (?St Gregory), possibly guiding singers with hand signs, holding an open book with the words 'Ad te levavi' (the introit for the first Sunday in Advent): detail of an ivory book cover (c875), probably from St-Amand

chants are for the most part negligible in the sense that they do not significantly alter the identity of the melody. These slight variations, moreover, conform to regional patterns that must have developed after the breakup of the Carolingian realm. It appears probable to him that the early manuscripts closely reflect the chant as it existed in the time of Charlemagne. One recognizes in Hughes's argument a remarkable analogy with Levy's claim for a Carolingian notated gradual; it might prove equally controversial, but will be incorporated none the less in the speculations that follow here along with the relevant aspects of Levy's proposal.

★

If chant scholars have devoted most of their efforts to the music itself, liturgical scholars have tended to concentrate on the history of the Roman liturgical year. Yet much remains to be done in this latter area;

while there is a 50-year-old, book-length study on the Sanctorale, there is nothing of the sort for the more important Temporale, not even a single major article in a modern reference work. Therefore the discussion of the origins of Gregorian chant that follows is necessarily a tentative one. It takes the form of a series of hypotheses, insights and outright guesses that are in some cases original to the present author and in others borrowed. They represent an attempt at a coherent, if incomplete and provisional, exposition of the subject.

The first of our speculations involves the period from roughly 450 to 600 in the West, from the close of Christian antiquity to the time of Gregory I, who died in 604. It is difficult to detect anything of permanent significance for the history of chant taking place; discontinuity seems to be the norm. One gains a general sense of this in reading how Bishop Caesarius of Arles (*d* 542) rejoices that the 'gift of psalmody' has come finally to his diocese and prays that his congregation will be able to persevere in it. We assume that psalmody would have been well established and consistently maintained in the principal ecclesiastical centre of all Gaul a century and a half after the psalmodic movement of the fourth century. A similar complaint is heard from Rome itself in the roughly contemporary apocryphal letter of Pope Damasus to Jerome: 'On Sunday', it reads, 'one epistle of the Apostle is read and one chapter of the Gospel, but the custom of psalmody is not observed'. Thus it was a struggle to maintain even the simple gradual psalm at Rome, and further reflection on the history of this primordial Mass chant serves only to confirm the impression of discontinuity. The conventional assumption is that it began as a simple responsorial psalm which, with the professionalization of the chant, became steadily more elaborate until it reached the full-blown melismatic state of the Gregorian gradual. At that point, because of its excessive length, it was necessary to drop all the psalm verses but one, leaving only the medieval respond and verse. What little evidence we have, however, seems to speak against such an assumption.

Dom Henri Leclercq drew up a list of 22 psalm verses that appear in the works of St Augustine as gradual psalm refrains,[8] but only seven of these figure as responses in the approximately 120 graduals of the early medieval repertory. Similarly, Michel Huglo recently described a remarkable sixth-century Italian psalter that has the letter 'R' inscribed in gold leaf before 70 of its psalm verses.[9] He made the obviously proper assumption that the 'R' indicated a refrain verse and went on to find 21 of the verses that were so indicated within the repertory of medieval gradual responds. Again, 21 from 70 may show a degree of continuity, but the unrepresented 49 show considerably greater discontinuity. Moreover, the seven verses from Leclercq's list and the 21 from Huglo's psalter simply appear somewhere within the medieval gradual repertory; with the exception of special cases like the Easter gradual *Haec dies* there is no way of knowing if a given verse was used on the same feast day in both its ancient and medieval appearances.

The so-called Leonine Sacramentary throws additional light on the question. This venerable book, dating from the seventh century and reflecting sixth-century Roman usage, has, as a sacramentary, only the texts recited by the celebrating priest at Mass, but it may tell us something about gradual psalms by analogy. It does not give a fixed set of prayer formularies for each feast day of the year, but rather a selection of formularies for various feasts. There are five sets for St Cecilia and no fewer than twelve for St Lawrence. When one considers that these prayers were composed with a particular feast day in mind, but that considerable room for selection was nevertheless maintained, it would seem that *a fortiori* freedom would have been exercised in choosing a gradual psalm from the existing resource of the Psalter. In sum, it seems anachronistic to attribute to this earlier period the very concept of the *circulum anni* or annual cycle that we know from eighth- and ninth-century sources, that is, the assignment of specific chants to each feast day of the liturgical year.

Finally, an examination of the medieval gradual texts themselves suggests discontinuity in the history of the genre. First, the verse is usually not the initial verse of the psalm, which we might expect to have been the case if the gradual had grown too long, and all but the first verse had been dropped as a result. Secondly, the texts do not reproduce word for word the texts of the Psalter; rather they show changes that suggest what might call the 'libretto principle', that is, the crafting of text with its musical setting in mind.[10] Finally, some of the most important festivals of the church year – days like the Epiphany and Holy Thursday – have gradual texts derived not from the psalms at all, as must have been the case originally, but carefully chosen from elsewhere in scripture.

These considerations, centring about the text of the gradual, suggest a different model for the origins of Gregorian chant. Rather than a slow and steady evolution from ancient psalmody, perhaps we ought to think of a relatively brief period of creativity, when it was decided to settle upon a cycle of texts for the entire church year and to match the texts with appropriate chants. Needless to say, much of the material for this enterprise, both textual and musical, would certainly have been at hand. And no doubt the tendency to indulge in elaborate song as opposed to simple psalmody would already have manifested itself to some degree. But the evidence suggests that the chant was fashioned into an organized repertory, textually and musically, more suddenly than gradually.

★

When might this have been? Was it in the time of Gregory I (*d* 604),

33. St Gregory dictating his sacramentary to two scribes: miniature from the Metz Sacramentary, School of Corbie (c870). Similar scenes were painted later to illustrate Gregory's involvement in music

who once was thought to have composed the chants himself under the inspiration of the Holy Ghost, and who even in this century was widely believed to have organized and edited them? It will be argued here, as the second in our series of hypotheses, that a more likely time would have been that of Gregory II, who reigned more than a century after his famous namesake, from 715 to 731. Actually François-Auguste Gevaert, writing towards the close of the last century, had already assigned Gregory I's traditional role to Gregory II.[11] His quasi-heresy, however, met with powerful refutation at the hands of the eminent Benedictine scholar Germain Morin,[12] which settled the matter for the next half-century, a period when chant scholarship was dominated by the Solesmes Benedictines. (Gregory I, as we shall see, was always admired especially by monks.) During the past three decades, a period of more pluralistic chant scholarship, the Gregorian question has been dealt with only peripherally; faith in Gregory I's traditional role has been badly shaken, but no scholar has seen fit to resurrect the cause of Gregory II in explicit fashion.[13] The attempt to do so that follows here makes no claim to a full treatment of the subject; rather it focusses on a single point – the date 608, just four years after Gregory I's death, a date that has been invoked, and continues to be, in affirmation of his role.

Before taking up this point, however, it is necessary to digress at some length on the methodological question of how one proceeds in seeking to date Roman liturgical events of the seventh and eighth centuries. One does so primarily by tracing the development of the church year during the period, one of those categories of evidence singled out above. It is a process, incidentally, that musicologists might find reminiscent of that used in the postwar period to establish the chronology of Bach's church cantatas. To start with there are a number of dates available from external evidence, such as Gregory II's incorporation of the Lenten Thursdays into the liturgy, but much of the work must be done with internal evidence. Fortunately, there are discernible chronological layers of text formularies, analogous to the layers one uncovers in archaeological excavation. One assumes, for example, that numerically ordered formularies are the product of revision and hence comparatively late. The most celebrated example of this involves the weekday communions of Lent which are derived in sequence from Psalms i–xxvi. Changes wrought in this sequence, along with the circumstance that Thursdays are the last day to be added to the Lenten calendar, allow one to discern no fewer than five chronological layers in Lenten communion antiphons (see Table IV.1).

The first layer is made up of Sundays in Lent; these display no numerical sequence and hence one assumes their priority to the weekdays. One observes the weekday sequence beginning with an antiphon derived from Psalm i for Ash Wednesday and closing with one derived from Psalm xxvi for Friday in Passion week. It constitutes the second layer. It must have been composed some time before Thursday was made a liturgical day because there is no provision for Thursdays in the sequence. It must also have been composed before the set of five communions with Gospel texts because clearly the five gaps in the numerical sequence – Psalms xii, xvi, xvii, xx and xxi – attest to the previous existence of the sequence. At some point in the eighth century, for reasons having to do with the preparation of Catechumens for Baptism on Holy Saturday, it was deemed appropriate to compose new formularies for these five days. Why they are assigned a date later than the Thursday communions, and thus constitute our fourth layer, will be explained after a brief reference to the three dates from our fifth layer. These three are very late, not yet appearing in the ninth-century unnotated graduals, where their absence is indicated by the rubric 'Sabbato vacat' or 'Dominica vacat'.

The reason for assigning the Thursday communions an earlier date than that of the five Gospel communions occasions another fundamentally important methodological digression. The British liturgical scholar Walter Frere originated the famous dictum that 'fixity means

Table IV.1: LENTEN COMMUNION TEXTS *c*800

Sundays	Weekdays		Thursdays (c725)	Gospel	(c800)
	Ash Wed	Ps i	Thur Ps xc		
	Fri	Ps ii			Sat Vacat
1st Sun Ps xc	Mon	Ps iii			
	Tues	Ps iv			
	Wed	Ps v	Thur *John* vi		
	Fri	Ps vi			
	Sat	Ps vii			
	Mon	Ps viii			Sun vacat
	Tues	Ps ix			
	Wed	Ps x	Thur *John* vi		
	Fri	Ps xi			
	(	)		Sat *Luke* xv	
3rd Sun Ps lxxxiii	Mon	Ps xiii			
	Tues	Ps xiv			
	Wed	Ps xv	Thur Ps cxviii		
	(	)		Fri *John* iv	
	(	)		Sat *John* viii	
4th Sun Ps cxxi	Mon	Ps xviii			
	Tues	Ps xix			
	(	)	Thur Ps lxx	Wed *John* ix	
	(	)		Fri *John* xi	
	Sat	Ps xxii			
Pass Sun I *Cor* xi	Mon	Ps xxiii			
	Tues	Ps xxiv			
	Wed	Ps xxv	Thur Ps cxviii		
	Fri	Ps xxvi			
	—	—			Sat vacat

antiquity',[14] that is to say, if the same formulary appears in many sources it must be relatively old. It is described, moreover, as having 'stability', whereas 'instability' exists where various texts appear from source to source for a particular liturgical item. One recognizes here, incidentally, the liturgical equivalent of Levy's 'paleaeographic common sense' described above, and also of Hughes's claim that melodies with little variation in the sources must have considerable pre-histories.

The application of 'fixity means antiquity' to Lenten communions is an easy task. The Thursday communions are quite stable in the sources, whereas the Gospel communions are very unstable, both with respect to text and melody, suggesting a significantly later date. The most notoriously unstable item in the chant repertory is relevant enough to our general purposes to warrant a prolongation of this digression. This is the alleluia. Several of the early graduals fail to assign specific alleluias to the Sundays after Pentecost; rather a list from which they can be selected appears as an appendix at the end of each manuscript. Eventually, individual churches established their own cycles with the result that alleluia assignments differ in chant books from diocese to diocese for centuries to come. Chant scholars like Peter Wagner and Willi Apel, faced with this situation but constrained by their misreading of patristic sources to attribute to the alleluia the same antiquity as the gradual, resolved the contradiction with the unsatisfactory proposition that a melismatic alleluia refrain was always a part of the Mass, and that a verse was added to it in the eighth century.[15] Certainly a more plausible hypothesis, one that negates neither the essential relationship between verse and refrain nor the literary evidence as discussed in the previous chapter, is that both alleluia verse and refrain made their way into the Roman liturgy under Byzantine influence. The most likely time for this to have happened is not easy to determine, although one thinks readily of the late seventh and early eighth centuries, a period of relative peace between the two capitals that saw considerable Byzantine liturgical architectural and artistic activity at Rome.

To return to the question at hand – the significance of the date 608 – the argument for its affirmation of Gregory I's role begins with the assertion that in 608 Pope Boniface IV had the ancient Roman Pantheon rededicated as a Christian church, Sancta Maria ad Martyres (fig.34). The formulary for the feast of Sancta Maria ad Martyres is that for the dedication of a church, beginning with the introit *Terribilis est*. The crux of the argument is that this is the last completely original Gregorian formulary. All other liturgical days that follow the first discernible layer of the liturgical year – days like the Sundays after Pentecost, the Thursdays in Lent and the group of four Marian feasts imported from the East in the seventh century – have either both texts and music borrowed from earlier feasts, or if for some theological reason new texts were composed, the music was borrowed. This warrants the conclusion that the formulary for the dedication of a church, the last wholly original formulary, composed for the dedication of Sancta Maria ad Martyres in 608, brings to a close the creative period of Gregorian chant, the 'golden age' of Gregory I.

The weakness of the argument lies not in the significance of the dedication formulary but in its assignment to the year 608. The date rests on two items of evidence. The first is a passage in the biography of Pope Boniface IV (608–15) from the *Liber pontificalis* that says 'he made [in the Pantheon] a church of the blessed Mary ever a virgin and of all the martyrs'.[16] The second is the appearance two centuries later in the first unnotated graduals of the dedication formulary *Terribilis est* for the feast of Maria ad Martyres on 13 May. The second establishes the genuine probability that at some point in the history of the church it was dedicated and that the formulary *Terribilis est* was sung; the first is alleged to fix that point in history at 608. However, the *Liber pontificalis* merely said that Pope Boniface remade the Pantheon into a Christian church; it did not say that he established an annual feast of Maria ad Martyres, let alone that he commissioned a Mass formulary to be composed for the day.

Before examining new evidence one might reflect briefly on the implications of this situation for Gregory's alleged liturgical involvement. We know that he dedicated numerous churches throughout his

34. *The Pantheon, Rome (118–c130), dedicated as the church of Sancta Maria ad Martyres under Boniface IV in 608: engraving by G.B. Piranesi (1720–78)*

fourteen-year reign. Now if it were he who saw to it that Mass formularies and chants were composed for the entire year, is it not unlikely
that he would have neglected a dedication formulary? Why should he
have left this single task to Boniface? But the case against the date is
more than speculative. There is to start with the quibble that Boniface
ruled from 608 to 615 and concomitant annoyance that chant scholars
generally cite the earliest of the seven years involved. The important
evidence, however, is found in eighth-century liturgical books, the first
to present the full Roman *circulum anni*. The feast of Maria ad Martyres
is missing from both the early eighth-century Würzburg Lectionary
and Rheims Gospel Book: it is missing similarly from the Old Gelasian
Sacramentary as well as other eighth-century Gelasians; its first
appearance is in the Hadrianum, the sacramentary Pope Hadrian sent
to Charlemagne in about 790. This suggests a mid-eighth-century

*35. Ivory cover (showing scenes from the life of David, purported author of the psalms) from
Dagulf's Psalter, one of several books given by Hadrian I (772–95) to Charlemagne*

origin of the festival, and we have, it turns out, a potential occasion for its creation from that period. The *Liber pontificalis* narrates in some detail the rebuilding of Sancta Maria ad Martyres during the pontificate of Gregory II's immediate successor, Gregory III (731–41), an event that would have in all probability called for a second dedication. It seems too neat to be true, but certainly the tandem of Gregory II and Gregory III matches the chronology far better than that of Gregory I and Boniface IV.

★

This is not the first time a post-Gregorian origin for the chant has been advocated; it is simply a new argument. Indeed, most chant scholars have held some post-Gregorian position or another since they began in the postwar period to pay proper attention to the Old Roman manuscripts mentioned above. During the first half of the century they were dismissed by the monks of Solesmes as representing no more than a decadent version of the Gregorian, but now they spurred a variety of theories on the relationship of their music to that of the so-called Gregorian. Just two of these will be summarized here, that of the Franciscan liturgical scholar S. P. Van Dijk,[17] and that of Helmut Hucke, already briefly outlined.

Van Dijk maintained that there were two Roman chants in the seventh century. One of these, the Old Roman, went back at least to the time of Gregory I and continued to be sung in the churches of Rome and its environs up to the thirteenth century. What we call Gregorian chant, that which appears in our early Frankish graduals, originated in the second half of the century under a series of musical popes beginning with Vitalian (657–72). They were motivated by the desire to produce a chant that was not provincial in character like the Old Roman, but worthy of a Rome that was beginning to look upon itself as a reawakening world force. This new chant was at first confined to the papal chapel and jealously guarded by the Schola Cantorum, but in the second half of the eighth century it was relayed to the Carolingian north despite the strenuous objections of the Schola and eventually came to be copied in our earliest extant Gregorian manuscripts.

Perhaps the chief virtue of Van Dijk's position is his emphasis upon the Schola Cantorum and his chronological placement of its major accomplishments not in the time of Gregory I but in that of later popes with verifiable musical and liturgical involvement. He cites Vitalian (657–72), Leo II (682–3), Benedictus II (684–5) and Sergius I (687–701). The weak link in this chain is the first, Vitalian, the principal figure in Van Dijk's view. He was not associated with chant until the twelfth century, whereas the other three popes were already cited as singers in the *Liber pontificalis*, considered reliable for this period because of its closely contemporaneous manuscripts. Possibly Van Dijk's chronology would benefit from an adjustment to a slightly later period, but there are more serious problems with his theory, and these have been pointed out by Hucke.[18]

Hucke notes that Van Dijk, as a liturgiologist rather than a musicologist, devoted little thought to problems of musical transmission. Van Dijk assumed that the Old Roman chant survived for five centuries unchanged without benefit of musical notation, from the time of Gregory I to the end of the eleventh century, and he assumed that the Gregorian version, similarly without benefit of notation, made the trip to the Carolingian north unchanged. Perhaps the chief implausibility is the existence of two distinctly different versions of the chant, existing again without benefit of notation, but set to the same texts and maintained within the same city by members of the same religion. Hucke counters with unimpeachable common sense that there could have been but one chant dialect sung in Rome during the seventh and eighth centuries. He makes no attempt to establish a date for its maturation, but he does express scepticism about Gregory I's musical involvement. His central point is that it is this single *cantus romanus* that was imposed by Pepin and Charlemagne on their Frankish realm, dooming the indigenous Gallican chant to oblivion, while changing itself substantially in the process. Inevitably, the Frankish singers translated it into their own musical idiom and, more than that, they reworked it to conform to the theoretical construct of the eight church modes. (This system, apparently unknown at Rome and borrowed by the Carolingians from Byzantium, where it was known as the *Octoechos*, classified all chants as possessing one pitch of central importance called the 'final'. There were four such finals: D, E, F and G. Four of the modes, those called 'authentic', had melodies which moved within the space of an octave or less above their finals, while the other four, called 'plagal' or false, had melodies of a lower range, that moved both above and below their finals.)

It is generally acknowledged that certain modifications to chant melodies were necessary to adapt them to the system, since the melodies existed in Rome before their subjection to the system in the north. The so-called Gregorian chant, transformed by modal system as well as by less tangible northern musical traits, is in reality, therefore, a Frankish chant. Adding plausibility to Hucke's position is the liturgical context: the history of the chant appears closely linked to that of the Roman liturgy, which underwent substantial modification at the hands of Carolingian scholars like Alcuin, Benedict of Aniane and Amalarius of Metz. Meanwhile, in Rome, the chant went its own way, absorbing, it is true, a measure of Gregorian influence, but by and large in isolation. Slowly, through centuries of oral transmission, it evolved, arriving finally at the state we know from the so-called Old Roman manuscripts.

In recent years Hucke has refined his position by adapting the oral transmission hypothesis of Leo Treitler to explain better the state of the chant from the time of the Frankish adaptation to the appearance of the first notated graduals. Treitler's hypothesis is presented in a series of publications appearing over the past decade; they are characterized by breadth of learning and an argument that is rich and subtle.[19] In an attempt to summarize the theory, and any such attempt will suffer from oversimplification, one starts by noting that it invokes the orally trans-mitted poetry of the legendary Homer and its modern counterpart in Yugoslavian folk epic, as described in the work of Milman Parry and Albert Lord. For Treitler each performance of the chant, like that of epic poetry, is more a unique performance than the replication of a completed musical composition; the singer remembers what he can, chiefly the overall pattern employed in a particular liturgical genre, fleshing out the piece with conventional formulae, adapting them to the exigencies of the text, always constrained by the need to keep the perfor-mance going. 'Reconstruction' is his term for the process. At times Treitler himself has suggested rather narrow limits of chronology and liturgical genre for the application of the theory, but his followers, including Hucke, have tended to interpret it more broadly, so as to cover most chant of the Carolingian period.

Hucke's overview of Gregorian origins, along with its incorporation of Treitler's oral transmission theory, provides a compelling model, one that has had considerable influence on both European and American scholars. Indeed, in its broadest outline – a single eighth-century *cantus romanus* that bifurcates into a Frankish Gregorian chant and an indigen-ous Old Roman – it has achieved a status that is virtually axiomatic; it is the framework within which various points of view are now free to contend. Where it has been called into question, however, is precisely in its application of the oral transmission theory to the Frankish Grego-rian chant of the ninth century. This application calls for a highly fluid existence for the chant, subject to transformation first in its journey to the north and subsequently during the century before becoming fixed in notation. But if there is any merit to Levy's claim for a notated Carolin-gian gradual and if Hughes is right in his assertion that the musical homogeneity displayed by the extant notated graduals can be explained only by a long-lived pre-existence for the melodies copied there, then the fluidity called for in the Hucke–Treitler view must be replaced by a conception involving greater stability. This is not to deny the overwhelming importance of oral transmission for the ecclesiastical music of this time. It goes without saying that the Old Roman chant was orally transmitted for many centuries, and more than that, some scholars have been quite successful in revealing certain aspects of the process at work.[20] The Gregorian chant was also transmitted orally to the north, and it continued, in a sense, to be orally transmitted long after the advent of notated chant books, whether these existed from about 800 or 900. It is generally agreed that for a number of centuries chant continued to be sung at liturgical services without benefit of notated chant books, while the books – those that survive are too small to have been of any use in an actual performance – must have existed somehow as reference works, perhaps to be consulted as a memory aid before the service. So the question is not whether or not Gregorian chant was transmitted orally during the crucial period of its emergence in the north, but what the character of that transmission was.

In considering this one ought to emphasize an obvious, yet insufficiently examined, distinction – that existing between choral and solo chants. It is one thing to say that a soloist reconstructs a chant each year, for example a gradual or an alleluia verse, but how does a choir reconstruct an introit or communion antiphon? It is hard to conceive of any practical manner in which they could have done so; surely they must somehow have sung such chants from memory. Might the Schola have memorized the choral chants while the cantor reconstructed the solo chants? There is an easy plausibility to this notion, but one can argue that the cantors were members of the Schola and that they were likely to have brought the same performance habits to the solo chants that they were accustomed to employing in the choral chants. Speculation aside, what does the musical evidence suggest? One can arrive at a provisional conclusion by examining Hendrik van der Werf's conveniently arranged transcriptions. He has provided transcriptions of some 30 introits and four graduals from a representative spread of manuscripts in a neat vertical alignment that greatly facilitates comparison.[21] Most chant scholars are inclined to emphasize melodic variation, but surely what leaps out at one from these pages is an impression of melodic homogeneity rather than diversity. One sees here manuscripts reproducing the same melodies with relatively minor variations rather than different reconstructions of a partially remembered melody. This is true especially of the large sampling of choral introits, but the small group of graduals represented does not present a radically different impression. Thus while common sense might suggest a more stable form of oral transmission for choral than for solo chants, van der Werf's transcriptions suggest relative stability for both.

But there is evidence available from which one might make the opposite case – that for melodic instability, whether of solo or choral chants. JoAnn Udovich's study of *Magnificat* antiphons, for example, shows melodic differentiation in this type of chant well beyond the introits and graduals of van der Werf's sample.[22] The observation leads in turn to a distinction that is probably far more crucial than that between solo and choral chants – the distinction between older and more recent chants, or, to be more precise, between a core repertory like the

Mass Propers of the more ancient feasts that were stabilized at an earlier date and a more peripheral repertory like *Magnificat* antiphons which, regardless of age, was standardized at a later period. Again one recalls Frere's dictum that 'fixity means antiquity' and also the proposition that the key to chant origins might very well lie in the history of the liturgical year. I have only just begun my own examination of the question, but the preliminary results are strikingly suggestive. A more ancient date in the liturgical calendar like the first Sunday of Advent provides an alleluia and verse that is remarkably stable in both textual assignment and music, while a later date like the fourth Sunday in Advent displays a variety of chants from manuscript to manuscript and substantial melodic variation when the same chant happens to appear. Thus one ought perhaps to think of a core repertory with the sort of stability that Hughes describes, and other layers of the repertory with degrees of instability corresponding to the relevant historical circumstances.

Any such core repertory will include literally hundreds of chants, and the faithful reproduction of it conjures up a feat of memorization that strains the credulity of present-day observers. The notion of literal memorization is not much in fashion today; indeed, Treitler cites a modern theory of memory that defines it as reconstruction rather than literal reproduction.[23] We all recognize this reconstructive memory as that employed in lecturing from notes, for example, or retelling a story, but literal memorization remains alive in at least some quarters. Actors, recitalists and conductors continue to perform prodigious feats of literal memorization, while certainly memory was relied on much more in the early Middle Ages than it is in this century. To take just the most obvious example, all clerics were required to know the Psalter by heart and to reproduce it verbatim. As for chant, one must keep in mind that it was sung as virtually a full-time occupation by many clerics for the better part of their lives, including early childhood. Weekly church-goers, incidentally, are capable of carrying about in their heads large hymn repertories, and while the typical Gregorian chant may be more difficult to retain than a metrical hymn, the medieval cantor, singing chant for hours every day, should have been able to retain a corresponding fund of chant. To complete this analogy with modern hymns, some hymn tunes show slight variations from denomination to denomination, while retaining their essential identity, just as chants show slight variations from region to region. It might even be that there is a small measure of consistency in these hymnic variations; for example, the tunes called 'St Thomas', 'Hursley' and 'Sicilian Mariners' in Anglican hymnals are not as florid as their counterparts in Catholic hymnals.

Finally, there were patterns of resemblance among many chants that must have made the process of memorization easier. Two technical terms come into play here, 'adaptation' and 'centonization'. Adaptation is the utilization of the same melody for different texts, making adjustments to match the accentual patterns and the length of the new text. Such adaptation can be said to aid memory by the simple expedient of reducing the number of melodies to learn. The term 'centonization' has been justly criticized by Treitler for lack of precise analogy with its literary namesake, but, as he explains himself, there is substance to the musical phenomenon behind the term.[24] Stock melodic formulae of varying lengths, what Peter Wagner called 'wandering melismas', appear in many chants. Obviously the presence of one or more of these formulae in a particular chant would make it somewhat easier to retain. It is true, on the other hand, that they are more a feature of solo than of choral chants; they are common, for example, in graduals and totally absent from introit antiphons. Indeed, it can be argued that they suggest a measure of improvisation in the performance of solo chants, but in view of what was written above, it might be better to think of such improvisation as having taken place at an early stage in the history of these chants, before their final stabilization.

In any case the argument made here for literal memorization is not meant to be absolute. Certainly many chants were sung differently from time to time and place to place. No doubt reconstructive memory somehow shared the task of oral transmission with reproductive memory. And memory lapses must have occurred frequently, due both to the fallibility of individuals and external circumstances. But it remains a plausible hypothesis, and one suggested by a provisional examination of the evidence, that a central portion of the Gregorian repertory, both choral and solo, might have been reproduced annually in substantially the same form during the century or two in question.

If it is reasonable to think of the memorization of stable melodies as a key element in the oral transmission of Gregorian chant, how does one think of their origins? When and how was the core repertory stabilized so that it could be transmitted? The 'when' has already been suggested here as closer in time to the reign of Gregory II (715–31) than Gregory I (594–604). The 'how' might be better imagined, perhaps, if one reflects on the task facing the Schola Cantorum. It was a magnificent and enormous enterprise that took the form of fleshing out the framework of the *circulum anni*.[25] Each day was to have its appointed text formulary and each formulary its own music. The age-old practice of selecting prayers and chants from a range of appropriate possibilities was finally abandoned in favour of set choices, to be recorded in liturgical books and repeated each year. It was to a great extent a process of organization and completion; much traditional textual and musical material would be retained, some would be abandoned, new material would be created, and all would be revised and synthesized. If this was the time the gradual was changed from a responsorial psalm to a single respond and verse of determined text, this would account for the need to apply the techniques of adaptation and centonization. Introits, on the other hand, retained their form of psalm with antiphon, and would have required less radical revision. The remarkably homogeneous style of the introit antiphons, however, suggests a deliberate programme of revision for the traditional melodies, while the expansion of the repertory could have called for entirely new compositions. All told, this is the sort of enterprise that could be accomplished only by a close-knit group of singularly talented individuals, caught up in the excitement of their movement for a generation or so. One is reminded of the creative ferment that produced Viennese Classical music, Gothic architecture, classical Greek drama or, for somewhat closer analogy perhaps, the historiographic achievement of the seventeenth century Maurist Benedictines.

The last in the series of speculations presented in this essay returns again to the Gregorian question. If the activity just now associated with the Schola Cantorum took place, say, from the late seventh century to the mid-eighth, with Gregory II playing a decisive part in it, why was it that it came to be falsely attributed to Gregory I? That the two pontiffs share the same name creates the potential for such a misattribution, but does not explain why it actually happened. The immediate cause of the confusion must have been the famous verse prologue that first appeared towards the end of the earliest unnotated graduals.[26] 'Gregorius praesul', it begins, 'meritis et nomine dignus' ('Gregory the leader, honourable in both name and deed'), a line applicable to either Gregory. It continues, 'Unde genus ducit, summum conscendit honorem' ('There whence his family derives, he achieved the highest distinction'). The verse goes on to specify that 'he composed this book of musical art of the Schola Cantorum', but it is that second line which requires explanation. Dom Morin and generations of chant scholars after him have maintained that the phrase 'Unde genus ducit', can be applied to Gregory I only, not Gregory II, but this is patently untrue. It means simply '[there at Rome] whence his family derives', and both Gregorys came from Rome; their biographies in the *Liber pontificalis* begin in precisely the same way, 'Gregorius natione romanus' ('Gregory, a citizen of Rome'). One might argue that Gregory I was a member of the nobility and Gregory II was not, but the verse fails to specify nobility, and more than that there is good reason why its author might have wanted to indicate the Roman background of Gregory II in particular. He was the only Roman pope from 685 to 752, the better part of a century when every other pope was of Eastern lineage.

An important factor in all this is the part played by the Schola Cantorum. The 'Gregorius praesul' prologue refers to the Gregorian antiphoner as a book of the Schola Cantorum, while John the Deacon, writing late in the ninth century, attributed the founding of the Schola to Gregory I. How likely is it that Gregory I founded the Schola? For one thing there is a chronological problem with the notion. The first hints of the Schola's existence appear long after Gregory's death with the *Liber pontificalis*'s references to late seventh-century popes, Leo II, Benedictus II and Sergius I, who had musical training in their youth. But perhaps the strongest argument that Gregory I did not found the Schola is that to have done so would have been quite out of character. The Schola was an important part of the Roman clerical establishment, and Gregory was at odds with that establishment. His sympathies were more monastic than clerical and he arrogated to his client monks many of the cherished duties and responsibilities of the clergy, a policy for which he was resented in Rome long after his death.[27] It seems unlikely that he would have augmented the forces of the clerical establishment by creating an institution which came to serve as a kind of Roman seminary.[28]

It is this question of Gregory's reputation in Rome that touches directly upon our final speculation – why it was that the ninth-century Franks mistakenly attributed to him the activities of Gregory II. In fairness to Gregory's memory, it should be said that he was always esteemed as an ascetic and spiritual author. It was as a churchman, a figure of ecclesiastical accomplishment, that he was so little regarded in seventh- and eighth-century Rome. His paltry biography in the *Liber pontificalis*, incidentally, occupies but one page in Duchesne's edition, while that of Gregory II occupies no fewer than fourteen.

Why then the shift in Gregory I's favour? The reason lies in the central role played by England in the Carolingian Renaissance. Gregory I had sent Augustine of Canterbury to England on what turned out to be a highly successful missionary effort, and the English remembered this with gratitude. As faded as was the reputation of Gregory at Rome, so it flourished in England. His first biographers were English, and the Venerable Bede mentioned him frequently with great warmth. Now it was these same English – figures like Boniface and Alcuin – who were chiefly responsible for bringing the Franks into line with the Roman Church. They were devoted to Rome with an intensity unequalled elsewhere in all Christendom, and for them the embodiment of Rome was Gregory. The Franks, in turn, imbibed this veneration for him from their English mentors; it is not surprising that in the ninth century they attributed the accomplishments of a by then indeterminate Gregory to the first pope to bear that name, the man who would eventually be called Gregory the Great.

★

To summarize, it is hoped that this series of speculations presents a view of Gregorian chant origins that is at least coherent and not entirely implausible, even if necessarily tentative and incomplete. It is a historiographically comforting view in that by leaning towards a less fluid conception of oral transmission during the ninth century it places the stabilization of chant close to the time of Charlemagne, a mere generation or two from its maturation under Gregory II and his contemporaries. Dare we think, then, that the chant of those two times and places was substantially the same? Certainly there are potential problems in the transference of so vast a repertory from the confines of the Schola Cantorum, across the Alps, to a greatly differing environment. But the more stable conception of oral transmission proposed here suggests that this might have been accomplished with less change to the chant than is frequently assumed. Moreover, an essential element in the eagerness of the Franks to share the celebrated *cantus romanus* was the peculiar Carolingian hankering after authenticity. They were, as Treitler observes, the first musicologists; they wished to establish an authoritative text, so to speak, and moved quickly to capture it within the Byzantine system of eight modes, completing the task by inscribing it on parchment with neumatic notation. It is true that the application of the modal system must have required adjustments to some chants, but there is nothing in the earliest accounts of modal theory to suggest that most melodies were substantially altered. Thus it is just conceivable that what we know today as Gregorian chant might be something marvellously close to its origins, rendering those origins knowable eventually rather than lost in centuries of darkness.

NOTES

[1] The *ordines romani* are edited by M. Andrieu, *Les ordines romani, du haut moyen âge*, Spicilegium sacrum Lovaniense, xi, xxiii–xxv, xxviii–xxix (Louvain, 1939–61).

[2] These appear in R. J. Hesbert, *Antiphonale missarum sextuplex* (Rome, 1935).

[3] Most notably the cantatorium *CH-SGs* 359, *F-CHR* 47 (destroyed in 1944) and *F-LA* 239. These are available in facsimile along with some twenty other important chant manuscripts in the collection edited by the Benedictine monks of Solesmes, PalMus (various locations, 1889–).

[4] K. Levy, 'Charlemagne's Archetype of Gregorian Chant', *JAMS*, xl (1987), 1–30.

[5] See H. van der Werf, *The Emergence of Gregorian Chant* (Rochester, NY, 1983), i, 1, 123–7.

[6] This hypothesis will be recognized as that of Helmut Hucke; citations appear below.

[7] D. Hughes, 'Evidence for the Traditional View of the Transmission of Gregorian Chant', *JAMS*, xl (1987), 377–404.

[8] H. Leclercq, 'Afrique', *Dictionnaire d'archéologie chrétienne et de liturgie*, i (Paris, 1907), 638.

[9] M. Huglo, 'Le répons-graduel de la messe: évolution de la forme, permanence de la fonction', *Schweizer Jb für Musikwissenschaft*, new ser., ii (1982), 33.

[10] The concept appears in K. Levy, 'Toledo, Rome and the Legacy of Gaul', *EMH*, iv (1984), 66. On the use of the Psalter in liturgical texts, see the important article of J. Dyer, 'Latin Psalters, Old Roman and Gregorian Chants', *KJb*, lxviii (1984), 11–30.

[11] F.-A. Gevaert, *Les origines du chant liturgique de l'église latine* (Ghent, 1890).

[12] G. Morin, *Les véritables origines du chant grégorien* (Maredsou, 1890).

[13] B. Stäblein comes the closest to doing so in his valuable '"Gregorius Praesul": der Prolog zum römischen Antiphonale', in *Musik und Verlag: Karl Vötterle zum 65. Geburtstag* (Kassel, 1968), 537. The prologue in question will be discussed below.

[14] W. H. Frere, *The Sarum Gradual and the Gregorian Antiphonale Missarum* (London, 1895), x.

[15] See W. Apel, *Gregorian Chant* (Bloomington, 1958), 378.

[16] *Le liber pontificalis: texte, introduction et commentaire*, ed. L. Duchesne, i (Rome, 1886), 317.

[17] The most complete exposition of his views appears in 'The Urban and Papal Rites in Seventh- and Eighth-Century Rome', *Sacris erudiri*, xii (1961), 411–87.

[18] Hucke became one of the principal protagonists in the controversy over chant origins at a surprisingly early age; there is a convenient summary of his views in 'Toward a New Historical View of Gregorian Chant', *JAMS*, xxxiii (1980), 437–67.

[19] See especially L. Treitler, 'Homer and Gregory: the Transmission of Epic Poetry and Plain-chant', *MQ*, lx (1974), 333–72.

[20] See for example E. Nowacki, 'The Gregorian Office Antiphons and the Comparative Method', *JM*, iv (1985–6), 243.

[21] See van der Werf, *The Emergence of Gregorian Chant*, ii.

[22] J. Udovich, 'The Magnificat Antiphons for the Ferial Office', *JPMMS*, iii (1980), 1–25.

[23] Treitler, 'Homer and Gregory', 344–7.

[24] L. Treitler, '"Centonate" Chant: *Übles Flickwerk* or *E pluribus unus?*', *JAMS*, xxviii (1975), especially 11–12.

[25] For the process at work in sacramentaries, see B. Moreton, *The Eighth-Century Gelasian Sacramentary* (Oxford, 1976).

[26] See n.13; Stäblein makes the telling point that the earlier Italian versions of the prologue fail to mention Gregory I's most characteristic accomplishment, his spiritual writings, while the somewhat later Frankish ones do.

[27] See P. A. B. Llewellyn, 'The Roman Church in the Seventh Century: the Legacy of Gregory I', *Journal of Ecclesiastical History*, xxv (1974), 363–80.

[28] What I find to be even more conclusive arguments against Gregory I's founding of the Schola Cantorum are developed in a study by J. Dyer to appear in a Festschrift dedicated to H. Hucke.

BIBLIOGRAPHICAL NOTE

In recent years most chant scholars have shied away from the central issue of chant origins and concentrated instead on more narrowly defined topics. For an overview of the subject one still begins with Wagner's admirable *Introduction to the Gregorian Melodies*, i, trans. A. Orme and E. G. P. Wyatt (London, 1901). W. Apel updated Wagner in his *Gregorian Chant* (Bloomington, 1958,3/1966), which is still useful, even if in need of updating itself. H. Hucke has twice, in article-length studies, moved the subject closer to an acceptable synthesis: 'Die Entwicklung des frühchristlichen Kultgesangs zum Gregorianischen Gesang', *Römische Quartalschrift*, xlviii (1953), 147, and 'Toward a New Historical View of Gregorian Chant', *JAMS*, xxxiii (1980), 437–67. The only recent book-length study that grapples with any of the larger issues is H. van der Werf, *The Emergence of Gregorian Chant* (Rochester, NY, 1983). D. Hiley has provided a useful summary of the issues involved and the most recent work on them in 'Recent Research on the Origins of Western Chant', *EM*, xvi (1988), 203–13.

More specialized chant studies are too numerous to cite. There has been an attempt to include as many as possible of the more important authors in the notes to this essay, but several who are worthy of mention have been missed.

Liturgical studies present an even larger bibliography than chant studies; a useful guide to the field is R. W. Pfaff, *Medieval Latin Liturgy: a Select Bibliography* (Toronto, 1982). The standard survey of the history of the Mass is J. Jungmann's *The Mass of the Roman Rite*, trans. F. X. Brunner (New York, 1951–5). For the Office, R. Taft's recent *The Liturgy of the Hours in East and West* (Collegeville, Minn., 1986) does much to make up for the deficiencies of S. Bäumer's *Histoire du breviaire* (Paris, 1905). The history of the Sanctorale was well served by W. Frere, *Studies in Early Roman Liturgy*, i: *The Calendar* (London, 1930), and his subsequent volumes in the same series on the lectionary and evangeliary, but there is nothing comparable for the Temporale. The closest thing to a comprehensive survey of the latter is the long article by A. Chavasse, 'Les plus anciens types du lectionnaire et de l'antiphonaire romains de la messe', *Revue bénédictine*, lxii (1952), 3–94; Chavasse, however, labours under a strong pro-Gregory I bias and tends to date virtually all liturgical developments more than a century too early.

The area of general history most relevant to the present essay is that of Rome in the early Middle Ages, and here one is grateful for a number of excellent recent works, including P. Llewellyn, *Rome in the Dark Ages* (London, 1971); J. Richards, *The Popes and the Papacy in the Early Middle Ages 476–752* (London, 1979); and especially T. F. X. Noble, *The Republic of St Peter* (Philadelphia, 1984). A highly readable survey that emphasizes the artistic and architectural aspects of the subject is R. Krautheimer, *Rome: Profile of a City, 312–1308* (Princeton, 1980).

Chapter V

Plainchant Transfigured: Innovation and Reformation through the Ages

DAVID HILEY

THE WRITING DOWN OF PLAINCHANT

At some time in the ninth century – perhaps as early as the end of the eighth century, but more likely in the latter half of the ninth – a decision was taken to make a written record of the melodies of the chant repertory. This step is as important for the history of Western music as the time and place when it happened are mysterious. Although the music now notated for the first time had developed without written aid, the device of notation was eventually to make possible the composition of music which could not have been conceived without it. That stage was reached some time later. It has been argued that the polyphony of thirteenth-century Paris is the first musical repertory which goes decisively beyond what improvisation can achieve, in the building of large musical structures and the accurate coordination of complex contrapuntal lines.[1] But that a notation of any sort should have been brought into use was decisive, one of the most significant events in Western culture.

    Why should it have happened, and who was responsible? These are difficult questions upon which scholars still disagree. I have already hinted at the disagreement about the date, and while the leading cultural centres of the Carolingian Empire were no doubt involved in the new activity, it is not at all clear if any one institution can claim precedence. One crucial area of disagreement is about whether the earliest surviving chant books, copied at the end of the ninth century, descend from one 'Ur-exemplar', or whether different musicians in different places each made their own recensions from memory. One would expect the problem to be easily soluble: can one not compare the extant sources and see how much or how little they agree with one another? Close agreement would support the notion of a master exemplar, disagreement would speak for independent redactions. Yet here, too, scholars interpret the evidence in different ways, some believing that the close (but not complete) agreement indicates written transmission from an archetype prepared perhaps at Charlemagne's behest, others preferring the idea of later, independent attempts to record the melodies from memory.[2]

The earliest examples of notation that have come down to us belong to the ninth century. Although very few are exactly datable, there is general agreement that none can be placed convincingly in the eighth century.[3] But all these examples are copies of but a few isolated pieces, perhaps only a single item. Quite a number, for example, are notations for the intoning of the Genealogy of Christ at Christmastide, when the deacon used a special melodic formula more solemn (which in musical terms means slightly more ornate) than the usual tones for Gospel lessons (fig.36). It should be noted that the music involved here is still simple, a reiterated formula used for each pair of verses, where the singer has only to decide on which syllable of his text he should make the traditional inflections for the ends of phrases, sentences and so on. In other words, the notation acts rather like a punctuation system.[4]

36. *Miniature of St Matthew, and part of the Christmas genealogy from St Matthew's Gospel, with English neumatic notation, from the 'Gospel Book of St Margaret', English, eleventh century. The book was owned by St Margaret (d 1093), wife of Malcolm III, King of Scotland*

The deacon was not the leading musician of the church. The more complex chants of Mass and Office were the province of the cantor and the trained Schola, and it appears that they did not at this stage rely on musical notation for the learning of their allotted chants. The earliest manuscripts which contain a comprehensive corpus of notated chants for the whole church year date from about 900. They are graduals, containing the chants of the Schola for Mass. Notated antiphoners, containing chants for the Divine Office, seem to appear somewhat later, and this may be connected with the greater variation between antiphoners which may be observed, in contrast to the relative homogeneity of graduals.

All notated chant sources earlier than the eleventh century, whether they be the isolated examples of the ninth century or the later complete books of chants, employ notational signs which do not indicate precise pitches. To a modern musician this may seem extraordinary: can signs which do not communicate one of the primary elements in music really constitute a musical notation? The implication is that a singer must have known the melody well when he performed a chant – well enough, in fact, for the notation to have been unnecessary during the performance itself. Although it is conceivable that one such as the deacon might use his simple notation as a guide, it is most unlikely that any of the early graduals, which record far more complex music, were used during performance. The notation in most of them is far too small, even for a single singer, quite apart from its lack of precision (when judged from a modern point of view). What purpose did it serve?

Early chant books were most likely reference books for cantors, to be consulted in the song-school and used during rehearsal. They specify clearly the number of notes for each syllable of text, and the direction of the melodic inflections (up, down, repeated notes). The notational signs are known as neumes, the group of signs for one syllable constituting one neume. They indicate not only regular melodic inflections but also certain special features of delivery, whose nature is now not entirely clear: the sign known as the *quilisma* may imply some sort of trill or turn, the *oriscus* another, and so-called liquescent signs warn of liquid consonants, diphthongs and other elements in the text which demand a particular manner of delivery. Some early books (those from St Gall, St Emmeram in Regensburg (fig.37) and Laon are prominent examples) are peppered with additional signs or letters which indicate rhythmic and dynamic nuances, and they employ a rich vocabulary of variations upon the usual basic signs to similar ends.

By 900, notations of the greatest sophistication were therefore in use in many different parts of western Europe. We should avoid the pitfall of regarding these notations as incomplete simply because they were not intended to specify pitch. Pitch was a preoccupation of eleventh-century musicians, just as rhythm was an overriding concern

37. *Chants for the Mass of St Stephen's Day, with German neumatic notation, from a gradual from the monastery of St Emmeram, Regensburg, c1000*

in the thirteenth century. It is clear that at the start of the ninth century pitches were well enough known to need no specification. Numerous melodies were employed many times over in the chant repertory, their outlines familiar from years of use during the mighty cycle of services each day, each week and each year. Some antiphon melodies might be used for over 50 different texts, some alleluia melodies likewise. The verses of Office responsories were practically always sung to one of eight rather ornate tones, different in complexity but not in kind from the tones the deacon had to manage for the Genealogy. Even elaborate chants like graduals and tracts show repeated reliance on standard procedures, traditional ways of beginning, continuing and ending chants, given prose texts (usually psalm verses) of differing length and construction. The singer needed guidance not in the pitches of the basic melodies, but in how to apply his musical expertise, his store of melodic types, to the delivery of different texts. We might use the analogy of punctuation once more, while remembering that neumes are applied to each syllable of the text and may consist not only of simple steps and segments of recitation but also of complex melodic figures, surges and

123

leaps, sequential descents, hoverings and roulades, and the 'tremulae vel vinnolae' which Adhémar of Chabannes, writing in the eleventh century, said were characteristic of Roman chant but were found difficult to perform by the Franks.

Already by 900 there were numerous different styles of musical writing. The three earliest graduals are from Brittany (manuscript *F-CHR* 47), Laon (*F-LA* 239) and St Gall (*CH-SGs* 359; see fig.28 above), and they use quite distinct notational shapes; and other styles are documented at an equally early date in less comprehensive sources. It is by no means clear that these should have evolved in some way from a common mother script. And, while the three graduals agree to an extraordinary extent on melodic detail, they do not agree perfectly. The disagreements might be explained by a gap of a couple of generations between the first codification of the repertory and the copies of around 900, which would give time for different calligraphic and melodic preferences to assert themselves. Yet one may be permitted to ask whether the concept of a centrally ordained master exemplar was not foreign to that age. There can be no doubt that enormous and painful efforts were made to revivify liturgical practice along Roman lines in Frankish lands. The scars left by the experience are discernible in the conflicting accounts by John 'Hymmonides' the Deacon (of Monte Cassino) and Notker 'the stammerer' (monk of St Gall) of the attempts by the Franks to learn from Roman singers: John thought the Franks were incapable, Notker accused the Romans of deliberately deceptive teaching. But notated chant books, which would have helped sort out disagreements, do not figure in the affair. Amalarius of Metz, who compared Roman and various Frankish books, found plenty of disagreement even in the choice of texts to be sung at various services. Again, notation is not mentioned, and it is unlikely that Amalarius (writing about 850) ever saw any completely notated chant books. Had he done so, he would no doubt have noticed plenty of discrepancies of detail in the melodies as well. When so many early sacramentaries (books which contain the Proper prayers of Mass to be intoned by the priest) differ from one another in textual details, it seems optimistic to suppose that the gradual and antiphoner could have achieved textual unification, or that such unification would have been thought a sufficiently important goal to aim for.

THE FRANKISH ENRICHMENT OF THE ROMAN CHANT REPERTORY

The chants recorded in the earliest graduals and antiphoners catch the repertory in a state of flux, a state in which, it may safely be said, it has always existed. There is considerable disagreement among both these and later sources, for example, as to which alleluias should be sung on which days of the church year, and it is clear that many new pieces entered the repertory throughout the Middle Ages, some achieving fairly widespread popularity, some remaining purely local favourites. This is a state of affairs encountered time and time again in the history of plainchant. The uniformity envisaged in Pius X's *Motu proprio* of 1908, and effectively discarded again at the Second Vatican Council, is unique, impossible to achieve before the present century and not dreamt of in the early Middle Ages.

The surviving manuscripts, no doubt only a fraction of what once existed, present a lively picture of local initiative and intercourse between institutions. Nowhere is this more evident than in the music composed for the feast days of the church year, which called forth a multitude of special items and special ways of performing the traditional elements of each service. The most important new genres were the sequence, tropes of various kinds and the rhymed Latin songs known as conductus, *versus* or *cantiones*. Wherever the first steps in these new directions were taken – and it is by no means clear from the surviving sources who may claim priority – scores of churches across Europe composed their own pieces and performed borrowed items according to their own liturgical requirements. The order of events seems to have been first the establishment of the Roman liturgy and its chant in Frankish territory, and then the further enhancement of the liturgy of high feasts with extra, non-Roman material. The two must of course have overlapped to some extent. The manuscript record is too incomplete, and begins too late, for us to be as certain of chronology as we would like. It will be convenient to refer to the Roman chant which the Franks codified as 'Gregorian' (which is what they believed it to be), to facilitate comparisons with the newer genres. The relationship of the new to the old is particularly interesting.

The sequence was performed after the alleluia at Mass. It was usually composed roughly according to a melodic scheme *a bb cc dd . . . x*, so that pairs of versicles had the same melody. The sequence is best known as a texted genre, with the odd characteristic that each syllable of text usually has just one note of the melody. Opinion is divided as to whether this was a feature of the sequence from the beginning. Some early sequences (perhaps the earliest) may have started life as ecstatic, purely melodic extensions of the alleluia jubilus, the jubilus being a rhapsodic vocalization upon the final syllable of the word 'alleluia'. (The normal pattern for the alleluia is (i) alleluia with jubilus, (ii) verse, (iii) repeat of alleluia and jubilus. The festal form would have been (i) alleluia with jubilus, (ii) verse, (iii) alleluia with sequence.) These sequence melodies are not traceable before the ninth century and were already being texted then. Indeed, many new texts and melodies were composed simultaneously. The method of texting was to provide a single syllable for each single note of the melody. Texts made by Notker were taken up with some enthusiasm in eastern territories (roughly from the Liège diocese in the north down to Constance, and lands east, together with some north Italian centres such as Nonantola), and some became current in western lands. In some cases Notker took pre-existing sequence texts as his starting-point, and these have been traced in west-Frankish manuscripts. A letter in which Notker describes his boyhood difficulties in learning the long textless melodies, and how he learnt the way to set texts to them, was often copied as a preface to his collection.

Our knowledge of the geographical dispersion of the sequence repertory is limited by the loss of manuscripts. Other places where new texts were composed for old sequence melodies include Winchester, whose period of greatest musical activity was initiated by Bishop Ethelwold (*d* 984). Particularly rich collections have survived from south-west France (Aquitaine). Some originated at the monastery of St Martial in Limoges; some came there as a result of the activities of St Martial librarians, and of these the provenance is often now unclear. The Aquitanian manuscripts with sequence collections also contain much other festive material, principally tropes for chants of Mass, and this is true of such manuscripts from other areas. The traditional, 'Gregorian' items of Mass would be copied in separate graduals. Many Italian manuscripts, however (those from Benevento in south Italy form a prominent group), copy the traditional items and the festive pieces side by side in performing order.

In the early years of this century, tropes (and often sequences as well) were regarded with a disapproving eye as excrescences, battening on the traditional chants rather like parasites, lacking the authenticity of 'Gregorian' chant. The desire to praise God in new and better ways has always brought forth original compositions, and tropes fulfilled an evident need to enhance the solemnity of greater feasts. We can now see the trope repertories (the plural indicates once again the local character of much compositional activity) as an ingenious compromise, for they succeed in enriching the liturgy without the danger of disruption which completely independent new items might have caused. This was achieved in two ways.

Texts might be sung to previously textless phrases. Such added texts are sometimes called 'prosulae' and are obviously somewhat similar in nature to the texts which were added to pre-existing sequence melodies (sometimes called 'prosae'). Melismas in alleluias, offertories and responsories were frequently texted in this way. Many aspects of the performance of plainchant are unknown to us today, particularly how matters stood before the advent of fully rubricated books in the thirteenth century. The later books tell us that prosulas for Office responsories were often performed by a select group of singers standing in a special position (such as mid-choir, facing the altar). Each of their

38. *Tropes for the introit of St Stephen, with English neumatic notation (and a miniature of the saint), from an English troper, mid-eleventh century, possibly made for King Edward the Confessor*

texted verses was echoed by the rest of the choir, who repeated the melody only (to 'a' or some other appropriate syllable). Whether this method of performance also obtained in early centuries is unclear, but the desire to raise the singing of the responsory to a new plane of solemnity is clearly evident.

The word 'tropus' in medieval books is most often used to indicate another type of addition, where new phrases of chant were sung before phrases of the traditional melody. This was most often practised with festal introits, but offertories and communions were also troped. 'Today the celebrated martyr Stephen ascends crowned with laurel to paradise', sang the leaders of the monastic choir at Winchester at the beginning of Mass on St Stephen's Day towards the end of the tenth

127

century, and the choir answered with the first line of the introit: 'Princes sat, and spoke against me'. The alternation continued: (cantors) 'The wicked people of the Jews rose up against me'; (choir) 'And the wicked persecuted me' – and so forth, with a total of no fewer than fourteen trope verses in all. Out of an introit no different in length or character from scores of other introits sung on less important days in the year an impressive and richly allusive entrance portal to the liturgical edifice has been built.

It is not always quite clear whether one is dealing with a troped chant or not. The Kyrie eleison of Mass provides examples. Its basic Greek text seems standard enough, but its melodies are many and varied. In the earliest extant sources, some melodies appear always and only with extra Latin text. It has therefore been argued that, instead of untroped and troped Kyries, we should recognize two distinct types, a ferial form with the Greek words only, and a festal form with Latin verses. The distinction was perhaps more important at the time when tropes still needed an advocate, but it serves to highlight some important points: the contrast between the liturgy of ordinary ferial days and the more splendid and solemn celebration of feast days, full of topical illusions to the event being celebrated. This is something not emphasized so much in early centuries. The text of the St Stephen introit *Etenim sederunt* ('Princes sat') is culled somewhat adventitiously from Psalm cxviii. As far as chant texts were concerned, the infinitely complex web of references linking every part of the year's liturgy was more important in the early centuries than the topicality of an individual feast. The high Middle Ages, by contrast, delighted in glossing and supplementing the neutral, ancient texts, piling allusion upon allusion in joyous reiteration of the day's theme.

The question about the Kyries (it also affects the Gloria, and has to be borne in mind whenever the distinction between trope and parent chant is made) reminds us again that the early manuscript sources catch the repertory in mid-career. We cannot plot all its early stages, for it is usually in the nature of the sources to record what is established, perhaps in danger of decaying, rather than what is being built up step by step. (Musical loose notes in preparation for the definitive copy, so to speak, have nevertheless been shown to survive among the St Gall manuscripts.)

To later generations, the original compositions of a previous age often seem all too earthbound and antiquated. Few manuscripts after the twelfth century contain introit tropes. Kyrie tropes and sequences, as a genre, survived reasonably strongly until the sixteenth century, when the singing of all tropes and all but four sequences was discouraged at the Council of Trent. Sequences nevertheless persisted occasionally, for instance when local loyalties to a favourite patron saint would not countenance the suppression of the sequence on his feast day.

Some important churches did not adopt all the festive genres. At Cluny, for example, sequences were sung with words only on the nine most important feasts, and left simply as melodies on other feast days; and apart from a troped Agnus Dei on Easter Day, tropes were avoided entirely.

Other genres also blossomed and faded. Some festal liturgies of the twelfth and thirteenth centuries are characterized by the inclusion of 'conductus', or 'versus', strongly rhythmic, rhyming Latin songs often sung as the deacon or subdeacon approached the lectern for a lesson, or as recessional anthems (see fig.39). Famous liturgies of this type were those celebrated at Beauvais and Sens on New Year's Day, the Feast of the Circumcision or the 'Feast of Fools', when a subdeacon assumed the 'baculum', symbol of office of the ruler of the choir, and much ceremonial and musical licence was permitted. The conductus genre persisted longest in eastern lands, usually under the name of 'cantio'. Another feature of these liturgies was the singing of 'farsed' (literally 'stuffed') chants, notably lessons, Credo and *Pater noster*. The traditional chant was interspersed with trope verses, often not newly composed but borrowed from sequences or other sources.

Regular rhythm and rhyme are features of new chant texts only

39. *End of the conductus 'Natus est, natus est/Igitur, igitur', to accompany the deacon to and from the altar for the intoning of the Gospel, and start of the farsed Credo, from a Circumcision liturgy, Beauvais Cathedral, early thirteenth century*

from the twelfth century onwards. The fashion proved irresistible. Early sequence texts were in prose, with lines of varied length. From the late eleventh and early twelfth centuries we have sequences with some (though not all) lines in regular accented trochees, with rhyme. Completely regular sequences, every verse in some such scheme as alternately accented 8 + 8 + 7 syllables, or 2 + 2 + 3 + 3 (mixed patterns can also occur), were composed in great numbers from the mid-twelfth century, many by Adam 'of St Victor', canon of Notre Dame in Paris

One favourite genre for the rhymesters was the Office. Newly composed Offices for local saints, and for some prominent internationally known saints such as Thomas of Canterbury and St Dominic, were often made with rhyming texts for responsories and antiphons. Clearly it was not often possible to adapt traditional 'Gregorian' melodies to metrical texts, and new music was composed. The music for Offices as well known as those of Thomas and Dominic was in its turn used for other saints. All the poet had to do was to compose new poetic texts with the same metre: the music would fit automatically. It may be observed of this procedure that no new items are introduced into the liturgy: the standard genres, responsory and antiphon, are simply composed in a new style.

The so-called liturgical dramas of the early Middle Ages are somewhat different in character. Up to the end of the first millennium, little more is recorded than brief dialogues between the Marys visiting Christ's tomb and the Angel. The popularity of this dialogue is remarkable, for it was sung all over Europe, in contrast to most tropes, for example, which usually had only local currency. The 'Quem quaeritis' dialogue was brief enough to be insertable in different places in the liturgy: either at the place where a procession formed before Mass on Easter Day, or at the close of Easter Matins, or prefacing Mass itself. In the next century the scope of the representational ceremony expanded dramatically. New material, and any existing antiphons and responsories which could be used, were drafted into longer presentations, and, although the Easter story dominated the attention of the medieval compilers, other events were also 'dramatized': the Christmas story, for example. Rhymed chants entered the repertory and some completely rhymed ceremonies were written, for instance the miracles of St Nicholas contained in the so-called 'Fleury Playbook', or the 'Play of Daniel' from Beauvais.

The festive liturgy in a great church of the high Middle Ages, then, might well be a kaleidoscopic mixture of chant in widely different styles and of differing age and provenance. (The parallel with the diverse architectural elements of medieval churches is striking.) The confection was complete when polyphonic performance was added as the ultimate musical enrichment of the liturgy.

40. Abbey of Mont-St-Michel (1024–1228 and later); liturgies, like architectural styles, were imported into England from churches such as this

CHANGES IN THE LANGUAGE OF MUSIC

Plainchant is music with a text: a mode of delivery for sacred words in the context of the liturgy. We have no knowledge from this time of abstract, textless, musical constructions (such as, say, the organ voluntary so familiar in modern worship), unless we choose to regard sequence melodies as such. (Whatever the early state of the sequence in Frankish lands, an analogous repertory, known as 'melodiae', was always sung without text in the Ambrosian Church of Milan.) It is often easier to characterize chants by their texts than by their music, as I have done for tropes above. But music naturally reflected the variety of the texts that it set. I shall try to describe some of its characteristics.

We can reconstruct the pitches of early manuscripts only by comparing them with sources of the eleventh century and later, when pitch-specific notation was used. A handful of sources of the eleventh and twelfth centuries provided alphabetic letters for each note of the melodies, but the favourite method of notating pitch became that

131

advocated by Guido of Arezzo around 1030, whereby the notational signs were deployed on a staff. It is clear from the widespread agreement between pitch-specific sources of very different provenance that not only the profile but also the pitches of the chants had indeed been transmitted astonishingly accurately by memory.

The differences between sources are nevertheless revealing. Among the thousands of antiphons sung during the Office Hours, for example, there are a few dozen which in different parts of Europe were understood to be in different tonalities, even though the basic shape of the melody remained the same. That is, at one church the chant would be in D mode, in another in E mode and so on. Nor do we have to wait for the advent of pitch-specific manuscripts to know that some chants caused some problems of modal identification. At the beginning of the tenth century, for example, Abbot Regino of Prüm, near Trier, complained of some antiphons that they started in one mode, continued in another and ended in a third, wherefore they were called 'nothas, id est, degeneres et non legitimas'. It was particularly important to have a sense of the mode of an antiphon because of its function as partner to a psalm or canticle. The psalms themselves were sung to one of eight tones, simple formulae which must have been the very first things learnt by a choirboy or novice monk and which he would use many times every day, thousands of times each year. Since the antiphon was sung before the psalm, that psalm-tone had to be chosen which would best fit musically with the antiphon melody; and because the antiphon was repeated after the psalm, one of a number of possible cadences had to be chosen for the psalm-tone so that a smooth return to the antiphon could be effected. Thus it became customary to compile long lists of antiphons grouped according to melodic type, indicating which psalm-tone and cadence they controlled. Such books, which sometimes include lists of other chants as well, are known as tonaries.

Through tonaries, and also through the modal signatures given in some early chant books, we can trace the modality of many chants back to the ninth century. An incomplete tonal list of Mass chants from St Riquier may even date back to the closing years of the eighth century. From theoretical writings too it is clear that the system of eight modes was a matter of great importance. The impetus to adopt such a system seems to have come from contact with Byzantine musicians, of which there is evidence in the *Musica disciplina* of Aurelian of Réôme and in the anonymous *Musica enchiriadis*, both ninth-century works. Yet its role in the West is not easy to understand. In the East the eight modes were integrated into an eight-week liturgical cycle, so that chants in mode 1 were sung in the first week, chants in mode 2 in the second week and so on. This arrangement is at least as old as the eighth century, if not older.

The West never adopted this arrangement. (The only pieces

arranged modally were the antiphons and responsories of new Offices, especially the rhymed ones, where the first responsory would be in mode 1, the next in mode 2 and so on. But here we are speaking of the chants within a single service, Matins, not of an eight-week period.) The Franks seem to have learnt the repertory from Rome without reference to any modal system. (Old Roman chant, if that is an indicator, does not seem to have known any modal classification.) And while the tonary was no doubt of some use to a cantor as a work of reference, his memory of the antiphon melodies would have served him equally well when decisions about psalm-tones had to be taken. The tonaries, like much theoretical writing of the time, are evidence instead of the intellectual curiosity of the Carolingian musicians, having newly mastered an immense repertory of liturgical music, aware both of some aspects of sophisticated Byzantine practice and of the classical theoretical knowledge transmitted by Boethius, and eager to understand, analyse and classify their own music. A didactic purpose is also present, for several theorists speak of their wish to rectify corrupt practices.

Although plainchant was divinely inspired – the image of St Gregory, dove on shoulder, having his scribes write down music rather than his commentary on Ezekiel, is an invention of the ninth century – it has perforce been entrusted to fallible human vessels. Writings on music are littered with references to inexpert singers and the need for 'libri bene emendati'. Some of the emendation was clearly inspired by knowledge of the modal system. Modally ambiguous chants were emended in order to remove uncertainty. This much becomes clear when the new sources with pitch-specific notation of the eleventh century and later are compared. Openings, troublesome internal phrases, cadences, could all be modified to suit the scribe's notion of modal propriety. This phenomenon should not be overemphasized, for very few manuscripts show evidence of such emendation; but they are typical examples of what may happen when it becomes important to legislate on something previously left unspecified. A melody was declared 'troublesome' because it did not conform to a system within which it was not originally conceived, and some chants (such as tonally adventurous offertories) appear to have caused considerable problems to scribes using staff notation, so that we are no longer certain of being able to perceive the full range of the original.

These are minor details, however, when set alongside the changes that were to come. When chant could so easily be led away from the correct path, those who thought themselves able to perceive a truer image of the divine original could instigate reform in the name of tradition. The first to attempt this with pan-European consequences were the Cistercians, in the mid-twelfth century.[5] They had already made an abortive attempt to adopt the musical practice of Metz, which they believed from old report to have been the leading exponent of Roman

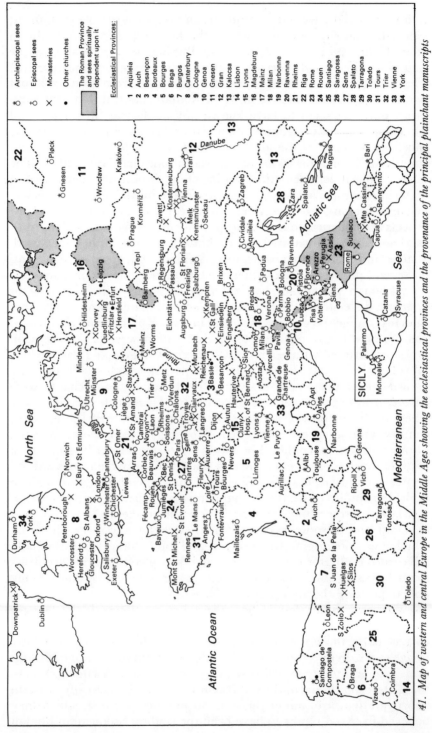

41. *Map of western and central Europe in the Middle Ages showing the ecclesiastical provinces and the provenance of the principal plainchant manuscripts*

chant in Charlemagne's time, and even to have had an authentic antiphoner sent from Rome. But Metz practice was found unsuitable, evidently having been corrupted in the intervening centuries. Eventually it was decided to create a new reformed repertory. Three aspects of the reform stand out: the concern for modal purity led to a strong separation of authentic and plagal modes (that is, passages which trespassed too much below the high authentic mode, or too much above the low plagal mode, were emended); B flat was excluded, once again being deemed a tonal impurity; chants were restricted to the range of ten notes, and passages which went beyond this were rewritten. It has to be admitted that not every instance of the above 'faults' was eradicated from Cistercian books, as extant manuscripts testify. The tenor of the reform is nevertheless clear.

Dominican books (a master-exemplar of the complete Dominican liturgy and music was compiled 1259–62) were strongly influenced by Cistercian musical practice.[6] Other recently formed religious orders were content to continue with the practices of the area where they originated, which in the case of the Carthusians meant following the Use of Lyons, whose liturgy had excluded all pieces of which the texts were not from Holy Scripture. Most other churches of Western Christendom continued with their own versions of the liturgy and its music. Occasionally, by comparing books for their choice of chants or for the musical and textual variants in those chants, we can trace the derivation of one use from another. Thus the order of items found in books of the monastery of St Bénigne at Dijon is reproduced in books from Jumièges and other Norman monasteries, refounded by William of Dijon in the early eleventh century; from Jumièges the same order was carried to Westminster in England. Such direct borrowings are, however, not common. The usual pattern is that geographically proximate churches tended to have similar liturgies and musical practices, with the interesting national differences that whereas in France and Italy uses tended to be somewhat diverse, German sources are relatively uniform. There is considerable fascination in comparing musical sources, especially from the point of view of their sequence and trope repertories, in order to discover just how much individuality was tolerated and in which direction interrelationships point. The overall picture is thus one of colourful variety between churches. One other instance of widespread uniformity should nevertheless be mentioned: the identity between Roman books from the thirteenth century onwards and those of the Franciscans.[7] The political implications of the unification of Franciscan and papal usage, which took place in the 1220s, are as important as the musical ones. But it is worth pointing out here that a necessary consequence of the adoption of a reformed liturgy by the curia was the abolition of Old Roman chant books, which were largely suppressed in the late thirteenth century.

From that time until the Council of Trent no major reforms were visited upon the chant repertory as a whole. The Council, however, initiated a major review of liturgical practice which resulted in the rewriting of the chants according to humanist principles, mostly the work of Anerio and Soriano. The chief witness to the changes was the graduale published in two volumes in 1614 and 1615 by the Medici Press in Rome (and thus usually referred to as the 'Medicean' edition). These versions persisted in Roman books and in those approved by the Vatican, down to the chant books printed by the firm of Pustet in Regensburg in the late nineteenth century. Apart from changes to the texts, melodies were made to sound less archaic tonally, melismas were curtailed (especially those on unstressed syllables) and stressed syllables were thrown into clear relief.

These reforms tampered with a repertory that was already formed. The new·compositions of these centuries also bear eloquent witness to changes in musical taste. Tropes tended deliberately to match their host chants by adopting a sort of all-purpose 'Gregorian' melodic style, but sequences were quite different. Some employ an astonishingly wide range, over two octaves, and their constant straining towards melodic climaxes and purposeful reiteration of a few cadences not found in the 'Gregorian' repertory give them a sectional, almost strophic character and a powerful sense of direction which contrasts strongly with the more static older melodies. Equally striking is the new tonal character of the conductus and the rhyming sequence of the twelfth century, which tended to skip up and down triads and generally favour the interval of a third. Such intervals are of course not absent from the older Gregorian melodies, and they maintain a significant presence in early sequences. But in the new compositions they shape the entire melody. There is none of the hovering, meditative quality of many older chants. The melodies range freely, boldly, through their compass, often stressing not only the upper fifth but also the octave as a melodic goal. The constant aiming at these perfectly consonant intervals, as well as the imperfectly consonant thirds (we are using contemporary terminology), is strongly suggestive of the polyphonic music of that time, which preferred these intervals to all others.

PLAINCHANT AND POLYPHONY

Polyphony might well have been discussed earlier, among the ways of enhancing the solemnity of the great feasts of the church year. Because it is potentially the more complex musical phenomenon, modern scholarship has tended to devote more attention to polyphony than to the plainchant that (at least in the early examples that have come down to us) it ornamented, despite the very meagre quantities that have survived from before the thirteenth century. The possibility should no doubt be reckoned with that polyphony, the sounding of two or more notes simultaneously, was also practised outside the church; but, as with so many aspects of medieval culture, it is at first only the church that made a written record of it.

Early polyphony, up to the eleventh century, emphasizes the static and ruminative qualities of plainchant. The most important source is a manuscript probably compiled by Wulfstan, the cantor of the Old Minster, Winchester, in the 990s, which contains added parts ('voces organales') for over 150 pieces of plainchant from festal liturgies. The technique is also described in a number of theoretical treatises, of which the latest and most explicit is Guido of Arezzo's *Micrologus*, written around 1030. *Vox organalis* and *vox principalis* (the original plainchant) usually begin and end on the same note, but in between the *vox organalis* seeks out holding notes, if possible no more than a fourth away from the *vox principalis*, which it reiterates beneath the more mobile *principalis*. Sometimes the two parts move in parallel fourths. The effect – Guido called it a soft or sweet sort of music – is to root the chant on structurally important notes (the holding notes). Since the plainchant itself often oscillates around structurally important notes the total impression is one of vibrant stasis.

From roughly the mid-eleventh century a new type of polyphony seems to have begun to replace the former. Here the emphasis was on opposite, contrary motion between the plainchant and added part. If the plainchant moved upwards, the *vox organalis* moved down, seeking out octaves, fifths and thirds; if the plainchant moved low, the added part rose above it. Now it is particularly striking that the new polyphony was used not only for traditional plainchants but also for the new conductus/*versus* repertory being created at the same time. And it is more than coincidental that the vertical consonances favoured in the polyphony should also be those intervals that dominate the melodic motion of the Latin songs.

Up to about the twelfth century, polyphony consisted nearly always in matching each note of the plainchant with an added note. The *vox principalis*, as the theorists' name for it implies, is paramount, the *vox organalis* often hardly more than its shadow. But in the twelfth-century books (the chant settings in the celebrated manuscript at Santiago de Compostela known as the 'Codex Calixtinus' or 'Liber Sancti Jacobi' are perhaps the best examples) we also find for the first time another type of chant setting, where the added part moves more freely, matching the chant not with single notes but with extended melodic phrases (fig.42). The independence of the added part and the possibilities it offered for the creation of musical structures were crucially important. It was but a short step from here to the grandiose chant settings of Pérotin in Paris at the end of the century. The function of the plainchant thus established, as 'tenor' (holding foundation notes), or as

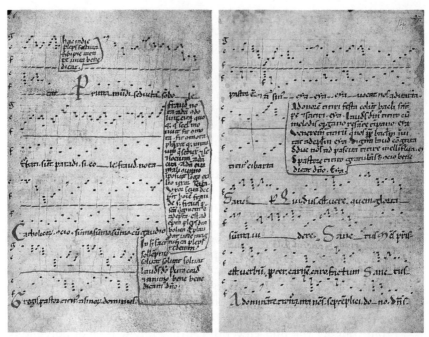

42. *Polyphonic conductus for two voices, and monophonic Sanctus, from a late twelfth-century manuscript relating to the Aquitanian repertory; note the visible (dry-point) pitch lines, pitch indicators (f, c, g in left-hand margins) and vertical lines to help align the parts (these are not bar lines)*

'cantus firmus', it remained important in church polyphony until beyond the Renaissance.

To a large extent we have lost contact with the liturgy of the medieval church. It is easy for us to forget the role of music as the servant of the liturgy. This is especially so when sacred polyphonic music is performed. The remarkable creations of Pérotin, Guillaume de Machaut, Guillaume Dufay and so many other composers are sufficient in themselves to occupy our attention and satisfy our aesthetic sense. The fact that they build upon a plainchant cantus firmus is of structural significance – we can well admire the ingenuity of its deployment within a complex construction – but little more. It is not easy for us to hear that plainchant in a wider context, as an integral part of the incessant prayer and praise which rose from ecclesiastical choirs all over Europe, now singled out to provide the ground-plan of a sumptuous polyphonic edifice. We must use our imagination, both to appreciate the liturgical context and also to understand the hierarchy of musical styles at whose pinnacle the polyphony stood: the simple tones of prayers, lessons and psalms; then the modestly inflected antiphons; the richly melismatic responsorial chants such as alleluia and offertory; and finally the crowning glory of polyphonic music, where the unison columns of plainchant, as it were, burst asunder into the multiple arches and ribs of church vaulting.

PLAINCHANT IN THE LAST HUNDRED YEARS

It is now just over a hundred years since Dom Joseph Pothier, monk of the Benedictine abbey of Solesmes, published a new edition of the Proper chants of Mass based on close study of authoritative medieval manuscript sources, the *Liber gradualis* of 1883. Twenty years later, on St Cecilia's Day 1903, Pope Pius X issued the *motu proprio* 'Tra le sollecitudini', which declared among other things that the highest type of sacred music was plainchant in the form recently restored. In the next few years the Vatican published chant books prepared by a commission of which Pothier was the head, which were to replace the editions published by Pustet and other versions then current.

Surely no other body of music has undergone such manifold and various transformations as the chant first codified some thousand years ago. This is of course a result of its liturgical function. Although it has been made to respond to changes of liturgical and musical fashion in sundry ways, it is not music composed to entertain or as a vehicle for artistic expression. It is for everyday use, not primarily for aesthetic enjoyment. It was from its earliest recorded appearance hallowed by tradition, and it has never entirely ceased to be sung.

The transmogrification that medieval chant suffered at the start of the seventeenth century was not the last change wrought upon it before the restoration by Pothier and his fellow monks and scholars. Rome in 1614 had no more power than in 814 to enforce use of any particular version of the chant, although the advent of printing naturally aided dissemination of the Medicean edition. In any case, it had been decreed at the Council of Trent that provincial synods should have responsibility for music, with due regard for the customs of local congregations. Much remains to be discovered about the practices of different dioceses up to the nineteenth century. But it is clear from the example of the church in France that local independence could assert itself vigorously. Hand in hand with the 'neo-Gallican' movement associated with Bossuet went the preparation of new service books, with plainchant that was part recast, and part new. More expert musical establishments cultivated an ornamented and instrumentally accompanied manner of performanmce, known as 'chant figuré'.

There was a strong political element in the turn taken by events in France. Yet even where such motivation did not exist, as in Germany, numerous revised chant books were prepared. Thus the restoration work of the nineteenth century took place against a background almost of anarchy, at least from the point of view of those who longed for unity of liturgical practice with Rome and a restoration of ancient tradition. The return to medieval practice was intimately bound up with the work of Dom Prosper Guéranger at Solesmes, not only a restorer of Benedictine monasticism in France and a liturgical reformer, but knowledgeable about medieval sources and propagator of the principle that agreement between manuscripts implies common descent from an earlier tradition. Knowledge of medieval chant books was of course not confined to Solesmes, but through Pothier from 1860 and André Mocquereau from 1880 Solesmes played by far the most important part in the restoration.

The aim of the restoration was to provide better service books for the use of the Roman Church. The results, the *Kyriale* (1905), *Graduale* (1908) and *Antiphonale* (1912), constituted an editio typica, not an editio critica. No critical edition of any of these books, in the sense of an edition which chooses the 'original', 'correct' reading from among those available in medieval manuscripts, has ever been made, and it seems improbable that this could ever be achieved, given the disagreement among even the earliest sources. Instead, a comparative edition, where several sources are edited in parallel, may answer scholarly needs. This is, of course, not of immediate practical use for the church. An edition conceived as a model for modern worship must inevitably legislate on problems whose solutions are, strictly speaking, irrevocably lost in history. It must choose between conflicting and equally authoritative versions.

Not surprisingly, more controversy has been aroused by the performance of plainchant than by any other issue connected with it in modern times. The authoritative new edition had, after all, been made for practical use. But no medieval source describes such features of the chant as speed of delivery, loudness and softness, and we have no precise information about medieval methods of voice production. The interpretation of some neumes is uncertain. Above all, the significance of the rhythmic indications in such as the early St Gall manuscripts has been hotly disputed. Pre-Restoration chant books had long and short notes. But Solesmes cultivated a smooth and supple style of singing free from any such rhythmic straitjacket. Since Pothier believed that the St Gall rhythmic indications were a local phenomenon, no account was taken of them in the new Vatican edition. Mocquereau, however, held a contrary view, and books published from Solesmes itself (the best known is the compendium *Liber usualis*, which first appeared in 1921) employed dots, bars over notes, and other rhythmic signs. The effect is nevertheless one of subtle nuances in the basic motion, quite the opposite of the rigidly metrical interpretations which have occasionally been heard as a counterpoint to the Solesmes method.

Intricate investigations of the early sources continue. To what end? The question is not entirely frivolous for there is an illogicality in seeking to pierce the veils which still obscure notations of the ninth and tenth centuries for liturgical ends. The liturgy in which the chant is now sung is hardly that of the ninth century. Liturgical research has naturally been able to penetrate well beyond that point in the past when the musical record begins. The reforms of the Second Vatican Council, in as much as they involved a recovery of past ideals, could not stop the clock in the ninth century. Yet this paradox should not deter us. If I have stressed the functional nature of plainchant, it has been in order to forestall misconception and disappointment that it does not fulfil the same cultural role as the art music of later centuries. That is not to deny its beauty and its significance in terms of human creativity. We admire medieval cathedrals and abbey churches without necessarily participating in the liturgy which they, like plainchant, were designed to serve. Plainchant will continue to hold pride of place in liturgical services, as the Constitution on Sacred Liturgy declares. But it will also continue to be of absorbing fascination to all who are interested in the roots of our musical culture, of which it is the earliest substantial record, and in the multifarious forms of expression which it embodies.

NOTES

[1] See the contribution (untitled) by L. Treitler to the symposium '"Peripherie" und "Zentrum" in der Geschichte der ein- und mehrstimmigen Musik des 12. bis 14. Jahrhunderts', *GfMKB, Berlin 1974*, 58–74.

[2] Compare the views on the one hand of K. Levy, 'Charlemagne's Archetype of Gregorian Chant', *JAMS*, xl (1987), 1–30, and on the other of H. van der Werf, *The Emergence of Gregorian Chant* (Rochester, NY, 1983), i, pt.1, p.165, and H. Hucke, 'Toward a New Historical View of Gregorian Chant', *JAMS*, xxxiii (1980), 437–67, especially 477. For a more extended discussion of their views see the previous chapter.

[3] See the lists and facsimiles in S. Corbin, *Die Neumen*, Palaeographie der Musik, i/3 (Cologne, 1977).

[4] See L. Treitler, 'Reading and Singing: on the Genesis of Occidental Music-Writing', *EMH*, iv (1984), 135–208.

[5] S. Marosszeki, *Les origines du chant Cistercien*, Analecta Sacri Ordinis Cisterciensis, viii (Vatican City, 1952).

[6] See D. Delalande, *Vers la version authentique du graduel grégorien: le graduel des Prêcheurs* (Paris, 1949).

[7] S. J. P. Van Dijk and J. H. Walker, *The Origins of the Modern Roman Liturgy* (London, 1960).

BIBLIOGRAPHICAL NOTE

So much vigorous new writing has appeared in the last two decades, chiefly in academic periodicals, that in many areas a synthesis has yet to be achieved. Thus W. Apel's *Gregorian Chant* (Bloomington, 1958, 3/1966) is still the most comprehensive survey, but it is out of date and gives inadequate coverage to sequences, tropes, rhymed Offices and other later chant genres. *The Early Middle Ages to 1300*, ed. R. Crocker and D. Hiley, *NOHM*, ii (1989), and D. Hiley, *Western Plainchant: an Introduction* (in preparation), attempt to fill the gap. Meanwhile the article 'Plainchant' by K. Levy and J. Emerson in *Grove 6* is by far the best survey, both incisive and comprehensive, and supplemented by an excellent bibliography. The articles on various chant genres in *Grove 6* are also generally excellent.

Antiquity and the Middle Ages

The most useful introduction to plainchant notation is still G. M. Suñol's *Introduction à la paléographie musicale grégorienne* (Solesmes, 1935). More recent are B. Stäblein, *Schriftbild der einstimmigen Musik*, Musikgeschichte in Bildern, iii/4 (Leipzig, 1975), and S. Corbin, *Die Neumen*, Palaeographie der Musik, i/3 (Cologne, 1977), since when a more critical attitude to the nature and origins of neumatic notation has been voiced in, for example, L. Treitler, 'Reading and Singing: on the Genesis of Occidental Music-Writing', *EMH*, iv (1984), 135–208, and K. Levy, 'On the Origin of Neumes', *EMH*, vii (1987), 59–90.

Writing on the sequence has yet to regain its balance after the attack on traditional ideas by R. Crocker, culminating in his book *The Early Medieval Sequence* (Berkeley and Los Angeles, 1977). A balanced introduction to tropes, with a complete edition of one collection, is to be found in P. Evans, *The Early Trope Repertory of St Martial de Limoges* (Princeton, 1970). An edition and exhaustive discussion of one of the extravagant festal liturgies of the twelfth and thirteenth centuries is provided by W. Arlt, *Ein Festoffizium des Mittelalters aus Beauvais in seiner liturgischen und musikalischen Bedeutung* (Cologne, 1970).

A good account of the standardization of a chant repertory in the Middle Ages itself, that of the Dominicans, is given by D. Delalande, *Vers la version authentique du graduel grégorien: le graduel des Prêcheurs* (Paris, 1949). On the aftermath of the Council of Trent see R. Molitor's *Die nach-Tridentinische Choral-Reform zu Rom: ein Beitrag zur Musikgeschichte des XVI. und XVII. Jahrhunderts* (Leipzig, 1901, 2/R1967). The opposing points of view at the end of the last century and the beginning of this may be seen in F. X. Haberl, 'Geschichte und Wert der offiziellen Choralbücher', *Kirchenmusikalisches Jb*, xxvii (1902), 134–92, and P. Combe, *Histoire de la restauration du chant grégorien d'après des documents inédits: Solesmes et l'édition vaticane* (Solesmes, 1969).

Chapter VI

The Polyphonic Music of the Medieval Monastery, Cathedral and University

MARION S. GUSHEE

Through one of those inexplicable vagaries of historical preservation, what might have been regarded as nothing more than a rather eccentric treatise, *Musica enchiriadis* ('A Musical Handbook'), is now known to every student of music history as the very source of a new concept in Western music – the simultaneous vertical combination of pitches in performance – which eventually led to the ultimate glory of Western art music: harmony. This treatise, presumed to be of northern European monastic origin from about AD 900, is the earliest extant European theoretical exposition of the basic craft of creating vertical combinations of sounds in vocal music.

It is difficult to believe that the *Musica enchiriadis* signals the actual birth of Western polyphonic music. There are too many tantalizing uses of terminology in earlier medieval literature that might be argued to refer to polyphony, and there is the experience of many ages and cultures that polyphonic playing and singing of some sort is virtually irrepressible. Yet this was a special time in the history of music; the discipline of music theory was struggling to apply the legacy of Greek musical science to medieval musical practice and was engaged in its first attempts to develop a system of musical notation equal to the task. It is not surprising, then, that a treatise of the period provides, in completely transcribable form, the earliest extant examples of European polyphonic music. Using an odd ideographic system based on modified Greek symbols, known as Daseian notation, *Musica enchiriadis* illustrates two procedures for 'organizing' chant in parallel intervals. In the first instance, the given chant (*vox principalis)* is placed above the added voice (*vox organalis*), which moves in strict parallel with the chant at the interval of a fifth. By extension, the author also recognizes the possibility of doubling each voice at the octave, resulting in a four-voice texture, still limited to strictly parallel motion.

The second type, moving in parallel fourths but beginning and ending on the unison, appears at first encounter to be of greater historical significance, since it introduces the possibility of non-parallel part-writing in the *vox organalis*. In truth, however, this procedure is nothing more than a theoretical necessity at this early stage of the game: oblique motion is allowed only in order to avoid the tritone (augmented fourth, nicknamed *diabolus in musica* by reason of its 'devilish' numerical ratio), which would otherwise occur as a result of the peculiar tetrachordal tonal system propounded in this treatise. The latter system, having departed from the Greek tetrachordal tradition which allowed (among its several genera) a diatonic scale, in fact resulted in the more obvious absurdity of augmented octaves, and required chromatic notes (unknown in the diatonic chant of the period) to perfect them. Thus the step towards independent part-writing was in fact very small, and it remained for later theorists to bring tonal theory back into line with practice, and to build on new concepts of consonance and part-writing which did eventually allow true independence in vocal counterpoint.

It has been suggested that the sensual impact of this earliest organum may represent, on the one hand, a dim reflection of secular or folk music, and on the other, a validation of the theoretical structural concept of the tetrachord and its mathematical bases.[1] Although the execution of the notation differs in detail from source to source, the principle remains the same: pitch is indicated by the Daseian symbols in a vertical column on the left side of the page; the individual syllables of the text are placed on the page consecutively at the appropriate pitch levels, and (usually) connected by directional lines (fig.43).

Two other early treatises give evidence of further refinements in thinking about organum over the rather troublesome presentation of *Musica enchiriadis*. The so-called Cologne treatise (also *c*900) remarks on the 'abusiveness' of passages in organum which contain thirds and seconds, even the former being considered at this date a dissonance. The 'Paris' treatise of the tenth century tempers this viewpoint with the idea that when such vertical sonorities occur in organum, as indeed they frequently did, especially at cadential points, 'legitimum organum' falls silent, or that 'responsum organum' is lacking.[2] In other words, the doctrine of organum required that it consist, in structure if not in detail, of perfect consonances only, that is octaves, fourths, fifths and of course unisons. It remains the case in treatises throughout the twelfth century that those perfect consonances are the only constituent intervals sanctioned in definitions or descriptions of organum. It should also be remarked that the specific matter of the added voice falling silent in order to avoid a dissonance is one which is encountered anew even in the highly developed polyphonic art of the Notre Dame repertory, and remains a subject of some scholarly dispute in that context.

The writings of Guido of Arezzo (*d* after 1033),[3] as famous for his 'invention' of the musical staff as *Musica enchiriadis* is for 'inventing'

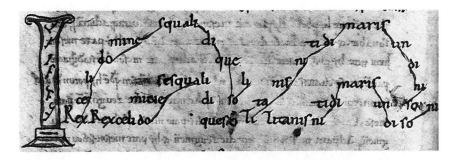

43. Sequence 'Rex coeli Domini' for two voices in the notation of parallel organum in 'Musica enchiriadis', from an early twelfth-century source of the treatise; the Daseian signs are in the left-hand column

polyphony, include major advances in polyphonic theory. In addition to basing his teachings, whether of monophonic or of polyphonic music, on a hexachordal system rather than the unsuccessful tetrachordal system of earlier times, and even while holding to the arrangement which calls for the *vox organalis* to lie below the chant and to observe rather strict rules of motion, Guido allowed for a number of 'exceptions' which, in sum, amount to a whole new approach to the construction – one might almost now say 'composition', with aesthetic connotations – of organum. The interval of the major third was now to be considered a consonance, and even the minor third tolerated; the voices were allowed to cross under certain circumstances, and it was permissible, in order to maintain good (mostly stepwise) part-writing, to form internal cadences at the fourth, and to add extra notes at the end of the *vox organalis* in order to cadence gracefully on the unison at the very end of a piece. While these may seem to be minute advances, in comparison with the rigid authority-based prescriptions of previous writers, Guido's lessons opened the door more than just a crack to freedom in composing part-music, and in essence, although he himself probably neither intended nor foresaw this result, placed this new art on a truly aesthetic footing.

Guido's advancement of the technique of musical notation (which amounted to an elaboration of methods which had gradually developed at varying rates in different dialects of chant notation) was primarily intended, according to his own claim, to make it possible to read music by sight, and thereby to facilitate the enormous task of learning the entire repertory of chant, which had previously depended almost exclusively on oral repetition and prodigious feats of memory. Now, Guido said, he could teach boys in two years what formerly took more like a dozen. Again, Guido may have been unaware of the major contribution he was making to the inventors of polyphonic music, who had been searching for practical written methods of specifying pitch, as was

44. The theorist Guido of Arezzo working on his treatise 'Regulae rhythmicae': miniature from a mid-eleventh-century source of his 'Micrologus'.

particularly necessary to their art.

In one further sense Guido of Arezzo's work represents a landmark in the history of polyphony and of the other aspects of music with which he concerned himself. Although relatively little is known about his life, there has never been any doubt about his existence, or of the secure attribution to him of several important writings, including the renowned *Micrologus* (*c*1025–6). It is reassuring to be able to attach an important document to a name, and moreover to a reasonably specific date, and to a hint of personal style. If we know nothing more than this about Guido, we are absolutely certain that his major concern was education; and in this effort he succeeded beyond his wildest dreams, for today his name is on the tongue of every student of music history and his teachings live on in the continuing pedagogical practice of *solfège* and in the omnipresent use of staff notation, though now generally more sober in aspect than Guido's innovatory multi-coloured lines.

★

While theoreticians, usually anonymous, were working on their erudite treatises in continental Europe, a prodigious repertory of organum was being produced (possibly by the cantor named Wulfstan) for performance in the services of the cathedral church in Winchester, England; this material will be dealt with in Chapter VII. Here we might add only this reflection. Although the Winchester books containing this repertory are referred to as 'tropers', a term normally used for books which contain music considered to be para-liturgical (i.e. not officially sanctioned in the Roman liturgy), the majority of the chants decorated with polyphony in this collection belong to the core of the official liturgy. Thus the use of the term 'troper' in this instance must be understood to refer to the inclusion of the organa, the added voices, thereby revealing the conceptual similarity in medieval understanding between horizontal and vertical accretions to the prescribed music for the Mass and Office.

Another important repertory of early polyphony developed, probably at a slightly later date, in another famous cathedral town: Chartres. During the central Middle Ages many of the most prominent musicians, known by name and reputation, made their careers in 'higher' fields such as law, theology or medicine. Among the most brilliant of such 'Renaissance men' of the Middle Ages one can certainly count Bishop Fulbert of Chartres, doctor, theologian, poet and teacher, who by all accounts was almost certainly a musician as well. One of his known protégés, Sigo of Saumur, was immortalized in poetry as a purveyor (whether composer or singer) of organum without peer:[4]

> Karitate Sigo noster plenusatque gratia
> Multa prebens ore, manu, advenis solatia
> Singularis organali regnabat in musica.
> (Our Sigo, full of grace and charity,
> Encouraged strangers by his words and good deeds;
> He reigned without rival in organal music.)

During Fulbert's tenure the schools of Chartres, those of the cathedral as well as those of several neighbouring churches and monasteries – most prominent among the latter was the Benedictine establishment of St Père-en-Vallée – appear to have cooperated to an uncommon degree in creating an atmosphere of high educational standards and notable aesthetic concerns. Serious attention was accorded to classical sources, thus engendering a somewhat more secular and humanistic aura than was normally encountered in church-dominated systems before the evolution of true universities.[5]

In Chartres, it is clear, polyphony flourished in a receptive community at a fairly early date. Unfortunately, the primary documents of the practice were all but destroyed in 1944 when a fire following an American bombing raid destroyed virtually the entire holdings of the municipal library, where all of the community's ecclesiastical documents had been deposited.[6] But evidence of a sophisticated and eventually prescribed use of polyphonic adornment of the community's religious observances has been preserved, largely through the efforts of two canons of the cathedral who, during the early part of this century, had the wisdom to publish and to photograph important portions of the pertinent manuscripts before they were destroyed.[7]

In Chartres, as elsewhere, polyphony found its first important role in the most significant church seasons, Easter taking precedence over all others in the remaining Chartrain musical sources. Only three manuscripts with notated polyphony are known to have survived before 1944, yielding a total of only nine pieces with completed notation, and several additional items for which provisions were made for polyphonic notation, although it is lacking. There is, however, another document crucial to the reconstruction of Chartrain polyphonic usage, an ordinal of the thirteenth century which, although somewhat later than even the latest written polyphony from Chartres, corresponds in

45. Bishop Fulbert of Chartres (c975–1028) surrounded by the canons, monks, nuns and choirboys of his cathedral: miniature from the 'Obituaire' of Notre Dame de Chartres, 1028

46. Polyphony from Chartres: the Easter alleluia 'Pascha nostrum' for two voices (top four lines of notated text), with an untexted chace for two voices in a fourteenth-century hand (below)

its assignments of polyphony to various parts of the rite almost exactly to those musical remnants.[8] Further, it gives precise instructions not only as to which pieces (including, of course, a number which have not survived) are to be used in the various ceremonies, but some quite detailed information about who is to sing, and exactly where the singing is to take place. In the latter regard it is most significant that in the Chartrain practice, which was a genuinely communal one on lesser holidays as well as greater, polyphony was most frequently sung in the context of a procession, sometimes within the cathedral, but more often out of doors, involving stops at one or several other churches and monasteries. As many as eight such outlying institutions are mentioned in the Chartres ordinal in specific conjunction with indications of polyphonic performance, which are often qualified with such phrases as 'as is customary', or 'if the succentor so chooses', which appear to pre-suppose pre-existent polyphonic compositions. One must also bear in mind, however difficult it may be, that Chartres Cathedral as we know it today was only in the initial stages of construction, on the site of several previous structures, when this polyphonic repertory was developing, so the cathedral may well not have been the most suitable location for elaborate musical performance.

Some individual pieces which we now consider to be 'fixed' in specific liturgical positions (especially alleluias) were obviously more movable at the period when they were first sung polyphonically – possibly for the very reason that, once having created such an elaboration, it was considered appropriate to use it more frequently than might otherwise have been the case. This habit of reassigning polyphonic

47. Musica (left, with instrumental attributes) and Grammaria (right, with pupils at her knee), two of the seven liberal arts: sculpture on the south portal (1225) of Chartres Cathedral

pieces to new positions may well relate to the emergence of the sometimes confusing designation 'processional antiphon' for a polyphonic composition the origin of which is not an antiphon at all, but more likely a responsory, an alleluia or a gradual.

Taking together the performance instructions of the Chartres ordinal and the written remains of polyphonic settings, it is possible to reconstruct a repertory of about twenty pieces whose liturgical assignments cover the important events of virtually the entire church calendar, from Christmas to early November, including Ascension, Pentecost, Assumption, All Saints' and several individual saints' days. Though pitifully small by comparison with the Winchester repertory, it is permissible on these grounds (and with the known loss of manuscript sources) to posit for Chartres a much larger practice of polyphony than can be precisely documented today.

Although a majority of the chants set polyphonically in the Chartres manuscripts are also included in the Winchester repertory, none of them can be identified as musically concordant. Despite a similarity of musical structure and style between the Winchester organa and those of the two earlier (mid- to late eleventh-century) Chartres manuscripts, the notation of each can at least be sufficiently decoded to arrive at this negative finding.[9] In both cases the polyphony is clearly based on similar theoretical premises, as recounted above.

The latest manuscript from Chartres, however, dating from about 1100, shows evidence of considerable change from earlier examples, both in its manner of notation (on dry-point lines, providing a focus for pitch determination) and in its musical style. Here we find a particular phase of structural procedure, emphasizing contrary motion to a great degree and resulting in what can be characterized as 'mirror-image' polyphony: the added voice tends to approximate a melodic inversion of the given chant.

This manuscript (*F-CHR* 109) contains the only polyphonic piece from before the Notre Dame epoch for which a musical concordance has been identified, the verse 'Dicant nunc iudei' for the Easter processional antiphon *Christus resurgens*. Its counterpart is found in a thirteenth-century manuscript whose provenance has recently been traced to a Benedictine establishment at Downpatrick, in what is now Northern Ireland.[10] Although only a portion of the Chartres version is transcribable, due to the poor condition of the folio at the time it was photographed *c*1910, it is sufficient to identify the piece as essentially identical with the Downpatrick version. The latter is also slightly mutilated (by page-trimming) at the very end, but essentially complete and easily transcribed since its neumatic notation is laid out in score with four-line staves and pitch indicators. Unlike other instances of settings of the same chant, this case presents such near-identity that it cannot be explained in terms merely of following the same theoretical precepts. It remains, however, to trace the route of transmission of this piece across the Channel: it surely must have involved a Benedictine connection.

The Benedictine monastery of St Maur-des-Fossés near Paris was another establishment from which evidence of polyphonic experimentation remains. Three manuscripts yield a number of polyphonic additions which, while not precisely decipherable, allow us to gain a general idea of their musical style as well as a knowledge of their text and genre. It is possible that further study of this difficult material might help to reveal a link between Parisian polyphonic practice and that emerging to the south of Aquitaine.

From the very beginning the singing of polyphony, or at least specifically of the newly invented parts of a polyphonically sung chant, was a soloist's art, reserved for the most gifted and highly trained singers of all, the *discantores, succentores* or *precentores*. This fact is reflected in very large measure by the choice of chants to be adorned with polyphony, which almost universally come from portions of the liturgy which in their original monophonic versions were sung by soloists rather than by choirs. It is further borne out by the fact that the largest early repertory of written polyphony (the Winchester organa) was recorded in a very small book suitable only for use by a single singer. Further, one must assume, since the generally scattered written representatives of early polyphony are widely acknowledged as the merest tip of the iceberg with respect to evidence of widespread 'improvisation' of polyphonic embellishments, that the *discantores* were at the very least well schooled in musical theory and knew the rules governing polyphonic structure.

As the eleventh century progressed, theoretical interest in

polyphony grew apace with, or perhaps a step or two behind, its practice. An anonymous treatise closely allied in content to Guido's *Micrologus*, usually cited as *Ad organum faciendum*, or more recently as the 'Milan Treatise', lays out five 'organum modes' which serve as a means of distinguishing various types of organum beginning and ending in different ways. The treatise, which consists of two sections, one in prose and one in verse, is preceded by (ostensibly) three two-voice pieces inscribed in pitch-letter notation. It has only fairly recently been discerned that the third of these 'compositions', a two-voice setting of the phrase 'Hoc sit vobis iter', is actually part of the incipit of the treatise itself; thus the true 'title' of the treatise translates as 'This should be your pathway to [the method of] making organum', with a welcome bit of polyphonic whimsy thrown in for good measure.

At least another half-dozen post-Guidonian treatises from before the twelfth century introduced more or less significant advances in 'harmonic' theory and flexibility in the construction of polyphony. What is perhaps most significant about the extant sources, theoretical and practical taken together, is that the latter consistently advance the aesthetic concerns of polyphonists at a more rapid rate than the former. (This has prompted one scholar to suggest that a more appropriate designation than 'theorists' for the writers of tracts would be 'teacher-reporters'.)[11] A case in point is provided by the later Chartrain polyphony, in which the interval of the major second, never sanctioned or even admitted by 'theorists', is statistically very prominent, as are major and minor thirds, which were only reluctantly admitted to the canon of permissible consonances. A chapter ('De diaphonia') in the very influential *De musica* of Johannes Afflighemensis[12] treats the traditional consonances with a clear eye on variety: voice-crossing is encouraged and contrary motion is much preferred to parallel or oblique (both increasingly consistent trends during this period). Now the *vox organalis* is permanently placed above the *vox principalis* and sometimes contains several notes for one note of the original chant, a clear reflection of the melismatic style of polyphony already established in southern regions.

It is worthy of note that during this period polyphony becomes a subject of discourse on its own, rather than, as had previously been the general rule, a mere adjunct to a broader discussion of music in either its intellectual (liberal arts) context or its practical (chant) aspect. In the following decades this shift of emphasis is to become even more pronounced. It was that and new and considered attention to the subject of polyphony which led musicians to experiment with forms of notation that would meet the needs of the art. The question of fixing metre or rhythm was, at least early on, apparently of no great concern; after all, before the evolution of melismatic polyphony (in which the added voice contains many more notes than does its melodic base) or the later discant style (in which the need for controlled rhythmic organization seems almost inevitable) polyphony consisted essentially of ornamentation of a given melody in a note-against-note (or neume-against-neume) fashion which presumes that the rhythm of the added voice matches that of the original plainchant.

A notation which dealt definitively with pitch was a more urgent desideratum, but for a long while scribes (as at Winchester, for example) continued to use a notation which indicated the direction of the melody but did not calibrate its steps. This lack of precision means that it is difficult even to determine which voice goes on top. Such notations could serve only as an aide-mémoire for singers. Letter notations (and here the Daseian system of *Musica enchiriadis* may be included) were completely accurate with regard to pitch, but they could not record expressive nuances; these are only infrequently encountered outside theoretical sources. There was also some experiment with score notation during the late eleventh century. The earliest examples, however, still often presented neumatic notation *in campo aperto* (i.e. without horizontal guidelines) and often without even a clear spacial division between the two melodic lines. More resourceful scribes made good use of parchment which had been prepared for non-musical purposes, with dry-point text-lines serving as guides for heightening the neumes. The routine use of letters as clefs was slow to materialize; presumably the scribes failed to recognize their potential usefulness.

A group of four manuscripts[13] containing a substantial repertory of polyphony now generally described simply as 'Aquitanian' was once ascribed to the Abbey of St Martial in Limoges, where indeed three of the manuscripts were deposited in the library for a long time, although there is nothing in them to suggest that they originated there. While we can no longer speak of a 'School of St Martial', the repertory of these manuscripts, which includes a total of some 60 to perhaps as many as 90 polyphonic compositions (depending on what one counts – of this more below), comprises a distinctive new phase in the history of polyphony which certainly merits a collective designation.

The hub of Aquitaine, Limoges, already in the eleventh century an ancient and highly industrialized city known for enamel, gold and leatherwork as well as the ceramics for which it is still noted, was divided – literally, by a fortified wall – into two distinct communities, under different governances. One sector was responsible to the bishop, the other (including the abbey of St Martial) was under feudal control, which engendered constant ecclesiastical conflict. Limoges was also the site, over a long period, of constant activity and turbulence: large- and small-scale warfare, international trade, ecclesiastical councils, papal synods, pestilence, Norman invasions, transient pilgrims, crusaders and more besides. It is all the more remarkable, therefore, that it should have been the centre of an unusually vigorous intellectual community.

Aquitaine was already renowned as the focal area of the enormous 'second wave' of sacred poetry and music – embodied in sequences, tropes, *versus*, hymns, rhymed Offices and their kin numbering in the thousands – well before the emergence of its characteristic and unique polyphonic repertory in the late eleventh and early twelfth centuries. Indeed, a major portion of the polyphonic repertory of Aquitanian origin is based on the rhymed accentual poetry of the region, which is a primary aspect of its distinctiveness.

In this worldly atmosphere it is perhaps not surprising that the thrust of musical creativity should have diverged from the earlier tradition of concentrating polyphony in the most thoroughly established portions of the musical liturgy, even though the principle of thus celebrating the most important calendar events held true. There are so few examples, among the *voces principales* of this repertory, of sanctioned chant melodies (although some may remain to be identified) that one can legitimately speak of a new stage of development based on newly composed tenor melodies as well as new texts.[14]

The abandonment of liturgical tenors in the Aquitanian repertory is only one of several new departures. Here we find, in addition, two clearly differentiated styles of polyphonic setting: on the one hand, a version of the note-against-note style previously seen – but in a new fashion which lies at the very root of the emerging distinction between 'discantus' so called and 'organum' as a species rather than a genre – which was to become increasingly significant in the ensuing decades; and on the other, a style commonly designated as 'melismatic organum', clearly the ancestor of that new species of organum which reached its full development in the Parisian sphere (see fig.42 above).

The new discant differs from its predecessors in part with respect to its relationship to the texts involved, which are rhymed, rhythmic and frequently strophic. The musical response to this verse, when the discant style is used, now exhibits a preoccupation with the control of form on a new level. While the previously discussed note-against-note settings proceeded from consonance to consonance – coinciding with beginnings and endings of prose phrases of varying lengths, but with relatively little concern about what happened in between – we now find great attention to small-scale phrase structure, exploiting the various techniques of contrary motion, imitation, melodic sequence, inversion, repetition, voice-exchange and all manner of combinations of the above, to the point of saturation. The resultant style is one of a very tightly knit texture which bears little resemblance to the rather free-flowing chant-like phrases of past – or better, of other – repertories, even though perhaps contemporary.

It is in the context of this new discant style in combination with metrical texts that the temptation arises to speculate, as many scholars have done, as to the likelihood that the trochaic rhythm which would eventually provide the basis of modal rhythm may be implicit in this style. Here, once again, the notational system, although it is generally quite pitch-specific (since the Aquitanian point-notation is for the most part carefully heightened and pitch indicators are generally used, if not indeed dry-point lines, and in the latest source inked lines), gives no hint of musical metre. On the basis of texture alone, however, the new Aquitanian discant can clearly be regarded as the forerunner of Parisian discant, the locus of development of the rhythmic modes.

Settings limited to this progressive discant style comprise only a small minority of the pieces in the Aquitanian sources, and those tend to be concentrated in the later stages of development (even though one such instance is included in the earliest manuscript source). The preferred style in this repertory is the melismatic one, also a forward-looking style in which the notes of the lower voice are elongated to accommodate a multiplicity of notes in the upper voice. Here we find another portent of things to come in the Parisian repertory: the style in which a rapidly flowing upper voice (or voices) moves over tenor notes so extended as to assume a drone-like quality in which the melodic contours of the given chant are for all practical purposes completely lost. This is the style which eventually came to be called *organum purum*, denoting a species, as distinct from the continued use of the generic term 'organum' for all polyphony.

In the Aquitanian repertory passages of the melismatic style often occur within a setting which may be for the most part in discant style, most frequently on the penultimate syllable of a verse, thus functioning as an elaborate, sometimes very extended cadential ornament. In some instances this florid closing involves both voices, that is, the lower voice adopts the guise of the upper, following it in pace and number of notes, usually in an imitative or inverted manner, or both. Models for this sort of cadential ornament in the polyphony are easily found in the monophonic repertory of the same sources.

In the Aquitanian sources we have a unique repertory, in terms especially of its texts, which, at the same time, anticipates the two primary styles to come in the Parisian repertory of the late twelfth and early thirteenth centuries. Although virtually no demonstrable historical, personal or bibliographical links have been established between the two repertories, the musico-stylistic affinities are manifest. Further, although the poetry of the Aquitanian sphere, especially the *versus* and *Benedicamus Domino* tropes, is very similar in style and spirit to the conductus of the Parisian repertory, only two textual concordances with the major Parisian manuscript sources have been identified, and neither of them is musically concordant.

It was once believed that a large manuscript from Santiago de Compostela in Spain might provide the missing link between the Aquitanian and Parisian repertories. Known as the Codex Calixtinus after Pope Calixtus II, to whom portions of the tome are ascribed,[15] this multi-partite volume includes various devotional works, a substantial monophonic Office for St James (whose relics were deposited in Compostela during the ninth century) and a polyphonic appendix containing nineteen two-voice pieces. One is ascribed to a 'Magister Albertus Parisiensis'. There was a cantor named Albert at Notre Dame during the approximate period of origin of this portion of the manuscript (probably late in the third quarter of the twelfth century), and this has been interpreted as a link with the Parisian repertory, but one might just as well attempt to link the manuscript to Chartres, since Fulbert of Chartres is accorded no fewer than seven attributions in its musical portions.

There is clear evidence of overwhelmingly French style in the Codex Calixtinus, both musical and notational, although the precise origin, particularly of the polyphonic appendix, has not been established. This is not surprising, since French influences on various of the arts in Spain, most notably architecture and poetry, are widely acknowledged. And it is also true that Limoges was one of the principal way-stations for pilgrims travelling to Santiago de Compostela, which by the end of the twelfth century was a centre of pilgrimage of equal rank with Rome and even with Jerusalem itself. So the possibilities for importation of Aquitanian musical habits to far north-western Spain were very real indeed.

It is common at present to include the Calixtine polyphony within the sphere of the Aquitanian repertory; there is, in fact, one contrafactum of an Aquitanian *Benedicamus* trope, *Noster cetus psallat letus*, with the incipit 'Ad superni regus decus', in the Codex Calixtinus. But the notation of the manuscript, both monophonic and polyphonic, with only one exception, is probably *not* of Aquitanian derivation: it is reminiscent more of a north-easterly dialect, possibly from the Autonois.[16] The repertory is noticeably different from that of Aquitanian sources, with a greater dependence on liturgical melodies. And there are a few linguistic anomalies (a Greek alleluia and a brief invocation to St James in German, both monophonic, but appearing at the very end of the polyphonic appendix) which are difficult to relate to Aquitanian practices.

Nevertheless, the musical style is certainly cognate with that of Aquitaine, emphasizing melismatic polyphony and evincing similar compositional procedures, including extended two-voice cadential melismas. A compositional 'first' still occasionally attributed to the Codex Calixtinus – the 'first' three-voice setting of a conductus-like text, *Congaudeant catholici*, which is the very piece ascribed to Magister Albertus Parisiensis – has actually long been recognized as spurious. The apparent third voice, which lies between the two outer voices but is not provided with its own staff, is recognizably a later addition and, if legitimate, undoubtedly represents an alternative second voice rather than a real third one. No doubt efforts will continue to close the factual gap between south and north within the realm of twelfth-century polyphony, but for the moment we must make the leap without benefit of a bridge.

★

Twelfth-century Paris was deep in the process of becoming the international capital of Europe. As its permanent population increased by leaps and bounds, so did its complement of visitors from all nations, especially those bent upon intellectual enlightenment. For Paris was also in the process of becoming the leading international centre of *Studia generalia*, attracting native and foreign students in great numbers, and teachers of enormous and lasting distinction in all fields. Even before the University of Paris *per se* was 'officially' chartered in 1200, the many and varied educational institutions of the city were providing a great breadth of instruction in the liberal arts and notable depth in several specialities, including medicine, canon law and theology. That music was another important area of specialization in Paris is abundantly clear from the numerous documents, both verbal and musical, which have survived.

As the university evolved, at least three distinct spheres of political influence held sway: the episcopate, the monarchy and the papacy. Although conflict among these powers was at times intense, in the end it was probably the struggle itself that engendered a vitality in the educational process that ultimately created the great university that became the model for all of the Western world.

The episcopal schools, centred in the close of the cathedral of Notre Dame de Paris on the Île de la Cité, where music was naturally one of the most important fields of study in the service of the cathedral, were well supported by the ecclesiastical hierarchy and by the now powerful central monarchy. There were, however, several monastic establishments on the Left Bank, most notably the abbeys of St Victor and of Ste Geneviève, which were highly involved in education and in music and which received direct support from the pope, especially in matters of student rights. In the middle, literally, between these frequently adversary factions, a third party intervened: the 'artiers', freelance professors of the traditional liberal arts, who held their classes on the Petit Pont linking the Île to the Left Bank.

The link was more than merely physical. Although both the monastic and episcopal establishments provided some general (secular) education for their students, the necessity for every student aspiring to the higher professions (or to teach the liberal arts) to acquire the equivalent of a bachelor's degree came about even before statutory requirements for the degree were established. This need was met for

157

virtually all Parisian students by the professors of the Petit Pont, whose high demand for space eventually forced them to spill over into Left Bank territory – establishing, in the process, not only the model, but also the actual site of the modern-day University of Paris. Thus the 'artiers', including the likes of Peter Abelard (*c*1079–1144) and John of Salisbury (*c*1120–80), who had previously sojourned at Chartres, came to wield considerable power in the intellectual community, not only through their teachings but also through personal alliance with students (and personal fees-for-service) which in fact led directly to the initial 'charter' of the university.

This document, signed by Philippe-Auguste in 1200,[17] guaranteed certain rights and protections to students and faculty, and was the direct result of events initiated by a tavern brawl between the servant of a group of German students and the tavern keeper; this eventually resulted in the deaths of several students whose friends and professors made a direct protest to the king. (It was not until a later document of 1215 that the official title 'Universitas' was introduced in Paris.)[18]

Music, among the other arts and sciences, therefore, developed in Paris in an atmosphere which was not only vital but volatile, both with regard to education (Aristotelian views were not well received at first) and to the concerns of daily life. It is significant that Bishop Odo of Sully decreed, in 1198 and 1199,[19] that the two now best-known compositions of Pérotin (the four-voice organa *Viderunt omnes* and *Sederunt principes*) should be performed at Notre Dame on the Feast of the Circumcision (New Year's Day – and, by extension, also on Christmas, since the liturgies were the same) and on St Stephen's Day, respectively, specifically to restore some semblance of decorum to those liturgical high holy days which had been thoroughly desecrated by the juvenile high-jinks of the infamous Feast of Fools tradition. But we anticipate.

Our primary witness to the development of music in twelfth-century Paris, and notably of polyphonic music, was an Englishman of monastic connections, known to us only as Anonymous IV.[20] Anonymous IV was evidently a student in Paris when (or before) he recorded, about a century after the fact, the information which has come down to us about the accomplishments of two Notre Dame composers, Léonin (*c*1163–90) and Pérotin (*fl c*1200). Léonin, according to this report, wrote a 'Magnus liber organi . . . to enhance the divine service'. Pérotin, his successor, who was 'the best discantor', is credited with having revised and shortened the *Magnus liber*, as well as composing many clausulas (i.e. textless polyphonic settings of fragments of melismatic plainchant in discant style), as well as the two four-voice organa already mentioned, several other three- and four-voice organa, and monophonic conductus. Moreover, according to our Englishman, this revised book was still in use at the cathedral of Notre Dame in his own time (*c*1285).

The lateness of Anonymous IV's information might well give pause to a conscientious historian were it not for the fact that it is corroborated in detail by three major musical manuscripts[21] containing versions of the *Magnus liber*, and a host of ancillary manuscripts from all over Europe, containing identifiable portions of its repertory, while also attesting to its great international significance. That we do not today have the original *Magnus liber* is unfortunate, but this has not deterred scores of scholars from attempting to reconstruct the precise nature of its contents. The clear intention, as witnessed by the extant manuscripts, was to provide polyphonic elaborations for the cathedral Masses and Offices for the entire liturgical year – an undertaking similar to those already witnessed in the Winchester tropers and in the unfortunately fragmentary documents from Chartres. In Paris, however, the dimensions of the project were enormous. In the earliest and most proximate manuscript (known as the Florence manuscript, although it was written in Paris, considerably later than the composition of the works themselves), there are well over a thousand pieces of music. The second major source is from elsewhere in France, and the third from Scotland, where it was copied (and provided with some locally specific additions) for use at the Augustinian priory at St Andrews.

The core of the Parisian repertory, which is attributed to Léonin, or at least to his generation of musicians, appears in varying forms in each of the three central manuscripts. It is a great cycle of two-voice organa consisting of responsories for Vespers and Matins, and alleluias and graduals for Mass, arranged in liturgical calendar order. The shortest version of this core repertory is in the manuscript from St Andrews, the longest in the Florence manuscript, which also includes the largest number (about 460) of the clausulas which Anonymous IV attributes to Pérotin. It is not yet possible, even after several generations of intensive scholarly probing, accurately to assess the degree of proximity of these sources to the missing original: the additions and revisions are too numerous and too complex to have yielded precise information in this quest. A great deal remains to be learnt about the sequence of events in the development of 'modal' rhythm (and its notational system), in order to sort out the chronology of this vast repertory with its numerous styles and categories of music.

The most honest statement that can be made about modal rhythm, without going out on any of the precarious limbs that seduce scholars at every notch of the central trunk, is that it clearly was the most significant development in music of the second half of the twelfth century. Again, Anonymous IV is one of our primary sources of information. He introduces his description of the rhythmic modes with the following words: '*modus* or *maneries* or *consideratio temporis* is the recognition [*cognitio*] of length and shortness in a melody [?song] or sound [?note]'.[22] For

Franco of Cologne, writing *c*1280 (slightly earlier than Anonymous IV, and speaking for his own generation), '*modus* is the recognition of sound [?pitch] measured in long and short time-values'.[23] Neither of these brief characterizations of the system includes the necessary descriptive facts made obvious in further definitions. Modal rhythm is essentially ternary in nature, and has often been described as 'dance-like'. Eventually the 'system' embraced six basic modes which fitted together in a patently scholastic, symmetrical and synthetic scheme. These six modes can be demonstrated most usefully by reducing them to modern time values, the crotchet representing the long and the quaver the breve of the then-current 'square' notational system:

MODE: I   II   III   IV   V   VI

Each example represents the shortest possible unit of each mode; each phrase, usually made up of several such units, is followed by a rest (in modern terms) whose length is determined within the context of its mode. In fact, as is evident from this illustration, the notation of modal rhythm is essentially contextual: the length of any given note is determined by its position in relation to its neighbours and to the basic underlying pulse. This can be seen most readily in modes III, IV and V, where the temporal values of the basic note shapes were of necessity modified by context, since only two values (long and short, the long exactly twice the value of the short) were initially recognized in this system. Thus in modes III and IV, each second breve needed to be lengthened (*brevis altera*) in order to fit the triple rhythm; in modes III, IV and V, of which the latter was principally used in the *tenores* (underlying chant), the longs were interpreted as *longae perfectae* (i.e. longs of three parts), while the longs in modes I and II were *longae imperfectae* (of two parts) – originally the proper value for this note shape.

It should be pointed out that in modern terms, although the six modes have here been described as essentially ternary in nature, there appears to be general agreement that there is also a clear-cut binary aspect to the overall rhythmic pulse. This is made evident in the fact that most present-day transcriptions of modal rhythms are cast in 6/8 metre (which is basically duple) rather than in 3/8 or 9/8, either of which might be fully justifiable on notational bases. Finally, it should be mentioned that even in their ternary aspects, the modes were susceptible to all sorts of modifications which blurred the distinctions between them. And, in fact, mode IV seems to be purely a product of the scholastic propensity to create balanced systems: it is rarely if ever discernible in the sources, and was even described by one contemporary writer as 'not in use'. On the other hand, Anonymous IV makes reference to various 'irregular' modes, of which he describes the seventh as unmeasured and very dignified: he calls it *organum purum*,[24] to which we shall return presently.

From what we can gather from various sources, *organum duplum* was the primary medium of Léonin and his generation, and is most prominent in the surviving Mass and Office responsories, as well as most settings of *Benedicamus Domino* (the closing chant of several liturgical rites, which by now had become strongly attached to the polyphonic processional repertory). Here again, however, as already noted with regard to the Aquitanian repertory, more often than not the melismatic organal style (now properly organum in the new sense) alternates with sections of essentially note-against-note discant. Here, indeed, we find the ultimate distinction between these two styles, in which the term 'organum' (sometimes modified with such adjectives as 'duplum' or 'purum') acquires the meaning of a particular species of polyphony, while still retaining its generic sense of *all* polyphony. In the Parisian repertory, based as it is on chant melodies, it is easier to rationalize the distinction of styles than in the case of the non-liturgical Aquitanian polyphony. As a general rule those chants which are melismatic in their original monophonic versions are set in discant style; those which were originally syllabic are set melismatically, or in the *new* organum. There are, of course, exceptions to this generalization; but there are few exceptions to the rule that only originally soloistic sections of chant are used as tenors for polyphonic settings. The art is still one for highly trained specialists.

In *organum duplum* or *purum* there are many tantalizing instances where apparently strict modal patterns make brief appearances, only to be shattered by 'irregularities' of the sort that Anonymous IV invokes to describe this genre. Among other things, one finds such extravaganzas as the following, from a *Benedicamus Domino* in the Florence manuscript:

[Benedi-]   ca-   – mus.

Such lengthy melismas, which include the diamond-shaped notes known as *currentes* (running notes), are most often found over penultimate syllables of the text phrases, as in the Aquitanian repertory: again, an elaborate extension of the cadence. All that is really known about such passages, in terms of rhythm, is that they are to be sung fast: there are no indications of precise metric values. But should we be so perturbed by such a phenomenon? Many twentieth-century composers leave similar matters, and sometimes even much greater liberties, to the discretion of the performer. Perhaps it is time that we made allowance for such thinking even in the context of such an authority-ridden intellectual milieu as that of the late twelfth century, especially since the art of polyphony was clearly based on an oral tradition carried forth by talented singers and because the gap between the practical sources (musical manuscripts) and theoretical ones (treatises) continued to prevail. In any case, *organum purum* can be regarded as a very free and somehow recondite form of polyphony of the Gothic style. So we have, in the Parisian repertory, two very distinct kinds of polyphony, related both in style and in musical context to the music of the Aquitanian region, but now even more clearly delineated. (There was, in addition, a third style mentioned by several theorists, called copula, which apparently was somehow understood to link the other two; but the nature of this style is still so controversial that it will be passed over here.)

The primary purveyors of the discant style, the clausulas, remain enigmatic as to function. In the past they have been designated 'substitute clausulae', implying that they were intended to be substituted, in their respective liturgical positions, for earlier and more prolix settings. But to date no consensus has emerged as to their precise significance, especially as they exist in such great numbers and often replicate the same liturgical tenors many times over. An alternative designation for these compositions, 'punctae' (clearly related to the later usage *punctus contra punctum* = counterpoint), ties this genre to that of the very different world of secular instrumental dance music via the *estampie*.

Thus modal theory, which is so critical to the interpretation of the Parisian repertory, is in reality an ingenious codification of a very gay and lively form of rhythmic expression which served to establish a close relationship to secular music and dance. Like the latter, modal rhythm is characterized by a distinct beat which comes much closer to 'common practice' rhythms of more recent centuries than do, for example, the enormously complex quantitative rhythms devised in the fourteenth and fifteenth centuries.

A genre which is very prominent in the Parisian manuscript sources, the conductus, has been much neglected by scholars, no doubt because it is so difficult to relate in terms of function to the core repertory, and also because its syllabic notation, in conjunction with accentual Latin poetry, is very difficult to interpret. The notation of conductus, because of its essentially one-note-per-syllable style, consists almost exclusively of single notes, usually longs. Some scholars are convinced, however, that modal principles are implicit in the poetic rhythm, and therefore should be applied in the interpretation of the notation.[25] Evidence for this position exists in the form of a number of instances in which untexted *caudae* ('tails') at the ends (and sometimes the beginnings) of conductus are notated in ligatures, and sometimes consist of exactly the same melodic structures as the compositions which they frame. The issue is, however, yet another in the realm of Parisian polyphony for which a resolution has yet to be found.

Conductus are found in Parisian sources in one-, two-, three- and four-voice versions, with and without textless *caudae*. Its primary distinctiveness as a genre resides in several particulars: it is not based on liturgical chant; many conductus texts are accentual poetry concerned with current events, ecclesiastical or other, often overtly political;[26] and when more than two voices are involved, a single text is used in all the upper voices and the rhythm of all the voices is essentially the same, with only minor ornaments to the basic syllabic rhythm. Some conductus were written to commemorate specific events (a function later to be taken over by the motet), such as victories in war or royal personal or public occasions. The exile in France and eventual murder, in 1170, of Thomas á Becket, for example, was the subject of several conductus. The performance of these works could hardly have had a place in a cathedral liturgy, but may well have figured in the entertainment of clerical dignitaries as well as courtly gatherings.

The manner of composing polyphonic conductus is addressed, specifically because it differs in one important respect from that of the chant-based genres, by the primary theorist of Parisian style, Johannes de Garlandia,[27] who pointed out that the first order of business was to fashion the most beautiful melody possible for the tenor, then to add the other voice(s) in concord with this newly composed melody. The procedure for constructing chant-based polyphony was clearly the same, once the chant tenor had been selected: each successive voice was layered, quasi-independently, over the chosen tenor, with regard only for its consonant relationship to that basic voice. Nothing in the written descriptions or prescriptions for constructing polyphony gives any hint of concern for vertical sonorities among the added voices (what we would consider 'harmonic' concerns) other than the required consonances at openings and closings of phrases. This is a melodically, horizontally conceived art, in which, with the emergence of the new genre known as the motet, each added voice eventually achieved its own rhythmic and melodic characteristics as they also came to be more and more clearly differentiated in character.

★

This process of layering and differentiation of voices is seen most clearly in the development of the motet, a new genre arising in the Parisian repertory whose progress can be fairly accurately charted. The word 'motet' (from the French 'mot') derives from the initial stage of adding words to the upper voice of previously composed discant clausulas. The earliest motets were literally nothing other than discant clausulas with non-liturgical Latin texts fitted precisely to the duplum (the added voice), which is henceforth referred to as motetus. This process can be verified by the presence in the sources of both texted and untexted versions of the same compositions.

During the early thirteenth century the motet took centre stage as the choice vocal medium, overshadowing the liturgical styles of previous generations. Although some early motets could quite conceivably have had a function within ecclesiastical rites, especially votive rites such as the increasingly popular Marian observances, the genre moved quickly into the secular province as the nature of the texts took on a new and unmistakably secular character.

The poetry of the 'classical' French motet is virtually indistinguishable in character and subject matter (*amour courtois* was the dominant theme) from that of the chanson, the music of the trouvères. In fact, the actual borrowing of monophonic songs for use in motets created a sub-species known as the *motet enté* ('grafted motet'), in very significant numbers.

Although there was an obvious kinship of both text and function between motet and conductus as the newer genre was emerging, the musical style of the motet evolved very differently from that of the older genre, which declined in popularity as the motet gained primacy. As more voices were added, as French vernacular poetry replaced Latin, as the music was re-ornamented, as added voices were replaced with new ones or joined with different tenors, a large pool of almost free-standing motet 'voices' gradually amassed, from which an inventive composer could pick and choose at his pleasure, while making his own contribution to the repertory.

Although some motets were included in the central manuscripts of the Parisian repertory, most are found in manuscripts dedicated primarily to this genre alone. A major motet manuscript written late in the thirteenth century, called the Bamberg codex,[28] contains a repertory of a hundred motets from the early part of the century and a few other compositions. Among the latter are seven textless pieces which may be the first written instrumental music: one of these pieces is entitled *In seculum viellatoris* ('*In seculum* of the vielle-player'). There is no consensus on this matter, however; since the textless pieces are based on liturgical tenors, like the motets in whose company they are found, they may be seen as just another (vocal) category of descendants of the clausula, with all the attendant questions of function and manner of performance.

48. Montpellier codex, late thirteenth century; this folio shows the motet 'Deus in adjutorium intende' in three-voice organum (the last verse is an elaborate alleluia) and a miniature depicting three singers

The principal repository of thirteenth-century motets is a large manuscript known as the Montpellier codex,[29] compiled very near the end of the century, which contains about 345 motets and is organized so as to reflect the entire process of development of the genre and of its changing notations throughout the century. The first fascicle of the manuscript contains liturgical polyphony of the Parisian repertory, but now recorded in mensural rather than modal notation. The succeeding four sections, each grouping in turn the various subspecies of motets (four-voice motets, motets which combine Latin and French texts, three-voice Latin motets, French motets of two, three and four voices etc), are all notated in some form of the emergent mensural notation, in which specific note shapes take on specific time values, unlike the contextual meanings of modal note forms. The final two fascicles of the manuscript are written in fully developed 'Franconian' notation, so named from Franco of Cologne, who codified the new system in his treatise *Ars cantus mensurabilis* of about 1280.[30]

It is also to be observed that in the earlier portion of the manuscript the motets, with only two exceptions, are based on liturgical tenors, a majority originating from alleluias or graduals, while in the two latest fascicles about a third have recognizably secular tenors. The latter, having finally achieved complete freedom from their liturgical origins, point the way to the total secularization of the motet at the end of the thirteenth century, as well as (from a technical point of view) to the intellectual complexities of the Ars Nova music of the early fourteenth century.

The 'classic' thirteenth-century French motet, then, represents a significant new departure in the sphere of written polyphony: for the first time a purely secular genre, no longer tied to the liturgy (although very probably still related to ecclesiastical personnel) gained ascendancy as the music of the intellectual élite, a group now increasingly centred on courtly and mercantile rather than ecclesiastical surrounds. It seems clear that cultivation of the motet during the thirteenth century was primarily a participatory entertainment, the product of singer-poet-composers working singly (as in the instance of Adam de la Hale) or in concert to produce these sometimes fiendishly clever and difficult works for their own amusement.

From our perspective, the difficulty of apprehending, in the three- and four-voice works, the several different texts sung simultaneously seems almost insuperable. But our perspective is, of course, irrelevant. It should perhaps be pointed out that there is, after all, a 'modern' analogy for this sort of multi-textual music in the infinitely pleasing and successful solo ensembles of Mozart and his successors in opera, which do not present a problem to the listener who has followed the plot. That the thirteenth-century motet seems to us to exist in a contextual vacuum is probably nothing more than ignorance. As more and more textual and musical borrowings, lendings and exchanges among motets are identified, their context begins to emerge, even at this distance. Surely we should assume that these borrowings were not only intentional but immediately recognizable to their audience, even without a plot to guide the ear. (A somewhat more removed analogy with the ever-popular *roman à clef* also suggests itself.) Similarly, the very frequent device in motet poetry of creating a text which complements or directly comments upon its companion text must have been easily recognized and appreciated (a favourite device in Latin/French motets was an invocation of the Virgin Mary combined with a typical courtly-love chanson text).

In this essay on the emergence of polyphonic music in the West, the focus has been almost exclusively on the music of what is now France. There is, of course, a legitimate historical reason for such circumscription, but this is not to say that polyphony existed only in that territory. Mention has been made of widely scattered evidence of polyphony in the very earliest phases of its development. In the last decade or so, an ever-growing number of sources of early polyphony from Italy, primarily from the late twelfth and early thirteenth centuries, has been discovered, again serendipitously, which may eventually attain proportions worthy of a whole new chapter in the history of early polyphony.

NOTES

[1] L. Gushee, 'Musica enchiriadis', *Grove 6*.
[2] Both treatises are included in E. Waeltner, *Die Lehre vom Organum bis zur Mitte des 11. Jahrhunderts* (Tutzing, 1975).
[3] His principal treatise, *Micrologus*, is available in English translation in *Hucbald, Guido and John on Music*, ed. C. Palisca (New Haven, 1978).
[4] The poem, which celebrates many notable personages of Chartres and elsewhere, is by Adelman of Liège, a student of Fulbert of Chartres. The first redaction dates from 1028–33, the second from 1048. See J. A. Clerval, *Les écoles de Chartres au moyen-âge du Ve au XVe siècle* (Chartres, 1895).
[5] Clerval, *Les écoles de Chartres*.
[6] This event is chronicled, and the precise state of the remains of the library's holdings documented, in *Catalogue général des manuscrits des bibliothèques publiques de France*, liii: *Mss. des Bibliothèques sinistrées de 1940 à 1944* (Paris, 1962).
[7] See Y. Delaporte, *Fragments des manuscrits de Chartres*, PalMus, xvii (1958). The three manuscripts known to contain polyphonic music are *F-CHR* 4, 109 and 130.
[8] See Y. Delaporte, *L'ordinaire chartrain du XIIIe siècle*, Mémoires de la Société archéologique d'Eure-et-Loir, xix (Chartres, 1953). Specific references to polyphonic performance are extracted in M. Gushee, *Romanesque Polyphony: a Study of the Fragmentary Sources* (diss., Yale U., 1965), appx. A.
[9] See A. Holschneider, *Die Organa von Winchester: Studien zum ältesten Repertoire polyphoner Musik* (Hildesheim, 1968), transcriptions.
[10] *F-Pn* lat.11631, 12584 and 12596.
[11] E. Sanders, 'Consonance and Rhythm in the Organum of the 12th and 13th Centuries', *JAMS*, xxxiii (1980), 271, n.25.
[12] See *Hucbald, Guido and John on Music*, ed. Palisca. Johannes's identity is still a matter of conjecture, as detailed in this work, where the phrase 'of Afflighem' is called into question.
[13] *F-Pn* lat. 1139, 3549 and 3719; *GB-Lbm* Add.36881.

[14] The term 'tenor', as an alternative for 'cantus firmus' to designate the base melody over which a new voice (or voices) was to be added, did not enter the medieval vocabulary until slightly later than the period under discussion, but it seems more appropriate here since the *voces principales* in this repertory are not chant melodies.

[15] See the facsimile and edition in *Liber Sancti Jacobi: Codex Calixtinus*, ed. W. Whitehill, G. Prado and J. Carro García (Santiago de Compostela, 1944).

[16] Personal communication from Solange Corbin, 1970.

[17] Paris, Archives nationales, M.66a, no.1.

[18] Document signed by Robert de Courçon, cardinal and papal legate of Innocent III, gave the 'University of Parisian Masters and Scholars' its first statutes. *F-Ps*, Archives universitaires, D 10b.

[19] That Odo was obliged to issue such instructions at least twice, with obviously little effect on the deportment of the minor clergy, has no bearing on the significance of the prescription of this important music for specific rites.

[20] So called from the position of his treatise (fourth anonymous treatise in the volume) in *CS*, i, 327. The most reliable modern edition, with commentary, is that of F. Reckow, *Der Musiktraktat des Anonymus 4: Edition und Interpretation der Organum purum-Lehre* (Wiesbaden, 1967).

[21] *I-Fl* Plut. 29.1; *D-W* 677 and 1206.

[22] See Reckow, *Der Musiktraktat*, or the translation, *The Music Treatise of Anonymous IV: a New Translation*, ed. J. Yudkin, MSD, xli (1985).

[23] Partial English translation in O. Strunk, *Source Readings in Music History* (New York, 1950/*R*1965).

[24] See n.20.

[25] See for example J. A. Knapp, 'Musical Declamation and Poetic Rhythm in an Early Layer of Notre Dame Conductus', *JAMS*, xxxii (1979), 383–407; and G. A. Anderson, 'Mode and Change of Mode in Notre Dame Conductus', *AcM*, xl (1968), 92–114.

[26] See L. Schrade, 'Political Compositions in French Music of the 12th and 13th Centuries: the Coronation of French Kings', *AnnM*, i (1953), 9–63; repr. in L. Schrade, *De scientia musicae studia atque orationes* (Berne, 1967), 152–211.

[27] See E. Reimer, *Johannes de Garlandia: De mensurabili musica: kritische Edition mit Kommentar und Interpretation der Notationslehre* (Wiesbaden, 1972).

[28] See *Cent motets du XIIIe siècle*, ed. P. Aubry (Paris, 1908); facs. with commentary.

[29] See Y. Rokseth, *Polyphonies du XIIIe siècle* (Paris, 1935–9), facsimile, edition and commentary.

[30] See n.20.

BIBLIOGRAPHICAL NOTE

Cultural background

Ecclesiastical architecture, which provides a necessary and appropriate background for the music discussed in this chapter, is impressively interpreted in two general studies notable for extending far beyond the physical structures themselves to include their uses and influences: G. Duby, *The Age of Cathedrals: Art and Society, 980–1420* (London, 1981), and O. von Simson, *The Gothic Cathedral: the Origins of Gothic Architecture and the Medieval Concept of Order* (London, 1956). The great American classic, H. Adams, *Mont St Michel and Chartres* (Washington, DC, 1901), has lost none of its spirituality or its meticulous architectural and poetic interpretations of its subjects, Chartres having been a very significant centre of polyphonic experimentation. A.E.M. Katzenellenbogen's exquisite *The Sculptural Programs of Chartres Cathedral: Christ, Mary, Ecclesia* (Baltimore, 1959, 2/1964) brings the symbolism, idealism and frequent realism to life in a remarkable fashion. In *Notre Dame of Paris: the Biography of a Cathedral* (London, 1956), A. Temko approaches his subject, as the title suggests, as if 'she' were in fact organically animated; his discussion includes information about musical composition and performance. O. Demus's superbly illustrated *Romanesque Mural Painting* (London, 1970) and E. Mâle's enormous series of works on religious art throughout the Middle

Ages (and well beyond) help to complete the image of Gothic splendour and its infectious influence on music, as well as other arts and intellectual endeavours.

C. H. Lawrence's *Medieval Monasticism* (London, 1984) is a helpful general account, outlining the major developments in the spiritual life of the time. E. Galtier's *Histoire de Saint-Maur-des-Fossés depuis les origines jusqu'à nos jours* (Paris, 1918), on the other hand, is representative of the hundreds of invaluable small-scale studies of local institutions which are often remarkably detailed and documented.

A further step in relating characteristic institutional structures to their denizens and their habits is found at its best in studies of 'ordinary people', such as J. Evans's *Life in Medieval France* (London, 1925), as delightful to read as it is factually solid, and filled with useful insights into 'ordinary' activities, including music-making; or U. T. Holmes jr's *Daily Living in the Twelfth Century* (Madison, WI, 1952). A more recent work takes a similar tack in somewhat more rigorous detail, and with its focus on music specifically: P. Gülke, *Mönche, Bürger, Minnesänger: Musik in der Gesellschaft des europäischen Middelalters* (Vienna, 1975, enlarged 2/1980). A different approach altogether, but equally fruitful, is that of A. Friedmann in *Paris: ses rues, ses paroisses, du moyen âge à la révolution* (Paris, 1959), which peoples the burgeoning city in such detail that the church in its natural habitat truly comes alive.

Musical learning in schools and universities

A very significant contribution to an understanding of the teaching and learning of music in the Middle Ages is J. Smits von Waesberghe's lavishly illustrated, provocative and entertaining *Musikerziehung: Lehre und Theorie der Musik im Mittelalters*, Musikgeschichte in Bildern, iii/3 (Leipzig, 1969). Von Waesberghe gives a great deal of attention to the teachings of Guido of Arezzo, perhaps the earliest professional teacher of music, whose name has come down to us as the 'inventor' of the musical staff.

The principal objective of musical studies at the primary levels was to furnish choirs for a variety of institutions, chiefly secular cathedrals, collegiate churches, household chapels, colleges and monasteries. F. Ll. Harrison's *Music in Medieval Britain* (London, 1958, 2/1963/R1980) furnishes an enormous amount of detail about early musical studies in the British Isles, which must surely be essentially transferable to French institutions by way of the Benedictine connection. N. C. Carpenter has contributed valuable information about music in higher education in her *Music in Medieval and Renaissance Universities* (Norman, 1958, rev. 2/1972). J. Dyer, 'A Thirteenth-Century Choirmaster: the *Scientia musicae* of Elias Salomon', *MQ*, lxvi (1980), 83, provides an interesting view of medieval choral instruction.

Music and musical theory

There is a vast literature on the polyphonic music of the ninth to the thirteenth centuries and its accompanying theory, much of it directed primarily to musicologists. It consists for the most part in facsimile editions of the principal manuscripts, transcriptions into modern notation of portions of the repertory and studies of varying length and scope on some aspect of the subject. The reader is best referred to a selective list of bibliographies, among which the most practical starting-point might be Andrew Hughes's *Medieval Music: the Sixth Liberal Art* (Toronto, 1974; suppl., 1980). More technical, but offering one the opportunity to grasp the special nature of the subject, are Gilbert Reaney's two volumes in the monumental international catalogue of musical sources, the Répertoire Internationale des Sources Musicales; these are *Manuscripts of Polyphonic Music: 11th – early 14th Century*, B/IV/1 (1966) and *Manuscripts of Polyphonic Music c.1300–1400*, B/IV/2 (1969). There are in addition many useful bibliographies scattered throughout *Grove 6*, among them 'Organum and Discant: bibliography', xiii, 808; 'France: bibliography of music to 1600', vi, 764; 'Notation, III, 2–3', xiii, 370; and 'Sources, IV, 2–4', xvii, 650.

Chapter VII

Medieval England, 950–1450

PETER M. LEFFERTS

The brilliant literary and artistic culture of the earlier Anglo-Saxon kingdoms, unmatched in western Europe in the seventh and eighth centuries, suffered devastating decline through successive waves of Danish invasions. Revival of culture and learning began under King Alfred at the end of the ninth century, reaching its culmination in the second half of the tenth century in association with the renewal and dissemination of Benedictine monasticism. It is this resurgence of later Anglo-Saxon England that provides the context for the first English musical repertory of which we have concrete knowledge.

Two key individuals in the revival of music were Dunstan and Ethelwold, scholars and teachers of learning and great energy who possessed considerable literary, musical and artistic skills. Dunstan (*c*908–88) was successively Abbot of Glastonbury (*c*940), Bishop of Worcester (957), Bishop of London (959) and Archbishop of Canterbury (961). He is recorded to have been a lover of music, a harper who always carried his instrument with him, and he is credited with the plainchant melody for the Kyrie *Rex splendens*. Ethelwold was a younger contemporary, a monk under Dunstan at Glastonbury who carried the programme of monastic reform instituted there to Abingdon upon his appointment as abbot (*c*954) and to Winchester when he became bishop and abbot of the Old Minster (963–84). There he was responsible for drawing up new regulations for the conduct of Benedictine monasticism, the *Regularis concordia* (*c*970).

Monastic reform necessarily had an important liturgical and musical component, for traditions in these areas had to be established in new houses and revitalized in older ones. The *Regularis concordia*, for instance, provides detailed information about the performance of liturgical drama at Easter. To ensure 'correct' practices, English church leaders turned to French houses for instruction. While at Abingdon, Ethelwold had expert singers sent from Corbie to teach his monks, and he sent monks on missions to Fleury to learn at first hand the implementation of the monastic rule and the proper singing of chant. Books were loaned from Fleury to Winchester during the reign of Ethelwold, and Dunstan invited the learned Abbo of Fleury to come to the newly founded abbey of Ramsey, where Abbo stayed two years instructing the monks (986–8). Based on their contents and notation, surviving service books of this era can be linked to practices at Corbie and St Denis.

Intimately bound to these reforms of the later tenth century are three events of great importance: the creation of a repertory of tropes at Winchester and Canterbury, the creation of a repertory of polyphonic organa at Winchester, and the installation of organs at Winchester and some other monastic churches.

A trope, in the broadest sense of the term, is any accretion to the Franco-Roman nucleus of chants for Mass and Offices that we call Gregorian chant, a repertory fixed by the early ninth century. More narrowly speaking, tropes *per se* are musical-textual versicles added as introductions to lines of Gregorian Propers and other material. A large insular repertory of tropes *per se* survives in three late Anglo-Saxon manuscripts. The first troper was copied *c*1050 at Winchester from an exemplar of *c*978–86; its repertory was assembled while Ethelwold was still bishop. The second was copied *c*996–1006, again at Winchester, during the bishopric of Aelphege II. The third troper was written at Canterbury half a century later, perhaps around 1050 (see fig.38 above). These tropers are collections of music for Mass and Office sung by the cantor, the chief soloist in the liturgy, and as a consequence they contain not only cycles of tropes for chants of the Mass, as their name would imply, but also cycles of untroped plainsongs of the Mass, including alleluias, sequences, proses, tracts and offertories. The Winchester tropers reflect Ethelwold's reforms and liturgical codifications at Winchester following his translation from Abingdon, so their repertory of tropes is probably directly based on the earlier Abingdon trope repertory. There was some expansion of this corpus in the second Winchester troper, and the Canterbury book contained a rich anthology of insular and continental material.

The Anglo-Saxon trope repertory was mainly a French or Rhenish heritage (about two-thirds of it appears in French sources) but its tradition is complex, with evident borrowings from other repertories such as those of Germany and Italy. It is probable that these other continental pieces came in through northern French and Rhenish sources, especially via Fleury and Corbie. Just under a third of the tropes are of demonstrable English origin, though the repertory must have been larger than that which survives, and the Canterbury collection undoubtedly preserves some unidentified English tropes among the pieces that are unique to it. The native tropes are mainly pieces in honour of local saints or for saints particularly venerated at Winchester, together with complementary additions to continental trope cycles. Furthermore, many continental tropes have been reworked textually and musically in a campaign of recomposition to suit local needs and tastes. English tropes bear some of the distinctively ornate literary Latin of late tenth-century Anglo-Saxon authors, but as the local tropes lack concordances in a readable, diastematic notation, they cannot be transcribed into modern notation and therefore reveal nothing about any possible English melodic dialect.

In the latter part of the second Winchester troper is a collection of organa consisting of the added voices only for a repertory of two-part polyphony based on the note-against-note counterpoint to a plain-chant. It is the earliest extant practical source of liturgical polyphony from western Europe, with no antecedents except for a handful of continental textbook examples. The organa testify to a flourishing polyphonic practice that must have relied on improvisation or memorization rather than notated sources. This oral tradition was surely brought from Abingdon to Winchester by Ethelwold and again ultimately reflects at some distance the Benedictine traditions of northern France, especially those of Fleury and Corbie. The organa are a corpus of material similar in size and liturgical coverage to the main contents of the tropers. Polyphonic elaboration was applied not only to the most ornate melismatic repertory of responsorial chants from Mass and Office, but also to newer, post-Gregorian repertory assigned to the soloist, including cycles of settings for Kyries, Glorias, tracts, sequences, alleluias, Matins responsories and processional antiphons.

As polyphony was the soloist's domain, these organa were in all likelihood composed by, and for, one man: Wulfstan of Winchester. Wulfstan was a pupil of Ethelwold and a noted literary figure in his own right; he was the precentor or cantor at the Old Minster and thus its chief musical and literary official in the later tenth century. Over 150 organa in the main series are written in a hand which is believed to be Wulfstan's own. Like the tropes, the organa were inscribed in staffless neumes so their transcription into modern pitch notation is difficult. However, most of the plainsongs on which the organa are based can be found in the tropers, with musical readings that are restorable by comparison with later sources, so it is possible to reconstruct many of the organa, given a few basic assumptions about the behaviour of the added voice in relation to the plainchant and the implications of the neumes of the organa for melodic direction.

In a metrical prologue to a poetic life of St Swithun (patron saint of the Old Minster), written c995 by Wulfstan the cantor and dedicated to Bishop Aelphege II, there is a vivid if hyperbolic description of a new organ installed in Winchester Cathedral. Apparently the organ was newly constructed as part of the rebuilding and refurbishing programme Aelphege undertook as a continuation of the work of Ethelwold. Ethelwold himself is credited with the building of an organ at Abingdon with his own hands, and in the later tenth century organs were also installed at other monastic churches including Ramsey and Malmesbury. Some suggestions as to how these organs were used is provided by the double musical notation of several proses in the second Winchester troper, in which there are not only plainchant neumes but also an alphabetic notation of pitch. It has been suggested that this form of notation is the earliest-known keyboard tablature, corresponding to the labelling of keys on the Winchester organ. The tablature evidence suggests that the first half of each double-versicle melody of the proses was played on, or accompanied by, the organ.

★

The Norman Conquest of 1066 was one of the most crucial events in the musical history of medieval England, for it initiated a period of over 300 years of relative cultural homogeneity across northern France and England in respect to courtly, intellectual and artistic pursuits. The most certain and most powerful impact of the Conquest on liturgical music came from the wholesale replacement of senior monastic officials by Norman monks, with a resulting Norman influence in liturgy, ceremonial and chant in which the practices of Cluny and Bec were particularly important. In English service books the influence of Norman chant with regard to choice of chants and melodic dialect can be detected as an overlay above pre-Conquest chant traditions from Corbie or St Denis. There was, however, tenacious and spirited resistance in some quarters to these changes. Eleventh-century English and Norman monks also continued the tenth-century Benedictine literary and musical tradition of writing hymns, sequences and full rhymed Offices for Anglo-Saxon saints, honouring now not only figures such as Cuthbert, Birinus, Guthlac and Swithun, but also great reformers not long deceased such as Dunstan, Ethelwold and Aelphege.

Only two isolated examples of polyphony survive from England in the late eleventh and early twelfth centuries, one each from Canterbury and Winchester, which remained centres of musical creation and scholarship. Both pieces reflect the general style of Romanesque polyphony also found *c*1100 on the Continent in fragments from Chartres, Fleury and Paris, a kind of note-against-note polyphony only slightly advanced over that of Wulfstan the cantor's organa for Winchester. Insular cultivation of organum in the twelfth century is affirmed by the observations of several writers, including Ailred of Rievaulx and John of Salisbury, who give us a glimpse of a more elaborate style. In a chapter of his *Speculum caritatis* (*c*1142–3), a work addressed to the novices at the Cistercian abbey of Rievaulx in Yorkshire, Ailred rails at the artificialities and excesses in the performance of contemporary church music in a spirit of true Cistercian austerity, and John, writing in his *Policraticus* (1159), engages in a similar diatribe to make an equally colourful condemnation. Beneath the rhetoric we find a testimony to singing in as many as three parts, as well as to the use of 'unnatural' (falsetto) vocal timbres and hocketing effects; both comment on the wide ranges and florid turns indulged in by singers. This highly decorated style probably pertains to the *ad hoc* ornamentation of slowly sung chant by one or more solo singers simultaneously. The resulting texture – a freely florid, melismatic, almost ecstatic incantation over a slowly moving, drone-like sustained-note accompaniment – was undoubtedly widespread as an orally transmitted, improvisatory practice before the mid-twelfth century, when its formulaic idioms and gestures began to be codified in the written record.

Given the well-drawn picture of the internationalism and relative homogeneity of Latinate intellectual culture in northern Europe provided by historians of the 'Renaissance of the twelfth century',[1] there is no need to detail at any great length the sustained contacts between northern France and England that exposed Englishmen to the new musical repertory which arose in Paris at the cathedral of Notre Dame in the second half of the century. The most impressive Parisian musical monument of this renaissance is the great cycle of two-voice polyphony for the responsorial psalmody of Mass and Office on all major feasts of the church year, the *Magnus liber*, that was composed by Léonin at Notre Dame in the 1170s and early 1180s. Our main source of information about the Notre Dame school is the music treatise of an anonymous Englishman writing about 1275, perhaps a Benedictine monk of Bury St Edmunds, who is referred to by historians as Anonymous IV. It is he who identifies Léonin and the later Pérotin with the surviving repertory and indicates how widespread was the performance of organa, with practitioners on the Iberian peninsula (Castile, Aragon, Navarre), in France and in England at the royal court, at Winchester and in the 'Westcuntre'. And he names specific English singers who were masters of the art, including Johannes Filius Dei of St Paul's, Makeblite at Winchester and Blakesmit at the court of Henry III.

The earliest surviving version of the *Magnus liber* is of British origin. This volume, known to music historians as W_1, was written in the 1240s for the Augustinian cathedral priory of St Andrews, Scotland. It is not known where W_1 was made, but if it was not copied at St Andrews then it probably was executed on commission in the south of England. To what extent the W_1 version of the *Magnus liber* preserves the closest surviving readings to Léonin's, and to what extent it preserves instead simply a local house-style, a version adapted to insular tastes that stands at some remove not only in time but also in musical dialect from the Parisian originals, remains to be fully elucidated. It is inconceivable that W_1 was the first book of its kind to circulate in the British Isles; it is likely that all monasteries and communities of secular clerks with sufficiently lively musical and intellectual traditions had such a volume by the early thirteenth century. Though most of our evidence is late, we know from library inventories that books containing the Notre Dame repertory were possessed in 1295 by the Royal Household Chapel of

49. Feast for the Prodigal Son, accompanied by rebec and organistrum (hurdy-gurdy): detail of a single sheet from a bible from Bury St Edmunds, second half of the twelfth century

Edward I and by St Paul's Cathedral. The St Paul's book had been in the library since 1255, and perhaps since 1245 or before. Volumes of two- and three-voice organa, perhaps Parisian or perhaps local products, were copied at Leominster by a monk of Reading, W. de Wycombe, in the 1270s. Organum continued to be widely practised in the British Isles in both monastic and non-monastic environments, though it was recognized that the modern style was a product of worldly clerks and canons, not the regular orders. In 1217 the General Chapter of the Cistercian Order censured the abbeys of Dore and Tintern for their singing in three and four parts 'after the manner of the secular clergy'. But there was no strong insular tradition of writing out entirely new organa in the sustained-note style of Notre Dame. W_1 provides a representative case. In it there are just two local additions to the two-voice organa of the *Magnus liber* cycle, namely two responsories for St Andrew. Indeed, the number of note-against-note (hereafter 'discant') settings of plainchants from English sources shows that in the thirteenth century this basically homorhythmic texture was cultivated in preference to the sustained-note style.

Organa are not the sole corpus of British liturgical polyphony from the later twelfth and early thirteenth centuries. Somewhat over-shadowed by the elaborate cycle of organa for Mass and Office is a substantial body of polyphonic settings of the Mass Ordinary and sequences. The English particularly cultivated these genres, and in fact W_1 combines both kinds of liturgical works between its covers. Especially noteworthy is the local British repertory of its eleventh fascicle, consisting of two-voice discant settings of chants for Marian masses: Latin-texted Kyries, a troped Gloria, alleluias, a tract, sequences and proses, and Sanctus and Agnus tropes. A substantial number of kindred settings, in particular of sequences and Sanctus and Agnus tropes, can be accumulated from fragments of other British sources of

175

the late twelfth and thirteenth centuries.

A third repertory within the covers of W_1 consists of conductus. This is not surprising, since Latin song collections with music circulated with the *Magnus liber* in several of its most important sources, and the conductus is intimately linked to the Notre Dame school by the lyrics of Philip the Chancellor, who collaborated closely with Pérotin. But in contrast to the narrowly Parisian compositional milieu of the *Magnus liber*, the internationally circulating repertory of monophonic and polyphonic conductus and cantio was no more uniquely Parisian than, for example, the trouvère repertory. Latin lyrics were a product of Latinate culture, not the product of a single milieu; their authors were members of a class of learned clerks and ecclesiastics of many nationalities, often Paris-educated, of course, but employed throughout the realms of France and England and beyond. Two of the greatest authors represented in the central conductus repertory, Walter of Châtillon and Peter of Blois, had careers associated closely with the Angevin court of Henry II, alongside other important English lyrical and satirical 'Anglo-Latin' poets. The corpus of conductus may be differentiated stylistically, geographically and chronologically, and it is possible to discern layers of material within the biggest collections, including a distinct stratum that circulated particularly in England. Precisely how much of this repertory may be of English authorship or bears specifically English features remains an open question. A significant number of Latin conductus and planctus are datable on the basis of textual content, and among these there are more datable pieces concerning English topics – royal deaths and crownings, the dynastic struggles of Henry II and his sons, and Henry's clash with Becket – than concerning the royal family of France.

In the course of the thirteenth century a distinctive insular musical dialect began to emerge in two-voice and three-voice liturgical polyphony through a process that might be termed 'subregional differentiation'[2] in respect to the wider musical culture-area embracing Anglo-Norman England and northern France. This differentiation was as natural and inevitable as the drift of Anglo-Norman away from mainland French dialects, and it is a process for which one can find parallels in politics, the fine arts, architecture and various intellectual disciplines, especially philosophy and science at Oxford. In music this trend can be analysed in terms of an English concentration on certain genres and aspects of style present in the earlier international repertory. Its result was the emergence of a vigorous, autonomous music culture of great originality.

The English musical dialect was distinguished foremost by the prevalent use of imperfect consonances as harmonies – thirds and sixths in two-voice textures, five-three and six-three sonorities in three-voice textures, often in parallel counterpoint. These sonorities began to appear frequently in the earlier thirteenth-century English two-voice sequence settings, though they are not striking in the discant chant settings of the insular eleventh fascicle of W_1. One sees the use of thirds in the continental conductus repertory and in the earliest Parisian motets, and this has been viewed as English practice or a mark of English influence. But it may be simply a trait of counterpoint at this stage in its development, a tendency isolated and intensified by the English. English music theorists were certainly more liberal about the admissibility of the third into counterpoint than their continental counterparts. Preference for this harmonic idiom may have been due in large part to the influence on learned musicians of distinctive regional styles of folk polyphony cultivated in the British Isles. We owe most of our knowledge of these to the ethnographic reporting of Gerald of Wales. In his famous descriptions of Wales *c*1200 he refers to the part-singing in close harmony of the Welsh and of those living north of the Humber and around York, which he suggests is a result of the contact of these societies with the Norse and Danes. Other evidence supports this, suggesting that there may have been related idioms of folk polyphony common to all the Germanic-Nordic races of northern Europe.[3]

There are further characteristic features of the emerging English musical dialect in addition to harmony and counterpoint. For one, an idiosyncratic English early mensural notation developed out of the 'modal' notation of the early thirteenth century. Rather than using a square figure for a breve, as on the Continent, it used a lozenge-shaped figure, a shape appearing in English sources as soon as compositions began to use free-standing breves to bear a syllable of text. There was also a marked English preference for trochaic (long–short) rhythms, in contrast to the predominance of iambic (short–long) rhythms in the thirteenth-century French repertory. The English also show a propensity for four-part writing, a texture virtually abandoned on the Continent after the first quarter of the thirteenth century. And a number of stylistic features derived from the conductus were prominent in English polyphony, including chordal textures and homogeneity of rhythmic activity, homorhythmic declamation of a single text, strophic structures and balanced, regular phrases.

These distinctive musical features emerged in conjunction with the cultivation of a wide variety of compositional genres, most of them peculiar to the English. The best-known example is the most famous single piece of medieval music, the delightful Sumer canon (*Sumer is icumen in*), a rota or perpetual canon at the unison whose repetitious harmonic structure is defined and supported by a *pes* of two voices constantly exchanging. But the rota is rare; the conductus, motet and troped chant setting were the predominant types. A large repertory of later thirteenth-century three-voice conductus circulated only in England; these normally had texted voice-exchange or rondellus

50. Excerpt from a three-voice conductus, with a rondellus section in which the movement of the text between the voices indicates the round: manuscript fragment, third quarter of the thirteenth century

sections (see fig.50). Rondellus technique, in which three voices permute a number of musical ideas, was also used to generate independent rondellus and rondellus-motets, while voice-exchange technique, in which two parts alternate material over a repeating tenor, spawned motets with strict or varied voice exchange over a freely invented, repetitive *pes*. The rota, conductus and rondellus were cultivated only up to the turn of the century, but the tradition of the voice-exchange motet, now in four voices as well as in three and built on a cantus firmus, survived well into the fourteenth century. Troped chant settings, intended to be directly substituted for many ritual texts from the Mass and Offices (especially alleluias, for which cycles of settings were written), show the influence of motet style in their texture of two upper parts over a single statement of the plainsong, with both added voices singing elaborate paraphrases of the chant text.

In regard to subject matter, the English polyphonic repertory was emphatically sacred rather than secular in orientation, setting either ritual texts or newly written Latin texts on religious themes – Mary, saints, feasts and homiletic topics. The Sumer canon is exceptional in being provided with both secular English and alternative sacred Latin lyrics. Only one motet has a text in Middle English, and a handful set Anglo-Norman. The few other polyphonic settings of vernacular texts of the thirteenth and early fourteenth centuries, whether of Middle English or Anglo-Norman, secular or devotional, are found in conductus-like strophic settings.

In the last third of the century, with the growing stylistic and generic breach between French and English music, we no longer find the widespread circulation of insular repertory on the Continent or vice versa. However, some English pieces do turn up in the vast Montpellier codex, a Parisian motet anthology of the later thirteenth century, and a few French motets, some recast in English mensural notation and Anglo-Norman orthography, are found in English sources of similar age. One amusing continental piece of the later thirteenth century that shows familiarity with the English style is a French motet, *Hare hare hye!/ Balaam! Gaoudalier on bien ouan*, over whose repetitive tenor is built clearly periodic phrasing and voice exchange, with texts that refer to the English, poking fun at them as 'ale-quaffers'.[4]

★

Surviving records of the musical life of medieval England reveal not only a vigorous tradition of sacred polyphony but also the long cultivation of secular and devotional song. And the variegated status of Latin, French and English as spoken and written languages in medieval England makes the history of song on this island a complex one. A unique glimpse of non-liturgical song in the monasteries of Anglo-

Saxon England is afforded by the 'Older Cambridge Songbook', copied at St Augustine's, Canterbury, in the mid-eleventh century. This educational compilation consists of a graded Latin reader plus additions, among which is a substantial collection of Latin song texts probably taken from a German exemplar. The lyrics, numbering over 50, include love songs, planctus, *fabliaux*, pious and celebratory or political verses. Some, perhaps all, were intended to be sung, though only a few of the lyrics are provided with neumes, which are unfortunately imprecise as to pitch. However, a modus or tune name is attached to four lyrics, suggesting that these, and perhaps others, were intended to fit well-known melodies.

Of Anglo-Saxon musical life outside the monastery we have no direct evidence. No musical settings of Old English texts survive. None the less, substantial literary testimony describes a secular society in which musical performance was a central component of work, public ceremonial and entertainment. The scop, a maker and performer of tales of heroic deeds, was a serious and respected member of the community, the holder of an office of standing that elevated him above the rank of mere entertainer; professional entertainers, the harpers and gleomen, were of a distinctly lower status. The normal public performance of heroic, epic narrative poetry was musical. It would seem, though, that the tradition of song for ceremonial and work occasions was probably distinct from that of shorter, lyrical genres, and the extent to which these briefer Old English poems were sung is an open question. Also open (and the subject of much scholarly hypothesis) is the manner of performance of all genres, their musical form and style, and the precise function of the ubiquitous harp as rhythmic or melodic accompaniment.

The first hundred years of Norman rule saw the introduction at the highest level of society of a new vernacular with its own tradition of secular entertainment music, of which at first there are few extant traces. During the reign of Henry II, however, the English court came to play a central and well-documented role in the development of Latin and vernacular song. Indeed, Henry II and Eleanor of Aquitaine

> were the recipients and ideal audience of an astounding range of literary works, vernacular and Latin . . . the Angevin and Norman court milieu harboured much of the most brilliant poetry of the mid-twelfth century, and . . . especially in the two decades from Henry's and Eleanor's accession to the English throne in 1154, to Eleanor's revolt against Henry and her consequent imprisonment in 1173, England was the highpoint of 'the Renaissance of the twelfth century'.[5]

The literary products of this environment included Anglo-Norman and Middle English verse chronicles, epics, romances by Thomas of England and Chrétien de Troyes, Provençal lyrics of Bernart de Ventadorn, lais and fables of Marie de France, and Latin lyric poetry by Walter of Châtillon and Peter of Blois, to mention only a few outstanding figures. To a very large degree their literary products, in their original creative milieu and performance contexts, were intended for music.

We have already had occasion to mention the Latin song repertory in conjunction with late twelfth- and early thirteenth-century polyphony. Here it should be stressed that monophonic and polyphonic conductus and cantio also circulated independently of the central manuscripts, surviving in numerous widespread and diverse sources that contain poetry of tremendously wide range, from devotional hymns and sequences to biting moral satire, intense love poetry, philosophical debates and humorous *fabliaux*. One important British collection of such Latin lyrics in musical settings is the 'Younger Cambridge Songbook' of the very late twelfth or early thirteenth century. This source has 22 monophonic songs, twelve for two voices and one for three voices. The collection is international in character and it is not likely that many of its pieces are English in origin, but it appears that they were copied in the British Isles for a learned community, perhaps in Leicestershire. The songbook has strong affinities to, and concordances with, the famous *Carmina burana* copied *c*1220–30 in southern Germany.

Sacred and devotional monophonic Latin songs continued to be composed by Englishmen well into the thirteenth century. The best known of these include the hymn *Dulcis Jhesu memoria* from the pen of an anonymous English Cistercian, Archbishop Stephen Langton's popular Pentecost sequence *Veni sancte spiritus* and the strophic devotional lyric *Angelus ad virginem*. Sustaining a longstanding Anglo-Saxon and early Norman tradition, devotional Offices continued to be written, as is witnessed by the great monastic rhymed Office for St Thomas of Canterbury written by Abbot Benedict of Peterborough in the later 1170s. Subsequent English saints or near saints of the thirteenth and early fourteenth centuries, including Simon de Montfort, Thomas of Lancaster and Thomas of Hereford, in their turn received Offices from the pens of both Benedictines and the mendicant friars. On a more mundane level there survive Latin verses penned by Bishop Ledrede of Kilkenny in the fourteenth century for his clerks to sing in place of less appropriate lyrics on great feasts; they are found in the *Red Book of Ossory* with short tags or snatches of verse by a number of them to indicate their familiar secular melody. Even the Latin carols of the later fourteenth and fifteenth centuries show that Latin was still a natural vehicle for music for a learned audience, and of course the English mystery plays that begin to emerge into the written record in the later fourteenth century are full of song that for the most part was familiar Latin liturgical music.

Though the steady growth of Middle English literature can be charted from the later twelfth century to its tremendous flowering in the later fourteenth century, French remained the predominant language of social intercourse and literature among the uppermost classes well into the fifteenth century. It comes as no surprise, therefore, that romance song was a significant element in medieval English musical culture. Indeed, from the twelfth century there is a particularly conspicuous repertory of songs in Provençal, French and even Italian – some lyrical, some political, some lamentory – written for and about Henry II, Eleanor of Aquitaine and their progeny. Bernart de Ventadorn is perhaps the greatest musical figure contributing to this output, but Peire Vidal, Bertran de Born and others also wrote and sang about the domestic and dynastic struggles of the Plantagenets. Richard I, Eleanor's eldest son by Henry, was a notable poet-musician in his own right, some of whose songs survive.

No correspondingly significant lyric repertory can be associated with the courts of the later Plantagenets, but there is ample testimony to the patronage of trouvères and minstrels by the secular and ecclesiastical aristocracy of England from the later twelfth to the early fifteenth century. The greater magnates kept staffs of household minstrels and might have one or more in personal attendance upon them, and there are plentiful payment records revealing the entertainment of minstrels at bishop's palaces and great abbeys. English household minstrels travelled widely on the Continent in the fourteenth and fifteenth centuries, where they can be documented playing for Philip the Bold of Burgundy, the Count of Flanders and others, and English minstrels were regularly given leave to attend the great Lenten *scolae* in the Low Countries. In the late thirteenth century, in England as on the Continent, the patronage of lyric song became a bourgeois pastime. The records of the London Guildhall preserve the regulations of a *puy*, or court of love, that was established by the traders; it had elaborate rules for the judging of songs and the crowning of a 'chanson roial' every year at a great feast after Trinity. Similar courts of love for the cultivation and judging of song were being established in the same era in northern and southern France at towns like Arras and Toulouse.

Strong parallels exist between the survival patterns for Anglo-Norman and Middle English lyrics, with or without music. These two languages occur together in many of the most famous poetic anthologies from England in the thirteenth and fourteenth centuries. However, the much rarer sources with music tend to be small and miscellaneous in content rather than homogeneous, extensive collections or sizeable, systematic anthologies. Typically they mix monophonic and polyphonic settings of French, English and Latin with textless instrumental pieces. Unfortunately, no great Anglo-Norman chansonnier survives that would define for us a securely insular repertory of courtly chansons, identify for us songs composed by Anglo-Norman musicians

51. *The minstrels who should solace a king: miniature from a treatise by Walter de Milemete, 1326.*
Their instruments are (from the top) double pipe, fiddle, gittern (citole), timbrel, bagpipes, shawm,
crowd, pipe-and-tabor, gong, portative organ and (centre) positive organ and harp

and make possible the isolation of an insular style. None the less, though they are not numerous, examples of Anglo-Norman songs survive together with their melodies in a variety of sources and have recently begun to be systematically collected and studied from a musical point of view.

Songs written in Middle English are even more elusive than those in French; they are indeed 'a fugitive kind of verse'.[6] And their tunes are correspondingly few in number. From before 1200 only St Godric's three short sacred songs of the mid-twelfth century survive with their melodies, and from the thirteenth and earlier fourteenth centuries roughly a dozen more devotional songs, and just five secular lyrics, are provided with musical notation. Only two of the latter, *Miri it is* and *Brid one brere*, are monophonic solo songs. However, the large corpus of Middle English lyrics surviving without music – secular, religious, historical, political – is believed to be mainly intended for singing. Further, English remained the native tongue of the lesser aristocracy, country gentry and lower classes of society, and traditional oral forms of musical entertainment in English flourished for them. The staple repertory of the itinerant minstrel consisted to a large degree of narrative verses, not refined lyrics, and there is ample evidence for the singing or chanting of popular, lengthy metrical romances in English as well as French. Not to be left out of account either are the shorter narrative rhymes in English, the ballads, the chronology of whose historical origin in oral tradition is obscure but which began to emerge into the written record in significant numbers (as texts only, without their music) in the fifteenth century.

On the Continent there appears to have been a hiatus in the composition of polyphonic settings of vernacular lyrics during the first four decades of the fourteenth century, and the motet in France reverted to settings of Latin. However, by the 1340s Guillaume de Machaut and others had begun to experiment with polyphonic settings of the recently refined dance songs with fixed refrain forms: the ballade, rondeau and virelai. And in trecento Italy there emerged into the written record for the first time almost simultaneously a repertory of vernacular Italian song in lighter forms: the madrigal and ballata. French and Italian composers produced hundreds of secular songs by the end of the century. No extant songbooks transmit a comparable body of polyphonic settings of vernacular lyrics, either Anglo-Norman or Middle English, from this era in England. The lack of musical sources from court circles is particularly remarkable considering that the international court culture of the later fourteenth century, which had such a strongly intellectual musical aspect on the Continent, flourished so conspicuously at the courts of Edward III and Richard II. The court was intensely Francophile in cultural outlook throughout the fourteenth century, and it is possible to document 'the constant interchange

52. Dance accompanied by fiddle and gittern (citole): miniature from an English book of hours, c1250–75

and cross-influence which took place in music and poetry in the late Middle Ages between England and France',[7] pre-eminently in the circle of Walloon artists and men-of-letters which gathered around Edward III's queen, Philippa of Hainaut, which included Jehan de la Mote and Jean Froissart.

Chaucer and Gower, who wrote French as well as English lyrics, are comparable as lyric poets to their direct French contemporaries Froissart and Deschamps, with whom they were well acquainted. All inherited the strong literary but not compositional patrimony of Machaut. On the Continent, the political or celebratory motet and *grande ballade* were a prominent part of 'the elaborate and competitive ostentation of late medieval court culture',[8] but to the extent that indigenous, written polyphonic music served these purposes in England it did so in the display of sacred polyphony as part of liturgical ceremony. However, there was undeniably a repertory of song and dance music at the English court and at the courts and houses of the nobility and gentry as well. Even Chaucer's squire 'could songes make and wel endyte' (Prologue to the *Canterbury Tales*, vv.94–6). A very indicative remark is made in Chaucer's *Parlement of Foules* (c1382), however, in which there is a reference to birds singing a 'roundel', or chanson in rondeau form, of which it is said, 'the note, I trowe, maked was in Fraunce' (vv.673 ff).

From the mid-fourteenth century to the 1470s there are tantalizing, scattered remains of repertories of polyphonic vernacular song that circulated in England, some by Englishmen and some continental in origin, on texts both French and English. The most important strand of song is French in its stylistic orientation. The earlier songs are of an international tradition of rather unpretentious settings in an Ars Nova

53. *Opening of the top part of a motet setting of the Latin drinking-song 'O potores', with illumin-*
ated initial, c1440

style akin to that of early or middle-period Machaut. Many such songs
circulated widely in a geographical swathe across England, the Low
Countries, Germany and northern Italy. One composer in this style,
Alanus, may be identified as the Englishman John Aleyn, a canon of
Windsor who died in 1373. A provincial collection assembled at
Winchester College between 1395 and 1401 provides a cross-section of
pieces in its repertory of Latin songs and canons, French-language
songs (mostly unique but some with international circulation) and
settings of English verse similar in form and style to the French. The
vernacular lyrics are mainly set in what might be described as trun-
cated virelai form (*ABB*); their melodic-contrapuntal style is simple,
often crude, and while they are written in Ars Nova mensurations, they
often lack strict metrical regularity. One of the songs in English,
definitely a local product, sings the praises of the city of Winchester.
From the later part of the era, the 1430s to 1470s, the small repertory of
songs extant in insular sources can be augmented with songs by
Englishmen that circulated mainly on the Continent, especially in the
fixed forms of the ballade and rondeau, and again with original texts in
French or English. Representative song composers of this later era
include John Dunstable, John Bedingham, Robertus de Anglia, Robert
Morton and Walter Frye.

Other kinds of insular song never crossed the Channel; the most important of these was the English devotional carol, which comprises the first truly substantial extant repertory of polyphonic vernacular song in English. (There are carols in Latin, too, as well as macaronic carols mixing both languages.) Over 500 carol texts survive from the fourteenth to the sixteenth century, with monophonic and polyphonic settings of over 130 from the late fourteenth and fifteenth centuries. Carols for one, two or three voices are united as a genre by a standard stanzaic pattern (*aaab*), a fixed form alternating a choral refrain (the burden) and solo verses, prevailing ternary metre and homorhythmic declamation whose notation is facilitated by writing the carols, conductus-like, in score. Their texts mainly concern Christmas and Easter themes.

> It seems most likely that they were conceived and sung as home-made entertainment, of a festal but edifying nature, round the firesides of the lodgings and refectories of the vicars choral and singing-men of the greater secular churches and aristocratic household chapels. Despite their vernacular texts (albeit commonly interspersed with phrases in Latin), it must be emphasized that . . . these carols and their manuscripts were by no means the music of the people, but exclusively of the educated and sophisticated élite.[9]

Another, lesser strand of purely local consumption was a distinct tradition of free-form partsongs in a more popular vein, of which the drinking song *Tappster, drinker, fille another ale* is a rousing example.

The indigenous tradition of sacred vocal music that had emerged over the course of the thirteenth century continued to flourish in the fourteenth and fifteenth, evolving in response to the demands created by the founding of new choral institutions and the cultivation of new services. As before, 'medieval England was part of Europe and not an island in the cultural sense',[10] and it remained true that English music continued to be affected by, and have an influence upon, the Continent. The greatest foreign impact on the insular repertory of the fourteenth century was notational. The adoption of the advances of Franco of Cologne and Petrus de Cruce around the beginning of the century caused English mensural notation to fall out of use, and the Parisian Ars Nova notation and mensurations of Johannes de Muris and Philippe de Vitry eventually supplanted all other practices, though certain anti-Franconian notation types and uniquely insular approaches characterized English notations to the end of the century. Conversely, English exploration of large-scale strophic structures and various forms of numerical periodicity in the motet may have had a great impact on the French, in particular on the motet technique of Vitry. Even before the great tidal wave of English music on to the mainland in the second and third quarters of the fifteenth century, English liturgical music may have had an influence on the Continent, especially on Flemish and northern Italian composers writing just before 1400, such as Egardus, Ciconia and Antonio Zachara da Teramo.

One of the most significant processes in the social history of English liturgical music, initiated in the later thirteenth century, was the rise of new musical establishments that were neither monastic choirs nor choirs of secular clerks associated with a cathedral. Their model was the choral establishment of Edward I, which to some degree may have been established on its new footing in emulation of the Sainte-Chapelle of Louis IX, founded in 1248. Radical changes were made during the 1270s in the constitution of the Royal Household Chapel (the Chapel Royal), which grew from three men to a force of sixteen (six chaplains, six clerks and four choristers) plus an ancillary staff. It is possible to chart steady further growth in the statutory membership of this body to 46 under Henry VI and Edward IV. These later numbers imply a huge staff of gentlemen and boys, but it was probably on a rota so that not everyone had to be present to sing every service, and the statutory number of positions was not always filled. Nevertheless, these were the largest forces of their kind in Europe; the *ampla capella* of the English kings, served by a number of active composers, was famed throughout Europe, admired by chroniclers and the target of raids for singers by other ambitious institutions.

Just as in France, the vogue for personal chapels spread beyond the king's household to those of other leading aristocratic and ecclesiastical magnates, especially in the generation of leaders reaching their maturity after the middle of the fourteenth century. In the early fifteenth century chapels were maintained, for instance, not only by Henry V but by his mother Joan, the dowager queen (widow of Henry IV), and his brothers Humphrey, Duke of Gloucester, John, Duke of Bedford, and Thomas, Duke of Clarence. In addition to private chapels, other kinds of choral institution were also established. In contrast to the Royal Household Chapel, which was an itinerant body always in attendance upon the king, two other major royal chapels of fixed abode were founded by Edward III: the royal chapels of St Stephen's at Westminster and St George's at Windsor, founded by similar letters patent in 1348. Aristocratic foundations also established new collegiate chapels, or raised parish churches to the level of collegiate church with an endowment sufficient for the performance of chant and polyphony. New foundations of colleges at Oxford and Cambridge in this period began to provide for endowed chapels and choirs, and collegiate statutes frequently refer to polyphony, as do the terms of appointment or payment for musical officials such as the organist and the master of the boys. Late medieval monasteries also often maintained a chapel outside the monastic choir, especially in the Lady Chapel, that might be endowed by lay patronage; such establishments sometimes were associated with a grammar or song school and might be staffed from outside the monastic community by boy choristers and laymen or clerks in lesser orders. At one time there were probably 50 or more major monastic institutions whose choirs sang the liturgy with great splendour and had the expertise to undertake complex mensural polyphony.

With the general long-term decline in the vitality of the monasteries balanced by the growth in new choral establishments, a similar number of major ecclesiastical choral institutions were to be reckoned with in the later fourteenth and early fifteenth centuries.[11] Two points must be made about these new choirs. First, whatever the size of choral forces provided for in these institutions, it is important to recognize that until the fifteenth century polyphony was performed mainly by small groups

54. Benedictine monks singing from choir stalls: miniature from the Psalter of Henry VI, French, c1450

of soloists and that polyphonic music was written under the constraints imposed by the capacities of ensembles whose main duty was to sing chant. English polyphony for three or four parts was normally sung simply by a soloistic ensemble of an equal number of men whose voices lay in ranges equivalent to the modern baritone, tenor and male alto or countertenor. Before the mid-fifteenth century, boy choristers only participated in the chant, not in polyphony. Second, the precise degree of musical literacy amongst these choirs, and the number that performed written part music, have yet to be charted in detail. Certainly, the capacity for singing complex composed polyphony cannot simply be equated with its realization in practice. Complicated mensural polyphony was probably not attempted by most choirs whose staple diet was plainsong. The sharp contrast between the occasions for which polyphony is specified in some liturgical books and the very much less extensive coverage afforded by surviving polyphony suggests the extent to which simple, extemporized forms of polyphony may have been the norm, especially at the secular cathedrals for which virtually no notated repertory is extant.

With the growth of new institutions, we can begin to document new career paths for musicians, free of the anonymity of the cloister. Composers, theorists and singing men might be priests or clerks in lower orders, or even laymen with a background at a song school or university. One remarkable later fourteenth-century English motet about music and musicians, *Sub arturo plebs*, provides us with fifteen names of men who were members of the Chapel Royal or who enjoyed the patronage of King Edward III and the Black Prince in the third quarter of the century, most of whom were clergy in lesser orders who can be traced in the public record by the granting of benefices and other favours.[12] Noteworthy also is the compositional activity of Roy (i.e. King) Henry, to whom a Gloria and a Sanctus setting are attributed in the Old Hall Manuscript, while a fragment of a Kyrie survives elsewhere attributed to Le Roy. All pieces are roughly of the same period but in such different styles that a consistent personal idiom cannot be derived from them. Historians are divided as to whether Henry IV (ruled 1399–1413) or Henry V (ruled 1413–22) was the Roy Henry skilled in the craft of composition. However, a fourth piece, an alleluia setting, survives with a creditable attribution to 'henrici quinti' and tips the scales towards the younger ruler.

The careers of Lionel Power (*c*1375–1445) and John Dunstable (*c*1390–1453), the two most important English composers of the first half of the fifteenth century, both show the kind of employment one might find in private service and demonstrate the new role played by Benedictine monasteries in such a career. Power and Dunstable are styled 'armiger' in existing documents, implying they were men of considerable standing, with a social status ranking just under that of

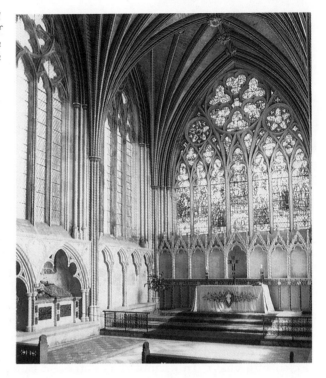

55. The Lady Chapel (east of the Choir) of Exeter Cathedral, begun (c1280) in the late English Decorated style

knight; that they were never awarded benefices suggests they were not in clerical orders. Power probably served Thomas, Duke of Clarence, as one of the Gentlemen of his chapel and for a time instructor of his boy choristers over the decade *c*1411–21. After the death of Clarence we may assume Power found employment in some other aristocratic household chapel, perhaps that of John, Duke of Bedford. By 1438 he had moved to Canterbury in semi-retirement, working there until his death as the first (lay) master of the singing boys who constituted the Lady Chapel choir. Dunstable may have been in the service of John, Duke of Bedford, before 1427; it is more certain that he worked for Joan, dowager queen of Henry IV, for some time before her death in 1437 and then went into the *familia* of Humphrey, Duke of Gloucester. All three patrons provide Dunstable with strong connections to the Benedictine house of St Albans through their benefactions in support of the abbey. Dunstable wrote several ceremonial isorhythmic motets on saints particular to St Albans, and one of his epitaphs was written by John Wheathamstead, Abbot of St Albans; it is conceivable that he sustained a relationship with St Albans not unlike Power's with Canterbury.

New liturgical services, as well as new institutions and the careers they provided, had a marked impact on later medieval English musical life. Devotions to the Virgin Mary were among the most important of these. In addition to the commemorative mass sung in choir on Saturday, Mary's special day, a Lady Mass increasingly came to be performed daily, celebrated in the Lady Chapel at the growing number of Gothic churches – monastic and secular – whose architecture incorporated this special place of worship. Indeed, in many places the master of the Lady Chapel's music became the highest ranking practising musician in ecclesiastical service. Another Marian devotion requiring polyphony was the Salve, a brief evening service after Compline for which settings of Marian antiphons were written. (Its name is derived from the popular antiphon *Salve regina*.) An alternative to the musical elaboration of Vespers at the end of the working day, this service was specifically designated for polyphony in the statutes of foundation of many new English choral institutions in the later fourteenth and fifteenth centuries. Where display was of primary importance, festal masses and ceremonial masses for coronations, royal marriages and births, treaties, victories, triumphal entries and like occasions were also now clothed in the splendour of increasingly long and elaborate polyphonic works.

In describing the styles of fourteenth- and fifteenth-century English liturgical music it is useful to distinguish three points along a continuum of compositional sophistication. The first and lowest was a means of extemporizing counterpoint in which one or two voices were added to a chant. In its most characteristic English form this was a rather mechanical three-voice technique called faburden, in which the added voices shadowed the chant at the fourth above and the third below, with the lowest voice occasionally inflecting the stream of parallel chords by dropping to the fifth below. Though this technique could be used to elevate the status of any chant, faburden particularly came to be associated with lengthy processional and antiphonal choral chants such as hymns, litanies, processional psalms, the *Te Deum* and the *Magnificat*.

The second, middle, style incorporates a large repertory of unpretentious, functional, written polyphony whose homogeneous texture is derived from the conductus. These strictly utilitarian settings were primarily for three voices, notated in score format with the text written only once under the lowest staff but sung homorhythmically by all parts. Two compositional techniques must be distinguished. One is discant, setting a plainchant that normally is laid out monorhythmically as the middle voice of three. The voices added above and below usually make varied counterpoint, more often than not moving predominantly in contrary motion, though in a few of the least elaborate examples they move primarily in parallel motion with the chant, almost like faburden. The other technique is a freely composed, melody-governed style usually termed 'cantilena style', in which two lower voices move predominantly in parallel with a treble melody, creating phrases harmonized by chains of parallel imperfect consonances. Discant and freely composed settings exist for a great variety of genres, including Mass Ordinaries, alleluias and other Propers for the Lady Mass, Marian cantilenas and antiphons, Office hymns, *Te Deum, Nunc dimittis, Magnificat* and items for Holy Week including Passion music and processional hymns and litanies.

The third and highest style includes a repertory of larger-scale, elaborate and ostentatious music written in separate voice parts rather than in score. The longest established genre taking this more sophisticated approach, the motet, thrived in England in the fourteenth century. English composers explored a greater number of well-defined archetypes for motet construction than are found on the Continent, including such types as the isoperiodic motet, the refrain motet, the five-section voice-exchange motet with coda, the varied voice-exchange motet and the duet motet with *medius cantus*. However, starting around mid-century, the influence of the mature type of French isorhythmic motet developed by Vitry, Machaut and others began to be felt, and after a period of hybridization and experimentation, this design fully supplanted indigenous varieties by 1400. Isorhythmic motets on Mary and individual saints continued to be written by composers such as Dunstable and Forest until about 1450.

In the second half of the fourteenth century, settings of the Ordinary of the Mass surpassed the motet as the most actively cultivated English polyphonic genre. Discant- or cantilena-style settings were the rule at first, but there was an increasing concentration on the high style. With no previous tradition for Mass Ordinary movements in such an elevated manner, composers of these complex and artful new settings drew on textures and procedures derived from other elaborate genres, employing canons of several voices over one or more supporting parts, the isorhythmic design and texture of the motet, and free, chanson-style, treble-dominated textures with rhythmic independence of parts and considerable rhythmic and notational subtlety. The greatest source of such mass music is the Old Hall Manuscript, compiled in the second decade of the fifteenth century for the chapel of Thomas, Duke of Clarence; Lionel Power may have played an important role in its production. Old Hall, now owned by the British Library, is a systematically arranged manuscript that puts together all settings of each successive text of the Ordinary. Within each such group, its scribes observed a strict division between pieces notated in score and parts, hence between the more modest and more ostentatious items.

Two types of polyphony important for Marian services, the cantilena and the antiphon, also advanced from the middle to the upper end of the stylistic continuum in the late fourteenth and fifteenth centuries, particularly in the works of Lionel Power, John Dunstable and their successors. In their substantial numbers, far outweighing the production of motets, they formed the most significant complement to the repertory of settings of the Mass Ordinary.

In the first few decades of the fifteenth century two important factors dominated the further evolution of style and technique in English sacred polyphony. First, in terms of performance practice, there was a major change from soloistic ensembles to choral forces with several singers on a part, with a concomitant shift from consistent musical textures to writing that introduced dynamic, textural and spatial contrasts by varying both the number of parts (alternating two- and three-voice writing, in particular) and the number of performers on a part (designating sections for chorus or for soloists). Second, settings of the Mass Ordinary began to be linked to one another in pairs or in cycles of three to five movements by various musical techniques, the most important of which was the use of a common cantus firmus as structural foundation.

The great Flemish music theorist Johannes Tinctoris, writing in the 1470s, regarded the new Franco-Flemish musical art of his day to have originated among a school of musicians writing some 40 years earlier, among whom the English, with Dunstable at their head, stood out as leaders. English polyphony composed in the decades immediately after Old Hall, including most of the large-scale antiphon settings and innovatory cyclic cantus-firmus masses of Power, Dunstable, Benet, Bedingham and others, circulated widely on the mainland for several decades starting in the later 1420s and 30s, and the greater part survives today only in continental manuscripts of Flanders, southern Germany, Austria and northern Italy. This innovatory repertory, with its smooth triadic melodies and distinctive cadential turns of phrase, flowing rhythms, pan-consonant harmonies and progressions, and new principles of formal integration, had an immense impact on the course of development of Netherlandish polyphony in the second and third quarters of the fifteenth century and helped give birth to the European-wide Renaissance in music.

NOTES

[1] See both R. W. Southern, 'The Place of England in the Twelfth-Century Renaissance', in his *Medieval Humanism and Other Studies* (Oxford, 1970), and R. M. Thomson, 'England and the Twelfth-Century Renaissance', *Past and Present*, ci (1983), 3–21.

[2] Thomson, 'England and the Twelfth-Century Renaissance', 4.

[3] On Gerald's famous comments about music in the *Descriptio Cambriae*, see S. Burstyn, 'Gerald of Wales and the *Sumer Canon*', *JM*, ii (1983), 135–50, and Burstyn, 'Is Gerald of Wales a Credible Musical Witness?', *MQ*, lxii (1986), 155–96.

[4] *The Earliest Motets*, ed. H. Tischler (New Haven, 1982), ii, no.131, pp.876–80.

[5] P. Dronke, 'Peter of Blois and Poetry at the Court of Henry II', *Mediaeval Studies*, xxxviii (1976), 185–6.

[6] The comment by Douglas Gray is in J. W. Bennett, *Middle English Literature*, ed. and compiled D. Gray (Oxford, 1986), 364.

[7] N. Wilkins, 'Music and Poetry at Court: England and France in the Late Middle Ages', in *English Court Culture in the Later Middle Ages*, ed. V. J. Scattergood and J. W. Sherbourne (New York, 1983), 183–4.

[8] R. F. Green, *Poets and Princepleasers: Literature and the English Court in the Late Middle Ages* (Toronto, 1980), 48.

[9] Roger Bowers, cited from his discussion of the Trinity College carol roll in *Cambridge Music Manuscripts, 900–1700*, ed. I. Fenlon (Cambridge, 1982), 88.

[10] M. T. Clanchy, *From Memory to Written Record: England, 1066–1307* (Cambridge, Mass., 1979), 7.

[11] R. Bowers, 'The Performing Ensemble for English Church Polyphony, c.1320–c.1390', in *Performance Practice: New York 1981*, 175.

[12] B. Trowell, 'A Fourteenth-Century Ceremonial Motet and its Composer', *AcM*, xxix (1957), 65–75.

BIBLIOGRAPHICAL NOTE

General
The first comprehensive account of the social and stylistic history of medieval music in England was provided by F. Ll. Harrison in his classic *Music in Medieval Britain* (London, 1958, 2/1963/*R*1980), whose narrative goes up to the reign of Henry VIII; a shorter, more recent survey of the same time-span that can be recommended is E. H. Sanders, 'England: from the Beginnings to *c*1540', in *Music from the Middle Ages to the Renaissance*, ed. F. W. Sternfeld (New York, 1973), 255–313.

Liturgical music
The sacred repertory of Anglo-Saxon England is reviewed in excellent monographs on Winchester by A. Holschneider, *Die Organa von Winchester* (Hildesheim, 1968), and A. Planchart, *The Repertory of Tropes at Winchester* (Princeton, 1977). For the thirteenth century, previous editions of the Worcester fragments and related music have now been entirely superseded by *English Music of the Thirteenth and Early Fourteenth Centuries*, ed. E. H. Sanders, PMFC, xiv (1979). For the English music in W_1, see especially M. Lütolf, *Die mehrstimmigen Ordinarium Missae-Sätze vom ausgehenden 11. bis zur Wende des 13. zum 14. Jahrhundert* (Berne, 1970), and D. Hiley, 'Further Observations on W_1: the Ordinary of Mass Chants and the Sequences', *JPMMS*, iv (1981), 67–80.

For the fourteenth century, there is still much of value in F. Ll. Harrison, 'English Church Music in the Fourteenth Century', *NOHM*, iii (1960), 82–106; a monograph by P. M. Lefferts, *The Motet in England in the Fourteenth Century* (Ann Arbor, 1986), discusses notation and other genres of polyphony in addition to the motet. The bulk of the surviving repertory has been recently edited, much of it for the first time, by F. Ll. Harrison in *Motets of English Provenance*, PMFC, xv (1980), and by F. Ll. Harrison, E. H. Sanders and P. M. Lefferts in *English Music for Mass and Offices*, PMFC, xvi–xvii (1983–6); these volumes have important introductions and bibliography.

For the fifteenth century, contextual and archival studies have been particularly enriched by R. Bowers, 'Some Observations on the Life and Career of Lionel Power', *PRMA*, cii (1975–6), 103–27, and A. Wathey, 'Dunstable in France', *ML*, lxvii (1986), 1–36. On repertorial and stylistic matters, the essay by M. Bukofzer, 'English Church Music of the Fifteenth Century', *NOHM*, iii (1960), 165–213, is still useful; and for the greatest figure of the first half of the century there is an exemplary monograph by M. Bent, *Dunstaple* (Oxford, 1981). Important editions of Mass Ordinary settings, motets and antiphons include *The Old Hall Manuscript*, ed. A. Hughes and M. Bent, CMM, xlvi (1969–73), *John Dunstable: Complete Works*, ed. M. Bukofzer, MB, viii (1953, rev. 2/1970 by M. Bent, I. Bent and B. Trowell), and *Four Anonymous Masses*, ed. M. Bent, EECM, xxii (1979). For settings of other liturgical genres for Mass and Office, one can turn to *The British Museum Manuscript Egerton 3307*, ed. G. McPeek (London,

1963), *The Music of the Pepys MS 1236*, ed. S. Charles, CMM, xl (1967), and *Fifteenth-Century Liturgical Music*, i, ed. A. Hughes, EECM, viii (1968).

Song

An excellent, wide-ranging study of monophonic song is J. Stevens's *Words and Music in the Middle Ages: Song, Narrative, Dance and Drama, 1050–1350* (Cambridge, 1986); in it, Stevens promises a forthcoming study devoted to songs of English provenance. N. Wilkins provides a context for fourteenth-century British song in 'Music and Poetry at Court: England and France in the Late Middle Ages', *English Court Culture in the Later Middle Ages*, ed. V. J. Scattergood and J. W. Sherbourne (New York, 1983), 183–204. For the fifteenth century, see M. Bukofzer, 'Popular and Secular Music in England (to *c*. 1470)', in *NOHM*, iii (1960), 107–33, and D. Fallows, 'English Song Repertories of the Mid-Fifteenth Century', *PRMA*, ciii (1976–7), 61–79. There is now a comprehensive edition of settings of English lyrics up to the early fifteenth century, by E. Dobson and F. Ll. Harrison, published as *Medieval English Songs* (London, 1979), which has an extensive and indispensable commentary. The texts of the English carols have been edited by R. L. Greene in *The Early English Carols* (Oxford, 1935, rev. 2/1977), and their extant music is available in two editions by J. Stevens: *Medieval Carols*, MB, iv (1952, rev. 2/1958) and *Early Tudor Songs and Carols*, MB, xxxvi (1975). The songs of perhaps the most important English chanson composer of the fifteenth century have been edited by A. W. Atlas in *Robert Morton: the Collected Works* (New York, 1981).

Chapter VIII

Court and City in France, 1100–1300

CHRISTOPHER PAGE

> He was a man of very high rank; a very gracious lord, he knew well
> how to compose songs, to play the fiddle and to sing. He was a fine
> knight in arms, a gracious speaker and a great success with women.

This is the troubadour Pons de Capdoil (*fl c*1200) as the scribes who
copied his songs imagined him several generations later.[1] They picture
him with all the qualities necessary for excellent behaviour at court,
and indeed their romantic vision of an aristocratic poet living in a castle,
gracious in demeanour and 'a great success with women', has lost none
of its allure in the six centuries which have elapsed since the last of the
troubadours, Guiraut Riquier de Narbona, faded into oblivion around
1300. In so far as any man of substance had a private life in the Middle
Ages, the castle keep was a private place, shielded from prying eyes by a
curtain wall. What could be more natural, therefore, than for the
aristocrat's residence to be called his court, literally his 'yard within an
enclosed space', and for the pleasant demeanour expected there to be
called courtliness?

It is customary to refer to the whole repertory of lyrics by the
troubadours and trouvères as a corpus of 'courtly' song, and yet this
term conceals a danger. It is part of the romance of courtliness that a
courtly society is readily imagined as one that is sophisticated because
it is enclosed and detached from urban values; the private and fortified
domain of a lord like Pons de Capdoil, in other words, seems to share
nothing with the modern concept of a city as an open, crowded and
democratically governed metropolis. And yet a glance at the medieval
vocabulary of courtliness shows how court and city were converging
during the twelfth and thirteenth centuries in both physical and psychic
terms. 'Courtoisie' was not the only word in use to describe what
Chaucer calls 'cheere of court'; there was also the Latin 'urbanitas', a
legacy from antiquity whose root meaning is 'the sophistication of mind
and manners bred by city life'. At first this confluence of words may
surprise us, but that is because the romance of courtliness is leading us
astray.

A court may have been 'an enclosed yard' in essence, but there was
often a thriving town on the other side of the walls. The period 1100–

197

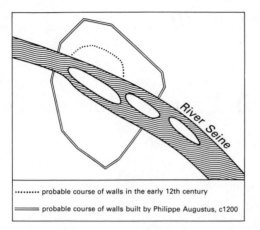

56. Map showing the expansion of Paris in the late twelfth century

········ probable course of walls in the early 12th century

═══ probable course of walls built by Philippe Augustus, c1200

1300 was a time of urban expansion in northern Europe – as a plan of thirteenth-century Paris readily shows (fig.56) – and it was increasingly the case during these centuries that a magnate's principal residences lay within the ramparts of some town or city within his patrimony. A castle of the troubadour Dalfi d'Alvernhe (*d* 1234), Count of Clermont and Montferrand, provides an illuminating example. It was not swathed in the silence and thyme of a rural domain, but rather sheltered by the walls of Montferrand. This *palaitz* survived long enough to be included in the fifteenth-century drawing of Montferrand by Guillaume Revel (fig.57, far left), and it was there that Dalfi held court during the principal feasts of the liturgical year. Dalfi was a cynosure of troubadours, and it would have been in the Great Hall of this castle that he entertained Peire d'Alverne, Gaucelm Faidit, Perdigo, Uc de Saint Circ, Peirol and many other troubadours with whom he is known to have had connections. Indeed, there are signs that many of the details recorded in the *vidas* (or 'lives') of the troubadours derive from stories told around Dalfi's marble couch by the fire in the Great Hall of Montferrand. Were the songs which the troubadours brought to this hall 'courtly' lyrics or 'urban' ones? Was the demeanour of the guests in Dalfi's castle *courtoisie* or *urbanitas*? In this context, at least, the meaning of such terms begins to dissolve.

We know so little about the social contexts of secular music during this period that it is unwise to draw a distinction between the supposedly sophisticated culture of courts on the one hand and what we may imagine to have been the coarser tastes of urban merchants and artisans on the other. Troubadour song is a case in point, for it is possible that the shoemakers, cutlers and notaries of Montferrand may sometimes have heard the songs of the troubadours who were entertained in Dalfi's castle. The diversified social background of the troubadours themselves suggests as much. Some were born into families of merchants and artisans. Peire Vidal, one of the most famous, was the son of a tanner in Toulouse, while Elias Cairel, who may have been a music scribe ('ben escrivia motz e sons', says the biographical note with his poems), was a goldsmith who became a minstrel.[2] These details, if accurate, suggest that we must keep many concepts fluid if we are to appreciate the full social context of this monophonic art – 'court' and 'city' being chief among them. As a worker in precious metals, Elias Cairel would presumably have been an urban tradesman with a tenement and a shop; as a minstrel and troubadour, however, he could seek entry into households of many kinds from the castles of great lords like Dalfi down to the domains of minor castellans who lorded over little more than a tower and a grange; as a music scribe (if this is the correct interpretation of the words in his 'biography'), Elias exploited a talent that is astonishing in a layman of *c*1210 whose primary skills lay with the hammer and pliers of his urban shop. Such troubadours as Elias and Peire Vidal, both lowly born, can only have learnt to compose by hearing the songs of established troubadours, and it may have been nothing unusual for a man of artisan or mercantile background in Occitania to develop such abilities. According to the Catalan poet Raimon Vidal (*fl c*1200), everyone wished to compose and to sing, even 'clerics, townsmen and peasants'. The travels of minstrels – many of

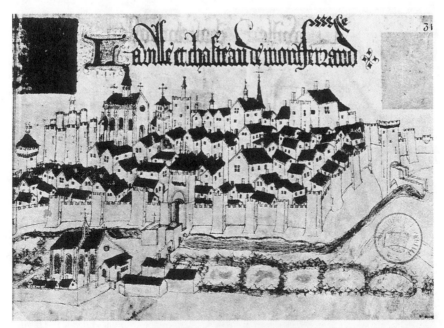

57. *The city of Montferrand: drawing from the Armorial of Guillaume Revel (mid-fifteenth century); the castle of Dalfi d'Alvernhe (built ?c1200) can be seen on the left. Even allowing for the expansion of the city between the thirteenth and the fifteenth centuries, the drawing may give a reliable impression of the essentially urban aspect of Dalfi's castle at the time of Raimon Vidal*

whom were troubadours themselves – may have done much to carry troubadour songs into the fine Romanesque houses that still survive in some southern towns (fig.58), and even perhaps into the taverns which some troubadours are said to have loved *oltra mesura*.

The circumstances which brought troubadour songs to the north, where the troubadours found able imitators in the trouvères, are unfortunately obscure, and it is unknown what literary appeal an Occitan lyric could have possessed for northern listeners when its text was garbled by a performer who could not understand the difference between 'lo cor de dezirier no.m fon', which is a line from one of the most famous songs by the troubadour Bernart de Ventadorn, and 'no coir dont desier non fon', which is how the line appears, reduced to rubble, in a romance of 1228 by a northern connoisseur of monophonic songs, Jean Renart. Despite the barrier of language, however, it is clear that a song possessed a certain mystique for northern listeners if it was associated in some way with the warmer and sunnier south. There were many varieties of Occitan lyrics circulating in *Fransa*, to judge by the writings of Old French poets who refer enthusiastically to 'sons limousins', 'sons gascons', 'sons poitevins' and 'sons auvrignaces', all terms that refer to regions south of the great linguistic divide between

58. *Romanesque house at Saint-Antonin (Haut-Languedoc), built c1155 for the Granolhets, a leading urban family in the area*

59. Map showing the principal varieties of the Langue d'Oc

France and Occitania (fig.59). No doubt itinerant minstrels did much to spread these southern songs; several narrative poems in French mention jongleurs who perform *sons poitevins* in the castles of northern barons – the epic of *Garin le Loheren*, for example, of *c*1200: 'It was a great feast that was made for Garin. Many a fine *son poitevin* was sung and played upon the fiddle'.

Personal contacts during the course of diplomatic business may also have inspired northern lords to imitate their southern counterparts. Several songs by the trouvère Conon de Béthune (*fl* 1180–1200) share their melodies with poems by the troubadour Bertran de Born (*d* 1204), Lord of Autafort; the two men may have met at a plenary court convened in 1182 by Henry II at Argentan in Normandy.[3] Contacts at this exalted level would explain the high rank of many of the early trouvères (such as Conon de Béthune himself, an important *seigneur*), and we should not imagine the spirit of such diplomatic meetings to have been inimical to poetry as contemporaries understood it; eloquence and wisdom (*biau parliers et sagesse*) were the virtues which delegates to plenary courts were expected to display, and these were exactly the qualities that were admired in the love-lyrics of the troubadours and trouvères.

During the decades after 1200 the trouvère community, dominated at first by men of high social standing, became as diversified as its southern counterpart had always been. Many of the trouvères who

60. Tristan teaches Iseut to play the harp: drawing after one of a series of English earthenware tiles (1250–70) depicting scenes from the Tristan story, probably designed for one of Henry III's principal residences.

flourished in the thirteenth century were urbanized clerics and townsmen. Arras was a literary centre of particular importance, and it is there that we find, for example, a prolific trouvère like Guillaume li Vinier, a cleric who was attached to the monastery of St Vaast (although he does not appear to have progressed beyond minor clerical orders). Such men as Guillaume attest to the widespread acceptance in urban society of the 'courtly' ideals which we met at the beginning of this chapter in the troubadour Pons de Capdoil.

The romances – tales of love and adventure which found willing readers throughout medieval society – exerted a powerful influence on musical interests. Time and time again these romances present themselves as a *vraye mirour* of chivalry and courtesy, and there is no doubt that these claims were often taken seriously by readers. The tremendous vogue for Arthurian romances with personable young heroes who sing well, and who sometimes play an instrument (fig.60), inspired many young men in the towns to prettify themselves to the extent of writing a little lyric poetry, composing music for it, and perhaps learning the harp or fiddle. Here, for example, is a thirteenth-century scholar named Henri de Malines, presenting an image of himself as a young man which has been 'romanticized' in more than one sense of the word:

> This servant of God knew how to rule himself when blowing wind into
> flutes and reed-pipes and instruments of that kind with varied artis-
> try. . . . Afterwards he entered the regions of philosophy and became

a pupil, cultivating his mind and disciplining his understanding; thus he did not wish to pursue wind instruments further, in line with what Aristotle reports in the *Politics*: Athene, having invented wind instruments, is said to have cast them away. This boy knew how to play a fiddle, bringing together, in harmonious fashion, a melodious touching of strings and drawing of the bow. . . . Further, he was familiar with (and willingly sang) all kinds of monophonic songs in diverse languages; he was a trouvère (*inventor*) of poems and melodies, and a merry and amorous leader of *caroles* and master of dances in wooded places.

Henri makes no mention of courts. He is referring to a period of his life passed in the town of Malines (now in Belgium) and in Paris as a young student; and yet the echoes of Pons de Capdoil are unmistakable.

Like Pons, Henri de Malines plays the fiddle. Bowed instruments existed in many shapes and forms during the twelfth and thirteenth centuries, but in all probability the *viella* of Henri de Malines was broadly similar to the *viola* of Pons de Capdoil: an oval-bodied instrument with the proportions of a modern violin or viola, played upon the shoulder and, in its classic form, possessing five strings of gut or occasionally, it would seem, of horsehair (fig.61).[4] The prevailing ethos of this instrument as the troubadours knew it in the twelfth century is captured in Gervase of Tilbury's account, based on an eye-witness report, of the Catalan troubadour Guiraut de Cabreira performing in the hall of a palace at Arles. 'Guiraut was of very high birth, dashing in warfare and gracious in manners', says Gervase, 'and furthermore he was in the flush of youth, charming, lively, highly skilled on musical instruments and madly desired by the ladies . . . in the sight of many princes this knight used to play the *viola*'. Much of this is present in Henri de Malines's romanticized evocation of his youthful self, and yet Henri de Malines goes further for he presents the fiddle as something that he learnt when his advanced education began and he 'entered the regions of philosophy'.

This is one of many pieces of evidence to show that among the urbanized clergy of the thirteenth century the fiddle had become swathed in a savant ethos which owed much to Aristotle (whom Henri cites). In texts such as the *Politics* and *Ethics*, for example, both of which became available in full to the Latins in the thirteenth century, Aristotle often speaks in passing of the classic instrument of the Greeks, the kithara, and for him this lyre is a worthy diversion for men who seek reasonable amusement as a rest from study or from the toils of government. Thinking of this sort was utterly different from anything in the writings of the Church Fathers, which had formed the foundation of monastic spirituality for almost a millennium. In the tradition of Gregory or St Jerome, for example, instruments were more likely to be regarded as 'the devil's heap of rubbish' than as a legitimate consolation to men in a fallen world. The philosophers and theologians in the urban schools knew this tradition well enough, but it was not their notion of perfection to rinse the mind, day after day, in the dye of the Fathers; they enjoyed an intellectual freedom which the monk, as a contemplative, did not seek, and many of these schoolmen transferred Aristotle's thinking about the kithara to the fiddle, an instrument which possessed dignified associations already.

As a result the fiddle emerged as the classic instrument of urbanized clerical culture in northern France during the later thirteenth century, and it is no surprise to find that two of our principal sources of information about the instrument derive from the largest of all medieval urban communities, the city of Paris. According to Johannes de Grocheo, probably a Master of Arts in the university, the fiddle was capable of playing every kind of music and was the instrument which reigned supreme above all others. Another Parisian writer, the Dominican Jerome of Moravia, gives three tunings that were used on the five-string fiddle. From these it is clear that the fiddle was often tuned to a concordant mixture of fourths, fifths and octaves in such a way that, when the player drew the bow over all the strings at once, a chord without a third resulted. This was done to make the fiddle a self-accompanying instrument; a common technique was therefore to bow a number of strings at once, fingering the melody in the 'home key' of the instrument and allowing adjacent strings to produce a drone.[5]

To some extent the passage of musical forms and styles between court and city was facilitated by the nebulous character of courts. Historians of medieval music are prone to speak of 'courts' as if they were places: temples of luxury and sophistication. For most of the year, however, a magnate's court existed as a column of carts carrying baggage, chancery records and chapel accessories, all supervised by a shifting personnel of knights, notaries and chaplains. Their task was to defend the lord, to record his business and to pray for him as he travelled through his domain, settling disputes and showing himself to his dependants. This court might take up residence anywhere when it paused for the night, although for major feasts of the liturgical year the magnate would hold a 'full court' in one of his great residences, as Dalfi d'Alvernhe did at Montferrand.

It is doubtful whether a household would have required much secular music as it travelled on its business. The only music consistently required was plainchant for the mobile chapel, but even that could be waived in favour of a spoken service if the progress had been undertaken with only a skeleton staff of chaplains. Some minstrels might be employed throughout the course of a journey, but their responsibilities appear to have been wide and by no means confined to music. String musicians, for example, were expected not only to play but also to carry letters, to run errands, to tell stories and to provide diverting conversation whenever it was required. The most specialized minstrels (that is to say the ones most obviously and consistently employed as musicians) were those whose purely musical importance was very low, namely the trumpeters who were required to play fanfares and signals. No doubt itinerant minstrels sometimes fell in with a lord's column in the hope of being admitted to his tent, and court rolls often include payments to performers who are clearly local to the town or region where a household had pitched its pavilions for the night. Their tasks might include singing or playing while members of the household were bled, or while they made offerings at shrines encountered on the way. On some occasions local minstrels might be commanded to perform the topical songs and ballads of the region so that a lord or king could sense the popular feelings of an area within his patrimony.

When the court came to a loyal town or city, however, the scene changed dramatically. Old French epics and romances show that a retinue could experience a rush of entertainment when gates and ramparts came into view. Raoul de Houdenc's romance of *Meraugis de Portlesguez* (*c*1200–1220) provides an example:

> They see the citizens issuing from the gate of the city that was securely surrounded by walls. They cover the land. There was not one lady that did not come, and they all went forward singing. The girls, of whom there were so many there, come forth singing and making *caroles* so large that you never saw the like at the May celebrations; before them come the agile knights on their swift and powerful horses.

It is impossible to miss the importance of dances, or *caroles*, in this celebration, and the way that Raoul de Houdenc compares them to the *caroles* of the May festivities, the *maieroles*. Danced in a ring, a chain or a procession (fig.61), company dances like these were a powerful force in the development of a common musical culture uniting court and city. During the period 1100–1300 more and more men of substance built town-houses and urban castles for themselves, and since all medieval life, in the towns as in the countryside, was structured around the great festivals of the church's year, a festive calendar developed which bound the greatest aristocratic courts, the town-houses of nobles, and the city squares and streets together.[6]

The principal musical entertainment in this festive culture, the *carole*, was danced to songs which the carollers usually provided for themselves. Sometimes, the dance was led by an instrumentalist (fig.61). Medieval romances, which offer so many suggestive portrayals of aristocratic musical life, show that *caroles* were a prominent feature of the full courts convened for Christmas, Pentecost and other great feasts of the liturgical year. For many of the families who attended these courts, however, the *caroles* which they enjoyed in the Great Hall of their host were only a more luxurious version of an entertainment which they

61. Carole accompanied by a fiddle: detail of a miniature from a French bible (?Paris, c1250). The illustration depicts the episode in Judges xxi:19–25 in which the sons of Benjamin steal wives for themselves

could also enjoy in the towns and cities. In any urban community of the Middle Ages there were local saints to celebrate, marriages to rejoice over, spring games to be played (the *maieroles*), harvest suppers to be eaten and so on through a calendar of seasonal pleasures. These occasions were often enlivened by carolling, as sermons, manuals of confession and many other kinds of writings reveal. Indeed, these dances became a characteristic feature of urban life during the twelfth and thirteenth centuries. A story recorded in the *Summa predicantium* by the early fourteenth-century cleric John Bromyard shows this clearly. Some churchmen approach a city and see a solitary devil sitting on the ramparts; 'I sit alone because I do not need any help', says the demon insolently in response to their questions, 'for all the city is obedient to my master'. Upon entering the city gates the clerics discover, to their horror, that the citizens are all dancing *caroles*.

This association between carolling and urban life was a direct consequence of the expansion of city walls. Before our period the boundaries of most walled cities and towns were set by ramparts built for protection against Norman marauders in the later ninth century. At that time, when the suburban land was kept shorn for reasons of defence, the cities rose like battleships in the sea, high-sided, dull-coloured and aggressive above the surrounding flatness, and with all the living quarters hidden from view. These cities were quite small, and by the twelfth century their suburban lands were crowded with hospitals, cemetery churches and dwellings, all unprotected. The years between 1100 and 1300, however, saw many towns and cities equipped with new, larger ramparts that engulfed some of the cemetery churches that had originally lain outside the walls (in accordance with both pagan and Gallo-Roman custom) like 'great dormitory suburbs of the dead' (fig.56 above).[7] The result was a large urban space within the physical and symbolic presence of new walls, containing many open spaces such as cemeteries, allotments, orchards and even empty land left clear to accommodate future expansion. The cemeteries around the churches were a favourite with carollers, and sermons of the thirteenth century contain many harangues directed against dancers who choose 'sacred places' for their sport or who congregate 'among the bodies of the dead'. To some extent, perhaps, this unlikely choice of setting for a convivial company dance may be explained by reference to the *caroles* that were performed to honour local saints, the dancers converging on a church dedicated to the saint in question and dancing in the only area of the ecclesiastical property where they could do so without gross irreverence.

As a company dance closely involved with the festive calendar, the *caroles* could be almost as socially diversified as the city itself. A Parisian sermon by the Dominican Humbert of Romans (*d* 1277) reveals that the young women who went carolling could include *ancillae*, or 'serving-women', a term that may include the girls who acted as handmaidens to the wives of wealthy burgesses. Other young women in Humbert's *carole* are more genteel and include girls living in private houses and taking lessons to learn their letters, the Psalter, the Hours of the Virgin and the Office of the Dead. Other carollers noticed by Humbert are higher still, for Humbert calls them 'the daughters of the rich' – the daughters of burgesses, no doubt, and young women belonging to noble families with town-houses. These were the *puceles* who might accompany their fathers to a noble (or even perhaps a royal) full court; they are the *puceles*, *meschines* and *damoiseles*, in other words, who so often appear in descriptions of great court festivities, singing and dancing *caroles*. There is little in either the poetical or the literary remains of *caroles* to suggest that the songs which they danced to at court would have been very different in either poetic form or musical style from the ones that they enjoyed in the city squares when their parents were in residence. Indeed, it may be that they often preferred the freer atmosphere of the city *caroles*. The English friar Thomas Waleys had seen these well-bred young women as they danced in the towns, and in an audacious passage in his manual for preachers he compares them to 'noble dogs':

> As a dog sits quietly by his aristocratic master, but fights with his fellows in town when he gets a chance, so the demure daughters who sit and say their Hours by the firescreen love to run free and dance *caroles* in the town when they can.

The *carole* was one of the most ancient enemies of the church. Another was the minstrel. His name, be it 'histrio', 'joculator', 'scurra', 'mimus' or whatever, was abhorrent to many churchmen; in their eyes he was a rodent who bore the twin plagues of lechery and sloth upon his back. The power and grandeur of this clerical tradition can leave us with a very distorted picture, however, both of the minstrels and of the attitudes which reasonable people took towards their craft.

The 'lives' of the troubadours, the *vidas*, are a better source of information. We have already seen that the *vidas* contain some illuminating biographies; they also reveal some striking patterns.[8] The social backgrounds of seventeen minstrels are given in the *vidas*. Five are clerics of some kind, while three are the sons of townsmen. Two are from merchant families, two are the sons of poor knights, two were formerly poor knights themselves and two were formerly craftsmen. It is noteworthy that this list includes a number of different social categories – indeed, all the categories which medieval authorities themselves were accustomed to distinguish when, following a favourite scheme, they divided society into those whose task it was to work, to fight or to pray. What is more striking than the social diversity of these minstrels, however, is the way that the *vidas* illustrate the operation within the minstrel community of social forces that worked within medieval society as a whole.

Consider the 'poor knights'. The cost of maintaining a knight's equipment with a horse, harness and armour could cripple knightly families experiencing a crisis in their revenues; alternatively, the cost of equipping and training a first-born son in knighthood could be prohibitive. What were the impoverished knights or their sons to do? To judge by the *vidas*, they sometimes turned to minstrelsy.

The biographies of the cleric-minstrels display another force for social mobility in the Middle Ages: the conflict of conscience and desire. In the monasteries desertion was a constant problem; a monk's faith might fade, or the 'boredom of the cloister', the *tedium claustri*, might crush him. Worst of all, he might see a woman, fall in love with her, and thereafter find himself unable to keep his vow of chastity. Sexual problems of this kind were constantly presenting themselves, and as a result men of monastic education, able to read and write, found themselves once more among the laity and looking for ways to exploit their skills for a living. Something of this kind seems to have happened in the case of the troubadour Gausbert de Poicibot. The son of a noble castellan, Gausbert was presented as an oblate to the monastery of Saint-Léonard-des-Chaumes near La Rochelle, no doubt because he was a second or third son (the first-born was usually put into training for knighthood). Gausbert left his monastery, however, 'because of his desire for a woman' (*voluntat de femna*). What was a man in this position to do? Gausbert decided to turn to minstrelsy. Wisely, he made his way

62. *Map showing a minstrel's itinerary, Christmas to spring, c1200 (names given in Old Occitan)*

FRANSA

Atlantic Ocean

ALVERNHE

• Riom
• Montferrand

• Lo Puoi

PROVENSA

GASCONHA • Toloza
• Cabardés
Castillon • Foix

NAVARRA

• Besalú

CATALUNYA

to the household of the magnate Savaric de Mauléon, a troubadour and a long-standing benefactor of the monastery of Saint-Léonard-des-Chaumes. Savaric must have sympathized with the former monk's predicament (what troubadour would not?) and he gave Gausbert 'a minstrel's equipment, clothes and a horse'. With these resources Gausbert travelled 'from court to court', composing and performing songs. Eventually Savaric de Mauléon knighted him and gave him lands, thus restoring the inheritance that was denied to so many second sons put into the church at an early age, their lives ever after turbulent and dissatisfied.

Other *vidas* reveal more ways in which the minstrel community could be enriched by the talents of men from a variety of social backgrounds. One began life as a cleric, became a minstrel, and then retired to a monastery. Another was sent to the schools at Montpellier by his brothers but abandoned his studies for the life of a *joglar*. Another 'could not live by his letters' (which probably means that he failed to find a post as a notary, a private chaplain or something similar) and so he became a minstrel. Clearly the lives of these men were ruled by a complex interplay of influences that we are habitually inclined to separate when we write the history of medieval music: court and city, monasticism and knighthood, literacy and illiteracy.

Most minstrels of the Middle Ages were itinerant for much of the year. The needs of households on the move were too lean and unpredictable for consistent employment to be offered. The phrase which the *vidas* regularly use for the minstrels' travels is 'he went round the courts'

*63. The castle at Lastours
(Aude)*

(*anava per cortz*). What does this vague expression imply in terms of real journeys, times and places? With the help of a Catalan poem composed around 1200 it is possible to frame an answer to this question.

Raimon Vidal's *Abril issia* ('April was leaving') describes a journey undertaken by a fictional *joglar* between Christmas and spring, narrated by the minstrel himself (see fig.62).[9] The progress begins in the Auvergne one Saturday morning. It is the Christmas season, and the minstrel has been in Riom, perhaps in the castle which belonged to Dalfi d'Alvernhe. Leaving Riom by the main north–south route through the province, he joins Dalfi's retinue as it travels towards Montferrand for Christmas. Few sights can have been more welcome to a travelling minstrel than a magnate's entourage en route to a castle for some great holiday of the liturgical year, and for any minstrel wandering through the Auvergne during the Calends there could be no better meeting than with Dalfi.

When they arrive at Montferrand, the minstrel is admitted to Dalfi's *palaitz* in the town (fig.57), a massive, quadrangular keep, equipped with corner-towers and placed within a curtain wall that is also reinforced with towers. At the end of the sixteenth century, when the keep was already in a poor state, there were four great, square rooms in it, one above the other, and each wall measured approximately twenty metres in length. Raimon Vidal's minstrel would have been led up a flight of external stairs to the second of these floors (the first, windowless, was normally used for the storage of provisions and weapons). According to the minstrel's own account, he found there Dalfi and his followers relaxing with minstrels:

> We came to and were at Montferrand, with no trouble, up in the Great Hall. And if you ever saw well-bred and joyful men, that were we there. And the night, as I saw, was very dark after dinner and next to the bright fire the company was large, knights and jongleurs, clever and accomplished and amiable and agreeable to courteous men. . . . And the knights, without any reminder, went to bed when they were ready, for my lord [Dalfi] wanted to remain with a companion near the fire.

In the opening section of *Abril issia* the minstrel proclaims that he knows verses and songs by many troubadours; this is his own proud description of the social context in which he might be expected to perform them. The scene is foreign to anything in modern experience. It is midwinter, the season of frost and rain, *gel et plotge*, as the troubadours say, and the Great Hall is lit by a bright fire. Every bowl of fruit and every garment would have been saturated with the aroma of wood-smoke; to move from one place to another near the fire would have been to plunge away from raw heat on the face into darkness and draught. The Count, Dalfi, reclines by the fire upon a bench of marble covered with samite; around him are *cavayers* in whom we easily recognize the knights of the *estage*: the men required to serve their lord in his affairs and to keep him company for a fixed period of the year.

The next day the minstrel leaves Montferrand, having received the customary largesse. 'It was a Thursday; I took my leave in the sight of everybody, and if ever you saw a man well taken of, and by a lord at that, I was he'. Going south-east, he passes through Le Puy and continues into Provence 'where I found many joyous barons and the good count and the countess', that is to say Raymond Berenguer V and Beatrice of Savoy. Next he turns westwards for a leg of the journey that even he, an experienced traveller, is forced to describe as 'very great', making his way to the lands of the Count of Toulouse. He finds the count 'and many gracious knights who are with him'. There he is given a suit of clothes. Leaving the Count of Toulouse, he travels south-east to the region of Cabardès, perhaps to the castles which still command the heights above the village of Lastours, due north of Carcassonne (fig.63). There he would have found Pierre-Roger, Jourdain de Cabaret and other vassals of the Count of Béziers.

The next stage of the journey reveals the precariousness of the minstrel life in an age when great lords were constantly travelling to consume produce, administer justice and negotiate with neighbouring *seigneurs*. If a minstrel wished to avoid the calamity of arriving at a magnate's castle and finding only lounging porters then he needed to know a lord's movements in advance. How was he to find out? Would minstrels, giving news in the wayside taverns of what they had learnt on the roads, help him? Would the lord's marshal at the castle gate give him the details of any forthcoming progress? We do not know; what is clear from *Abril issia*, however, is that a minstrel's source of information could sometimes run dry, for at Foix Raimon Vidal's *joglar* finds that the count has left his residence there and gone to Alberu. After this disappointment he pushes on to the west in the direction of Castillon, and finally, 'last Monday', he crosses the Pyrenees into Catalonia. At the court of Mataplana he is received by the troubadour Uc de Mataplana and finds in him a lord who is 'gracious, frank, gentle, and a ready critic to listen to all good knowledge'. At last he turns his footsteps towards Besalú in Catalonia. The entire progress has taken four months.

At almost every stage this would have been a journey taking in courts and cities in equal measure. At Riom, Le Puy and Montferrand, the *joglar* would have found urban centres with thriving markets, while at Toulouse (if this is where he met the count) he would have found himself in one of the most prosperous cities of the Midi. Even at Foix, where the fortified comital residence stands aloof on a rock, any minstrel might console himself for the disappointment of missing the count by leaving the empty *castrum* to seek business in the *bourg* below.

In the dawn of the thirteenth century most of this journey could have been undertaken on important roads, allowing a minstrel to benefit from the hostels which sprang up all over France in the twelfth century to cater for the merchants, couriers, pilgrims and knightly retinues that travelled the roads in ever greater numbers. Trees falling in the woodland to make highways, new cisterns for horses by the road-side – these were the things that meant easier travel and richer pickings for the mounted minstrels who could exploit such advantages. As the roads improved, so the distances between the major urban centres shrank; there was more chance of getting to Montferrand by the Calends, or of stabling in a town just before the feast of a favourite saint when the citizens would be in holiday mood. The gap which had always existed between the relatively poor jongleurs who worked a cluster of villages on foot, for example, and the wealthier minstrels with a mount, widened; the mounted jongleurs could ride between cities and win both the lavish presents and the ready coin which allowed them to subsist without losing time and dignity by singing in the streets.

The interest of Raimon Vidal's *Abril issia* does not end with its description of a minstrel's itinerary, however, for the poem also offers an insight into the nature of minstrel experience at court. The social aspects of court experience in all times and places have been intensively studied by historians. Here, for example, is Norbert Elias on the delicate and circumspect art of courtly conversation in seventeenth-century Versailles:[10]

> it is those of relatively low rank who become masters of the tactics of conversation . . . he is the one most at risk in such a conversation. The prince can always break the rules . . . he can, if he likes, break off the discussion and the relationship for any reason he chooses without losing much.

In many social contexts during the twelfth and thirteenth centuries a minstrel, being a paid entertainer, was the lowest in rank when he entered a room. 'If you were the son of an emperor', says the narrator to the minstrel in *Abril issia*, 'you would still be no more than a jongleur as long as you enjoyed travelling back and forth.' A castellan could send a minstrel packing at no cost to himself. The *joglar*, therefore, needed to be what Norbert Elias calls 'a master of the tactics of conversation'. How should he conduct himself in this hazardous environment?

Raimon Vidal's poem reveals that the first requirement was eloquence. Above all a *joglar* had to be a fluent speaker. Yet a mere facility with words was only the beginning; to make his conversation truly beguiling the minstrel needed wisdom (*saber*). On one level this wisdom is the tact which makes a man able to secure his own advantage. Thus Raimon Vidal advises that a minstrel, with an eye to his eventual reward, should not praise himself nor overpraise others, nor must he preach to knights about knighthood; he must also make a point of appealing to the younger members in the company, 'for the heart leads young men to be generous', and at all times he should preserve a delicate balance between wit and raillery in his conversation. He must maintain a measure of professional decorum, never speaking ill of a troubadour's work nor disparaging another jongleur.

Many of the narrator's counsels in *Abril issia* touch upon matters of courtly tact. Here it becomes plain that a minstrel was much more than a professional musician who arrived, performed and left as his modern counterpart is accustomed to do. He was required to converse, to tell stories and to judge when it was time for his fluent tongue to stop. This required him to be a skilled judge of the feelings which people concealed behind their expressions. The *joglar* also needed the ability to gain a swift impression of who mattered in a gathering and who did not; to be seen lingering with those whose stock was falling could damage his prospect of reward.

How was a minstrel to deport himself when he had troubadour songs to perform? Here the narrator in *Abril issia*, apparently a minstrel himself, gives detailed advice to the minstrel who has come to consult him. In his view the art of performing troubadour songs is not so much a matter of musical expertise as a question of tact in dealing with court experience. The minstrel's strategy must be to move from silence to complete control of the conversation. At first he must say nothing; then, little by little, he must work his way into the conversation by exploiting his *saber*. In the first instance this was his wit and his ability to turn his travel experiences to good account. By these means a *joglar* who was truly beguiling could 'increase the wisdom and learning' of select people, according to Raimon Vidal. Next, the minstrel must discern when the company has lost its independent momentum and has come under his sway; then he should tell stories in rhyme (*novas*). Finally, if he senses that his listeners are ready for *chantars*, he should offer them troubadour songs.

In the twelfth and thirteenth centuries many churchmen were exposed to the moral and social complexities of life in the expanding towns and cities. They included mendicant friars, theologians in the urban schools and secular canons. It fell to these urbanized clerics to devise a Christian interpretation of city life with the essentially pastoral and contemplative materials bequeathed by monasticism.[11]

Broadly speaking, these churchmen began to accept the existence of at least certain kinds of minstrels. For one thing, some minstrels were becoming respectable citizens. The urban merchants with money to spare could turn a wedding, a homecoming, a harvest dinner or a local saint's day into a festival where minstrels could find a ready welcome and good business. Some of them prospered, and in thirteenth-century writings we begin to hear more of the apprentices or attendants who carried a minstrel's instruments, for example, and stabled his horse; there are also references to the town-houses which some minstrels possessed. In cities like Arras, where the tradition of minstrelsy was strong, there existed a sense of communal welfare that could be guarded by communal piety – a sense that was so powerful in the cities of the later Middle Ages – and this drew the more prosperous minstrels together with local merchants and townsmen – to judge by the Confrérie des Jongleurs et des Bourgeois d'Arras, whose origins may perhaps lie as early as the first decades of the twelfth century.

If some minstrels prospered, however, many did not. At its lowest, minstrelsy was the refuge of the poor who knew no other way of putting food in their bellies. The great cities inevitably attracted them in huge numbers. In Paris during the reign of St Louis, for example, the number of poor minstrels is reputed to have been vast. In the public pulpit, as in the private confessional, many priests began to advise their flock that it was legitimate to take pity on a destitute minstrel, especially if he had a family to support.

We should not underestimate the currency of minstrel skills among both the urban and the rural poor of the twelfth and thirteenth centuries. For the pauper, every minstrel who passed by, filling his purse with coins before he moved on, was an object lesson in self-help. A story in a thirteenth-century sermon tells how a simpleton 'in a certain French village' became envious of a minstrel who earned much money by singing; the simpleton asked the minstrel if he could buy some songs for himself. The musician promised to sell him a sack full and the next day he duly appeared in the village square, where all the rustics of the place were accustomed to gather, with a sack full of wasps whose humming was taken by the simpleton as a sure sign that the bag was indeed full of songs. Another revealing story in the same source tells of a pauper who lived under the stairs of a house belonging to an avaricious burgess in Montpellier. 'The pauper had a fiddle', the story relates, 'and when he was tired of his work, he played it and sang songs therewith in a spirited fashion. When he had five or six denarii he purchased meat, made some sauces, and had a wonderful time in this manner'. Clearly, it was not unknown for a pauper to keep the wolf from the door, or to provide himself with a few modest luxuries, by becoming a minstrel for a day.

NOTES

[1] This account is from the *vidas* or 'lives' of the troubadours. The original texts of the *vidas* are printed in J. Boutière and A. H. Schutz, *Biographies des troubadours* (Paris, 2/1973). There are English translations in M. Egan, *The Vidas of the Troubadours* (New York and London, 1984). For the poems of Pons de Capdoil which survive with their music see the editions by I. F. de la Cuesta, *Las cançons dels trobadors* (Toulouse, 1979), 552f, and H. van der Werf, *The Extant Troubadour Melodies* (Rochester, NY, 1984), 282f.

[2] Boutière and Schutz, *Biographies*, 351ff and 252–4.

[3] For full details see W. D. Paden jr, T. Sankovitch and P. H. Stäblein, *The Poems of the Troubadour Bertran de Born* (Berkeley, Los Angeles and London, 1986), 47–8, 52–4 and 97.

[4] On the medieval fiddle see W. Bachmann, *The Origins of Bowing* (Oxford, 1969), and C. Page, *Voices and Instruments of the Middle Ages: Instrumental Practice and Songs in France 1100–1300* (London, 1987), *passim*, but especially 55f and 126ff.

[5] Bachmann, *Origins of Bowing*, 93f, and Page, *Voices and Instruments*, 126ff.

[6] On the *carole* see Page, *Voices and Instruments*, chap.6, and *The Owl and the Nightingale: Musical Life and Ideas in France 1100–1300* (London, 1989), chap.5.

[7] P. Brown, *Society and the Holy in Late Antiquity* (London, 1982), 223.

[8] For the original texts on which the following paragraphs are based see Boutière and Schutz, *Biographies*, and for translations Egan, *The Vidas of the Troubadours*.

[9] Raimon Vidal's text is edited, with translation, in W. H. W. Field, *Raimon Vidal: Poetry and Prose*, ii: *Abril Issia* (Chapel Hill, 1971).

[10] N. Elias, *The Court Society* (Oxford, 1983), 108.

[11] This subject is discussed in Page, *The Owl and the Nightingale*, *passim*.

BIBLIOGRAPHICAL NOTE

The renaissance of the twelfth and thirteenth centuries

There are comprehensive and well-documented essays on many important topics in *Renaissance and Renewal in the Twelfth Century*, ed. R. L. Benson and G. Constable (Oxford, 1982). R. W. Southern's *Medieval Humanism* (Oxford, 1970) is an eloquent account of spiritual and intellectual changes, and C. Brooke's study *The Twelfth-Century Renaissance* (London, 1969) is a masterly piece of popularization. The philosophical and intellectual interests of the period are discussed in M. Haren, *Medieval Thought: the Western Intellectual Tradition from Antiquity to the Thirteenth Century* (London, 1985), and *A History of Twelfth Century Western Philosophy*, ed. P. Dronke (Cambridge, 1988). Amid so much change it is well to be reminded of the monastic traditions of the period; J. Leclercq's *The Love of Learning and the Desire for God* (New York, 3/1982) is sublime. R. I. Moore's *The Formation of a Persecuting Society* (Oxford, 1987) is an illuminating account of the 'dark underside' of the twelfth-century renaissance.

Urbanization and mentalities

The outstanding general account of urbanization in France during the period 1100–1300 is now A. Chédeville and others, *La ville médiévale*, Histoire de la France urbaine, ii (Paris, 1980). See also F. L. Ganshof, *Etude sur le développement des villes outre Loire et Rhin au moyen âge* (Paris and Brussels, 1943). There are illuminating discussions of the social and mental consequences of this urban expansion in J. Le Goff, *Time, Work and Culture in the Middle Ages* (Chicago and London, 1980); A. Murray, *Reason and Society in the Middle Ages* (Oxford, 1978); L. K. Little, *Religious Poverty and the Profit Economy in Medieval Europe* (London, 1978); and J. Baldwin, *Masters, Princes and Merchants: the Social Views of Peter the Chanter and his Circle* (Princeton, 1970).

Courts and courtliness

J. Dunbabin, *France in the Making 843–1180* (Oxford, 1985), and E. M. Hallam, *Capetian France 987–1328* (London, 1980), provide excellent guides to the political and administrative background to court life in northern France. G. Duby's *William Marshall* (London, 1986) provides a vivid complement to these studies with its many insights into the social and mental world of the English and northern French aristocracy *c*1200. The phenomena of courtesy and 'courtly love' (which are to be distinguished), so often celebrated in the lyrics of both the troubadours and the trouvères, have been much discussed; see C. S. Jaeger's *The Origins of Courtliness: Civilizing Trends and the Formation of Courtly Ideals 939–1210* (Philadelphia, 1985) and for a review of earlier literature (much of it concerned with the origin of 'courtly love' – a tedious term that has now outlived its usefulness) see R. Boase's *The Origin and Meaning of Courtly Love* (Manchester, 1977). For the place of music in the medieval French literature of courtliness see D. Kelly, *Medieval Imagination* (Wisconsin, 1978), and C. Page, *Voices and Instruments of the Middle Ages: Instrumental Practice and Songs in France 1100 – 1300* (London, 1987).

The troubadours and trouvères

The corpus of troubadour poems surviving with music has been edited twice in recent years: by I. F. de la Cuesta, *Las cançons dels trobadors* (Toulouse, 1979), and H. van der Werf, *The Extant Troubadour Melodies* (Rochester, NY, 1984). Both editions abandon the 'modal' theory of rhythmic transcription and present the melodies in stemless noteheads. The former edition has an advantage in that it is complete (i.e. it includes the lais and the *dansa*/virelai pieces) and it reproduces the note forms of the original notations above the staff. It contains errors, however, and normalizes the texts in a way that makes them almost useless to the modern scholar or performer. In this respect the edition of van der Werf is more helpful, and it also contains several important essays presented as prolegomena to the edition. The *vidas* or 'lives' of the troubadours are translated in M. Egan, *The Vidas of the Troubadours* (New York and London, 1984). Since the trouvère repertory is much larger than the troubadour corpus there is no comprehensive edition. The best introduction is through the texts and melodies of the important trouvères Gace Brulé and Adam de la Halle since their works are now available, with melodies, texts and facing translations, in S. N. Rosenberg, S. Danon and H. van der Werf, *The Lyrics and Melodies of Gace Brulé* (New York and London, 1985), and D. H. Nelson and H. van der Werf, *The Lyrics and Melodies of Adam de la Halle* (New York and London, 1985).

On poetry and music in twelfth- and thirteenth-century France the outstanding study is now J. Stevens's *Words and Music in the Middle Ages: Song, Narrative, Dance and Drama, 1050–1350* (Cambridge, 1986). See also H. van der Werf, *The Chansons of the Troubadours and Trouvères* (Utrecht, 1972), and M. L. Switten, *The Cansos of Raimon de Miraval* (Cambridge, Mass., 1985). There is no social history of music in twelfth- and thirteenth-century France, although an attempt has recently been made to provide one: C. Page, *The Owl and the Nightingale: Musical Life and Ideas in France 1100–1300* (London, 1989).

Chapter IX

Ars Antiqua – Ars Nova – Ars Subtilior

DANIEL LEECH-WILKINSON

From the viewpoint of the modern writer the second half of the thirteenth century seems to have been one of the last periods of music history in which old and new existed comfortably together. In a clear reflection of the brief equilibrium of peace and prosperity achieved in contemporary society, we see in music a unique balance between the cultivation of the old Notre Dame styles and the developing tradition of the motet. Perhaps the best evidence for this is the apparently tireless enthusiasm of the anthologists. The later thirteenth century saw the compilation of huge collections of Notre Dame music – collections on which our knowledge of that repertory is very largely based – at much the same time as the copying of a series of magnificent manuscripts devoted to more recent developments in the motet. The extent of this activity is a witness both to pride in the past and to satisfaction with the present, a combination of which there was to be little sign in the century that followed.

At the same time, the abundance of surviving material, and the fact that progressive compositional activity seems to have been restricted largely to one form (the motet), can be misleading. Leafing through the massive collections which have come down to us it is easy to overlook their variety; what we see, page after page, is not so much a reflection of obsessive hidebound uniformity as of subtle diversity and apparently unstoppable creativity.

Of the many developments traceable through this mass of material, the most immediately obvious is a trend away from the Notre Dame repertory. Musical sources from the later thirteenth century contain fewer and fewer reworkings of Notre Dame clausulas, and an ever-increasing number of newly composed works. And, in contrast to the Notre Dame motets, new pieces tend not to be reworked by later composers. It is as if the concept of a musical work as fixed, having an integrity of its own as its composer left it, is finally becoming widespread.

It is clear, also, that for the composers of the earliest motets one of the most stimulating features of the new form was its openness to the addition of new voices with new texts. One of the first manuscripts devoted to motets ('La Clayette'), its repertory dating from before 1250, already contains works in four parts in which the upper voices have three different texts, in two languages (Latin and French). But this trend towards textural and linguistic complexity seems to have reached its zenith here. There is barely space within the vocal compass of an adult male ensemble for even four separate parts if dissonances are to be kept within conventional limits; and from the mid-century onwards composers seem to have been content to settle for a norm of three voices – a plainchant-derived tenor supporting a newly composed motetus and triplum, each with its own text and in a single language (usually French). From a musical point of view three voices represented the most satisfactory compromise between the desire for harmonic and contrapuntal elaboration, on the one hand, and the need for control of dissonance and clarity of texture, on the other.

More surprising for the modern listener is the consensus in favour of two simultaneously sounding upper-voice texts. To our ears the result is often unintelligible; and while it is tempting to assume that comprehension was not an ideal for the medieval composer, it seems probable, in view of the motet's status as the most complex of thirteenth- and fourteenth-century musical forms, that striving to follow both texts simultaneously – like following the repetitions of rhythms and phrase-patterns – was part of the intellectual challenge offered by the motet.

That the later thirteenth-century motet was aimed at connoisseurs is made abundantly clear by the well-known remarks of Johannes de Grocheo and Jacques de Liège:

> This kind of song ought not to be propagated among the vulgar, since they do not understand its subtlety nor do they delight in hearing it, but it should be performed for the learned and those who seek after the subtleties of the arts.[1]

> In a certain company in which some able singers and judicious laymen were assembled, and where modern motets in the modern manner and some old ones were sung, I observed that even the laymen were better pleased with the ancient motets and the ancient manner than with the new.[2]

In this sort of learned context it is not so hard to accept double-texting and repeating form-schemes as engaging challenges for the expert listener, despite Jacques's attempt to use double-texting – a prominent feature of the older motets he preferred – as a stick with which to beat the moderns:

> In a great company of judicious men, when motets in the modern manner were being sung, I observed that the question was asked, what language such singers were using, whether Hebrew, Greek,

Latin or some other, because it could not be made out what they were saying. Thus, although the moderns compose good and beautiful texts for their songs, they lose them by the manner of their singing, since they are not understood.[3]

At any rate, the Parisian motet shows every sign of being a university product, and this helps to explain the curious contrast between the licentious frivolity of most of the texts and the rigorously academic techniques with which they were set.

A further trend, which becomes apparent near the end of the century, is towards an increasingly clear rhythmic distinction between the two texted voices. The upper voice (triplum) tends to have a longer text more rapidly declaimed than before, the lower voice (motetus) a shorter text set to longer note values. Because the tenor, at the bottom of the texture, tends to be stretched out into the longest of the traditionally available note lengths, the three voices become much more distinct to the listener. The difficulty of following the faster word-flow of the triplum, however, cancels out any gain in comprehensibility from the slower motetus. And this rather suggests that the changed relationship among the voices occurred less in the interests of comprehensibility than as a reflection of a change in musical style, towards a more elaborate upper-voice melody line accompanied by two more harmonically conceived lower parts. Together with this, inevitably, went developments in notation, so that a greater range of upper-voice note values became available to the composer.

Of the motets which show this development most clearly, a number are associated with Petrus de Cruce – one of the first names since Pérotin to be associated with particular polyphonic compositions. As usual, we know almost nothing of Petrus other than that he was a composer and theorist. Jacques de Liège cites as examples of his innovations two motets which survive among the later entries in the encyclopedic Montpellier Codex. These, and about a half-dozen like them, stand out from their more conventional contemporaries not just on account of their rhythmic layering but also – and more memorably – for the way in which the reflective quality of their texts is mirrored in their musical style, the more extended lower-voice foundation matched by harmonic progressions which seem to encourage the more subdued effect of the flat seventh scale-degree. The result is a style more thoughtful than in the racy concoctions of earlier Parisian composers.

★

In the development of the thirteenth-century motet from relatively free expansions of existing material towards wholly original compositions with an ordered hierarchy of voices, it is tempting to see a reflection of trends in the intellectual life of the period. The rapid expansion of the

University of Paris during the thirteenth century made a sophisticated education available to a much wider slice of society – laymen as well as clerics – and as a result created a wider market for writings of all sorts. The transfer of the motet from the world of the cathedral to that of the university undoubtedly reflects this.

But far more significant for developments in music was the increasingly 'scientific' turn taken by philosophical writings as the thirteenth century gave way to the fourteenth. As traditional metaphysical interpretations of the world lost ground to logical and mathematical pursuits of evidence, so in music the overloaded notational system of the thirteenth century, owing more to tradition than to practicality, was subjected to radical reorganization on logical principles. And the labels applied to the old and new philosophical approaches – 'via antiqua' and 'via moderna' – were adopted by musicians as banners of their own allegiance.

Thus it was in a treatise entitled *Ars nove musice* that Johannes de Muris, in about 1320, set out these rethought principles of notation, relating them to the mathematics of sound and time, and to the practices of the *antiqui* which they extend. By contrast, at about the same time, the traditionalist Jacques de Liège was directing the whole of the final part of his *Speculum musice* to an embittered denunciation of the *moderni* for their scornful treatment of the old ways. The bitterness of his argument is vivid testimony to the strength of feeling on both sides; and even Johannes seems to have found it hard to be generous in victory: 'Perhaps in the course of time there will happen to us what is now happening to the *antiqui*, who believed that they held the end of music'. But his earlier prediction that 'there are many other new things latent in [the new] music which will appear wholly plausible to posterity'[4] was to be amply justified by the longevity of the reforms of Ars Nova.

The first hint of Ars Nova in practice dates from five years or so before Johannes's definitive theoretical summary, appearing, as no more than a small step beyond the innovations of Petrus de Cruce, in one of the most extraordinary musical and poetic documents of the Middle Ages, *Le roman de Fauvel*.

Fauvel originated in 1310 as a 1200-line poem satirizing the moral condition of France. Under Philippe IV habits of government, stable through most of the thirteenth century, had been radically revised as the king worked to strengthen his administrative powers at the expense of the nobility and the church, appointing a new breed of educated bureaucrats loyal to his political and financial advantage; *Fauvel* reflects the bitter divisions which his policies engendered. In 1314 the text was more than doubled in length by the addition of a second book by one of Philippe le Bel's new men, the notary Gervais de Bus. It was a further revision in 1316, however, which turned *Fauvel* into a document

64. *Scene from the satiri-cal allegory 'Le roman de Fauvel' (early fourteenth century): Fauvel, dressed as a man, is going to bed with Vaine Gloire (daughter of Fortune) when they are disturbed by a carnival procession*

crucial for the history of music. Together with another 3000 lines of text, Chaillou de Pestain (tentatively identified with another court functionary) supervised the insertion of 169 musical items whose texts point up the narrative. These pieces cover a huge range, both chronologically and formally, suggesting that a great deal of early thirteenth-century music remained current a hundred years later. Together with plainchant, monophonic conductus, lais and refrains are 34 polyphonic works, most of them early to mid-thirteenth century, but others clearly of very recent vintage; and it is these last which hint at radical new developments in rhythm and texture, clearly linked to the theoretical stance of the *moderni*.

The connection is most obvious in the large range of note lengths kept in play, from the newly defined minims used in the upper voices to notes as much as 24 times as long in the tenor. This extension of the rhythmic contrasts suggested by the generation of Petrus de Cruce brings with it changes in harmonic practice. The very slow tenor (still derived from plainchant) offers its pitches as supporting pillars over which the upper voices define arches of intertwined melodic decoration, returning always to a new consonance at the next tenor support. For the composer, control of harmonic direction has to be more rigorous in order to make sense of these constraints; while repetition of the tenor's rhythmic and melodic patterns allows varied upper-voice treatments of an internally coherent fundamental structure. The new style has an intellectual logic and a harmonic and contrapuntal clarity that reflects as accurately as any development in the arts the new empiricism of contemporary thinkers and the newly rationalized organization of early fourteenth-century government.

But if the latest *Fauvel* motets are the first fruits of the new style, their notation – though later updated – was not yet quite as advanced as that set out by Johannes de Muris. It corresponds closely, however, to principles laid down in a group of treatises claiming to preserve the teaching of a notary in the royal household, Philippe de Vitry. Their essential innovation concerns the relation of smaller to larger note values. In the Ars Antiqua tradition the unit of measurement, the breve, was subdivided into triple groups of smaller notes, but according to the new teaching each note value, from long to semibreve, could be worth either two or three of the next smaller note value. As a result the composer had at his disposal not only a new level of small note values (the minim) but also a range of combinations of metrical relationships from which to choose. Duple values were available at all levels for the first time, and in addition, red coloration was introduced to change short passages of notes from triple to duple or vice versa. The result was a system of impeccable logic which at a stroke made a wide range of new metrical possibilities available to composers. Indeed, it is hard to think of any development in music which changed so much so quickly.

The treatises (some of them little more than lecture notes) in which these momentous innovations are set out cite several of the *Fauvel* works in illustration, and it has been generally assumed that Vitry was their composer. This may well be so. Vitry was applauded by his contemporaries and successors to a quite exceptional degree as an innovator in the field of music, as the founder of a 'new manner of motets' and of 'the four prolations and red notes and the novelty of proportions' – all first appearing in *Fauvel*. In addition, the texts of these new works, angry commentaries on recent political events, are very much in the style of later, more securely attributed works of this composer. If Vitry was already connected with the court by 1316 (as seems possible, though the first documentary reference dates from only 1321) it is easy to see why Chaillou de Pestain should have found in him the ideal collaborator in revising and adding music to *Fauvel*.

Certainly the secure works of Vitry are uncompromisingly modern, revelling in all the features which Jacques de Liège so despised – rapidly declaimed texts, minim note values, duple metres, proportionally diminishing formal structures marked by rapid upper-voice exchange of notes and rests ('hocketing') – and in view of the vicious sarcasm of much of Vitry's writing it is not difficult to suppose that it was he who denounced Jacques and the *antiqui* as rude, idiotic and ignorant of the art of singing,[5] a remark which seems to have been responsible for much of the *Speculum musice*.

In works written after *Fauvel* Vitry standardized the motet so successfully that his works provided models for a stream of motets by his immediate followers. Typically, the isorhythmic motet was made up of two sections, each of which was constructed around one statement of the plainchant chosen to provide the melodic material of the tenor voice. The chant was set to several statements of a repeating rhythmic pattern (hence 'isorhythmic'). Each rhythmic statement ideally corresponded to one stanza of each of the texts which were to be set in the upper voices. Where the structure of the texts allowed, the second section was usually based upon repetitions of the tenor in half-length note values. The upper voices were also partially isorhythmic, repeating at the same time as the tenor rhythms, most literally so wherever there was a particularly memorable upper-voice figure, such as a passage of hocket. Clearly it was part of the game for the listener to attempt to follow this selfconsciously rational process. The effect was sometimes enriched by a second lower voice, a contratenor, which was constructed in the same fashion as the tenor, providing a two-part harmonic framework for the triplum and motetus to decorate.

This approach to motet composition seems to have been standard – at least in northern France – throughout the 1320s and 30s; but from the 1340s there was a trend towards greater complexity, with shorter values in the lower voices obscuring the layering of parts and increasing the rate of harmonic change. It may be only coincidental that Vitry would have had little time left for composition by then. His career which, so far as we can tell, began quietly enough in the government bureaucracy, had taken him by the mid-1340s to one of the most influential positions in the king's household, and close to the heir to the throne, Jean, Duke of Normandy. Soon after Jean's accession in 1350 Vitry accepted the bishopric of Meaux; and it was the chief lament of his great admirer, Petrarch, that Vitry would now be so weighed down with work that there would be no peace left for study.

Certainly by Vitry's death in 1361 the motet was developing in ways quite opposed to his earlier principles, in particular the pursuit of continuous isorhythm in all voices, and we must assume that his direct influence had long since ceased.

★

Posthumous tradition credited Vitry with not only a 'new manner of motets' but also of 'ballades, lais and simple rondeaux'. Of these nothing is known. Indeed, the earlier history of fourteenth-century polyphonic song is still very obscure, probably because there are few music manuscripts of any sort surviving from the period of increasing political disruption from the death of Louis X in 1316 to the temporary upturn in France's fortunes after 1360. Of the songs surviving from that period the most likely candidates for Vitry's authorship are the chaces – three-voice canons setting light courtly-love texts enlivened with mimetic descriptions of animals and musical instruments. In these the rhythmic style, at least, is close to that of the Ars Nova motet.

Much more important for the development of fourteenth-century song, however, are the compositions which set poetry in one of the *formes fixes*, principally virelai, ballade and rondeau. Some of the earliest of these have features in common with the motet and chace – which may suggest a line of development – but their patchy survival, in much later manuscripts, has so far made attempts at establishing a chronology unreliable. In such a context, any composer who left a substantial body of work in ascribed and datable manuscripts would be assured of a dominant position in any history of the period. Such a figure is Guillaume de Machaut (*c*1300–1377).

65. Woman singing to a harp, with the opening of the popular three-voice ballade 'De ce que fol pense' by Philippe des Molins (chancellor to the Duke of Berry in 1368): detail of an Arras tapestry (1420)

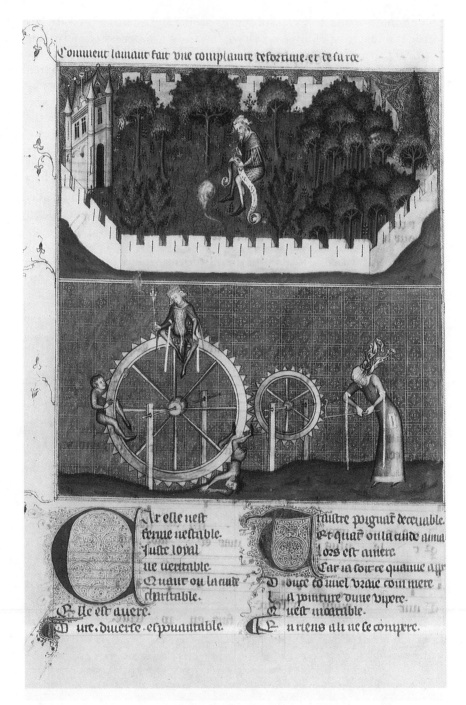

66. *The poet (? Guillaume de Machaut) composes a complainte to Fortune, seen below turning her wheel: folio from Machaut's narrative poem the 'Remede de Fortune' (c1350)*

Like Vitry, Machaut emerges from the shadows in the early 1320s, and again like Vitry, his career seems to have begun as a clerk in a royal household – in Machaut's case that of Jean, Duke of Luxembourg and King of Bohemia. One of the more colourful figures of the age, Jean was a tireless campaigner for the expansion of his Bohemian territories and a regular traveller between eastern Europe, Luxembourg and France. In his service Machaut must have seen more of the world than most clerics of his time. After Jean's heroic death at the battle of Crécy (1346) Machaut settled as a canon at Rheims Cathedral, and it is from this point onwards that documentation of his activity as a poet and composer begins to survive. For this the catalyst may perhaps have been the Black Death.

In 1347–9 something like a third of the population of France died. It is no wonder that after surviving such a disaster, and already an old man by medieval standards, Machaut should have begun around 1350 to collect together his life's work into what would prove to be the first of a series of luxurious manuscripts for his wealthy patrons. The contents of this 450-page book (Machaut manuscript *C*) show an extraordinary range of poetic and musical activity: five long narrative poems (averaging 3000 lines each); ten lais, twenty motets, 24 ballades, 25 virelais, nine rondeaux, all set to music; and almost 200 such poems not set. All this work, of course, dates from the period since *Fauvel* and the earlier works of Vitry, testifying to the success with which polyphonic song had developed a tradition and language independent of the motet, during the intervening 30 years.

Of the *forme fixe* settings the simplest are the virelais, whose short-lined, relatively popular-style texts are set to two-section musical forms according to the following pattern:

Text refrain	R				R	
Text groups	1	2	3	4	5=1	
						etc
Music section A	A			A	A	
Music section B		B	B			

Here each text group consists of two or more lines, each set as a separate musical phrase, mostly with one note for each syllable. All the virelais in manuscript *C* are monophonic, emphasizing their kinship with popular unwritten traditions.

Even the simplest rondeaux, however, are already considerably more complex. In these a two-voice texture is spun out over larger expanses of music, with extended melismas, often at several points within one line of text. And the sense that these are more elaborately 'artificial' works is encouraged by the less regular poetic form shown below:

R	R		R			R	R
1	2	3	4=1	5	6	7=1	8=2
A		A	A	A		A	
	B				B		B

Not long before the compilation of manuscript *C*, however, Machaut began to set rondeaux with three and four voices; and although the latter is a temporary phenomenon (coinciding with a temporary simplification of his harmonic language) three parts became the norm in his later settings.

1	2	3
A	A	B

That Machaut should have used the ballade for his most adventurous explorations beyond the beaten track of fourteenth-century harmony may be due to the form's ancestry in the High Style of the thirteenth century. And throughout his life it is in this most open-ended of the closed forms that he shows the exceptional breadth of his musical imagination.

Finally, the lais of manuscript *C* offer an equally impressive demonstration of Machaut's ability to control large-scale forms. These huge lyric texts, typically twelve stanzas of sixteen lines each, required twelve separate sections of music, composed so as to allow each to repeat but at the same time to play its part in the shape of the whole. In addition several of the later lais allow successive stanzas to be combined polyphonically – a remarkable compositional achievement.

Clearly, then, by 1350 Machaut had created a substantial body of work, much of it highly original. He enjoyed sufficiently secure patronage to collect together all his work and have it copied into a beautifully illuminated manuscript for sale to (or on commission from) one of his several noble patrons. And, perhaps the most revealing commentary on contemporary priorities, he enjoyed this level of security at a time when, beyond the walls of Rheims, France was disintegrating under the blows of military defeat, administrative chaos and plague.

For Machaut, having survived the Black Death, the condition of France cannot have been more pitifully obvious than during the winter of 1359–60, when Rheims was besieged by the English armies intending to crown Edward III King of France in Rheims Cathedral. It may well have been at this time that Machaut wrote his last three motets, whose texts call on God, the Duke of Normandy and the Virgin Mary for help, and seem to allude to several of the misfortunes suffered by France at the time: the English invasion, the siege of Rheims, the revolt of the Jacquerie and continuing recurrences of plague.

In the end the siege of Rheims failed, as did that of Paris the following April, and the signing of the Treaty of Brétigny on 8 May marked the start of four years of relative peace. For Machaut this was an Indian summer of creativity. As well as his setting of the Ordinary of the Mass, which probably dates from these years, his increasingly amorous correspondence with the young Péronne d'Armentières gave rise to an exquisite group of late songs in which the harmonic and rhythmic innovation of his earlier works is held in perfect balance. That Machaut admired them too is endearingly clear from the letters with which they were enclosed; on ballade 33:

I've made the tune for *Le grand desir*, as you asked me; and I've made it

67. Singers performing from a note roll (rotulus): miniature from Machaut manuscript E, compiled for the Duke of Berry in the 1390s

like a *Res d'Alemaigne*; and truly it seems to me very strange and very new. . . . And by God, in my opinion, it's a long time since I've made anything so good; and the tenors are as sweet as unsalted gruel.[6]

On rondeau 17:

My very sweet heart; I send you the music of the rondeau where your name is [as an acrostic], and would have sent it before, but the visitors who've been in Rheims wouldn't leave me in peace. And you can be sure that for seven years past I've not made so good a piece nor one so sweet to hear, on account of which I have great joy when I've succeeded so well for love of you.[7]

The letters also contain valuable information on the copying of his collected works:

My most sovereign lady; I would have brought you my book to amuse you wherein are all the things which I have ever made, but it is in more than twenty pieces, for I had it made for one of my lords; and so I am having the notes put to it, and that is why it has to be in pieces.

68. Love introducing her children Sweet Thought, Charm and Hope to Machaut (seen here in old age): miniature from Machaut manuscript A (1370s)

And when the notes have been put to it I shall bring it or send it to you, if it please God.[8]

Although we know nothing more of this manuscript or of the patron for whom it was copied, owners of similar collections included Juan I of Aragon, Amadeus VI of Savoy, Jean, Duke of Berry, Philip the Good, Duke of Burgundy, and Gaston Fébus, Count of Foix. Judging by its twenty sections, it probably contained substantially more than manuscript *C* (surviving sources compiled near the end of Machaut's life contain about 50 per cent more) and most of this new material is likely to have been written since *c*1350.

With so much music and such wide and influential distribution it seems strange that Machaut should be so little represented in the more typical 'repertory manuscripts' of the period. Of his 143 musical works only 22 are recorded in manuscripts originating outside Machaut's circle. Yet his influence can be traced in songs of the last third of the century, and his poetry played an important part in shaping the literature of the next generation. It seems probable, then, that Machaut guarded his work jealously, perhaps to discourage faulty copies from being made and circulated (his original melodic progressions being particularly susceptible to alteration by conventionally minded scribes), but probably also because demand for the authorized complete works thereby increased.

★

It is likely to be no coincidence that large music manuscripts containing a general repertory begin to appear once more from *c*1360. The reign of Charles V (1364–80) saw France at last take military initiatives in the fight against England, and the consequent (if temporary) recovery in her fortunes seems to have encouraged some resurgence of artistic activity.

A manuscript now at Ivrea, dating from about 1365, contains a large repertory of isorhythmic motets, songs and also mass movements, the motets reaching back as far as the post-*Fauvel* works of Vitry. A large number of motets related to these, presumably by younger composers, and many of the songs, must date from the period 1320–60; and the diversity of styles is a useful reminder that Machaut, for all his genius, was both socially and stylistically on the periphery of French musical life.

Some fragmentary manuscripts now at Cambrai, probably written in the 1360s, seem to be the remains of collections of similar scope, though perhaps representing a slightly earlier stage of development. Unlike the Ivrea manuscript (possibly compiled for the southern courts of Foix and Béarn), the Cambrai manuscripts were probably northern in origin, as was the Trémoïlle manuscript, a large collection similar to

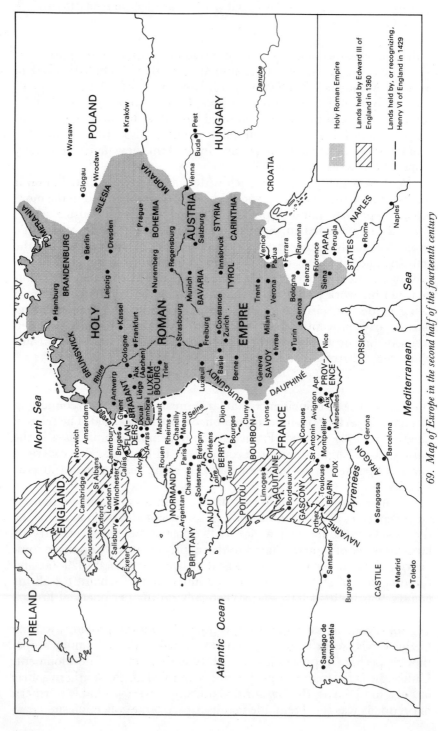

69. Map of Europe in the second half of the fourteenth century

that of Ivrea, compiled in 1376 for the court of Charles V (little more than its index survives).

This wide geographical distribution of three major collections emphasizes the extent to which Ars Nova innovations had spread during the half-century since *Fauvel*. There can be little doubt that Paris was the place of origin for the new style and the notational developments which made its creation possible. *Fauvel* was compiled there; Philippe de Vitry was almost certainly based there during the crucial years (approximately 1314–24). But already in 1336 an important treatise on composition (the *Compendium* of Petrus frater dictus Palma ociosa), in which the new counterpoint has been assimilated thoroughly enough to be presented as a technique course for students, was being written in a community at Cercamp, near Abbéville. Two motets probably written before *c*1350 list musicians from Bruges, Tirelemont, Aix, Bailleul, Thérouanne, Douai, Valenciennes, Arras and Cambrai – all in the area between northern Belgium and the Somme – and also from Luxeuil and Cluny on the main route south.

Turning east, towards Poland, Bohemia and Hungary, it is no surprise to find in the latter part of the thirteenth century, as far east as Stary Sącz (Poland), imported Notre Dame compositions alongside flourishing local traditions of polyphony. Much of this simple, mostly two-voice music continued to be copied into new manuscripts throughout the fourteenth century and was clearly a popular ingredient in festive, and especially Christmas, liturgical celebrations.

To judge by surviving material, Ars Nova innovations seem to have reached east central Europe only in the second half of the century. Ars Nova notation was being taught in Prague (Bohemia) by 1369; French isorhythmic motets and songs (including a composition by Vitry) were known in Wrocław (Silesia) by the late fourteenth century, and by about 1400 quasi-isorhythmic mass settings were being written in Poznań (Poland). By the mid-fifteenth century, fairly recent French and Italian works – by Ciconia and Zachara, among others – were circulating alongside much older works by Vitry, Machaut and their contemporaries; and Polish composers were working in similar styles.

But alongside all this progressive, Western-dominated activity, local traditions of 'popular polyphony', usually for two voices and using only the simpler features of modern notation, continued to be widely practised, and these surely accounted for most of the composed polyphony heard in central and east central Europe until well into the fifteenth century.

By contrast, the spread of French music southwards seems to have been rapid. At the very beginning of the fourteenth century, scribes at the convent of Las Huelgas (Burgos) were copying one of the last great sources of thirteenth-century motets, including rehearsal cues which clearly indicate that the manuscript was intended for current use. The ruling houses whose kingdoms lay immediately to the south of the Pyrenees had family ties with the Valois, and despite the hazards of travel through fourteenth-century France contacts must have been continual. It is no surprise, today, to find increasing amounts of Ars Nova music turning up in Spanish archives.

★

Family ties and the mechanisms of trade and administration, however, cannot adequately explain why, during the last quarter of the fourteenth century, the whole focus of progressive musical activity should have shifted from northern France south to the borders with Spain and Italy. The origins of this development lie in policies pursued by Philippe IV back at the beginning of the century. In 1309 the newly elected French pope Clement V settled his court not in Rome but in the Provençal city of Avignon, where the activities of the church could be more effectively influenced (and protected) by the French king. Conveniently sited between France and Italy, well away from the English–French wars in the north and the quarrels of the Italian states in the south, Avignon developed into a powerful political centre. The papal palace grew steadily in size and splendour, and despite fluctuations caused by the varying tastes and means of successive popes, the quality and reputation of its chapel slowly increased.

The daily liturgy, of course, prescribed the chanting of large parts of the service; and to that extent, like any religious institution, the papacy was bound to provide for music and for singers competent to perform it. How far beyond that basic requirement each pope chose to go was very much a matter of preference, and at first the Avignon popes seem positively to have discouraged polyphonic elaboration of the essential plainchant minimum.

Clement V condemned the 'severe disturbance' by which many clerics 'presume to say or to sing the canonical hours either cursorily or syncopatedly, even intermingling a great number of extraneous, meaningless, worldly and shameful texts'.[9] In 1324–5 his successor, John XXII, brought his characteristic sarcasm to bear upon:

> Certain disciples of the new school [who], much occupying themselves with the measured dividing of time, seek to invent new notes, preferring to devise ways of their own rather than to continue singing in the old manner. Thus the Divine Offices are now sung in semibreves and minims, and peppered with small notes. Moreover they cut up the melodies with hockets, they lubricate them with discant, sometimes they even cram in Tripla and Moteti in the vernacular. ... We strictly command that from now on no one shall presume to attempt these methods, or anything like them, in the said Offices.[10]

John, however, went on to recommend the occasional use of simple two-voice polyphony which left the plainchant intact – another clue that this style remained a norm throughout the period.

Clearly Ars Nova had reached Avignon without much delay; but the city had to wait another twenty years for a pope prepared to encourage it. Clement VI (1342–52) had been a senior colleague of Vitry's – in that they both undertook diplomatic missions for the state during the 1320s and 30s – and Vitry worked for him during the 1340s. His motet *Petre clemens/Lugentium* heaps extravagant praise upon Clement, and does so in the newest style of the second generation of Ars Nova composers. Clement proved to be a similarly extravagant patron of the arts, leaving considerable financial problems for his successors: spending on music was cut back after his death and seems to have recovered only very slowly.

By the later 1370s, however, not only the pope, but also many of his cardinals were supporting chapels of their own, and it is an indication of their quality that in 1379 the heir to the throne of Aragon looked to Avignon when recruiting singers for his court and collecting books of mass music and songs for them to sing. It was in 1379, also, that the antipope Clement VII initiated the last great expansion of the papal chapel. Elected as a rival to the Roman pope Urban VI, Clement probably saw his investment in the palace and its personnel as an effective means of demonstrating the cultural and financial superiority of Avignon. He employed some of the most talented composers of the day, several of whom duly set texts supporting his position.

But whatever the political forces felt by the Avignon musicians, they were employed primarily to sing services, and much of their creative activity seems to have involved providing music for the chapel. A great deal of polyphonic mass music survives from this period; and although much of it must have originated in Avignon, the chief surviving witness is a manuscript from the cathedral at Apt, some 30 miles to the east. Like almost every large manuscript of the fourteenth century, it includes a selection of Vitry and other Ars Nova motets; but its main contents are mass movements, and these cover a wide range of styles from complex isorhythm, through song-like settings, to simple chordal writing. A number of composers' names are known, most as yet unidentified from other sources; but of the three with documented careers, 'Pellison', an alias of Johannes de Bosco, was probably trained in Tournai in the 1360s and was employed as a papal chaplain by 1393; while 'Tapissier' (Jean de Noyers) and Baude Cordier were both composers to Philip the Bold, Duke of Burgundy, visiting Avignon with him in 1391 and 1395. Several of the others may very well have been local – Jacobus Murrin, for instance, may possibly be identified with a cleric living in Aix-en-Provence in 1419 – and it has to be admitted that some of their work, and that of the anonymous composers in the manuscript, is less than scintillating.

This rough picture, of a repertory of mass music composed partly by contemporary northerners and partly locally, can be refined a little by comparing Apt with the Ivrea manuscript. We have already seen that this is an important source for northern French Ars Nova motets. At least some of its mass settings (including some also in Apt) are likely to be northern; but its much earlier date (?the 1370s as opposed to Apt's *c*1400) shows that Ars Nova mass settings were in use in the far south (at any rate, in the court chapel of Gaston Fébus) at very much the same time as the final flowering of the papal chapel at Avignon, and reminds us, too, that even the local repertory was but a continuation of a much older French tradition.

★

Whatever their official duties, it is clear that many of the papal singers were deeply involved in the composition of secular songs. Court life, whether in the papal palace or in the households of the cardinals, offered daily opportunities for musical entertainment. It is no surprise, then, to find that 'Hasprois' (Johannes Symonis), 'Franciscus' (?Johannes de Gemblaco), Johannes de Haucourt and Matheus de Sancto Johanne, all papal singers, are known from surviving songs – Matheus, indeed, was one of the finest song composers of the time. Further, the many musicians, such as Baude Cordier, who visited Avignon in the entourages of dignitaries – the kings of France, Navarre, Sicily, Spain and Portugal, the dukes of Anjou and Burgundy and the Count of

Savoy among them – were the agents for regular exchange of music and ideas.

With such a concentration of talent, song styles were bound to evolve rapidly as composers vied with one another in extending harmonic, rhythmic and (therefore) notational practices to produce ever more sophisticated artefacts. The resulting Ars Subtilior, as it is now known, produced some of the most rhythmically complex works conceived before modern times. For precedents (whose authority was always essential, even in so radical a development as this) the Ars Subtilior composers looked directly back to Machaut, who, by the middle of the century, had already developed a taste for extended syncopations, displacing a melodic phrase by a half or a third of a beat relative to the accompanying voices; and a great many Ars Subtilior pieces depend for their effect upon an extension of this technique over longer passages

71. Gaston Fébus, Count of Foix, surrounded by his huntsmen: miniature from his treatise 'Livre de la chasse' (early fifteenth century)

and in more than one voice. A fair number, however, go further than this, inventing new notations (including several kinds of colour, variously decorated tails and new signs for reduction or augmentation of the written note lengths) to produce complex durations or whimsically irregular proportional relationships between the different voices.

The chief source for this remarkable repertory, a southern French manuscript now kept at the Château of Chantilly, names composers for most of its hundred compositions. As well as Baude Cordier, Haucourt, Matheus, Hasprois and Taillhandier (mentioned in connection with Avignon) are Jacob de Senleches, employed during the 1370s and 80s at the courts of Gerona, Castile and Navarre, and Gacien Reyneau, who was a member of the royal chapel at Barcelona in the 1390s; this emphasizes the northern Spanish courts' strength. A surprising number of compositions refer to Gaston Fébus and his successor Mathieu, whose court of Foix and Béarn, based at Orthez, was possibly the manuscript's first home and surely an employer of several of the Chantilly composers of whom nothing is yet known. The manuscript also looks back: there are three compositions by Machaut, drawn from among his most unconventional ballades, emphasizing his position as the root of the new, more subtle style; and a number of the more recent pieces, notably by Philippus de Caserta, acknowledge their debt by quoting from Machaut songs.

The range of styles cultivated by the Ars Subtilior composers is exemplified in the figure of Solage who, with ten compositions ascribed to him, is the best-represented composer in Chantilly. Several of these songs are close in style to the more experimental works of Machaut, particularly in their syncopated decorations of a single chord and in their unexpected harmonic twists. Others are much simpler, with neatly turned melody lines supported by relatively straightforward lower voices; and these seem to be approaching the new simplicity of the early fifteenth century. But a third group, including three pieces whose texts seem to link them to Jean, Duke of Berry, is much less conventional: complex rhythms, adventurous use of flats and exceptionally low voice ranges contribute to a style which has hardly lost the power to shock six centuries after its creation.

It is pieces like these which have led to so much misunderstanding of the Ars Subtilior, for however advanced it may be, this music is never, as has sometimes been claimed, irrational or fundamentally dissonant. Although a distressing number of editions and performances have produced senselessly discordant results, it has invariably been through misreading the notation. However complex the rhythmic ingenuities, and however unconventional the contrapuntal displacements, the underlying progressions always prove, when correctly transcribed, to be entirely logical.

Similar problems must surely have arisen when the music was new.

The notation, after all, was so complex that only a small circle of the most highly trained musicians could have performed from it; the style was so abstruse that only a handful of the most enlightened connoisseurs could have appreciated it or could have wished to support it. And by 1403, when the papacy left Avignon for good, taking from southern France its most important focus for musical activity and exchange, it must have been clear that the Ars Subtilior had only a very limited future. Its final monument, the Modena manuscript, is Italian; and henceforth it was to Italy and to the tastes of Italian patrons that the most gifted French musicians were to turn their skills.

NOTES

[1] *Johannes de Grocheo: Concerning Music*, trans. A. Seay (Colorado Springs, 1967, rev. 2/1974), 26.
[2] O. Strunk, *Source Readings in Music History*, i (New York, 1950/R1965), 189.
[3] ibid, 190.
[4] ibid, 178.
[5] ibid, 185 and 180–90 *passim*.
[6] F. Ludwig, *Guillaume de Machaut: Musikalische Werke*, ii (Leipzig, 192?), pp. 54*–5*.
[7] ibid, 57*.
[8] P. Weiss and R. Taruskin, *Music in the Western World: a History in Documents* (London, 1984), 76.
[9] A. Tomasello, *Music and Ritual at Papal Avignon, 1309–1403* (Ann Arbor, 1983), 5.
[10] H. E. Wooldridge, *The Oxford History of Music*, i (1901, rev. P. Buck, 1929), 294–6.

BIBLIOGRAPHICAL NOTE

History, politics and ideas
As an introduction to the historical and political background D. Waley's *Later Medieval Europe* (London, rev. 2/1975) is useful on the later thirteenth century; outstanding on the fourteenth century are D. Hay, *Europe in the Fourteenth and Fifteenth Centuries* (London, 1966), and G. Holmes, *Europe: Hierarchy and Revolt, 1320–1450* (London, 1975).
    On early fourteenth-century France, J. R. Strayer's *The Reign of Philip the Fair* (Princeton, 1980) and J. Favier's *Philippe le Bel* (Paris, 1978) give usefully different views of the same period; likewise J. Favier's *La guerre de cent ans* (Paris, 1980) and C. Allmand's *The Hundred Years War* (Cambridge, 1988) for later in the century. The most approachable primary source is *Froissart's Chronicles*, selected and trans. G. Brereton (Harmondsworth, 1968), a vivid record of the Hundred Years War up to 1400.
    On intellectual trends a valuable introduction may be found in G. Leff, *The Dissolution of the Medieval Outlook* (New York, 1976).

Music history, theory and notation
There are still no recommendable surveys of medieval music covering less than the whole Middle Ages. Thus R. Hoppin, *Medieval Music* (New York, 1978), and F. A. Gallo, *Music of the Middle Ages*, ii, Eng. trans. K. Eales (Cambridge, 1985), remain the best starting-points.
    There are several excellent 'document-based' studies of limited geographical areas; outstanding among them are M. C. Gómez Muntané, *La música en la Casa Real Catalano-Aragonesa 1336–1442* (Barcelona, 1979); C. Wright, *Music at the Court of Burgundy 1364–1419: a Documentary History* (Henryville, 1979); A. Tomasello, *Music and Ritual at Papal Avignon 1309–1403* (Ann Arbor, 1983); C. E. Brewer, *The Introduction of Ars Nova into*

East Central Europe (Ann Arbor, 1984); and (although mostly concerned with the fifteenth century) R. Strohm, *Music in Late Medieval Bruges* (Oxford, 1985).

On Vitry see A. Coville, 'Philippe de Vitri: notes biographiques', *Romania*, lix (1933), 520–47, and E. H. Sanders, 'Vitry, Philippe de', *Grove 6*.

On Machaut's biography the only detailed study is A. Machabey's *Guillaume de Machault: la via et l'oeuvre musicale*, i (Paris, 1955). For an example of his narrative writing see *Guillaume de Machaut: the Judgement of the King of Bohemia*, ed. and trans. R. Barton Palmer (New York, 1984). More on his correspondence with Péronne may be found in S. J. Williams, 'The Lady, the Lyrics and the Letters', *EM*, v (1977), 462–8. *Guillaume de Machaut, poète et compositeur* (no editor; Paris, 1982) contains essays on many aspects of his life and work; while G. Reaney, *Guillaume de Machaut* (Oxford, 1971), makes a useful introduction to his musical language.

Two valuable anthologies of medieval writings on music are O. Strunk, *Source Readings in Music History* (New York, 1950/*R*1965), and P. Weiss and R. Taruskin, *Music in the Western World: a History in Documents* (London, 1984). Johannes de Grocheo's treatise is available in a translation by A. Seay, *Johannes de Grocheo: Concerning Music* (Colorado Springs, 1967, rev. 2/1974); and the treatise *Ars nova* is translated by L. Plantinga in *JMT*, v (1961), 204–23.

The clearest guide to medieval notation is R. Rastall's *The Notation of Western Music* (London, 1983).

Music

The repertory of newly made Ars Antiqua motets may be sampled most conveniently in *The Montpellier Codex*, ed. H. Tischler, i–iii (1978), iv, texts and translations by S. Stakel and J. C. Relihan (1985). Editions of the other main manuscripts are all by G. Anderson, *Motets of the Manuscript La Clayette*, CMM, lxviii (1975); *Compositions of the Bamberg Manuscript*, CMM, lxxv (1977); and *The Las Huelgas Manuscript*, CMM, lxxix (1982).

Le Roman de Fauvel and *Philippe de Vitry: Complete Works*, ed. L. Schrade, were originally issued in vol.i (1956) of the series PMFC, but are now available as separate reprints (Monaco, 1975). Similarly, *Guillaume de Machaut: oeuvres complètes* were issued as vols. ii–iii of PMFC, but are now available in a five-volume reprint (Monaco, 1977).

Almost all the whole surviving repertory of fourteenth-century French motets was published as *Motets of French Provenance*, ed. F. Ll. Harrison, PMFC, v (1968). Five have been reissued as *Musicorum collegio: Fourteenth-Century Musicians' Motets* (Monaco, 1986). Most of the mass music will be found in *Fourteenth-Century Mass Music in France*, ed. H. Stäblein-Harder, CMM, xxix (1962), and MSD, vii (1962), excepting only the Barcelona, Toulouse and Tournai collections issued in PMFC, i.

The complete repertory of fourteenth-century French song is published as *French Secular Music*, ed. G. K. Greene, PMFC, xviii–xxii (1981–9). Less convenient to use but more easily available is *French Secular Compositions of the Fourteenth Century*, ed. W. Apel, CMM, liii (1970–72).

Chapter X

Trecento Italy

MICHAEL LONG

Italian polyphonic music in the fourteenth century has been likened to a 'dazzling meteor',[1] suddenly flaming into existence against an obscure background and, its fireworks spent, disappearing just as abruptly. Characterized by an unprecedented union of structural clarity with melodic and rhythmic inventiveness and often spectacular virtuosity, the musical settings of the trecento adorned a new type of text lyric, equally fresh in outlook and technique. Vernacular literature in thirteenth-century Italy, bound to the models of imported traditions for its style and even its language, was still in its infancy. The courts of northern Italy provided a home for the *fin-de-siècle* Occitanian courtly lyric; the south, also visited by emigré troubadours, witnessed the development of a corpus of Sicilian poetry rooted in the Arabic conventions and language which permeated courtly society in that region.[2] Aside from the sketchy remnants of the Siculo-Arabic school, most native vernacular literature before the very end of the duecento reflected in its style and content the central concerns of literate Italians of the period: religion, law and government. The composition of sacred vernacular poetry (encouraged especially by the Franciscans), and the occasional production of vernacular translations of civic statutes or notary manuals, may have provided some impetus towards the establishment of a loftier body of vernacular literature, but it took the conscious efforts of the leading figures of the next century (most notably the *tre corone*: Dante, Petrarch and Boccaccio) to unite the sound of the mother tongue with the courtly models provided by non-Italian poetry.

The paths of development traversed in the trecento by vernacular song and by polyphonic music in general were conditioned by the diversity of Italian culture itself. Any notion of a single 'Italy' was essentially geographical, an accident of topography. The Italian peninsula contained an array of sub-cultures, distinguished from one another by particular modes of political and social organization, diverse international loyalties and varied linguistic traditions. That diversity, savoured as a source of local pride, was attributable to the lack of a central royal administration (other than an absentee emperor)

72. *Singers, accompanying themselves on psaltery (left) and gittern, entertain a queen and the ladies of her court: miniature from a manuscript compiled (1352–62) for Louis II, titular King of Naples*

and to the topographical features of the peninsula itself – most notably the divisive spine of the Appenines – both of which encouraged the development of related, yet independent, cultural aggregations. The history of fourteenth-century Italian music is inseparable from the idiosyncratic social and political units in which it thrived. The two forms of medieval political organization in Italy – the familial dynasties, entrenched in geographically dispersed pockets of power, and the city-republics – each lent their characteristic flavours to the genres and styles which came to dominate trecento musical composition. The dynastic centres of the north, including Scaligeri Padua and Verona and Visconti Milan, witnessed the first flowering of Italian trecento polyphony, and embraced the dominant musical culture of the first half of the century. Judging by the extant body of music, republican Florence rose to prominence in the middle of the century, her composers cultivating a more virtuoso version of the established northern musical style, but favouring texts of a more identifiably Tuscan character. After about 1360, not only the style but also the genres which characterized the earlier courtly culture gave way to a more distinctly Florentine repertory. Towards the end of the century, an increasing recognition of the utility of music as an enhancement of large-scale political and ecclesiastical occasions brought northern Italian polyphony outside Florence into line with the 'international style' of the contemporary French dedicatory motet and ballade.

The decidedly regional character of trecento musical styles is underscored not only by the nearly exclusive reliance upon toponymic surnames in musical source attributions, but by modern scholarship's traditional classification of the repertory. In spite of the survival of the names and works of more than 30 individual composers, many of whom have left legacies of a considerable number of polyphonic compositions as well as historical, biographical traces, their works have continued to be subsumed under general regional rubrics, as representative of the 'northern' or the 'Florentine' style, respectively. This tendency is not the result of a lack of recognition on the part of scholars for the accomplishments of the individual figures involved. Rather, it reflects the medieval world's own understanding of the links between artistic endeavour and *patria*, and of the self-awareness (and ultimately, self-aggrandizement) which characterized Florentine historiography of the early fifteenth century. It is largely to the Florentine historical consciousness that we may attribute the impetus for the compilation of several of the most valuable and complete sources of trecento music, most notably the Panciatichi (Florence, Biblioteca Nazionale Centrale 26) and Squarcialupi (Florence, Biblioteca Medicea-Laurenziana 87) manuscripts. These major musical collections are (completely or in part) geographically and chronologically ordered 'historical anthologies'. Together with the manuscripts British Library Add.29987 and the Bibliothèque Nationale fonds italien 568, also compiled at the very end of the fourteenth century or in the first decades of the fifteenth, they record an already moribund tradition of compositional practice and represent the first stage in an inherited historiography which to this day has been more place- than person-orientated.

The trecento musical repertory, as preserved in those sources, is marked by a notable lack of generic diversity. Throughout the first two-thirds of the century, one genre predominates: the madrigal. Its origins and the reasons behind its popularity with fourteenth-century composers remain unresolved issues. Unlike most medieval song forms whose origins as monophonic dance accompaniments necessitated the development of refrain structures, the madrigal was polyphonic (and refrainless) from its inception. It arrived on the scene, at least in its written form, with a fully developed system of textual conventions, and was rapidly established as the primary vehicle for the compositional efforts of Italian musicians – and this in spite of its low status among Italian poets. Other secular song forms, including the caccia (similar to the madrigal in its textual structure, and consisting of two upper voices in canon over an untexted supporting tenor; see fig.73) and the mono-phonic ballata (a refrain form virtually identical to the French virelai) were cultivated during the same period, but with not nearly the same intensity.

Examples of forms other than the madrigal, caccia and ballata are infrequent. With no royal residence, no Avignon and no established tradition of mathematically based musical speculation as at Paris, the expansive and learned structures of the isorhythmic motet did not thrive. Occasional compositions, inspired for the most part by aristo-cratic pretensions, flourished only in a few supportive environments. For instance, two motets by the madrigalist Jacopo da Bologna, *Lux purpurata radiis/Diligite justiciam* and the fragmentary *Laudibus dignis merito laudari*, pay homage to Luchino Visconti of Milan through textual acrostics. Florence, the principal centre for polyphonic activity after mid-century, was after all a republic, and was legislatively hostile to displays which honoured individuals or specific families. In addition, the most prestigious and well-established academic centres of medieval Italy, Padua and Bologna, were far removed from the cathedral school tradition of French urban institutions, in which the teaching of 'numerical composition' had gained such a stronghold in the fields of music and literature. The reputation of the northern Italian universities was based on the study of civil law, rather than theology. Before the less than successful foundation of the University of Florence in the middle of the fourteenth century, the city boasted a respected and well-attended notarial college. Thus most Italian academics pursued their professional studies without entering the ranks of the clergy. Just as the corpus of 'learned' or written medieval polyphony beyond the Alps was transmitted within the academic sphere of the educated cleric, to a large extent so must the Italian universities have played a role in nurturing the primarily secular bent of trecento music.[3]

Outside the university, the nature of Italian religious experience was in no small way responsible for the character of the relatively few surviving examples of the sacred motet and polyphonic settings of the Mass Ordinary. Public religious observances, especially in the wake of the Black Death and (in Florence) the papal interdict of the late 1370s, were informed by a high level of lay participation as manifested in the growth of the confraternities and companies of *laudesi*, more than by formal ecclesiastical spectacle. Representational art and literature were both affected by the expanding base of non-institutional devotion. Fourteenth-century religious expression, written and pictorial, was marked above all by the secularization and humanization of artistic representations of the events and personages associated with the Christian narrative.[4] Appropriately, the few polyphonic mass movements that survive (mainly from the second half of the century) are stylistically more closely allied to the melodic and contrapuntal structures of contemporary secular polyphonic genres than to those highly technical edifices that marked the isorhythmic construction of French sacred music. A telling example of the extent to which the secular style could be employed in the service of piety is the anonymous *Cantano gli angioletti*, preserved in the British Library manuscript. The text of this three-voice work is a vernacular trope of the Sanctus and Benedictus, and is set in the form and style of a madrigal. Other liturgical or para-liturgical compositions exhibit similar stylistic links to the corpus of vernacular polyphony, at least with regard to counterpoint and phrase and cadence structures. Such a lack of distinction between polyphony in the sacred and secular realms argues not so

73. The caccia 'Tosto che l'alba' (top part, with textless tenor below) by Gherardello da Firenze, with a miniature depicting the composer, from the Squarcialupi manuscript, probably produced at the monastery of S Maria degli Angeli, Florence (early fifteenth century)

much for the wholesale appropriation of an alien or inappropriate style by composers of sacred music as for the existence of a continuous tradition joining the two spheres of composition. The links between the sacred and secular styles were already forged in the early trecento. The earliest secular vernacular polyphony, almost exclusively for two voices, relied on the same contrapuntal principles that informed the simple *cantus binatim* settings of Latin texts in the previous century.[5]

To account for the absence of those genres and styles which flourished outside Italy is considerably less difficult than to explain the origins of the few popular trecento song forms. A tradition of polyphony arose, seemingly independent of ultramontane musical influences, in the first decades of the fourteenth century, only to be submerged in the wave of ultramontane polyphonists who found employment in the Italian court and chapels of the early quattrocento. This situation distinguishes the Italian development sharply from the contemporary French Ars Nova, which was linked formally, stylistically and technically to the practices of the preceding and following centuries. However shadowy its musical origins, the rise of a native school of polyphonic art music occurred more or less simultaneously with the conscious formulation of a theoretical basis for Italian vernacular poetry, and with the proliferation of treatises justifying the position of Italian as a literary language. The establishment and rapid expansion of a written repertory of sung poetry after 1300 seems to have been inspired by, and dependent upon, the development of paradigms and theories in support of a literary vernacular. Much of our knowledge of the polyphonic musical world of the first half of the trecento is drawn, in fact, from descriptions of music and musical forms provided by poetry treatises. The musical manuscripts, all retrospective anthologies, do not serve as contemporary witnesses, and preserve very few works from the first decades of the century. Only one of the major sources of trecento vernacular polyphony, the Rossi-Ostiglia manuscript (Rome, Biblioteca Apostolica Vaticana, 215/Ost), was compiled well before the end of the century, and even it postdates a significant portion of its repertory by as much as three or four decades.

Dante, the *prima corona* of trecento literature, reveals little concerning contemporary polyphonic practice. The notion that poetry is a musical pursuit is frequently set forth in his treatise on vernacular poetry, the *De vulgari eloquentia* of *c*1306,[6] but for the historian of early vernacular polyphony, Dante's treatise is frustrating by its incompleteness. Several times he promises a discussion of the 'mediocre vernacular', which includes the ballata, the sonnet and 'other forms that are incorrect and irregular', among which may have been counted the madrigal. The treatise never proceeds, however, beyond a discussion of the loftiest vernacular form, the canzone, a type never set by trecento polyphonists, who concentrated their efforts on the mediocre forms. Dante's work is still valuable for the light it sheds on the development of a tradition of vernacular poetry, now for the first time validated by theoretical authority. In devising a theoretical foundation for a body and style of poetry which had coalesced in practice as the *dolce stil novo* of the late thirteenth century, Dante drew upon two established and respected sources: the ancients and the troubadours. The classical heritage, represented primarily by Virgil and Ovid, furnished authoritative paradigms for poetry governed by compositional rules. Dante's application of the term 'poeta' to practitioners of the vernacular lyric (*rimatori*) represented a critical step towards legitimizing the artistic efforts of Italian poets:

> Several times I have called the vernacular *rimatori: poeti*. And I have dared to utter this word without doubt for a reason: because they are indeed *poets* if we consider the true meaning of poetry, which is nothing other than the making of a poem (a creation of the imagination) according to the principles of rhetoric and music. But they [the vernacular poets] differ from the great [classical] poets in that the great poets composed according to an established system of language and style, and these [new poets] compose at random. For that reason it happens that when we try to imitate the great poets more closely, we compose poetry more properly. And I, who aim at writing a work on the rules of [vernacular] poetry, ought to emulate the rules of the great Latin poets.   [*De vulgari eloquentia*, ii, 4:10–19]

The regulated element which, more than any other, brought Italian vernacular prosody into the realm of *poesia* was syllable count. Scansion, the quantifying of lines according to syllable count, serves as the focus for the *Summa artis rithimici vulgaris dictaminis* by the Paduan jurist Antonio da Tempo.[7] Da Tempo's treatise on vernacular poetry, dated 1332, is our most valuable link, and one of very few contemporary witnesses, to the nascent tradition of secular art music in the first decades of the trecento. Da Tempo's theory of the vernacular lyric is founded on the same assumption that Dante set forth in the *De vulgari eloquentia*: a body of texts governed by rules (in this case, of syllabic quantity) must be taken as true poetry. The *Summa* presents a method for the scansion of Italian poetry and models for the construction of the madrigal, ballata, rotundellus (i.e. the rondel, a French import), and sonnet according to enumerative principles. Few of the extant madrigals with musical settings reflect da Tempo's model types with precision. But the musical works do agree with the general outline of da Tempo's 'second category' of madrigal, displaying a preponderance of seven- and eleven-syllable lines and a formal structure consisting of two tercets (*terzetti*) followed by a one- or two-line ritornello. That the madrigal was an inherently polyphonic form, and not a polyphonic elaboration of an earlier monodic lyric type, is indicated by the early treatises. Da Tempo calls for performance by at least two voices. The

247

anonymous *Capitulum de vocibus applicatis verbis*, a brief but highly instructive treatise on musico-poetical forms, dating from as early as the second decade of the trecento, is more specific in its description of a musical setting that matches precisely the style of those works which survive, consisting of two or more voice parts: a florid upper line (cantus) or lines over a slower-moving tenor (*'Mandrigalia* are texts set to several melodies, of which one is primarily of longs and is called tenor, while the other or others is primarily of minims').[8]

Even if the production of a madrigal text was governed by a system of compositional rules, the madrigal was by definition a 'rustic' or 'mediocre' genre. Poetic and musical style were both fixed by theoretical dicta. While its rustic or pastoral trappings no doubt contributed to its popularity within the courtly culture of suburban villas of northern Italy, the virtual explosion of the madrigal on to the literary scene in the fourteenth century, and the rapid coalescence of a system of conventional vocabulary and imagery, would not have been possible without a preceding tradition of long standing. The source for much of the madrigal's bucolic imagery may well have been provided by classical pastoral poetry.

In the *Bucolics* of Theocritus and Virgil, the shepherds and cowherds, around whose musical and amatory activities the pastoral lyric is woven, exist in a *locus amoenus*, or ideal landscape. Literary depictions of the *locus amoenus*, like other poetical or rhetorical topoi, shared a conventionalized descriptive vocabulary.[9] The ideal pastoral setting is a beautiful shady locale (often a grove or forest) including a tree (or trees), a meadow and a gentle flowing source of water. To those required ingredients might be added lovely flowers, sweet breezes or the songs of birds. Natural settings of precisely this sort characterize early trecento madrigal poetry. We find in the anonymous *Capitulum* the instruction that 'the texts of madrigals should be about shepherdesses, flowers, orchards, garlands, fields and similar things'. Often the opening tercet or tercets of a madrigal consist of nothing more than a catalogue of the constituent elements of a *locus amoenus*, as in an anonymous piece from the Rossi manuscript:

> Quando i oselli canta
> Le pasturele vano a la campagna
> Quando i oselli canta
>
> Fan girlande de erba
> Frescheta verde, et altre belle fiore
> Fan girlande de erba.

A well-known group of works by the three leading figures of the northern musical tradition reflects the crystallization of the ideal landscape as a literary topos in the madrigal. The texts of Maestro Piero's

All'ombra d'un perlaro and *Sovra un fiume regale*, Giovanni da Cascia's *Apres' un fiume chiaro* and Jacopo da Bologna's *O dolce, apres' un bel perlaro fiume* consist of little more than a set of permutations upon a single *locus amoenus*, the central features of which are the shady grove containing flowers, beautiful ladies, the *perlaro* tree, a stream and its bank. It has been suggested that most or all of these works were conceived as part of a competition at the Scaligeri court towards the middle of the century.[10] The fourteenth-century chronicler Filippo Villani reported that:

> Giovanni da Cascia, when visiting the halls of Mastino della Scala lord of Verona as a postulant, and competing in artistic excellence with Master Jacopo da Bologna, who was most expert in the art of music, intoned (while the lord spurred them on with gifts) many madrigals, many soni and ballate of remarkable sweetness and of most artistic melody.[11]

Such musico-poetical competitions may represent the survival in Italy of the old French tradition of the *puy*, in which competitors created songs upon a given topic.

There is much in the madrigal that recalls the world of troubadour song, which found its way to Italy in the last decades of the thirteenth century in the face of a hostile political environment in its native region. The most characteristic element of the formal structure in the madrigal is the concluding one- or two-line ritornello which stood apart from the rest of the poem conceptually, poetically and musically. The ritornello typically expressed a summary reflection upon the preceding pastoral narrative, or even a proverbial moral. It was usually marked by the introduction of a new rhyme sound and of a shift in poetic stance, at times involving direct address, a turn from the narrative to the vocative posture. The ritornello text is heard only once, at the conclusion of the poem; it is by no means a refrain, despite the implications of return inherent in the term. Functionally and formally, the ritornello was similar to the envoy, a direct address to a poem's intended 'recipient', which often concluded troubadour poems. Those Provençal envoys (as in the *sestina*, a form developed by the troubadour Arnaut Daniel) were termed 'tornadas', and it is likely that therein lies the root of the Italian term for the concluding couplet of a madrigal. Dante, of course, cites Daniel as a model in the *De vulgari eloquentia*, naming him as a master of the art of vernacular poetry. However, Dante's treatment of the troubadour model for vernacular poetry is limited to the lofty genres of the Provençal *canso* and Italian canzone, shedding no light on the background of the forms which received mensural musical settings.

The implication that Daniel may have been recognized as a progenitor of the northern musical tradition is present, however, in an illumination in a fourteenth-century Bolognese legal treatise (Fulda,

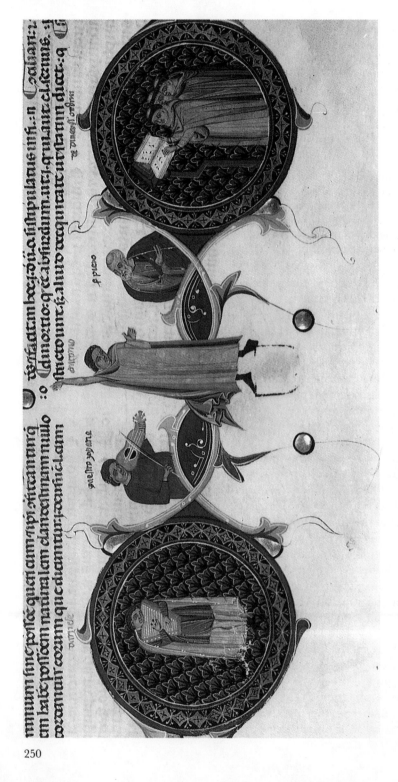

74. *Miniatures depicting (left to right) Arnaut Daniel, Giovanni da Cascia, Magister Piero and a group of singing monks, from a fourteenth-century Bolognese legal treatise*

Hessische Landesbibliothek D23).[12] Depicted at the centre of the illustration (fig.74) are the three masters of the northern madrigal style: Giovanni, Piero and Jacopo. To their left, encircled by a laurel wreath, is a singing figure in French courtly dress identified as 'Daniele', evidently the troubadour. The musical style of the polyphonic madrigal may have been far removed from the monophonic texture and free rhythms of troubadour lyrics, but it appears to have been considered a part of the same courtly tradition in Italy.

A further link to troubadour practice is revealed by the 'perlaro' madrigals by Giovanni, Piero and Jacopo cited above. In each ritornello, the name 'Anna' (possibly a noblewoman of Verona who participated in the judging of the musical competition; perhaps simply a literary representation of the ideal beloved) is hidden within the text as a *senhal*, a device used in Provençal poetry to disguise the name of the beloved for whom the song was intended. Rather than resorting to the troubadour ploy of identifying the female beloved by a masculine name, the Italian poet embeds the woman's name within the syllable structure of the words of the poem, as in the ritornello couplet of Giovanni's *O perlaro gentil*:

> Ai, lasso a mme, non vuol più ANNAmorarmi
> La bianca mano che solea tocarmi.

Even the selfconscious structural games which typified the elaborate *trobar clus* of the more accomplished troubadours is not without an echo in the artificially simple, rustic style of the early madrigal. Like Virgil's *Eclogues*, in which classical tales of bumpkins and animals transcended their mediocre characters and props through literary style and grace, the madrigal offered an opportunity for exploiting the poetic tension between rusticity (as a topic) and ingenious, if not elegant, textual structures. The anonymous *Piançe la bella Iguana* consists of an unusual three-strophe format, each strophe concluding with a ritornello couplet. The last word of each ritornello serves also as the first word of the following strophe, and the verbal chain is closed by the last word of the final strophe, 'piançe', linking the end of the poem with its beginning. References in the text to 'Iguana' and 'Euguana' suggest a provenance for the work in the Verona–Padua orbit, home to the mythical nymphs who supposedly populated the Colli Euganei.

Cultivation of troubadour and trouvère poetry was a feature of the courtly life of the Veneto, and references to collections of trouvère chansons appear in Florentine library inventories of the trecento. Courtly predilection for Gallic touches is even apparent in the several bilingual madrigals which turn up rarely but consistently throughout the trecento. An early madrigal in the Rossi manuscript is built of alternating Italian and French lines:

> L'antico dio Biber fra sette stelle,
> Che tout ior vont intor a tramontaine,
> Som spirt a mis et s'amisté sovraine.
> [Rit.] I lor aspetti son trini e sestilli. *etc*

Evidence for the Gallicization of trecento musical tastes is even more striking in the Florentine tradition of the second half of the century, and includes an anonymous French-texted caccia, *Quan je voy*, based on a trouvère song, and Landini's polyphonic ballata/virelai, *Adieu adieu, dous dame*.

Italian awareness of French musical culture extended to details of musical style and notation. Marchetto da Padova, whose *Pomerium musices* (written in the early 1320s in the residence of Raynaldus de Cintiis, a wealthy citizen of Cesena) furnishes the most extensive outline of the Italian notational system,[13] discusses the difference between Italian and French rhythmic notation at some length, occasionally exhibiting a bias towards the rules of the 'more logical' French system. The Italian system permits the incorporation of French gestures into madrigal and ballata settings, most notably the French preference for 'major prolation' (i.e. the theoretical division of the pulse into three equal parts). In Italian musical sources, instances of this sort of metrical organization are often signalled by the letter 'g' for *gallica*. An anonymous monophonic ballata written entirely in this rhythmic style acknowledges its French orientation in the deliberately ambiguous first line of its refrain: 'Amor mi fa cantar ala francescha' ('Love makes me sing to Francesca/Love makes me sing in the French manner'). Rhythmic variety in both the madrigal and ballata was often effected through shifts in the organization of the smallest note values between the French (*gallica*) grouping by threes, and the Italian (*ytalica*) by twos or fours.

Such techniques of rhythmic organization were supported by poetry theorists, who offer specific advice on the subject. The anonymous *Capitulum de vocibus* advised that in composing an Italian madrigal, 'if anyone should wish at some time to mingle in some measure in the French system, it would be good; but if he did so at the end of a line, that would be better'.[14] The intermingling of French and Italian metrical characteristics created a rhythmic kaleidoscope, particularly within the virtuoso melismas which fell most often (as suggested by the *Capitulum*) on the penultimate syllables of lines. The character of the madrigal is expressed completely and essentially by florid, melismatic passages in which the composer's gift for invention was most decidedly tested. Florid writing, confined mainly to the cantus part, alternated with passages in syllabic or nearly syllabic style in which both voices declaimed the text syllables simultaneously. In those syllabic passages, the extremely simple polyphonic framework of the madrigal as conventional two-voice counterpoint is exposed most baldly, supporting the theory that the madrigal may have evolved (in musical terms) from the simple *cantus binatim* associated primarily with native Italian sacred forms such as the *lauda*.

The extent of the correlation between poetical and musical structure in the madrigal is quite extraordinary. Not only the structural frame of the poem, but its subject matter and narrative nuances were consciously reflected in the *sonus*, or musical setting. In the case of what came to be the conventional madrigal structure, two tercets, each sung to the same music, were followed by a ritornello which was provided with new music. The change of narrative stance typical of the ritornello portion of the poem was often highlighted by a change of metre at the opening of the ritornello music, which created an audible sense of disorientation, as the listener is pulled out of the sphere of pastoral narration and placed in the present world of reflection, moralizing or invocation. According to da Tempo, the change in the music served as a complement to the change in rhyme (*consonantia*) which he called for in the ritornello. Within the tercets, each line-ending was marked, at least in the madrigals of the first half of the century, by a firm cadence. The cadence at the end of the tercet was usually of the contrary-motion variety, with cantus and tenor converging to a unison. While the placement of melismatic passages within the setting was determined by the composer's own preference, they regularly accompany the penultimate, and often the first syllable of each line of text, with the most extensive melisma usually reserved for the end of the tercet music.

The earliest extant madrigals, which probably originated in the 1330s (roughly contemporaneous with da Tempo's treatise), display a certain amount of restraint in the application of melismas to the text. The madrigal style was still in something of an embryonic stage, although each conventional element of musical structure was present. Since melismas are in some cases rather minimal, there is often a close correspondence between the number of syllables in a line and the number of *tempora* (bars) in the musical setting of a line. This feature of the early style seems to reflect da Tempo's dictum that the musical setting should reflect the composer's correct scansion of the poem (i.e. the counting of syllables). As melismas expanded, adding textless bars to the setting of each line, the relationship between line length and phrase length became incidental. That the composition of florid polyphony should have seized the imaginations of Italian composers with such vigour is not surprising if we view such musical *fioriture* as audible projections of the flowery landscapes of madrigal poetry. The music of the madrigal was, in a very real sense, draped across its text like the floral *ghirlande* of which poets and theorists were so fond. Northern madrigal settings of the 1340s and 50s were characterized not only by the further spinning-out of melismatic material, but by an increasing tendency towards textural complexity, which often obscured the underlying structure of the text. In the works of the great mid-century master

Jacopo da Bologna, the introduction of imitative exchanges between the cantus and tenor voices undermined the principle of simultaneous declamation of text syllables, while the threefold division of the strophe was rendered less distinct as simultaneous cadences in cantus and tenor were replaced by solo passages which linked one text line to the next in a musical enjambment.[15]

The madrigal continued to thrive among the first generation of Florentine composers shortly after mid-century, but its original profile took on features engendered by Florence's republican social milieu. Florentine madrigal texts exhibit a wider range of options with regard to both imagery and tone. The pastoral scenario was never abandoned, but was joined by satirical, didactic and even autobiographical topoi. The caccia, which had thrived in the first half of the century, appears to have inspired less interest on the part of Florentine composers. Formally related to the madrigal by its concluding ritornello, the caccia depicted in naturalistic fashion the sounds of the countryside, often of the hunt (dogs barking, horses whinnying) in its upper texted voices (fig.73 above). Florentine cacce (e.g. Francesco Landini's *Cosi pensoso*) are more wryly humorous, often choosing as their subject matter the daily activities of the lower classes rather than the pastimes of the nobility. The social context for the performance of Florentine polyphony no doubt contributed to the establishment of new textual and musical conventions. Republican Florence lacked the dynastic establishments which supported such activities as the courtly *puy* described earlier; the urban environment encouraged the production of texts which reflected the interests of an urban artistic élite. Hunting cacce and madrigals centring on shepherdesses, birds and garlands of flowers, appropriate to the ambience of a country stronghold, were often replaced in Florence by texts founded in the exigencies of daily life in the city: the making and keeping of money, personal relationships and the comical aspects of the lesser artisan and peasant.

Amateur performance of music (especially simple secular monophony) was apparently a favourite activity of well-bred Florentines. But the business of teaching and composing polyphony was essentially reserved for clerics who were, in most cases, drawn from the class of Florentine artisans or lower middle class. Despite their humble origins, these composers were linked to the leading families of the city in various ways. Some served as pedagogues, instructing the children of prosperous citizens in the rudiments of music.[16] Often figuring in the legacies of Florentine businessmen, the churches and convents to which composers were attached served both the spiritual and academic needs of the Florentine financial and industrial *haute bourgeoisie*. Existence in the conventual and capitular churches in Florence was orientated as much towards the city as the church, and clerics participated fully in Florence's secular intellectual life.

The musical activities of important composers such as Ser Gherardello, Francesco Landini and Nicolò da Perugia are unambiguously, if haphazardly, documented in the extant records of the Vallombrosian monastery of S Trinità? Landini and Lorenzo Masini were attached for much of their careers to the church of S Lorenzo.[17] Across the Arno, the Augustinian convent of S Spirito provided a cosmopolitan environment that was extremely hospitable to intellectual and artistic endeavours. The S Spirito circle embraced not only the resident composers Corrado da Pistoia and Guglielmo da Francia, but many leading Florentine literary and political figures, including Nicolò Niccoli, Coluccio Salutati, Luigi Marsili, Roberto Rossi and Martino da Signa.[18] The presence of a body of interested consumers for the elegant music of an international group of polyphonists may be attributed to the vitality of the academic courses of study offered by such institutions. The University of Florence, unable to achieve the status of the established centres of learning in Padua and Bologna, was often passed over by the scions of the upper strata of Florentine society in favour of the monastic *studium*, S Spirito's *studium* providing a model for proto-humanistic education.[19] That the tradition of Italian polyphonic music in the latter part of the trecento was largely in the hands of the monasteries is graphically emphasized by the Bolognese illumination discussed earlier which depicts Arnaut Daniel at the far left, the northern triumvirate of Giovanni, Jacopo and Piero to his right, and to their right a group of monks with the identifying label 'dei diversi ordini' (fig.74 above). The illustration provides a contemporary time-line of the development of Italian secular music. No greater testimony to the role of the monasteries in the propagation and preservation of trecento polyphony exists than the Squarcialupi manuscript, probably produced in the workshop of the Florentine monastery of S Maria degli Angeli.[20] More systematically organized than any other later medieval retrospective anthology, it is arranged by composer (after the fashion of troubadour and trouvère collections), grouped more or less geographically, with each composer's works announced by a masterful portrait. Most striking is the care taken in pictorially identifying the institutional association of individual composers by the colours of their clerical robes. In most cases, the orders indicated by the garb in the illuminations have been corroborated by modern investigation of institutional archives.

More difficult to assess, however, is the role played by polyphonic music, particularly the madrigal, outside the walls of monastic institutions. As suggested by Boccaccio's *Decameron*, socially orientated 'domestic' musical activities, enjoyed by the well-to-do in villas like the Alberti's Paradiso, probably centred more on the playing and singing of dance-songs, notably the monophonic ballata. The madrigal was probably confined to circles of musical connoisseurs, as reflected in the self-referential nature of some madrigal texts dealing with the teaching or composing of music. The ten monophonic ballate (five each by Lorenzo and Gherardello) transmitted in the Squarcialupi manuscript, and five earlier works transmitted anonymously in the Rossi manuscript, provide the only written remnants of what must have formed a significant and characteristic element of Italian musical life. They represent rare examples of the intersection of the sphere of the professional composer with the social sphere in which music functioned as a means of entertainment.

Musical accompaniments for dancing, one of the most popular medieval social pastimes, could be either sung or played on instru-

75. *Circle dance (the leader plays a tambourine and may be singing a monophonic ballata) depicted as one of the manifestations of the 'Effects of Good Government' (c1348), by Ambrogio Lorenzetti, in the Palazzo Pubblico, Siena*

ments. Vocal accompaniment was provided by the monophonic ballata which, like other medieval refrain forms, was originally a simple dance-song, although the extant written examples are quite sophisticated. Dances performed to the ballata were probably circle dances, similar to the French *carole*, with one dancer designated as leader (fig.75). All of the dancers participated in singing the refrain (*ripresa*), while the internal portions of the song – the *piedi* and *volta* – were entrusted to the leader. The monophonic ballate that have survived in musical manuscripts probably represent especially sophisticated extensions of a simple melodic genre. It is difficult to imagine that amateur dancers or musicians in a social situation could have successfully performed the rhythmically intricate melismas that appear in many of the written ballate.

Instrumental accompaniments for dancing all fell under the umbrella term 'soni'. The greatest repository for such works is the British Library manuscript, which includes a collection of dance tunes most of which bear generic designations: 'istanpita', 'saltarello', 'trotto'. One title, 'Lamento di Tristano', suggests a literary inspiration, and another, 'La Manfredina', prefigures the fifteenth-century practice of naming instrumental works with feminized male names. Both dances are followed by a contrasting *rotta*, suggesting an early establishment of the tradition, usually associated with the fifteenth and sixteenth centuries, of pairing dances in contrasting metres and tempos. The same manuscript includes a group of four melodies identified as 'chançonete tedesche'. These monophonic pieces, all written in a very simple and square rhythmic style (all are in duple metre and employ only breves and semibreves), may have served as foundations for improvised polyphony, performed by accomplished instrumentalists. Judging by the designation 'tedesche', those instrumentalists would most likely have been wind players. By the end of the fourteenth century, the realm of professional wind music was already dominated by performers from Germany and the Low Countries, who were establishing a dynasty which would last for more than a century. As early as 1375 the term 'piffaro', of German derivation, had replaced the native Italian 'cennamela' in many quarters and referred to wind players and to double-reed wind instruments (of the shawm family).[21] Simone Prudenzani, in *Il Solazzo*, praises a sound like that of a 'pifero venuto di Fiandra'.[22] Florentine records of the last decades of the century show that most of the *piffari della Signoria* were 'da Alemania', and musicians 'da Alemania' or 'da Fiandra' dominate the rolls of the *piffari* of the great musical patrons of the fifteenth century, most notably the Estense of Ferrara, whose library inventories document the existence of collections of *tenori todeschi*, probably similar to those of the London manuscript.[23]

Within the domain of the madrigal, the peculiarly Florentine taste

76. Tournament scene with trumpeters and (unusually) a group of musicians playing shawms, flute and fiddle: detail of a painted chest (Florentine school, early fifteenth century)

and temperament distinguishes the products of Lorenzo Masini (Lorenzo da Firenze, as he is identified in most musical sources) and his contemporaries from the original madrigals of the north. Florentine poets, more than their northern predecessors, were apparently willing to accept the madrigal as a serious vehicle for their literary efforts. Very few of the extant musical works by northern composers represent settings of texts attributable to known poets. The only such works, Jacopo da Bologna's setting of Petrarch's *Non al suo amante* and Giovanni da Cascia's *La bella stella* on a text by Lancilotto Anguissola, are both relatively late.[24] In Florence, however, Sacchetti and his circle cultivated the 'mediocre' genre with greater vigour, and it is, in fact, the Florentine, 'Sacchettian' madrigal which marks the absolute crystallization of the formal structure of two tercets plus ritornello and the standard rhythm scheme of *abb, cdd, ee*.

While the portrayal of a *locus amoenus* was not abandoned in the Florentine madrigal (for example, Lorenzo's *Nel chiaro fiume* and *Sovra la riva*, the latter on a text by Sacchetti), texts were often more pointedly classicized by reference to mythological figures such as Narcissus and Helen. Some were removed from the pastoral domain entirely.

Lorenzo's setting of Soldanieri's madrigal, *Dà, dà a chi avaregia*, provides a clear example of a quintessentially Florentine non-pastoral work. The text is moralistic, even proverbial, in tone. The pragmatic language is as typical of the Florentine mentality as it is distant from the bucolic descriptions that delighted the aristocrats of Lombardy and the Veneto in the first half of the century:

> Give, give, even to him who hoards for himself
> If bad times come his way at the whim of a she-bear
> Because without a purse one does not find a friend.
>
> You, O you who have a good position, listen to me:
> He has a chance to make a friend for himself
> Who has his foot in the water, his beak in the millet.
>
> Think now, think that he who falls slowly helps himself to rise again.
> Woe to him whose turn it is.[25]

The careful hand of the composer is evident throughout the musical setting. Gone are the abstract, meandering musical 'garlands' which adorned the early madrigals. Every melisma is carefully constructed upon sequential repetitions of a single musical idea; each phrase commences with a lively bit of imitation between cantus and tenor. Lorenzo's predisposition for coherent motivic organization within a work, for spinning out long melodic phrases through the manipulation and development of a single melodic motif, contributed to the eventual collapse of the older madrigalistic style in which the melismas that framed each line of text were little more than ornamental appendages to the simple two-voice counterpoint that served as the foundation of the work, and audible ornaments of a conventional text. The Florentine madrigals of the 1350s and 60s paved the way for the more 'organic' style (in which entire works were unified by varied repetitions of motivic 'cells') that characterized the polyphony of the last part of the century, most notably the works of Landini.[26]

Composers may already have been impatient to expand their musical horizons beyond the traditional genres before the advent of the polyphonic ballata on the Florentine musical scene. Lorenzo's madrigal settings include experiments not only in musical style, but in formal structure as well. The madrigals *Come in sul fonte* and *Sovra la riva* incorporate open and closed cadences into the ritornello music, among the earliest appearances of this characteristically French practice in Italian polyphony. More unusual still is his setting of *Povero zappator*, built on an isorhythmic tenor, the melody of which is constructed entirely of two-bar motifs followed in every case by a one-bar diminution of the same music. In *Ita se n'era star nel paradiso* the melismatic style is carried to its extreme.[27] Not only are the florid passages among the most expansive in the trecento repertory, but the rhythmic variety and complexity within those passages pose unusual notational dilemmas, attacked by Lorenzo in typically innovatory fashion. As the first composition in the section of the Squarcialupi manuscript devoted to Lorenzo's works, *Ita se n'era star nel paradiso* is transmitted in a bizarre, hybrid notation, undoubtedly of Lorenzo's own invention, which is completely unique to this piece. All these experimental and unusual works suggest creative struggle within a conventional system which was ready to burst its fetters, and which would soon be replaced by a new set of stylistic ideals in which the polyphonic ballata stood as centrepiece.

Lorenzo stands simultaneously as the most paradigmatic and most idiosyncratic representative of the Florentine musical style in the first two decades after mid-century. The son of a second-hand dealer, a representative of the lower stratum of the middle class, Lorenzo was a product of an urban world (as were many of the troubadours), and his works reflect the pride and independent spirit for which the Florentines were famous. His adult career, as a cleric in the church of S Lorenzo until his death shortly after 1370, was typical of a Florentine musician, attached not to a great cathedral or a wealthy patron, but to a religious institution with a decidedly local orientation.[28] Lorenzo is named, along with his compatriot and contemporary Gherardello (*d* 1364), as a 'faultless master of music' in Franco Sacchetti's nostalgic encomium to his native city, *Lasso, Fiorenza mia, ch'io mi ritrovo.* Among the composer's extant works are settings of poems by Sacchetti, Giovanni Boccaccio, Niccolò Soldanieri and Gregorio Calonista. Poems by Sacchetti and Soldanieri in particular constitute a significant portion of song texts set by Lorenzo and his contemporaries (including Gherardello, Donato da Cascia and Nicolò da Perugia), suggesting a closely interwoven relationship between local musicians and literati. An autograph manuscript of Sacchetti's *Libro delle rime* includes annotations which identify composers of settings for more than 30 of the poet's works, as well as a poetic correspondence with the younger Florentine composer Francesco Landini.[29] Lorenzo's setting of Boccaccio's *Non so qual i' mi voglia* is the only surviving monophonic musical treatment of a ballata by the poet, in whose *Decameron* the genre plays such an important role in the depiction of musical activities in a social setting, each day's narrative closing with the performance of a ballata by one or more of the assembled company.

Whether the madrigal or the ballata and other dance music represented the largest component in the auditory musical experience of a trecento Florentine, the former continued to enjoy favoured status among composers until roughly the decade of the 1360s, when its popularity was eclipsed by that of the polyphonic ballata. The new Florentine style was cultivated primarily by Francesco Landini. In the light of Landini's virtual abandonment of the madrigal, it is somewhat curious that his name stands out among all others as representative of the music of the trecento. His historical visibility is no less a function of his productivity as a musician than of his near-mythical stature in the Florence of his own day. With an output of more than 150 works, primarily polyphonic ballate, he was apparently (judging from the music that has survived) the most prolific Italian composer of the century. Owing to the Florentine provenance of the musical sources, and the Florentine bias of early quattrocento Italian historiography, it is difficult to assess the extent of Landini's reputation and influence outside his native Tuscan orbit. Certainly within the musical world of late medieval Florence, Landini represented the central musical personality for several decades. His works constitute a formidable proportion of the repertories transmitted by the primarily Florentine musical manuscripts, accounting for more than a third of the collection in the Squarcialupi manuscript, and more than half of the repertory in Panciatichi 26.

The evidence of written and iconographical sources suggests that during his lifetime Landini was recognized primarily as an organist. Florentine musical and archival sources identify the composer not by his family name, but as 'Franciscus de organis' (or 'horghanista') and 'Francesco degli orghanij', the latter being the name recorded in the official Florentine register of deaths for 2 September 1397. The portrait of Landini in the Squarcialupi manuscript shows the composer holding an organetto (fig.77), as does the carving on his tombstone in the church of S Lorenzo. Villani's capsule biography of the composer dwells above all upon his technical abilities as an organist. Landini's facility as a performer, colourfully depicted in Orphic trappings (as Francesco's playing holds sway over the birds in the trees) in Giovanni Gherardi da Prato's *Paradiso degli Alberti*,[30] was apparently matched by his skill as a technician, judging from his recorded involvement in two major organ construction projects at Ss Annunziata in 1397 and at S Reperata in 1387. Filippo Villani attributed to Landini the design of a string instrument which he called 'serena serenarum'.

Landini's reputation as a musician was enhanced by his expertise as a theorist and poet. Giovanni Gherardi da Prato, Cino Rinuccini and Coluccio Salutati praised his erudition in all aspects of the liberal arts.[31] Despite his popularity among the first generation of Florentine civic humanists, Landini's academic profile was rather conservative, as revealed in several of his own texts. The tritextual madrigal *Musica son/Già furon/Ciascun vuoli* (which introduces Landini's portion of the Squarcialupi manuscript) laments the state of music as practised by those without the requisite scholastic training. Another madrigal, *Tu che l'oper altru*, and a ballata, *Contemplar le gran cose*, both reflect the composer's interest in the philosophy of William of Ockham, a subject which provoked considerable controversy in the monastic schools of late trecento Florence. Landini's Latin poem written against detractors of Ockham testifies to his considerable erudition.[32] Much (or most) of Landini's music was fitted to texts which the composer may have written himself. According to Villani, Landini's excellence as a poet earned him the *corona laurea* (which he wears in the Squarcialupi manuscript portrait, fig.77), awarded by King Peter of Cyprus at Venice upon the recommendation of a jury which included Petrarch. If the story is not apocryphal, it suggests that Landini enjoyed a wider reputation than that indicated by the musical sources.

Despite the relative wealth of general testimony to Landini's fame and accomplishments in the last 30 years of his life, little is known of his earlier career or his musical or academic training. Francesco's father, Jacopo del Casentino (*d* 1349), was a painter of some repute, albeit within a geographically limited area, and a founding member of the Florentine painters' confraternity. The family name Landino or Landini apparently derives from Jacopo's father, Landino di Manno of Casentino. The composer's modest origins placed him within the same stratum of Florentine society as his musical compatriots Lorenzo, Jacopo Pianelaio (the slipper maker) and the painter-composer Bonaiuto Corsini, the son of a painters' guild associate of Jacopo del Casentino.

77. *Francesco Landini with an organetto, wearing the corona laurea: miniature from the Squarcialupi manuscript*

Some of his madrigal texts indicate the possibility of an early connection with the northern tradition, perhaps at the Visconti court, in
which case his first exposure to secular polyphony may have come at
the hands of Jacopo da Bologna or Giovanni da Cascia.[33] In a less
speculative vein, we may reasonably assume that the Florentines
Gherardello and Lorenzo played a significant role in the shaping of
Landini's musical style. The case for Lorenzo's influence on the
younger composer, perhaps in a teaching capacity, is particularly
strong. Lorenzo was a canon at S Lorenzo from 1348 until his death,
and Landini embarked on a long-term attachment to that same institution beginning in 1364. Lorenzo's works, particularly the humorous
madrigal *Dolgomi a voi, maestri*, addressed to fellow singing-teachers,
and the *Antefana*, a monophonic exercise in solmization and avoidance
of the tritone, reveal him to have been a witty and learned pedagogue.
While neither Lorenzo nor Gherardello composed polyphonic ballate,
the most characteristic gesture of Landini's style, the under-third
cadence (also termed the 'Landini cadence' because of the frequency
with which it appears in his works), was an important component of
Gherardello's musical vocabulary in his monophonic ballate composed
in the 1350s.[34]

Roughly two-thirds of Landini's ballate are for two voices, the
remainder for three. Most of the three-voice works are presumably
products of the composer's later years. Stylistically, Landini's ballate
diverge sharply from the madrigals of earlier generations. In all but a
few, madrigalistic virtuosity and metrical variation are abandoned in
favour of a simpler, more graceful rhythmic vocabulary. Mensurations
remain constant throughout a work. In modern terms, the sonorities
are enriched by an increase in parallel motion in thirds and sixths.
Since the refrain form of the ballata (*AbbaAbbaAbbaA*) required that the
ripresa music (*A*) allow for a smooth transition to the *piedi* (*bb*) and back
to itself at the end of the *volta* (*a*), and that the *piedi* lead coherently into
the *volta* (musically identical to the *ripresa*), both formal musical units
tend to end on the same pitch. This created a sense of coherence foreign
to the madrigal aesthetic, which called for a deliberate and audible,
often jarring, contrast between the music of the tercet and that of the
ritornello, a contrast effected through a change in mensuration and an
ultimate cadence on a pitch other than that which concluded the tercet.
Similarly, the shift in poetic stance encountered in the madrigal ritornello does not figure in the unified voice of the ballata texts. Topically,
the ballata is less narrative and less pictorial than the madrigal, tending
towards more personal and even self-revelatory expressiveness.

Landini's mature ballate and those of his contemporaries Paolo
Tenorista and Andreas de Florentia (Andrea dei Servi) reflect the
increasing Gallicization of Florentine musical style which informed the
last decades of the trecento. Florence's contacts with French cultural

and business centres were well established, suggesting that the incorporation of French elements into Florentine music may have been inspired in part by the tastes of the Florentine audience. Those elements include a reliance on three-voice polyphonic structures (in contradistinction to the native madrigal style, which was primarily two-voiced), the incorporation of open and closed endings into the *piedi* of the ballata (as in the *ouvert* and *clos* endings of the French *formes fixes*) and abandonment of the kaleidoscopic metrical structures which characterized earlier Italian polyphony. Not only the style and sonority, but also the techniques of notating music were affected. Florentine sources display such French features as texting in only the top voice of a three-voice composition, a hybrid notation which includes several characteristically French elements (such as the dot of addition) and five-line staves (as in the British Library manuscript) rather than the traditional Italian six-line staves. Several of the important Florentine manuscript sources even include French works.

S Spirito, perhaps the most cosmopolitan of Florence's monastic establishments, provided a convenient locale for the international exchange of ideas and probably played a significant role in the hybridization of Italian and French musical styles in Florence. It housed representatives of the Augustinian order from all over Europe, and the convent's centrality in Florentine intellectual history is illustrated by the Ockhamist debate which inspired Landini's composition of verses in praise of Ockham. Much of the propaganda serving both the conservative scholastic and the 'proto-humanist' sides was put forth within the walls of S Spirito in the last quarter of the century.[35] The only French composer who can be placed with certainty in the Florentine milieu is Guglielmo da Francia, an Augustinian residing at S Spirito in the 1360s and 70s. While few works by Guglielmo survive, they include a setting of Sacchetti's madrigal *La neve, el ghiaccio* (c1365). The limited number of compositions by Guglielmo do not permit more than a speculative assessment of his role in the importation of French elements into Florentine music, but his presence in Landini's circle during a crucial and transitional period in Italian style is surely significant.

Peripatetic Italian clerics and businessmen must have been no less instrumental in encouraging an interchange between French and Florentine musical culture. French was the second language of the Florentine businessman, and banking families like the Alberti maintained branch offices in Paris, Avignon and Bruges.[36] The Florentine clerical presence abroad was equally strong. During the 1360s and 70s, Florentines outnumbered all other Italians at the papal court, and among those the majority were members of the Augustinian order.[37] A manuscript compiled in the fifteenth century (Modena, Biblioteca Estense α.M.5,24), exemplifies the musical tastes of the papal courts in the last quarter of the fourteenth and the first decade of the fifteenth centuries. It includes within its diverse, Ars Subtilior repertory two works by a Frater Corradus de Pistoria, an Italian Augustinian who was a member of the S Spirito circle in Florence in the mid-1380s. The pieces are not Italian at all, consisting of a French and a Latin ballade, testifying to the increasing internationalization of the polyphonic repertory at the end of the trecento. In fact, some of the most difficult French-texted 'mannerist' music of the period was composed not by French composers, but by Italians, including Anthonellus and Philippus de Caserta and Matteo da Perugia.

The final chapter of the history of trecento polyphony in fact belongs to the fifteenth century. The primary genres, the madrigal and polyphonic ballata, remained viable throughout the first decades of the quattrocento and are represented in the works of the Italians Paolo Tenorista and Matteo da Perugia and the Fleming Johannes Ciconia. Their Italian-texted works, written very much in the international style of the turn of the century, represent vestigial traces of a musical universe on the verge of extinction. The wealthiest Italian patrons of music soon turned their attentions towards the newer motets, mass movements, ballades and rondeaux produced by foreign composers. In Florence, where secular music had long been the province of clerics, trecento musical style was not so much supplanted by something new and alien as it was transformed by cultural tendencies which had been gathering strength for decades. The increasing popularization of religion in Tuscany provided a hospitable climate for simpler polyphonic forms like the *lauda* to advance to the forefront of musical life. Art music was affected from two directions. On the one hand, secular songs displayed evidence of a reawakened interest in simple note-against-note counterpoint, as in the ballata *I' senti' matutino* by Andrea Stefani, a singer and composer of *laude* in the company of the Bianchi Gesuati.[38] At the same time, pieces from the existing ballata repertory were contrafacted and fitted with devotional *lauda* texts.[39] Most interesting in the light of these musical tendencies is the intensification of the production of manuscript anthologies containing musical works from the previous century. Motivated perhaps by purely historical interest, or, since the most complete sources were produced in Florence, by a desire to demonstrate Florentine superiority in the arts, the manuscripts suggest an abiding interest in trecento polyphonic music. Simone Prudenzani's set of sonnets, *Il Saporetto* (c1415),[40] depicts the performance of works from the first portion of the quattrocento as well as items from the earlier mainstream trecento repertory. Perhaps this indicates that the best of trecento music survived as a 'concert' repertory and was still a living part of Italian musical life. But literary references of this sort, and the musical sources themselves, may have been little more than nostalgic reminiscences of a lost 'golden age' (as in Giovanni Gherardi da Prato's *Paradiso degli Alberti* which describes, decades after the fact, Florentine cultural life in the late 1380s). Such questions lie in the domain of a 'reception history' of trecento art music that has yet to be fully explored.

NOTES

[1] N. Pirrotta, 'Ars Nova and Stil Novo', *Music and Culture in Italy from the Middle Ages to the Baroque* (Cambridge, 1984), 28.

[2] Concerning some surviving traces of the Sicilian musico-poetical tradition, see N. Pirrotta, 'Polyphonic Music for a Text Attributed to Frederick II', *Music and Culture in Italy*, 39–50, and 'New Glimpses of an Unwritten Tradition', ibid, 51–71. For a general discussion of the Arabic tradition in medieval Italy, see M. R. Menocal, *The Arabic Role in Medieval Literary History* (Philadelphia, 1987), especially 116–22.

[3] The role of secular education in medieval Italian culture is discussed in D. Hay, *The Italian Renaissance in its Historical Background* (Cambridge, 1970), 68–72.

[4] See M. Meiss, *Painting and Florence in Siena After the Black Death* (New York, 1951), 125–7.

[5] As in the two-voice *Verbum caro factum est* in PMFC, xii (1976), 158. See the introduction to the volume by the editors; also F. A. Gallo, 'Cantus planus binatum', *Quadrivium*, vii (1966), 57–84.

[6] *Dante Alighieri: De vulgari eloquentia*, ed. A. Marigo (Florence, 1968).

[7] *Antonio da Tempo: Summa artis rithimici vulgaris dictaminis*, ed. R. Andrews (Bologna, 1977).

[8] Cited in F. A. Gallo, *Music of the Middle Ages*, ii, Eng. trans., K. Eales (Cambridge, 1985), 121.

[9] E. Curtius, *European Literature and the Latin Middle Ages*, Eng. trans. W. Trask (Princeton, 1973), 190–200, and C. Segal, *Poetry and Myth in the Ancient Pastoral: Essays on Theocritus and Virgil* (Princeton, 1981).

[10] *The Music of Fourteenth-Century Italy*, ed. N. Pirrotta, CMM, viii/1 (1954), i.

[11] Cited in Gallo, *Music of the Middle Ages*, 128.

[12] K. von Fischer, '"Portraits" von Piero, Giovanni da Firenze und Jacopo da Bologna in einer Bologneser-Handschrift des 14. Jahrhunderts?', *MD*, xxvii (1973), 61–4.

[13] *Marchettus de Padua: Pomerium*, ed. G. Vecchi, CSM, vi (1961).

[14] Cited in Gallo, *Music of the Middle Ages*, 121.

[15] See for example the madrigals *Non al suo amante, O cieco mondo* or *O dolce apress' un bel perlaro*.

[16] F. D'Accone, 'Music and Musicians at the Florentine Monastery of Santa Trinita, 1360–1363', *Quadrivium*, xii (1971), 146.

[17] D'Accone, *Music and Musicians*, 136–8, and F. A. Gallo, 'Lorenzo Masini e Francesco degli Organi in S. Lorenzo', *Studi musicali*, iv (1975), 57–63.

[18] H. Vonschott, *Geistiges Leben im Augustinerorden am Ende des Mittelalters und zu Beginn der Neuzeit* (Berlin, 1915), 22–3.

[19] Concerning the educational and cultural life of S Spirito in this period, see D. Gutierrez, 'La Biblioteca di Santo Spirito in Firenze nella metà del secolo XV', *Analecta Augustiniana*, xxv (1962), 6–7; R. Weiss, 'An English Augustinian in Late Fourteenth-Century Florence', *English Miscellany*, ix (1958), 18; and R. Arbesmann, *Der Augustinereremitenorden und der Beginn der humanistischen Bewegung* (Würzburg, 1965), 73ff.

[20] K. von Fischer, 'Paolo da Firenze und der Squarcialupi-Kodex (*I-Fl* 87)', *Quadrivium*, ix (1968), 5–24.

[21] B. Migliorini, *Storia della lingua italiana* (Florence, 1962), 230.

[22] Cited in D. Heartz, 'Hoftanz and Basse Dance', *JAMS*, xix (1966), 13–36.

[23] See L. Lockwood, *Music in Renaissance Ferrara 1400–1505* (Cambridge, 1984), 218.

[24] See F. A. Gallo, 'Antonio da Ferrara, Lancillotto Anguissola e il madrigale trecentesco', *Studi e problemi di critica testuale*, xii (1976), 42.

[25] Translation from *Anthology of Medieval Music*, ed. R. Hoppin (New York, 1978), 151.

[26] For a discussion of this aspect of Landini's compositions, see M. Long, 'Landini's Musical Patrimony: a Reassessment of Some Compositional Conventions in Trecento Polyphony', *JAMS*, xl (1987), 46–9.

[27] See M. Long, '*Ita se n'era a star nel paradiso:* the Metamorphoses of an Ovidian Madrigal in Trecento Italy', *L'ars nova italiana del trecento, vi: Certaldo 1984*.

[28] Gallo, 'Lorenzo Masini'.

[29] *I-Fl* Ashb.574; *Franco Sacchetti: Il libro delle rime*, ed. A. Chiari (Bari, 1936), 284.

[30] *Giovanni Gherardi da Prato: Il Paradiso degli Alberti*, ed. A. Lanza (Rome, 1975), 164ff.

[31] A. Lanza, *Polemiche e berte letterarie nella Firenze del primo quattrocento* (Rome, 1971), 39ff.

[32] On Landini's 'Ockhamist' texts, see K. von Fischer, 'Ein Versuch zur Chronologie von Landinis Werken', *MD*, xx (1966), 42, and M. Long, 'Francesco Landini and the Florentine Cultural Elite', *EMH*, iii (1983), 88ff.

[33] Von Fischer, 'Ein Versuch zur Chronologie', 38.

[34] See Long, 'Landini's Musical Patrimony', 33–4.

[35] Long, 'Francesco Landini', 90ff.

[36] Y. Renouard, 'Le compagnie commerciali fiorentine del Trecento', *Etudes d'histoire médiévale* (Paris, 1968), i, 519–26.

[37] B. Guillemain, *La cour pontificale d'Avignon (1309–1376)* (Paris, 1962), 598–601.

[38] *The Music of Fourteenth-Century Italy*, ed. Pirrotta, CMM, viii/3 (1964), p.iii.

[39] K. von Fischer, 'Kontrafakturen und Parodien italienischer Werke des Trecento und frühen Quattrocento', *AnnM*, v (1957), 44ff.

[40] The passages concerning music are included in S. Debenedetti, *Il 'Solazzo': contributi alla storia della novella, della poesia musicale e del costume del trecento* (Turin, 1922).

BIBLIOGRAPHICAL NOTES

Cultural background

The best introduction to trecento music viewed from an informed and sensitive cultural perspective remains the series of articles by N. Pirrotta, 'Ars Nova and Stil Novo' (1966), 'Dante *Musicus*: Gothicism, Scholasticisim, and Music' (1968), 'Polyphonic Music for a Text Attributed to Frederick II' (1968), 'The Oral and Written Traditions of Music' (1970), 'New Glimpses of an Unwritten Tradition' (1972) and 'Novelty and Renewal in Italy: 1300–1600' (1973); all have been reprinted in N. Pirrotta, *Music and Culture in Italy from the Middle Ages to the Baroque: a Collection of Essays* (Cambridge, 1984).

An interesting first-hand view of Florentine polyphonic song in a contemporary literary context is provided by Franco Sacchetti's *Il libro delle rime*, ed. A. Chiari (Bari, 1936), in which Sacchetti's marginal attributions identify the composers of many settings and suggest a chronological outline for at least a portion of the trecento musical repertory. The other chief literary witnesses to contemporary musical life are Giovanni Gherardi da Prato, *Il Paradiso degli Alberti*, ed. A. Lanza (Rome, 1975), and Simone Prudenzani, *Il Saporetto*, ed. S. Debenedetti in *Il 'Solazzo': contributi alla storia della novella, della poesia musicale e del costume del trecento* (Turin, 1922), both of which include references to specific musicians and musical works. The former is discussed in a historical context in H. Baron, *The Crisis of the Early Italian Renaissance* (Princeton, 1966).

The classic of late medieval/early Renaissance Florentine historiography, *Philippi Villani Liber de civitatis Florentiae famosis civibus*, ed. G.C. Galletti (Florence, 1847), is the primary source for biographical information concerning fourteenth-century composers. Recent contributions in the area of composer biography include F. D'Accone, 'Music and Musicians at the Florentine Monastery of Santa Trinità, 1360–1363', *Quadrivium*, xii (1971), 131–51, and F. A. Gallo, 'Lorenzo Masini e Francesco degli Organi in San Lorenzo', *Studi musicali*, iv (1975), 57–63. While modern historians have rarely incorporated music into their reconstructions of the fourteenth-century Italian cultural milieu, useful background material on society, politics, religion and the other arts may be found in D. Hay, *The Italian Renaissance in its Historical Background* (Cambridge, 1970); G. Brucker, *The Civic World of Early Renaissance Florence* (Princeton, 1977); L. Martines, *Power and Imagination: City-States in Renaissance Italy* (New York, 1979); and M. Meiss, *Painting in Florence and Siena After the Black Death* (Princeton, 1951). For a specific discussion of the relationship between musical culture and contemporary society, see M. Long, 'Francesco Landini and the Florentine Cultural Elite', *EMH*, iii (1983), 83–99.

Music and texts

Virtually the entire trecento musical repertory has been edited in Polyphonic Music of the Fourteenth Century (PMFC) (Monaco, 1958–), vols. iv (Landini complete works), and vi–xiii. Most of the attributed madrigals are in volumes vi and vii. PMFC is more complete than Nino Pirrotta's earlier *The Music of Fourteenth-Century Italy*, CMM, viii/1–5 (1954–64), but Pirrotta's edition is still useful for its introductory remarks on historical, textual and technical issues, and for the transcriptions themselves, in which the large-scale metrical structure of the music is emphasized through a unique system of barring.

A useful tool for the study of the trecento musical repertory is K. von Fischer, *Studien zur italienischen Musik des Trecento und frühen Quattrocento* (Berne, 1956), which includes an alphabetical listing of works by genre, along with information on manuscript sources, attributions (music and text) and text disposition.

Several of the most significant musical manuscripts are available in facsimile editions: *Il codice musicale Panciatichi 26 della Biblioteca nazionale di Firenze: riproduzione in facsimile a cura di F. Alberto Gallo* (Florence, 1981); *The Manuscript London B.M. Additional 29987: a Facsimile Edition*, ed. G. Reaney, MSD, xiii (1965); and *Il canzoniere musicale del codice Vaticano Rossi 215*, ed. G. Vecchi (Bologna, 1965).

The primary theoretical work from the period is Marchetto da Padova's notation treatise, *Pomerium*, ed. G. Vecchi, CSM, vi (1961). For background, see N. Pirrotta, 'Marchettus de Padua and the Italian Ars Nova', *MD*, ix (1955), 57–71, and F. A. Gallo, 'Marchetus in Padua und die "franco-venetische" Musik des frühen Trecento', *AMw*, xxxi (1974), 42–56. Gallo's *La teoria della notazione in Italia dalla fine del XIII all' inizio del XV secolo* (Bologna, 1966) presents a thorough and penetrating survey and explanation of notational issues.

Many of the texts set to music by trecento composers can be found, along with enlightening notes, in G. Corsi, *Poesie musicali del trecento* (Bologna, 1970).

Sources for the literary theory of the early trecento include Dante's *De vulgari eloquentia*, ed. A. Marigo (Florence, 1968), also available as *Dante in Hell: the 'De vulgari eloquentia': Introduction, Text, Translation, Commentary*, ed. W. Welliver (Ravenna, 1981); *Antonio da Tempo: Summa artis rithimici vulgaris dictaminis*, ed. R. Andrews (Bologna, 1977); and S. Debenedetti, 'Un trattatello del secolo XIV sopra la poesia musicale', *Studi medievali*, ii (1905), 59–82.

Chapter XI

The Close of the Middle Ages

REINHARD STROHM

The close of the Middle Ages was also an opening towards the Renaissance and the Modern Age. Cultural traditions did not simply die out, to be replaced by altogether different ones; the old and the new lived together over long stretches of time, while it remained uncertain where the future would belong. The struggle for survival generated, occasionally, what we call 'progress'; at other times it re-established the status quo. It is only historical hindsight which gives these debates a larger meaning. The following pages endeavour to describe what musical culture in the fifteenth century felt like when it was fresh.

We can, of course, see this period as part of a larger historical process, coming from somewhere and going somewhere. It was an age of transition, like all ages, and the more so when viewed in relation to two important modern concepts. The first is that of 'Europe'. The material and spiritual integrity of Europe was at stake in the fifteenth century as never before. The balance of the medieval 'world' – i.e. Christian Europe – was shattered by the conquests of the Turks, who entered Constantinople in 1453 and besieged Vienna in 1526; by the discovery of America in 1492 which initiated European imperialism around the world; and by the increasing separation of the Greek and Russian churches from the West. Also, the spiritual unity of Europe was at breaking-point during the great papal schism (1378–1417) and the religious reform movements which it generated or nourished. They anticipated the loss of a religious consensus which has never been recaptured. Even deeper imbalances between Europe's own inhabitants were revealed in 1492 when the Spanish monarchs expelled the Jewish communities from the territories in which they had lived in peace for centuries. Long-range trade, capitalist forms of industry and, most important, the introduction of paper and then printing provided huge opportunities for individual enterprise, for critical thought and also for closer communication.

The second important concept is communication. Music, which is essentially communication, thrived in this enterprising age. In the fifteenth century, written music begins to claim to represent music in general, people begin to ask who composed a certain piece, and musicians separated by space and time recognize the achievements of their colleagues by studying their music in written form. In the 1470s the Flemish music theorist and composer Johannes Tinctoris concluded that nothing worth hearing had been composed until the appearance of John Dunstable about 40 years before. In his wisdom, gained by hindsight, he characterized Dunstable's music as a 'new art'.[1] But his effort to show how music had reached ever greater perfection during his own lifetime is still part of a traditional conception: that of music as an *ars perfecta*, serving only its own rules and goals. A more modern conception, that of music as a vehicle of ideas, was not yet formulated, but it was developing in the works of Josquin Desprez (*c*1440–1521).

This is not to say that medieval music had been 'art pour l'art'. It had always served as a secondary and relatively humble vehicle of ideas, especially when tied to words. It received its dignity by reflection, as it were, by carrying sacred words in the plainsong of the church, or by accentuating and ornamenting a poet's thoughts in written and unwritten song. As wordless music for instruments it was heard in the context of other forms of communication: civic and courtly ceremonies, collective activities such as dance and theatre, and the sacred ceremonial when that included organ music. But in the fifteenth century music had begun to emancipate itself. It incorporated those external references by drawing them into its own structure, so that it could ultimately be understood also in their absence. This process led to the communicative power of Josquin's music, which has its own 'rhetoric' and performs its own ceremony; it also emancipated music from its medieval status as one of the disciplines of natural science (the Quadrivium) and as a humble reflection of the harmony of the spheres. Music had now soaked up the images of the spiritual and material world and had become a messenger of the human subject.

CENTRAL AND LATERAL TRADITIONS DURING THE SCHISM

In order to absorb the world into its own structure, music had first to acquire such a structure, at least in principle. This happened – only on the level of written art music, to be sure – in the theory and practice of the French Ars Nova. Philippe de Vitry's boldest step away from purely referential music was the creation of the isorhythmic motet.[2] In this genre, the tenor (the essential voice) consists of rhythmically manipulated notes from a pre-existing melody, usually a plainsong. It thus represents plainsong, but is itself musical material. The upper voices carry their own texts and are restrained by poetic structures, but in essence obey the musical material arithmetically laid out in the tenor. This music 'plays its own game', while referring to the world directly or symbolically. A concomitant development was the organization of

musical rhythm through the comprehensive system of mensural notation. It tried to accommodate the greatest variety of rhythmic situations
within a minimum of arithmetical data: only the ratios between the
whole numbers 2, 3 and 4. Its point was, therefore, not merely to reflect
musical sounds as they might arise, but to be consistent and rational in
itself. A work composed in this notation could now assume an indi-
vidualized and fixed structure, making it transparent how the composer had manipulated the constraints of the system. This was 'composition' proper, not just 'style' – a minstrel's performance could have
style.

The isorhythmic motet was often used for ceremonies, or acts of
homage to a patron, but it was also the genre in which the best composers recognized and emulated each other. This was still the case in the
early fifteenth century. The two greatest composers of that period, John
Dunstable (c1380–1453)[3] and Guillaume Dufay (c1400–1474),[4] distinguished themselves from their contemporaries and became compan-
ions (although separated by tradition and environment) in their
isorhythmic motets. The genre ended with them; but they were both
largely responsible for transferring its structure and self-respect as composition to another genre, the cyclic cantus firmus mass.

Compositional self-respect was extended to secular song by
Guillaume de Machaut (d 1377). His polyphonic chansons guided two
generations of composers after him, who concentrated on elaborating,
individualizing and complicating Machaut's structures. They cultivated what has aptly been called an 'Ars Subtilior':[5] a relative advance
of the art towards greater subtlety of intervallic and rhythmic relationships between voices, but also between music and words. It is not
difficult to recognize personal styles, problem-solving approaches to
composition or selfconscious innovation in the works of Solage,
Philippus de Caserta, Jacob de Senleches (fl 1380–90) and many
others, whose strangely beautiful music is enjoying a major revival
today. 'Subtlety', originally a theological or philosophical quality, was
seen as the road to the future in courtly and clerical circles of southern
France, especially at the papal court of Avignon. Its musical entertainers were intelligent, creative artists: they handled structures, not just
sounds.

The composers of the Ars Subtilior provided southern French
courts and their allies in Aragon, Navarre, Lombardy, royal France,
Savoy, Naples and Cyprus with chansons, isorhythmic motets and also
much liturgical music (of a partly comparable nature). They represented
a 'central tradition', not only in the geographical sense within Europe,
but also because they elaborated the main heritage of the founders of
the Ars Nova.

The road to the future turned out to be a different one, however,
The great schism separated the central culture from the remaining

areas of Christendom, which supported not the popes of Avignon but those of Rome: England, the Low Countries, Germany, Italy, Bohemia, Poland and from 1409 also royal and northern France and Burgundy.[6] The degree of this separation varied according to the cultural activities concerned, but it was very high in music, an art still largely exercised by clerics and intellectuals. An ecclesiastic aspiring to a higher career, and many musicians did, would now have to choose whether to seek advancement through the papal curia of Rome or that of Avignon, at the risk of being seen as a heretic by the opposing administration. It was only natural that musicians from the peripheral countries of Roman obedience would redirect themselves to their foremost centre of music, the papal chapel in Rome. Already by *c*1380 the Roman chapel was filled with Netherlanders (as the Avignon chapel had been before); the epochal migration of Netherlandish musicians to Italy, which characterizes the whole Renaissance period, began in this way.[7] By *c*1400 some leading Netherlandish composers seem to have found a home in Italian institutions: Johannes Ciconia from Liège (*c*1370–1412) as cantor at Padua Cathedral, Johannes Egardus from Bruges probably in the Roman chapel (1394), Hmybertus de Salinis from the diocese of Liège probably at Florence (*c*1400–1415). Their music, with the exception of very few works in which they showed their mastery of Ars Subtilior idioms, is radically different from that of a Senleches or Philippus.

To use but one word, it is 'simpler' music. What resounds in their mass settings and motets are the straightforward rhythmic patterns, the declamatory word-setting and the clarity of phrasing and form which the Ars Subtilior had abandoned. These composers were still the heirs of Vitry and Machaut but had also adopted, in their host country, the Italian tradition. Ciconia,[8] in his Italian madrigals and ballatas, went a step further in developing also the secular music of the Italian trecento, as exemplified in the works of Francesco Landini (*d* 1397). He absorbed popularizing elements which were the fashion of northern Italian society around 1410, headed by the poet and singer Leonardo Giustiniani of Venice (1390–1446).

It is significant that even within Italy the native tradition did not rule alone. Whereas the most significant Italian-born composer, Antonio Zachara of Teramo,[9] followed native styles in all but one of his works, even to the point of overt folklorism, Matteo da Perugia and Anthonello de Caserta went to extremes in the imitation of the Ars Subtilior.[10] The reason seems clear: Antonio Zachara served the Roman popes from 1391 (and the chapel of Pope John XXIII at Bologna during the period of the three-fold schism, 1413–14), Matteo worked mostly in the Avignon-orientated duchy of Lombardy (he died in Milan in 1418), and Anthonello probably served Anjou rulers in Naples (*c*1415). It is rare in history that musical tastes so closely reflect large-scale political alignments.

Not only parts of Italy, but also other regions of Roman obedience outside France represented what may be called 'lateral traditions'.[11] Their relationship with the French Ars Nova corresponded at first to the model of 'centre and periphery': the Ars Nova radiated out to these countries, whether their own traditions of written music were as strong and developed as in England and Italy, or as hesitant and conservative as in central Europe. In the Low Countries, situated on the border between the Holy Roman Empire and royal France, French musical culture dominated at first almost exclusively. Precisely from the beginning of the great schism, the scene changed. Netherlandish musicians went to Italy, as we have seen, especially if they were from the dioceses of Liège, Utrecht or Cambrai; the Burgundian court of Philip the Bold (1369–1404) and his successor John the Fearless (1404–19) established itself as a northern power with the acquisition of Flanders in 1384, and its music began to differ considerably from that of the central tradition.[12] The Dutch, Flemish and also French-speaking musicians of the Burgundian court and its neighbours (Holland, Brabant etc), as well as those in the cities and cathedrals, lost interest in the complexities of the Ars Subtilior. From the earlier roots of the central tradition itself, and from local variants of the style, they developed idioms more analogous to the English and Italian traditions. This may seem surprising, given the geographical distances, but the Low Countries and their large commercial cities especially in Flanders were, in fact, inhabited by many merchants, diplomats and intellectuals from Italy, England and Germany. The dukes of Burgundy fostered these international connections which strengthened their economic and political independence from royal France; in the early reign of Philip the Good (1419–67), Burgundy had almost become an ally of the English who occupied Paris and much of northern France.

Some of the foreigners in the Low Countries were actively interested in local music, especially in the sacred sphere. The Bruges confraternity of the 'Dry Tree', with many Florentines among its leading members, observed the custom of hearing a polyphonic Lady mass in their chapel every Saturday from before 1396; the Lucchese banker Dino Rapondi, a main financier of the Burgundian court, instituted a polyphonic mass for his soul in St Donatian's, Bruges (1417).[13] Manuscripts of secular music completed in Italy around 1400–1420 show strong northern influences; many of the French chansons collected there may have been sung in the houses of Italian nobles and merchant families with business connections in the Low Countries. Musical exchanges across the Channel also existed. An establishment which facilitated them was the Carmelite friary of Bruges, which served as the continental headquarters of the English Merchant Adventurers, as well as for the Scottish, Hanseatic and Aragonese merchant colonies.

The greatest contribution of the Franco-Netherlandish culture to early fifteenth-century music was the development of the Burgundian chanson, and particularly of the small-scale rondeau for two or three voices, the words of which were unambitious love-poetry and had little to do with the great Ars Subtilior ballade. Symptomatic of this renewal of music and poetry was the aristocratic association of the 'Cour d'amour', founded in 1401 in the Parisian residence of the Duke of Burgundy with the participation of musicians and poets of his court.[14] Resembling not only the medieval orders of chivalry but also the middle-class associations of *rhétoriqueurs* (or *chambres de rhétorique*) in northern France and the Netherlands, the 'Cour amoureuse' had the specific goal to praise and defend the ladies. The poetry of Christine de Pisan (*c*1363–*c*1431) and Alain Chartier (*d* 1429) with its stylish and gallant emotionalism expressed the same socio-artistic spirit.

Among the chaplains, *valets de chambre* and minstrels of these courtly circles, Baude Cordier seems to be the most interesting figure (the more so if he can be equated with Baude Fresnel, a harper of the Burgundian court who died in 1397 or 1398).[15] His secular songs are by no means untouched by the extravagances of the Ars Subtilior, but Cordier uses his skills in a more elegant fashion, almost with understatement.[16]

Cordier's rondeau *Belle, bonne, sage* is famous for its pictorial notation in the shape of a heart (fig.78). (Another pictorial song by Cordier is the circle canon *Tout par compas suy composés*, notated in circular form.) Despite the notational artifice, the rondeau has the more modern traits of simple, flowing rhythm and balanced phrases, as well as poignant word-setting (declamatory imitation at the beginning) and a strict economy of motifs. It belongs to a genre of popular origin much appreciated at the Burgundian court (in stylized form, of course): the dedicatory chanson. The point of the text and notation is that the author presents his own heart, in a song, to his lady as a New Year's gift (*estrenne*). Such musical-poetic presents for the *jour de l'an* as well as for May remained a fashion throughout the next generation; Dufay, Binchois and many of their colleagues contributed to it. Dedicatory songs are just as frequent in a large collection of Flemish monophonic songs, the Gruuthuse manuscript of the 1390s, which originated among bourgeois and aristocratic *rhétoriqueurs* of Bruges.[17] Other genres of popular origin appeared at this time in written and stylized forms, for example the convivial or drinking song and the improvised canon or *rondellus*. There are pastoral and theatrical songs on the ostensibly humble social levels of the 'Robin et Marion' plays, mostly in the *formes fixes* of rondeau and virelai. The 'realistic virelai' of the Ars Nova had a late flowering, which is characterized by naturalistic imitations of birdsong, trumpet-calls or other sounds of the external world. Some of this aesthetic is reminiscent of the pastoral fashions and the illustrative music of the French *ancien régime* in the early eighteenth century.

78. *The three-voice ron-deau 'Belle, bonne, sage' by Baude Cordier, in the shape of a heart*

Much of this music became an almost European vogue, being culti-vated also in Italy, Germany and even England. This is even more the case with genres which did not have to overcome a language barrier, such as sacred music and polyphonic arrangements of songs for the keyboard. The latter practice seems to be the combined achievement of musicians in England, the Netherlands, Italy and Germany – the central tradition did not contribute to it.

It was not only stylistic idioms and actual pieces, but also compos-ers that travelled back and forth between the countries of the 'lateral traditions' during the time of the schism. This new internationalism in music came to a climax in the great assemblies of the Council of Constance (1414–18).[18] We know that the (Italian) papal chapel regu-larly performed there in public, and must assume that its Netherlandish and Italian repertory was distributed from Constance to institutions in southern Germany, Austria and Poland. Visiting musicians from England were admired by the locals for their polyphonic singing in church, and also their polyphonic wind-band performances. Native and foreign instrumentalists apparently learnt there how to compose for ensembles of shawms and slide-trumpets (similar to trombones). The Tyrolean knight and Minnesinger Oswald von Wolkenstein, then at Constance in the service of King Sigismund, eagerly collected French, Netherlandish and Italian chansons in order to adapt them to his own, highly original, poetry.[19] What happened in Constance, and in this whole internationalist period, was a chaining together of all the musical traditions which had hitherto been satellites of the French Ars Nova. Two of the immediate results of the Council for the course of European music history may be mentioned: English chapel members very probably took home Italianate and other continental music which changed the development of their native idioms, as attested by the music of the Old Hall manuscript (compiled *c*1413–*c*1420, with later additions);[20] Guillaume Dufay and probably other Franco-Nether-landish composers of the young generation now found again their ways to Italian courts and particularly to the papal chapel in Rome.

MUSICAL LIFE AND MUSICAL SCRIPT IN THE LATE MIDDLE AGES

Our views of past ages are inevitably determined by the nature of the available evidence. The late Middle Ages have for us a much more realistic flavour than earlier periods, because the introduction of paper in the later fourteenth century gives us incomparably more detailed insights into the realities of life, whether they be of administration, politics, intellectual life or art. It is almost paradoxical, however, that the enormous increase of archival evidence for this period also tells us to what a large extent cultural life still functioned without script. This was particularly so in music. As it is essentially aural communication, the best part of it cannot be recovered, only reconstructed. In the fine arts and architecture, there are material witnesses of past ages; the messages of literature, philosophy and science come to us relatively unimpaired in their written form. Performing arts other than music, such as dance and theatre, can be better appreciated from their pictorial and written testimonies, as their means of communication are visual and verbal. Musical notation is only a secondary witness. What is more, much of the music actually heard in the late Middle Ages was never written down at all. The music historian deals not only with loss of evidence, but also with phenomena which were never 'evident'.

Again paradoxically, we know much about music of that time through written records, such as archival sources, which mention it. We must rely heavily on this 'tertiary' kind of information, as well as on analogous kinds such as pictorial or archaeological evidence. Although the painting of a singer tells us almost nothing in comparison with that of a dancer, we may reconstruct a musical instrument from a good, naturalistic illustration (of which there are many); we may identify the physical surroundings of music-making such as rood-lofts in churches or minstrels' balconies in courtly halls. This is relevant information. A recent reconstruction suggests that the performance of Dufay's motet *Nuper rosarum flores* for the rededication of Florence Cathedral in 1436 took place from two platforms, about ten feet high, which had been erected at the eastern corners of the church crossing.[21] The singers were divided in two groups of between three and five each (this information is indirectly archival). The procedure matched what has been identified as the famous double-choir arrangement of St Mark's, Venice, in the sixteenth century; a similar division of singers is also shown in pictures of the performances of the papal chapel at the Council of

79. *Papal chapel divided into two groups at the consecration of Oddo Colonna as Pope Martin V in 1417: miniature from the 'Chronik des Konstanzer Konzils' by Ulrich Richental*

Constance (fig.79).[22] There are, in fact, pieces of sacred music of this period which distribute the material between a (perhaps smaller) group of falsetto soloists and another group with the lower voices. Some of these pieces may have been in the repertory of the papal chapel at the time, to judge from their texts.

Another possible reconstruction (or approximation) rests on a combination of archival and pictorial sources. Polyphonic masses were performed in the private chapels of Netherlandish cathedrals by groups of about six singers and a small organ.[23] The group leader, the succentor of the church, usually sang the tenor; the one or two contratenor lines were provided by adult assistants, one singer per part. The organ may have doubled the tenor – and just possibly also the top line, which was sung by two or more choirboys or falsettists.

There is relatively less information about all the other music which filled daily life: music heard in the streets and taverns of cities, in princely chambers and ballrooms, in monastic refectories and schools; music for the market-fair, jousting, hunting, processions and war; performances of minstrels on wagons, on horseback, on ships; the 'music' and the urban sounds of church-bells, organs, cymbals, signal trumpets; the tunes sung in the countryside by pilgrims, peasants and shepherds. Most of the music was vocal, since the human voice is the most natural instrument and available to anyone at no cost.

Without archival,[24] literary and iconographic[25] sources, we would know almost nothing about standard forms of music-making. The professional musician who made a living from his above-average skills, the minstrel,[26] did not perform from written music. He had to be an excellent singer (*ménéstrel de bouche*) or a specialist on a costly instrument to make his way as a solo performer. Apart from commanding a superb musical memory, he may have deployed related skills such as making poetry (*faiseur*), acting, telling jokes, dancing, or indeed reading and writing, which qualified him for administrative jobs at court and which he may ultimately have used to write his creations down. Courtly solo performers were often harpers, using the instrument so dear to the noble amateurs themselves. Harp, lute and gittern could be employed to accompany oneself while singing. (This kind of performance is so natural, and has so much historical depth, that it seems absurd to maintain that it happened only exceptionally in the late Middle Ages.) Performances involving a duo are also widely documented: dancer and singer/instrumentalist (married couples performed in this way), two singers (for example man and boy, who could sing polyphony for a low and a high part), singer and accompanist, and rather often, duets of two lutes or harps.

A larger standard ensemble was that of the *alta* group (*haute musique*), consisting of shawms in one or more registers, and trumpets or slide-trumpets. The size of these loud ensembles ranged from an essen-

80. Pygmalion entertains his lady by singing to the accompaniment of an organetto (his other instruments, harp and mandora, lie on the table): miniature from 'Le roman de la rose' by G. de Loris and J. de Meun (French second half of the fifteenth century)

tial three to several dozens of players performing together; they served for military music, civic signalling (the city waits), heraldic functions, processions and other outdoor music, but also played for entertainment in ballrooms and at banquets. The *bassa* group (*basse musique*) was even less standardized. The softer instruments employed here could be string instruments like vielle, rebec, gittern, hurdy-gurdy, but also flutes and portative organs. They suited the more private forms of entertainment; narrative sources praise the sensuality of this suave music, which aroused the affections and chased melancholy. Keyboard instruments[27] are often mentioned in the context of solitary pastime and meditation. The most intimate soft instruments, the eschiquier (chekker) and clavichord, were dear to princes and philosophers. These keyboard instruments, as well as the chamber-organ, also had the polyphonic potential which made them tools of composers. Blind musicians such as Francesco Landini, Konrad Paumann (c1410–1473) and Jean Fernandes, a Parisian philosophy professor (fl 1450–90), found expression at the keyboard. Johannes Tinctoris in his treatise *De inventione et usu musicae* (c1485) praises the meditative sweetness of the vielle and tells us that he admired Jean Fernandes on the vielle in a duet with his blind brother Carolus. Very little of this music survives in written form – unless we assume that some of the regular, written polyphony of the period was indeed played by such performers in their own way.

We do have manuscripts of polyphonic keyboard music, however – probably because keyboard players were often literate clerics and intellectuals. The largest source of keyboard music from the early fifteenth century, the Faenza codex, was probably compiled by an educated musician, perhaps a friar of the Carmelite house in Ferrara where the codex has been found. Its contents are arrangements of French and Italian polyphonic songs, liturgical settings for the organ and appa-

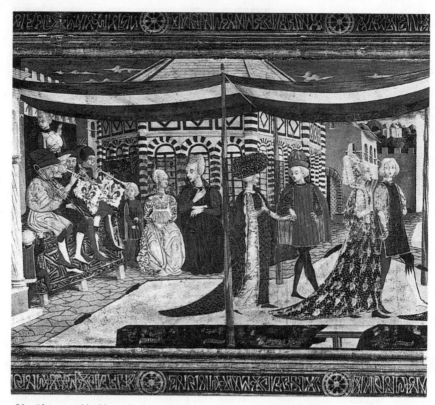

81. Alta ensemble (three shawms, one trombone) accompany dancing while a lutenist (of the bassa ensemble) waits behind (the two groups probably alternated according to the type of dance music required): detail of painted-chest (the Adamari wedding cassone, c1450)

rently a few courtly dance-tunes. Many pieces are known compositions circulating in northern Italy around 1410. The embellished forms in which they occur here are partly suitable for the organ or clavichord, partly also for lutes or gitterns. But the notational form, in score, with vertical lines separating rhythmic units, suggests solo performance.

A repertory including many of the same compositions is documented in Simone Prudenzani's epic *Il Saporetto* of *c*1425, which narrates musical pastimes in a middle-Italian aristocratic household.[28] The main performers named here are fictitious but they sing and play (on all kinds of instruments) many pieces by actual composers of the day, which survive in contemporary manuscripts. Surely some pieces were extemporized (such as regional dance-tunes from various parts of Europe), but the poet does claim that the leading performer owned a written source (in roll-form) for 'all these and more pieces'. He did not use it in the performance itself.

Musical script served these performers as a memory-aid, in rehearsal, for teaching and transmission to others. Organ manuscripts often had a didactic function: German organists wrote down not only their pieces and arrangements, but also so-called 'fundamenta': set examples or lessons in standard playing formulae to embellish a given melody polyphonically. The church organist had to know how to extemporize upper lines over a plainsong. Liturgical organ music must have been polyphonic more often than we can reconstruct today. Solo polyphony on the organ is documented as early as 1384, and it is likely that organists combined with singers of polyphony. The angel playing the organ in Hubert and Jan van Eyck's *Adoration of the Lamb* (Ghent, *c*1430) is clearly pressing three keys (*F*, *c* and *a*) simultaneously, whether or not the other instrumentalists in the same panel (or even the singers in the opposite panel) produce sound at the same moment.

Musical life and musical script are dialectically related: each contains elements which the other is lacking. Musical notation is intended to record what is not part of life in any case – an artist's individual ideas, for example. What it fails to transmit, on the other hand, must be presumed to be accessible to the performer through other channels – custom, oral transmission, ad hoc agreement between musicians. Musical notation is thus open to life: its apparent limitations or anomalies can tell us about musical practices beyond the manuscripts.

The regular mensural notation of the time, although a 'perfect' system in itself, left many aspects to the decision of the performer. They concerned pitch, rhythm, tempo, instrumentation and other categories. There were no general pitch standards, but the musicians chose pitch-levels convenient to them – a freedom more fundamental than that of transposing. Nevertheless, the concept of transposition was also known, as in English sacred music where plainsongs could appear on different pitch-levels within the same piece, or in keyboard arrangements of songs. Inflections by a semitone were largely left to the performer's application of *musica recta* and *musica ficta* (the addition of 'accidentals' according to certain rules). Especially in cadences, performers typically raised the pitch of one or even more 'leading notes' by a semitone. These practices often produced sonorities which we would hear as non-harmonic or strange, although they were more often consonant than the pre-cadential chords of Classical and Romantic music.

Rhythms not covered by the mensural system of the French Ars Nova, particularly smaller note values, found their way into script from about 1380 in the most divergent forms: alterations of note-shape (flags, double stems etc), colour (void, red and blue in addition to full black), new mensuration signs and numerical proportions were concurrently introduced, leading to many overlapping or redundant uses of symbols. The same rhythm could be heard, performed and indeed notated differently by different musicians. But in comparison with the actual sounds a piece could have in different performances, the divergent notational forms in the manuscripts are harmless. Notation was the basis from which the piece had to be developed (in rehearsal, for example), and not a written record of the finalized sound.

Tempo, the arithmetical ratio between note value and duration, was implied rather than expressed by the mensurations and proportional symbols, and that only within homogeneous repertories. For this whole period, a general trend of slowing down of tempos must be assumed. A minim, for example, would last much longer in 1480 than in 1380. But this trend affected different types of music to different degrees. Also, notational innovations to counteract this trend (by deliberately writing larger note values but performing them faster) did not catch on everywhere. One wonders how musicians from different areas could agree on tempos for specific pieces, or indeed how they understood the implied tempos of foreign or older music.

The choice of performance medium (instrumentation) must have depended to a lesser extent on the character of the piece, to a greater extent on the training of the performers and on external circumstances. Minstrels, for example, were widely prohibited from performing in church, where sacred music was sung and perhaps accompanied by the organ only. But wind bands played sacred music outdoors (in processions, for example) and, from the 1480s at the very latest, even polyphonic motets. In the context of princely ceremonies, on the other hand, the use of wind instruments in church is documented already in the fourteenth century – although what they played can hardly have been liturgical.[29]

In secular music, everything that could be sung could also be played, and vice versa. Manuscripts practically never answer our question, 'vocal or instrumental?'. Social circumstances, convenience, regional traditions determined far more than did the technical features of the music. While singers of English liturgical polyphony around 1400 did not need to manage ranges much beyond an octave, Italian and French contratenor specialists of the same time mastered two octaves. The tenor range of most European polyphony in our whole period, however, rarely exceeded the written ranges of plainsong. Also, secular monophonic song is often notated in a limited tenor range. Strangely enough, the performers of the rhythmically complicated contratenor lines had a lesser status in standard performing groups than the tenorista who was often the leader of the ensemble. Perhaps he was expected to have a better or stronger voice. The leading function of the tenor accords with compositional procedure, and the emancipation of the low contratenor (bass) as an essential voice can be observed in the works of Johannes Ockeghem who had a celebrated bass voice.

Doubling of lines by more than one singer may have been widespread, but choral performance was traditionally reserved for plainsong, and not even all of that. Specialized chapel singers, even if as many as sixteen to twenty (as in the Chapel Royal, the Burgundian or papal chapels at certain times) were soloists, not a 'choir'. The 'choir' was the clerical community, seated in the choir-stalls and performing plainsong. 'Choir' and 'chapel' were essentially distinct types of musical environment, rather like 'church' and 'chamber' in the Baroque era.

Doubling of a texted line in secular music with instruments was probably on the wane. Also, alternation between voice and instrument on the same line is less likely than has sometimes been assumed. The frequent untexted phrases in the top line of a chanson, for example, are excellently suited for singing.[30]

When there are so many aspects of aural significance which the manuscripts do not determine, what can be said at all about music which was not even written down? Our chances of reconstructing it lie not only in tertiary (archival, iconographic) information, but also in the anomalous and sometimes curious forms which this music shows when it first finds its way into script.[31]

Polyphony had begun well before notation. As extemporized music, it was practised before the Middle Ages, and outside Europe. In our period, the organum practice of singing in strict parallel with a plainsong was still very much alive, and not only in provincial areas. Singing *supra librum* (extemporizing a counterpoint against the plainsong as read in the liturgical book) was taught in major centres and was mostly used for simple, repetitive liturgical music such as hymns and psalms. The parallel techniques of faburden (in England) and fauxbourdon are variants of this practice, as are other 'discanting' techniques which add one voice to a plainsong in note-against-note counterpoint, aiming at contrary motion.

These techniques increasingly found their way into script as general musical literacy increased. An important dividing line between unwritten practice and written composition is whether the plainsong itself was individually rhythmicized (in mensural notation), so that it could no longer be read from the liturgical book. Interesting borderline cases have been found where the chant is given equal note values throughout, so that it could be performed by an unskilled choir or by the organ in the loft – without access to the polyphonic manuscript.[32] The discanting singers could embellish this monorhythmic chant with mensural counterpoint. The practice is found from England to central Europe and Italy, and has influenced the techniques of major composers such as Obrecht, Isaac and Josquin.

Primitive types of rhythmic notation are another borderline group. Stroke notation[33] in its various forms knows only one value-unit, a little stroke or semibreve. To achieve unequal rhythms, these signs were simply repeated at pitch, so that they added up to values of two, three or more units. Sometimes, stems were added to indicate half-values. In a sense, this was deteriorated mensural notation (drawing also on

82. *Polyphonic chanson performed from written music (which the lutenist cannot see): miniature representing the Garden of Love from a Flemish manuscript of 'Le roman de la rose', copied (c1500) for Engelbert of Nassau, Lieutenant of the Realm in Flanders during the minority of Philip the Fair*

elements of neumatic notation), although the adding-up principle goes against the divisional principle of the Ars Nova system. We find it in different forms not only in primitive vocal polyphony but also in monophonic song, and it shares essential features with instrumental notation, as used, for example, in the sources of the courtly basse danse.[34]

   The transmission of song relied more on written texts than on written music. Although extemporized poetry existed as well, poetry enjoyed a higher status of literacy than did music. Poets very often wrote texts to be sung to pre-existing tunes. The whole medieval tradition of the contrafactum (new text to old tune) was very much alive. Sacred contrafacta (as in the repertory of the Italian *lauda*)[35] and courtly uses of popular material are often the only written witnesses of tunes which had never been notated in their own right. They were also incorporated by composers in polyphonic settings, whether with a popularizing intention (as in French chansons) or simply for musical reasons. It is uncertain which intention was behind the secular and popular tunes used as mass cantus firmi, which became frequent from the mid-fifteenth century. The original form or status of such tunes is often unknown. The famous *L'homme armé* song, the cantus firmus of many mass cycles, sounds like a folksong to us, but may have a more literate origin. There is a subtle relationship between its text and music, and the symbolic integration of a trumpet-call on the very words 'L'homme armé' is reminiscent of the realistic virelai of the Ars Nova.[36]

What appears in the written sources as possibly popular in origin, and may seem the tip of an iceberg of unwritten music, can quite often be identified as 'deteriorated' art music. This is true for basse danse tunes derived from polyphonic chansons, for example. A tune with the name of 'Sciuch' quoted in *Il Saporetto* among instrumental and dance melodies, can possibly be followed back via vocal and instrumental arrangements for the eschiquier in central Europe (*Schack melodye, Skak,* i.e. *Schachpret*) to the French rondeau *Qui contre fortune*. Such 'dismantled polyphony' also appears in a manuscript of the 1440s which actually served a trumpeter for performances on a Venetian galley, in simplified notation and without proper counterpoint. It is well known, in any case, that voices (mostly tenors) extracted from polyphonic pieces could become independent as monophonic tunes, or serve as the basis for polyphonic improvisation or new composition. I suggest that much 'unwritten music' as performed in the fifteenth century indeed survives under other guises in manuscripts of the time.

Finally, we may consider the varied uses of music manuscripts themselves. Indirect methods (archival research and philological reconstruction) indicate that very many music manuscripts have been lost, so many, indeed, that the assumed level of musical literacy should be revised upwards. Also, a primary function of music manuscripts, undervalued today, seems to have been to record and transmit music to distant places, to future generations or for the benefit of students. This work was done not so much by the composers as by other members of musical institutions, officially appointed scribes, schoolmasters and bibliophiles. Music manuscripts experienced much the same patterns of production and usage as other books, and their types are partly analogous. The small, courtly chansonnier with costly illuminations corresponds to the *livre d'heures* or poetry collection of a prince or princess; the large polyphonic choirbook used by church singers corresponds to the gradual or antiphoner; the small-sized miscellaneous volume of mixed music and theory is the vade-mecum of the intellectual or friar. Unbound leaves with musical notation, small fascicles and rolls were useful not only in performance but also for transport; by the end of the fifteenth century we have actual music sheets which must have been sent by 'post'. Music books were used as master copies for reference only, as librettos to be read by a patron while the performers sang without script, as teaching aids in schools for rehearsal only, as wedding gifts, display copies and as purely commercial objects. Some people just owned them to look at the illuminations, or to have a record of the poetic texts. Evidence of institutional ownership, particularly by the church, and modest physical make-up, sometimes suggest practical use; from about the middle of the fifteenth century we also know of part-books – first in church, for part-singing in processions, and then for secular and social song.

Music books used in performance were often corrected or revised and re-bound, and this was often the case when they changed owners. Music manuscripts were passed on by bequest or endowment, lent to individual members of an institution or to far-away friends. Some people re-used the parchment or paper for other purposes, some stole or defaced music manuscripts. Probably more music books than other codices were actively destroyed in the sixteenth century, either because people had no more use for the music or simply because they could not read the old notation; religious reformers attacked liturgical manuscripts as much as paintings or statues of saints or the Virgin. King Henry VIII tried to delete the memory of St Thomas of Canterbury by having his feast eliminated from all liturgical books, an acknowledgement of the authority of the plainsong book and of script in general. It is not clear whether a music manuscript was ever put to the same use as the personal breviary of Duke John of Bavaria (*d* 1425): his enemies poisoned the pages so that he died after kissing them.

THE EARLY FIFTEENTH CENTURY

The identity question concerning Baude Cordier (see p. 274) has somewhat wider implications. If Maistre Baude Cordier was the same man as the harper of Philip the Bold, Baude Fresnel, this *valet de chambre* would have had a university degree as well as the astounding musical intelligence exhibited in Cordier's chansons. It is true that Cordier was not the first sophisticated composer to emerge from the ranks of musical entertainers: Jacob de Senleches seems to have been a harper and *valet de chambre* for all his life, but his six surviving songs are masterpieces in the most complex idioms of the Ars Subtilior. Baude Fresnel and his colleague and travelling companion at the Burgundian court, Jean de Noyers dit Tapissier,[37] were both laymen. About 1400 Tapissier ran a private music school in Paris, where he also educated ducal choirboys. These are but some indications that art music was now finding a respected place somewhere between the church service and profes-

83. *The Hunt of Philip the Good: painting, believed to be a copy of a lost original by Jan van Eyck*

sional minstrelsy. This happened in the courtly sphere. Most of the known composers of the Franco-Netherlandish orbit in the early fifteenth century served princes: Cordier, Tapisser, Jean Carmen, Jacques Charité, Jacques Vide, Nicolas Grenon and Pierre Fontaine the dukes of Burgundy;[38] Johannes Cesaris the dukes of Anjou and Berry; Gilet Velut probably those of Bourbon; Richard Loqueville the Duke of Bar. Some of them, such as Grenon and Loqueville, were also active at Cambrai Cathedral, the most important ecclesiastical centre of music. The princes took their civil servants wherever talents were available, and benefited from the intellectual and musical training which their chaplains had received in the cathedral schools. These ecclesiastics (whether musicians or other courtiers) could be paid through church benefices such as canonries or curateships. Other careers began differently: Gilles Binchois started out as a harper and probably squire of Netherlandish and English princes; about 1429 he became a Burgundian chaplain and collected his first church benefices, but he took holy orders as late as 1437.

The pattern was not dissimilar in the papal curia itself, a secular court which even employed laymen as *scriptores* and chapel singers (Antonio Zachara united all these functions). In all these cases it was the secular organization of a court which provided a living space for the arts. Not simply talent, but organization and patronage pushed the musical art forward. Even if learned humanism played a lesser role at the court of Burgundy than in Italian circles, its music could at least now assume the cultural function and dignity which it was to maintain in post-medieval societies. A famous painting of a hunting party at the court of Philip the Good (1419–67), believed to be a copy from a lost original by Jan van Eyck (fig.83), leaves a twofold impression: all the ingredients of medieval courtly pastimes are there (including the three wind players), but the aristocratic figures to the right actually seem to sing a polyphonic piece, from written music. Counterpoint is no longer beneath their status.

Guillaume Dufay and Gilles Binchois

The most prolific composer of the earlier fifteenth century, and arguably the greatest, passed through all the types of institutions which fostered art music. Dufay[39] spent about half of his career in the service of his home cathedral, Cambrai. For most of the years 1428–37, he sang in the private chapel of the pope. Intermittently, he worked for secular rulers (the Malatesta family of Rimini and Pesaro, *c*1420–1425; the court of Savoy, 1434–5 and 1452–6, probably also around 1438; the Burgundian court, 1439–40 and occasionally later). On his many travels he visited centres such as Laon, Bologna, Florence, Padua, Besançon, Geneva, the Council of Basle and certainly Paris (although it is not equally certain that he visited all of these). He was in contact, by letter or in person, with the Medici family, the Este court of Ferrara, possibly King Charles VII of France, Duke René d'Anjou, with Burgundian nobles (de Croy, d'Archy, d'Estampes), with fellow musicians (Binchois, Jacobus de Clibano, Johannes Ockeghem, Johannes Regis and the Florentine organist Antonio Squarcialupi) and with bankers and merchants such as the Florentines Francesco Sassetti and Tommaso Portinari – both also patrons of the fine arts.

His sacred compositions were usually written for the immediate needs of the institutions he served, but Dufay must also have worked on commission from outside. One of his motets, *Magnanime gentis* (1438), celebrates a peace treaty between the cities of Berne and Fribourg; in Florence he wrote two in honour of the local ladies. In Basle or Savoy, he composed a satirical motet on the rivalry between the Councils of Basle and Ferrara – in a juridical jargon perhaps reflecting his newly obtained degree in canon law (*Juvenis qui puellam*, 1438). He could well do so, as at this time both the pope (Eugene IV) and the antipope (Felix V) coveted his service. The motet *Nuper rosarum flores* celebrates Florence Cathedral after the completion of Filippo Brunelleschi's magnificent new dome. Dufay's mass cycle for St Anthony of Padua was probably performed for the dedication of Donatello's new altar in the Franciscan basilica (1450). His *Missa 'Se la face ay pale'* was probably written for a Savoy wedding (1452), the *Missa 'L'homme armé'* perhaps for the Burgundian aristocratic 'Order of the Golden Fleece' towards 1470. At the most famous festival of the Order, the *Banquet du voeu* at Lille in 1454, a musical lament on the fall of Constantinople (1453) was performed which may be by Dufay. He certainly wrote as many as four such laments, as he tells in a letter to Piero and Giovanni de' Medici of 1455. In that letter, he also offers these patrons some new songs, and in 1467 Lorenzo de' Medici asked him to set one of his own ballatas. The composer surely wrote chansons for distant friends and patrons, as presents for the New Year or May, or as celebratory works (for the court of Ferrara). Acknowledged or hidden addressees include musical colleagues, his mother Marie and perhaps other relatives, and very probably mistresses and patronesses who remain anonymous. There is also what may have been a lament on the death of Binchois from 1460, and the motet and *Missa 'Ave regina celorum'* which Dufay addressed to the Queen of Heaven for his own soul. The motet was sung at his death-bed, as stipulated in his will – one of the most fascinating documents about any musician of the age.

Dufay's stylistic development could be followed within any of the genres which he cultivated during several decades: masses, motets, other liturgical music, chansons. The many datable works span half a century from *c*1420 to *c*1470. Dufay's most private 'workshop', however, was set aside for the creation of about 80 French chansons, datable between 1423 and 1460. Although their textures, metres and contrapuntal techniques are more varied than in any other composer of his generation, he assiduously worked with the problem of the three differentiated voice-types – cantus, tenor and contratenor – and with the affective and structural challenge of French poetry in the *formes fixes*: ballade, virelai and above all rondeau. Dufay was the most universal song composer of his century. In the 1420s he learnt from the older Burgundian composers. In the 1450s he participated in a stylistic renewal also connected with the younger composers Johannes Ockeghem and Walter Frye.

The names of Ockeghem, from 1453 *magister capelle* of the King of France, and of the Londoner Walter Frye remind us that the Burgundian chanson was never only a regional speciality. The one composer who may be said to represent it with his whole career, Gilles Binchois, had made important contributions to it before entering the service of the Duke of Burgundy (*c*1429). But there is little of a stylistic development in his output of about 55 chansons (mostly rondeaux),[40] which is to say that Binchois had his mannerisms well established when he was about twenty years old. Similar artistic concentration characterizes the chanson output of the three major contemporaries of Dufay and Binchois: Hugo de Lantins, Arnold de Lantins[41] and Jacques Vide.[42] Dufay collaborated with the two Lantins in northern Italy in the 1420s;[43] they were both from Liège and represented a long series of excellent musicians from that area, which begins before Ciconia and ends with such figures as Johannes Brassart, the chapelmaster of the Emperors Sigismund, Albert and Frederick. Jacques Vide was perhaps the most important model for Binchois, if any individual need be mentioned; but the younger man became the fashion of all Europe perhaps also by his fame as a courtly singer and harper. Nobody's music, not even Dufay's, engendered as many imitations, paraphrases and allusions in the works of other composers. They range from dismantled or recomposed songs in basses danses, German organ arrangements, the contrafacta of Oswald von Wolkenstein (*Je loe amours*), to hidden allusions in English works (Lionel Power's *Anima mea* quotes the rondeau *De plus en plus*,[44] and an anonymous English Kyrie, erroneously attributed to Dufay,[45] does the same) and to cantus firmus masses over his chanson tenors (John Bedingham's *Dueil angouisseus* and Ockeghem's *De plus en plus* masses). *Deuil angouisseus*, in fact, has a fullness of sonority and a melodic grandeur which many would associate with English sacred music of the period.

This ballade is probably a lament on the death of a patron or patroness, and uses a poem written by Christine de Pisan on the death of her husband. Binchois also set poems by the other leading figures of his day, Charles d'Orléans and Alain Chartier. He was well connected in a way Dufay was not: Jan van Eyck painted what may be a portrait of him in 1432, with the motto 'Leal souvenir' (probably as a genuine *souvenir* for a former patron, the Earl of Suffolk), which makes him a legendary figure at the age of less than 35. Binchois composed two ceremonial motets for the Burgundian court (*Domitor Hectoris* and *Nove cantum melodie*) and also a good deal of simple, functional church music – all of it is beautiful in a somewhat leisurely, English-sounding manner, but nothing shows the great cultural and intellectual breadth of Dufay.[46] I believe, however, that there are a few late chansons which explore new territories (as in Dufay's case): they include *Pour prison ne pour maladie*, which the flexible but minor composer Jean Pullois mimicked in one of his songs, and *Comme femme desconfortée*, which still fascinated Josquin's contemporaries. Binchois' authorship of the latter song has been doubted, and even contemporary sources give his best later songs to other composers (*Tout a par moy* to Walter Frye, *Je ne vis onques* to Dufay), as if the musicians of the next generation could not have imagined that Binchois' art could gain a second wind.

English music on the Continent

Martin le Franc, a poet and diplomat of the court of Savoy, has left us irreplaceable testimony in his epic *Le champion des dames* (c1435 or 1440–42).[47] In some often-quoted lines, he claims that the music of Tapissier, Carmen and Cesaris had once astounded all Paris, but was then out-done by Dufay and Binchois who adopted English idioms and followed the model of John Dunstable. The poet later claims, however, that even Binchois and Dufay felt ashamed when hearing the blind viellists Jehan Ferrandes and Jehan de Cordoval, Catalan minstrels who served the Burgundian court from 1433 to at least 1457. Despite the exaggerations and the unverifiable comparison of composers with performers, le Franc puts his finger on very significant and repeated changes of musi-cal fashion. They all happened within the Burgundian orbit. The poem, dedicated to Philip the Good, was perhaps written under the influence of a visit which his chapel (including Binchois) made in 1435 to Savoy, where Dufay was then *magister capelle*. A manuscript copy of the poem (of 1451) contains a miniature showing both composers with their characteristic instruments, Binchois with the harp and Dufay with the chamber organ (fig.84).

It is impossible to single out specific works by Dufay or Binchois as those which 'follow the model of Dunstable'. It is even more difficult to define the English idiom or idioms which le Franc dubbed the 'conte-nance angloise'. It would be most convenient if he had meant a distinct technique such as faburden: the age-old scholarly debate about the priority of English faburden or continental fauxbourdon could then perhaps be settled.[48] But these strict, unwritten practices were not really observed in English composed works of Dunstable's period, and

84. Dufay (left) and Binchois: miniature from 'Le champion des dames' (c1435 or 1440–42) by Martin le Franc

also their continental variant had long outgrown unwritten practice. Around 1420, the strength of English music already lay elsewhere. The composers of the Old Hall manuscript had assimilated more continental influences than ever before. They operated with French and Italian techniques such as ornamenting the chant in the cantus, with isorhythm, canon, proportions and duet passages in works for more voices. The native English discant was transformed into continental chanson format with tenor and contratenor.[49] In turn, the English made a fresh impact on the Continent with their most mature works in the chanson idioms, particularly mass settings and the free antiphon or 'motet' in three parts. Such pieces were usually performed as votive or 'set' antiphons outside the regular liturgy.[50] The settings of Dunstable, Lionel Power (c1370–1445), Forest (d ?1446) and some lesser-known composers, with eminently singable lines for all voices, with full, consonant harmony and a relaxed, flowing rhythm, made the earliest and greatest impression abroad. The wealth of English musical thinking also included the opposite phenomenon, however: absolute strictness of cantus firmus treatment in the isorhythmic motet and the tenor mass.

The mass cycle, comprising the five Ordinary chants – Kyrie, Gloria, Credo, Sanctus and Agnus Dei – had been known in the Ars Nova period and was taken up again in the 1420s by Dufay, Arnold de Lantins and other Franco-Netherlanders. Isorhythm in the mass (i.e. rhythmic identity of successive tenor statements) and the idea of 'borrowing' a mass tenor from a non-mass chant, can also be found on the Continent before 1400. It was the combination of these three devices which characterized the cyclic tenor mass of the English. First steps are discernible in the Old Hall manuscript (mass pairs over related, isorhythmic antiphon tenors). The earliest actual cycle on a single cantus firmus may be Dunstable's Mass *Da gaudiorum premia*, written perhaps for the wedding of Henry V with Catherine de Valois in 1420, and again performed in Paris in 1431 for the coronation of Henry VI as King of France – an event presided over by Dunstable's probable employer, John, Duke of Bedford. Between those years, a dense network of Anglo-French musical interactions developed in the occupied parts of France, and further north. John of Bedford, brother of Henry V and regent in France, and his younger brother Humphrey, Duke of Gloucester, as well as William de la Pole, Earl of Suffolk, shuttled between London and France; musicians connected with them included Dunstable and Binchois. Lionel Power and perhaps Forest may have visited Flanders in the retinue of Cardinal Henry Beaufort of Winchester, an uncle of Henry V. English music on the Continent soon reached local cathedrals, collegiate churches and choir-schools: Bruges, Lille, Cambrai, Antwerp, Vienna, Trent, Vicenza, possibly also Padua, Liège and Lausanne, and by the 1450s the chapel of St Peter's in Rome. A major 'collecting point' for English music was the Council of Basle (1431–49). Here, the representatives of developing European chapels (Savoy, Habsburg, Ferrara) used it to fill their voluminous choirbooks.[51] If we had any Franco-Burgundian choirbooks from the 1430s and 40s, they would surely confirm the dominance of the English in sacred polyphony.

Besides *Da gaudiorum premia*, the only other undisputed contribution by Dunstable to the tenor mass may be the Gloria–Credo pair *Jesu Christe Fili Dei vivi*. In these works the rhythm and pitch of the cantus firmus are strictly repeated in the mass sections. A different aesthetic is found in the Mass *Rex seculorum*, variously ascribed to Dunstable or Lionel Power. Here, the tenor has different rhythms in each section and is sometimes ornamented. This so-called 'isomelic' principle (restatement of only the tenor pitches) is actually the most frequent in early fifteenth-century cycles. A main contributor is John Benet, with fragments of a Mass *Jacet granum* for St Thomas of Canterbury and a cycle also attributed to Lionel and Dunstable. In the latter work, a cantus firmus is either absent or disguised by excessive ornamentation. John Bedingham (*fl* 1440–60) and Walter Frye (*d* 1475) experimented with various stricter and freer isomelic techniques. The masses *sine nomine* by ?Benet and Bedingham were imitated in a free cycle (but with recurring tenor formulae) by Jean Pullois, written probably at Antwerp in the 1440s.[52]

Five more isorhythmic cycles survive (predominantly in central European manuscripts). The earliest of them may be Power's Mass *Alma redemptoris mater*, a strange work which combines absolute strictness of tenor repetition with Power's unpredictable, chanson-like upper-voice style.[53] Many duets enliven the texture.

The four other cycles are anonymous.[54] *Salve sancta parens* may have been written for recurrent Lady Mass services in an English (or even continental) Lady chapel, as the tenor is the introit regularly used for such 'votive' masses. This work, and *Quem malignus spiritus*, are for three voices – and might very well be the last examples of the three-voice isorhythmic mass. *Caput*[55] and *Veterem hominem*, two very similar four-voice cycles, fully exploit the contrapuntal methods of the four-voice isorhythmic motet (the low contratenor supports fourths between the cantus firmus and the upper voices).

Since continental musicians knew and copied all these works, what was their response? The idea of the cyclic tenor mass seems to have caught on slowly, whereas the sound of English music was eagerly imitated. This also refers to English procedures such as faburden and English discant. The characteristic sound of faburden (parallel six-three chords) resembles the aural effect of Dufay's early fauxbourdon pieces (from *c*1427), but they are constructed in a different and deliberate way, raising the common liturgical practice to the status of individual compositions. Some liturgical settings by Dufay and Binchois are known which have the plainsong in the middle, as in English discant, but it is handled like a high contratenor, not as an essential voice.

Early fifteenth-century cycles on the Continent usually lack a cantus firmus. They have too often been measured against the yardstick of musical unification, and have, in the absence of a common, borrowed tenor, sometimes failed the test. That similar clefs and ranges were used in all sections, that their modes and finals, mensuration schemes and perhaps initial motifs ('mottoes') corresponded, have been considered as tentative steps towards musical unity.[56] But these cycles cultivate variety, and their unifying devices were partly a matter of practical convenience only. The Parisian composer Estienne Grossin (documented in 1417–21) wrote a *Missa 'trompetta'* whose unity is concentrated on trumpet-like motifs in the contratenor. The point was to display this somewhat bizarre type of singing in all mass sections (probably because a specialist performer was at hand), not the formal coherence of the cycle.

Some works have, or seem to have, borrowed tenors, however. Three mass sections by Loqueville and Dufay are built over the same chant, a mensural Sanctus with the nickname of 'Vineux' (it was popular in a region near Cambrai),[57] and there are some other isolated mass sections over borrowed, occasionally secular, tunes. In one of them, a Gloria from Ghent (*c*1390), the antiphon tenor is even repeated in isomelic fashion.[58] An almost complete cycle which originated perhaps at Savoy in 1434 (surviving in the famous Cypriot codex at Turin) seems to use a secular tenor in a lighthearted style, although its order of phrases is never quite the same in the mass sections. The

Liégeois composer Johannes Franchois wrote a Gloria over *Alma redemptoris mater* in a similar vein. This is interesting because he seems otherwise to have known English music: his motet *Ave virgo* clearly imitates a canonic five-voice Gloria by the little-known Pycard, which survives only in the Old Hall manuscript.[59]

By the 1440s, musicians in central Europe used more specifically English cantus firmus techniques in individual mass settings or pairs. Most of them are isomelic, but one of them has the strictest form of patterning, on the melody *Herdo, herdo*. The full isorhythmic cycle appears first in the Netherlands: in Petrus de Domarto's *Missa 'Spiritus almus'* which is modelled after the English *Caput*. Domarto probably wrote this at Antwerp when Ockeghem was there in the 1440s, and it was Ockeghem who soon afterwards composed a *Caput* mass of his own.[60] This celebrated work uses the chant not only in the same general layout, but also duplicates its rhythms exactly. The cantus firmus is transposed into the bass line, however – seemingly undoing the English four-part technique. But this is deceptive, as Ockeghem freely allows fourths between the tenor and the upper voices as well. He understood the idea of his model, but immediately turned it into something else. The *Caput* melody is particularly unsuitable to the bass function, as it never reaches its finals by a fourth or fifth. Ockeghem showed how he could nevertheless use it in bottom position, generating harmonies different from the original, and very strange to our ears (exx. 1 and 2).

Around the middle of the century a short-lived but important contact between English and continental secular music was established. Apart from occasional secular uses of the carol, very few chansons (whether with French or English words) of English origin survive from this century.[61] Dunstable wrote two or perhaps three French songs, conceivably for circles in Paris; Walter Frye and John Bedingham actually became famous song composers. Frye's ballade *So ys emprentid in my remembrance* occurs in many manuscripts and formed the basis of two mass cycles: one by Frye himself and the other by the Burgundian chaplain Guillaume Le Rouge. In the 1450s this composer served Duke Charles d'Orléans – poet, ex-prisoner of the English, friend of William de la Pole and just possibly an ex-patron of Binchois. The 'remembrance' or 'souvenir' of youthful days, renewed by the talent of Walter Frye, seems to have stimulated these earliest chanson masses. Closely coeval is Bedingham's Mass *Deuil angouisseus* over the ballade by Binchois, a remarkable work which exceeds all previous cycles in its florid ornamentation of the model, of which more than one voice is used in the texture. This procedure initiates the Renaissance tradition of the parody mass – unless, of course, Frye's Mass *So ys emprentid* preceded it, as it also seems to paraphrase the upper voice of its model.[62]

Bedingham also set the ballata *O rosa bella* – 40 years after Ciconia – and thus joined the current fashion of the *Giustiniane* or *Veneziane*. This

Ex.1
(a) *Missa 'Caput'*, Gloria (English, Anonymous)

(b) *Missa 'Caput'*, Gloria (Ockeghem)

Ex.2 *In Adventu ad missam Rorate*, Hohenfurt songbook

may well have been when he was in northern Italy; a certain 'Johannes ab arpa de Anglia' visited the court of Ferrara in 1449–50.[63] Bedingham's setting became immediately famous; it gave rise to contrafacta, reworkings (one by Ockeghem), citations in musical pot-pourris (quodlibets) and three cantus firmus cycles. The first two of them are of Flemish origin and of the 1450s. The first resembles Le Rouge's variety of the isomelic technique, but the second repeats the artifice of Ockeghem's *Caput* in strictly duplicating but transposing the borrowed line.[64] *O rosa bella* also led to some other Anglo-Italian compositions, partly by Englishmen residing in Italy; the Fleming Gilles Joye contributed an Italian ballata in this style, while Bedingham himself wrote other songs which could be performed with either English or French words. He may just possibly be the composer of a macaronic (Latin–English) ballade in praise of the Este arms (*Agwilare habeth standiff*) for the accession of Duke Borso d'Este in 1450. For the middle of the century at least, it can be maintained that the best of English music, and the most progressive ideas, were created from Anglo-continental exchanges, and from an intertwining of stylistic features which we can hardly unravel today.

THE LATER FIFTEENTH CENTURY

The development of polyphonic music in the first half of the century largely coincided with a migration of techniques, ideas, but above all musical works, from the west and north of Europe to the east and south. In the latter areas, the music of Dunstable, Power, Dufay, Binchois, Bedingham and their colleagues was received and soon imitated with a readiness which demonstrates as much the artistic maturity of the recipients as the quality of their models; only on this double foundation was an all-European musical Renaissance able to rise. But the musical specialists in the wealthiest court chapels and cathedrals of central, eastern and southern Europe were an élite, capable of transcending their own native traditions; those musicians who were not, continued to cultivate music of older types and of a more regional, vernacular flavour. Even in England and in the Franco-Netherlandish area, such music by no means died out, but continued to fulfil vital functions in social life. This 'vernacular music' (in languages other than Latin and French) and 'everyman's music' (accessible to all layers of the population) now merged with the written culture of the educated classes by mutual assimilation. This process spans the whole of the later Middle Ages, and has repeated itself in other ages – but it has special significance for the later fifteenth century, with its dissemination of paper and literacy, its accumulation of capital wealth and its many new channels of communication. Gustave Reese's distinction between the 'central musical language' (i.e. of Franco-Netherlandish composers) and the 'diffusion of the language' (i.e. to all other areas)[65] may pinpoint a specific phenomenon of the early fifteenth century, but by the end of that century has all but lost its meaning. It also ignores the fact that the diffusion of music moves not only horizontally but also vertically, up and down through social layers. This vertical diffusion of the art can be observed in central as well as other areas.

Central Europe

Musical culture in central Europe – the territories of the Holy Roman Empire with the exception of the Netherlands – was separated from the French Ars Nova not only by a language barrier but also by a less mature level of musical literacy on the one hand and by a more intensive cultivation of unwritten and especially instrumental music on the other. To overcome both barriers was the mission of three important Germanic composers around 1400. The monodic and polyphonic songs of the Monk of Salzburg (perhaps identical with Archbishop Pilgrim II of Salzburg, *d* 1396) exhibit a curious mixture of indigenous and primitive musical styles with educated poetry,[66] for example in his *Tagelieder*. They correspond to the alba (farewell of lovers at dawn), but incorporate external sounds (the horn of the watchman) and primitive instrumental practice (*bordun* or 'organ point' of a wind instrument) with naive freshness. The Monk of Salzburg, and a priest of Freiburg, Heinrich Laufenberg, also led a large-scale movement for translating Latin plainsongs into German. Laufenberg left many dozens of translated sequences, hymns and rhymed prayers, as well as newly composed sacred songs (all monophonic) in German. The nobleman Oswald von Wolkenstein (*c*1377–1445) represents the Germanic feudal world and the heritage of the Minnesinger.[67] Unlike his contemporary Hugo von Montfort, whose poems were set to music by his squire Bürk Mangolt, Oswald is an original composer – the author of new monophonic tunes for about 50 of his *c*130 lieder (many other poems were sung to the same tunes). Oswald also 'wrote' over 30 polyphonic songs, most of them arrangements of Western and Italian chansons (see p.290): these contrafacta modify the musical models to suit his immensely varied metrical structures and highly individualistic poetry Oswald even rivals Machaut (perhaps consciously) in having his poetic and musical *opera omnia* written together in representative codices. The earlier of the two (now in Vienna) was compiled *c*1422–30, the later about 1432, with alterations and accretions.[68] It contains a portrait of the author, which is thought to have been painted by Pisanello (fig.85).

An innovation of Oswald, surely based on popular practice, was to assign the leading, texted voice to the tenor (Tenorlied). This polyphonic genre characterizes much German song throughout the century, particularly in Oswald's native Austria. From about the middle of the century, several collections document the swift assimilation of western counterpoint to native singing practices: the Lochamer and Schedel songbooks, both compiled by Nuremberg patricians around 1460, the Rostock songbook and the Glogau songbook (*c*1480), which is the earliest set of partbooks to survive on the Continent. Instrumental polyphony exists in many sources, notably in organ tablatures from Silesia, north Germany, Austria and in the large collection of the Buxheim organ book (*c*1460), which probably originated in the circle of Konrad Paumann from Nuremberg, court organist at Munich from 1450 (*d* 1473). Original compositions are here confined to organ versets and *fundamenta*, but between the Western chanson models for these arrangements there are also many German Tenorlieder.[69] The organ pedal is frequently used, which indicates an advanced technique of playing (and organ building); Paumann was also a master of other instruments and is said to have introduced polyphonic playing on the lute (i.e. with the fingers instead of a plectrum) in Italy about 1470.[70]

Several large choirbooks and private manuscripts attest to the growth of sacred polyphony in chapels and choir-schools between *c*1420 and *c*1480. They come from cathedrals such as Strasbourg, Vienna, Trent and probably the Habsburg court. The seven Trent codices (copied *c*1435–80) are the largest collection of mid-fifteenth-century polyphony; besides the major Western works, they contain hundreds of local anonyma.[71] Many of these belong to liturgical genres which typify preferences in this area: devotional motets, hymns, sequences and introits. But the borderline between foreign and native contributions is also very fluid in the stylistic sense: a mass cycle on the German *Leise Christ ist erstanden* is so similar to the English *Caput* mass that English origin has been considered, and there are many analogous examples. The music was largely copied, and used in the school and cathedral choir, by the priest Johannes Wiser. He stands for many musical schoolmasters across Europe whose university education and pedagogical zeal have preserved for us a large part of the courtly repertories as well. A whole series of Innsbruck schoolmasters is probably responsible for assembling the Nicolaus Leopold codex over the decades from *c*1465 to *c*1515; here we encounter the courtly and cathedral repertories of the Tyrol, Vienna, Ferrara, Milan and perhaps other centres.[72] The cadet branch of the Habsburgs in the Tyrol was a more important patron of music than even the imperial court under Frederick III (1439–93); both were eager to attract Netherlandish musicians. One of the greatest (and least known) of these composers working in the area was Johannes Touront (*fl* 1450–70). Heinrich Isaac visited Innsbruck in 1484 (later to be employed by Emperor Maximilian I), and Johannes Martini, Alexander Agricola and Jacob Obrecht also seem to have contacts with

85. Oswald von Wolken-stein: portrait by ?Pisanello, frontispiece to the manuscript B of his collected songs (c1422–30)

the Habsburg patrons.

A repertory closely resembling that of the middle Trent codices survives in the probably Moravian Strahov codex (c1470–80)[73] – but it does not represent the mainstream development in what is now Czechoslovakia. The militant anti-Roman Hussite movement of the 1420s and 30s had separated Bohemia quite radically from the Catholic community and, to some extent, even from its own cultural past under the Luxembourg emperors. This led to a multi-layered musical culture which combined primitive, inherited styles not only with an élitist reception of some Western music but also with strongly nationalized idioms.[74] Two early manuscripts which contain polyphony already show such a mixture, the Jistebniče Cantional (c1420) and the Hohen-furt (Vyšší Brod) Cantional (1410).[75] This type of manuscript was pre-dominantly liturgical, but filled with many newly composed tropes, *cantiones* (sacred Latin songs), hymns and motet-like pieces. Polyphony is marginal, retaining Ars Nova notation and even more archaic counterpoint, but the creativity in sacred monophonic song in these and many later sources is immense. Monastic clergy, cathedral musicians, university intellectuals from Prague and especially the lay confraternities (*Rorate* fraternities) of the Czech merchant towns all contributed to vernacular music, and the stylistic bands are often juxtaposed, as in the large Specialník codex of Hradec Králové (*c*1500), with archaic pieces as well as masses and motets by Josquin, Weerbeke, Obrecht, Agricola, Morton, Frye and other Westerners. Apart from Johannes Touront, who seems to have been in Bohemia for some time (perhaps at the court of the pro-Roman King Georg Podiebrad, 1458–71), Magister Petrus Wilhelmi de Grudencz (*fl* 1440–70) is the only named composer active in Bohemia. His curious polytextual Latin motets represent only one of the musical traditions of the country. The sacred songs of the Bohemian reformers (beginning with some by Johannes Hus himself) strongly influenced the Lutheran Reformation, mainly through the musical culture of the 'Bohemian brothers', an offspring of Hussite circles. A spirit of collective devotion and much congregational singing separated them from more orthodox religious traditions. In one such piece, the *Salve regina* trope *Ave yerarchia*, both the derivation from the medieval liturgy and the survival into later Protestant music can be demonstrated.

This beautiful melody was sung – perhaps by laymen as well as choristers – in the *Rorate* masses in Advent, special services attended by urban fraternities and exactly equivalent to the 'Golden' or 'Missus' masses of the Low Countries at the same time. The verses of *Ave yerarchia* (according to the Hohenfurt Cantional) were inserted between the verses of the *Salve regina*, as these services (beginning with the introit *Rorate celi*) were Marian masses for Advent. The Lutherans took over the melody for the Advent hymn *Gottes Sohn ist kommen*, removing only the Marian destination.

Musical culture in Poland and Hungary (two nations intermittently ruled by the same dynasty) was structurally different because of the continued adherence to Rome and the stronger feudal and monarchic influence. But the repertories overlapped to some extent with those of Bohemia, Silesia, Austria and Moravia. In Poland,[76] the important university in the royal city of Cracow and also the flourishing commercial centres to the north absorbed much Western music soon after 1400, stimulated by the Councils of Constance and then Basle. Apart from this, one major composer is known by name, Nicolaus de Radom, who about 1440 wrote in the style of the Ciconia generation but also used Dufay's technique of fauxbourdon. Polyphony with Polish texts increasingly appears from that point onwards. The Hungarian kingdom was closely tied to the West under the Anjou kings in the fourteenth century (manuscripts with Ars Nova music date from that period)[77] and to Bohemia/Austria under King Sigismund of Luxembourg (1410–

37). But an almost completely Westernized courtly musical life emerged in the reign of Mathias Corvinus (Hunyadi), 1459–90, whose palace in Buda was frequented by Italian humanists and scribes as well as Netherlandish composers and singers. This culture was 'borrowed' from the courts of Naples and Ferrara, with whom the king was related through his wife, Beatrice of Aragon. No choirbook from Mathias's chapel has survived, in contrast to many beautiful literary codices; but the Strahov codex mentioned above seems to show the repertory in use at Buda in the 1470s, with sacred polyphony coming from Italy as well as from the Habsburg orbit. Mathias Corvinus was partly successful in his wars against Emperor Frederick, and he even resided in Vienna during the years 1485–90. It was there that the celebrated Ferrarese lutenist and singer Pietrobono visited him and the queen (1488).

86. Singers rehearsing four-part music from a choirbook: miniature illuminating the initial C of 'Cantate domino canticum novum' (introit for the fourth Sunday after Easter) from a French gradual (c1487) used at the court chapel of Mathias Corvinus in Buda

Another famous performer well known to the court (whom Beatrice wished to recruit in 1488–9 through the services of his friend Johannes Martini) was the Innsbruck organist and composer Paul Hofhaimer.[78]

France and the Low Countries

Throughout the fifteenth century, musical life and institutions in the French-speaking areas benefited from the interplay or rivalry between the royal French court and that of Burgundy, like two magnetic poles. Cultural realities were, of course, more complex than that, for France encompassed many ducal and other territories, from the royal *apanages* Anjou, Berry and Burgundy to the almost independent duchies of Bretagne, Bourbon, Savoy, Lorraine – all provided with major musical institutions such as court chapels, cathedrals and abbeys. The Valois court of Burgundy was special insofar as it controlled many territories outside France (in the Low Countries) and because its economic and political power increased at the expense of royal France during the time of the English occupation. But when Charles VII had reconquered most of the crown lands (Rouen in 1441, Bordeaux in 1451) and transferred his primary residence from Bourges to Paris, the royal chapel and all the affiliated institutions (the Sainte-Chapelle du Palais, for example) gained fresh cultural energies.

The appointment of Johannes Ockeghem as *premier chapelain* in 1450 is one symptom of this. This composer, probably a native of Dendermonde in Flanders, had worked at Antwerp in the 1440s and at the court of Bourbon around 1450; when he joined the royal household, his fame and musical experience must already have reached a first peak. Endowed with the dignity of treasurer of the 'abbey' of St Martin of Tours (in reality one of the biggest collegiate churches of the period) and other benefices including one at Notre Dame, Paris, he represented the musical patronage of a proud dynasty and a powerful ruler, Louis XI (1461–87). Of his thirteen known mass cycles and 'only' nine motets and 22 chansons, a significant part must have been written before *c*1470, including such ingenious and highly individual works as the *Caput* mass, the masses *De plus en plus* (on Binchois' rondeau), *Ma maistresse* (on Ockeghem's own virelai) and *Au travail suis* (on a rondeau also ascribed to him but more probably by Barbingant) and the path-breaking chansons *Ma maistresse*, *Ma bouche rit* and *L'aultre dantan*. His *Missa 'L'homme armé'* is actually datable before 1467–8, composed perhaps at the same time (? and for a similar occasion) as the cycles by Dufay and Antoine Busnois on the same tune.

Ockeghem lived until 1497, and in the laments on his death there is also the complaint that he had not reached the age of 100: his date of birth may indeed be closer to 1400 than to 1420. In the 1450s he was clearly the leading member of an innovatory movement in the French chanson, to which even Dufay and Binchois belonged. There are formal novelties, such as the revitalization of the polyphonic virelai and its monostrophic, symmetrical variant, the bergerette, and stylistic ones, such as a bold exploration of unusual modes including the Phrygian and (*ante litteram*) the Aeolian. Ockeghem was a mentor and probably teacher of Antoine Busnois at Tours about 1460.[79] This great composer, who served the Burgundian and, later, Habsburg courts from before 1467 until his death in 1492, created a nucleus of spirited and complex chansons – together with Ockeghem himself and Barbingant, of whom nothing is known – which already fills French chansonniers of the 1460s. Much of the complexity (and difficulty) of his chansons and also his sacred works depends on a seemingly infinite rhythmic variety: within the simple basic mensuration of ○ (3/4), rhythmic groupings change all the time, forming irregular patterns (such as five-note units) and avoiding the successive use of the same note value over long stretches. Canon and declamatory imitation are used but often disguised; phrases often overlap in the voices, and the 'Burgundian' aesthetic of balanced phrases with predictable if varied cadential sonorities is further refined. The standard chanson format is often at risk: the addition of a contratenor bassus, with or without the result of a reworking of the altus, pervades the output of Busnois and also Ockeghem, although the status of an essential cantus-tenor framework is rarely questioned. But there are three-part works, partly canonic in technique, which remove every inequality between the voices, for example Ockeghem's *Prenes sur moy* (with canon at the upper fourth) and Busnois' *Bel acueil*. The latter piece opens the famous Mellon chansonnier,[80] copied *c*1475 for the wedding of Beatrice of Aragon with Mathias Corvinus, and probably in the Neapolitan circle of Tinctoris. The chanson text, one of the last to use the allegorical figures of the *Roman de la rose*, may have been written expressly for the princess, featuring her initials 'B. A.'

At the other end of the artistic spectrum, 'popular' and even folkloristic elements were welcome to these sophisticated composers and patrons. In continuation of preferences also shown by Dufay, they work with cantus firmi of pre-existent secular (or even sacred) material, and some of this comes from the monophonic repertory of dance-tunes and perhaps the theatre. Ockeghem's *Petite camusette* and Busnois' *Corps digne/Dieu quel mariage* are but two examples of this widespread new fashion. In his *déploration* on the death of Binchois (1460), Ockeghem uses a sacred cantus firmus, while the main text, 'Mort, tu as navré de ton dart', tells us much about Binchois' life and personality. Exchanges of ideas between composers – an aspect of 'intertextuality' already known to the Ars Nova – now go as far as a sort of musical and poetic 'correspondence' by way of chansons (in which women were also involved), and social games such as amorous rejection and reconcilia-

87a Angels with the music of Walter Frye's motet 'Ave regina celorum' (detail of fig.87b)

tion in a series of related songs. They also extend to sacred music. Ockeghem's motet *Ut heremita solus* and Busnois' motet in his honour, *In hydraulis quondam Pythagoras* (an offspring of the old 'musicians' motets') are musically related, and the network of 'intertextuality' spreads back to the *déploration* for Binchois, *Mort, tu as navré*, forward to Josquin's *Missa 'L'homme armé super voces musicales'* and, indeed, to his own *déploration* for Ockeghem, *Nymphes des bois*. Mass cycles over famous chansons round out this artistic universe. Like *O rosa bella* by Bedingham, *Le serviteur* by Dufay and several famous songs by Ockeghem (*D'ung aultre amer, Fors seulement*) and Busnois (*Fortuna desperata, In myne zin, Quant che viendra, Quant j'ay au cuer*), as well as the anonymous master-piece from their circle, *J'ay pris amours*, were used in many mass cycles, sometimes by more than one composer. Besides, the reworking of such songs into different formats, or the addition of totally new counterpoint to one or two of their voices, becomes a regular feature in this genera-tion.

The Burgundian court under Philip the Good and his son Charles the Bold (1467–77) participated as intensely as possible in this musical network. It had its own major song composers, such as the Englishman Robert Morton and the *valet de chambre* Hayne van Ghizeghem; Busnois joined the household of Charles shortly before 1467. Because of his musical authority (and that of Ockeghem), no separate stylistic fea-

87b Mary, Queen of Heaven: painting (c1485) by the 'Master of the Legend of St Lucy'

tures can be observed in this late flourishing of Burgundian chanson culture. After the death of Charles in battle, his daughter's death in 1482 and the related French-Habsburg campaigns for the Burgundian lands, all major European courts divided this splendid musical heritage among themselves.

   Nevertheless, the Burgundian Netherlands maintained a leadership in the art which was not generated merely by its court. We may almost reverse what has been said above in stating that even the courtly patronage of the early Renaissance could not live without civic and ecclesiastical roots. Patronage, after all, needed talents, and these were produced in the choir-schools and indeed in the streets. The continuing source for the successes of the Netherlanders at the Renaissance courts was the eager cultivation and public encouragement of music in lesser social contexts. This cultivation had a long history. The bourgeois fraternity of Our Lady at 's-Hertogenbosch, for example, had financed sacred polyphony from the 1330s.[81] Many similar civic groups in the commercial centres of the Low Countries, and the civic authorities themselves, did the same in the fifteenth century. Parish churches (in Ghent, for example) owned 'motet books' before 1400; by 1480 the city minstrels of Bruges gave daily concerts of polyphonic music for everybody who wanted to listen. The numerous religious fraternities (for example of the 'Salve regina' in Antwerp) could employ good composers and perform their works. Johannes Regis (*fl* 1450–85) and Jacob Obrecht (1450–1505) emerged as the greatest composers of this 'secondary level' of musical culture, and Alexander Agricola (1446–1506), Loyset Compère (*c*1440–1518), Gaspar van Weerbeke (*c*1440–1509) and, indeed, Josquin Desprez (*c*1440–1521) left their cathedral backgrounds in the Low Countries for posts in Italy.

Jacob Obrecht, composer of some 30 mass cycles and numerous motets and (French and Flemish) chansons,[82] is sometimes regarded as a 'northern' representative of this generation, in contrast to the 'Italianized' Josquin. But it is dangerous to identify his speculative, often symbolic and cryptic ideas as 'medieval' or 'Gothic' traits, as they are just as familiar to us from Josquin. Rather, Obrecht's sumptuous sounds and rational structures (especially in the patterning of cantus firmi) reflect a tension of mind and matter which, in totally different terms, recurs in Johann Sebastian Bach. A social parallel, rather than a merely aesthetic one, may be suggested here. Obrecht worked mainly for urban institutions (collegiate churches in Bergen-op-Zoom, Antwerp, Bruges) and their middle-class congregations; he almost certainly wrote instrumental polyphony for civic minstrels (his textless pieces and those ever-popular songs) and certainly for bourgeois fraternities and individuals. One of the works which comes almost directly from such a context is his *Missa 'Ave regina celorum'*. It is based on Walter Frye's very famous motet of the same title (really a votive antiphon), which was demonstrably well known to the citizens of Bruges in the 1480s: the civic wind band must have played it in public,[83] and two altar paintings of the Bruges school actually incorporate its musical notation in the picture of an angels' concert. (A third such painting reproduces, in the same way, a closely related *Ave regina* setting.)[84] The painter of one of these panels, the 'Master of the Legend of St Lucy', is connected with the Bruges church of St James for which also Obrecht worked in the late 1480s (fig.87).

Obrecht also composed a four-voice motet over Frye's piece, which is less closely related to its model. His mass cycle is not a parody mass in the sense of quoting several voices of the model at once (a procedure already common at the time), but a true tenor mass which extracts every possible idea from the tenor of the model alone. There are quotations of shorter and longer phrases in the same or augmented note values, ornamentation, interpolations, new rhythmic shapes and transpositions to all the other voices. The Benedictus has Frye's top voice in long note values in the cantus; the Sanctus and Agnus I have Frye's tenor in imitation or canon (see ex.3).

Is this luxuriant and free tissue of sound 'medieval'? It is like some of the magnificently embroidered robes which Renaissance princes liked to wear, or to present as ornaments to their churches. All lines are equal, but the sacred tenor is doubly present — a puzzle for the eye as well as the ear. This artifice is almost totally disguised. Rather than seeking in Obrecht a borderline between the Middle Ages and the Renaissance (which has in fact been done), we should recognize in him the musical spirit of the fifteenth century itself — a spirit originating with the great English composers and Dufay, and shared by their audiences, burghers and princes, in devotion, rational thought and entertainment. What music shares with mankind is that they both have access to the spiritual as well as the material world.

Ex.3 (a) *Ave regina celorum* (Frye)

(b) *Missa 'Ave regina celorum'* (Obrecht)

NOTES

[1] 'Novae artis fons et origo' (*Proportionale musices*, c1473). See R. von Ficker, 'The Transition on the Continent', *NOHM*, iii (1960), 134–64, especially 149. Other fundamental studies and surveys of fifteenth-century music include: H. Besseler, *Bourdon und Fauxbourdon: Studien zum Ursprung der niederländischen Musik* (Leipzig, 1950); H. M. Brown, *Music in the Renaissance* (Englewood Cliffs, 1976); M. Bukofzer, *Studies in Medieval and Renaissance Music* (New York, 1950); I. Cazeaux, *French Music in the Fifteenth and Sixteenth Centuries* (Oxford, 1975); A. Pirro, *Histoire de la musique de la fin du XIVe siècle à la fin du XVIe* (Paris, 1940); G. Reese, *Music in the Renaissance* (New York, 1954, rev. 2/1959); and R. Strohm, *The Rise of European Music, 1380–1500* (London, 1990).

[2] For a more detailed explanation, see pp. 223–5.

[3] M. Bent, *Dunstaple* (Oxford, 1981). Works edited in *The Works of John Dunstable*, ed. M. Bukofzer, MB, viii (1953, rev. 2/1970 by M. Bent, I. Bent and B. Trowell).

[4] D. Fallows, *Dufay* (London, 1982). Works edited in *Guillelmi Dufay: Opera omnia*, ed. H. Besseler, CMM, i (1951–66).

[5] U. Günther, 'Das Ende der Ars Nova', *Mf*, xvi (1953), 105–20.

[6] N. Valois, *La France et le grand schisme d'Occident* (Paris, 1896–1902).

[7] R. Strohm, 'Magister Egardus and other Italo-Flemish Contacts', in *L'ars nova italiana del trecento vi: Certaldo 1984*.

[8] *The Works of Johannes Ciconia*, ed. M. Bent and A. Hallmark, PMFC, xxiv (1985).

[9] J. Nádas, 'New Light on Magister Antonius Dictus Zacharias de Teramo', *Studi musicali*, xv (1986), 167–82.

[10] The works of most Ars Subtilior composers are edited in *French Secular Compositions of the Fourteenth Century*, ed. W. Apel, CMM, liii (1970–72).

[11] Strohm, *The Rise of European Music*, chap.2; see also R. Strohm, 'The Ars Nova Fragments of Gent', *TVNM*, xxxiv (1984), 109–31.

[12] C. Wright, *Music at the Court of Burgundy 1364–1419: a Documentary History* (Henryville, 1979). Generally on the Burgundian court, see R. Vaughan, *Valois Burgundy* (London, 1975); Cartellieri, *The Court of Burgundy*; and J. Marix, *Histoire de la musique et des musiciens de la cour de Bourgogne sous le règne de Philippe le Bon (1420–1467)* (Strasbourg, 1939/R1972).

[13] R. Strohm, *Music in Late Medieval Bruges* (Oxford, 1985), 15.

[14] A. Pirro, *La musique à Paris sous le règne de Charles VI (1380–1422)* (Strasbourg, 1930); Wright, *Music at the Court of Burgundy*, 134–7.

[15] Wright, *Music at the Court of Burgundy*, 124–33.

[16] *Early Fifteenth-Century Music*, ed. G. Reaney, CMM, xi/1 (1955). For the notation, see W. Apel, *The Notation of Polyphonic Music 900–1600* (Cambridge, Mass., 1942, rev. 5/1961).

[17] *Het Gruuthuse Handschrift*, ed. K. Heeroma and C. W. H. Lindenburg (Leiden, 1966).

[18] M. Schuler, 'Die Musik in Konstanz während des Konzils, 1414–1418', *AcM*, xxxviii (1966), 150–68.

[19] His polyphonic songs are edited in *Die mehrstimmigen Lieder Oswalds von Wolkenstein*, ed. I. Pelnar (Tutzing, 1982).

[20] *The Old Hall Manuscript*, ed. A. Hughes and M. Bent, CMM, xlvi (1969–73). For music manuscripts quoted, see generally *RISM* and *Census Catalogue of Manuscript Sources of Polyphonic Music 1400–1550*, RMS, i–iv (1979–)

[21] D. Baumann, in *L'ars nova italiana del trecento vi: Certaldo 1984*.

[22] For a facsimile edition, see U. Richental, *Chronik des Konstanzer Konzils 1414–1418* (Constance, 1964).

[23] R. Strohm, *Music in Late Medieval Bruges*, 15.

[24] The most significant and recent studies of archival material include Wright, *Music at the Court of Burgundy*; K. Polk, 'Instrumental Music in the Urban Centres of Renaissance Germany', *EMH*, vii (1987), 159–86.

[25] A representative study of iconographic evidence is J. McKinnon, 'Representations of the Mass in Medieval and Renaissance Art', *JAMS*, xxxi (1978), 21–52; see also E. A. Bowles, *La pratique musicale au moyen âge* (Geneva, 1983).

[26] A standard work is W. Salmen, *Der Spielmann im Mittelalter* (Innsbruck, 1983) (with 141 plates).

[27] Y. Rokseth, *La musique d'orgue au XVe siècle et au début du XVIe* (Paris, 1930).

[28] Simone Prudenzani, *Il Saporetto*, ed. S. Debenedetti, in *Giornale storico della letteratura italiana*, suppl. xv (1913).

[29] S. Žak, *Musik als 'Ehr und Zier'* (Neuss, 1979).

[30] Further on performance practice, see *Performance Practice: New York 1981* (with contributions by Arlt, Hasselman and McGown, Fallows, Bowers, Planchart, Günther).

[31] The basic notational usages are described in Apel, *The Notation of Polyphonic Music*.

[32] A. Hughes, 'The Choir in Fifteenth-Century English Music: Non-Mensural Polyphony', in *Essays in Musicology in Honor of Dragon Plamenac on his 70th Birthday* (Pittsburgh, 1969), 127–45.

[33] M. Bent and R. Bowers, 'The Saxilby Fragment', *EMH*, i (1981), 1–27.

[34] D. Heartz, 'The Basse Danse: its Evolutions circa 1450–1550', *AnnM*, vi (1958–63), 287–340.

[35] E. Diederichs, *Die Anfänge der mehrstimmigen Lauda vom Ende des 14. bis zur Mitte des 15. Jahrhunderts* (Tutzing, 1986).

[36] Strohm, *Music in Late Medieval Bruges*, 129–31.

[37] Wright, *Music at the Court of Burgundy*, 124–34.

[38] Marix, *Histoire de la musique et des musiciens*, editions of the music in *Les musiciens de la cour de Bourgogne au XVᵉ siècle* (Paris, 1937); and *Early Fifteenth-Century Music*, ed. Reaney.

[39] The fundamental study is Fallows, *Dufay*.

[40] *Die Chansons von Gilles Binchois*, ed. W. Rehm (Mainz, 1957).

[41] Music of both Lantins edited by C. van den Borren in *Pièces polyphoniques profanes de provenance liégeoise*, Flores musicales belgicae, i (Brussels, 1950), and *Polyphonia sacra* (Burnham Wood, 1932, rev. 2/1962).

[42] Chansons edited in *Les musiciens de la cour de Bourgogne*, ed. Marix.

[43] A. Planchart, 'Guillaume Du Fay's Benefices and his Relation to the Court of Burgundy', *EMH*, viii (1988), 117–71.

[44] S. Burstyn, 'Power's *Anima mea* and Binchois's *De plus en plus*: a Study in Musical Relationships', *MD*, xxx (1976), 55–72.

[45] C. Monson, 'Stylistic Inconsistencies in a Kyrie Attributed to Dufay', *JAMS*, xxix (1975), 245–67.

[46] A. Parris, *The Sacred Works of Gilles Binchois* (diss., Bryn Mawr College, 1965).

[47] Reese, *Music in the Renaissance*, 12.

[48] B. Trowell, 'Faburden – New Sources, New Evidence: a Preliminary Survey', in *Modern Musical Scholarship*, ed. E. Olleson (Stocksfield, 1978), 28–78; A. B. Scott, 'The Beginnings of Fauxbourdon: a New Interpretation', *JAMS*, xxiv (1971), 345–63.

[49] A. Hughes and M. Bent, 'The Old Hall Manuscript: a Re-appraisal/an Inventory', *MD*, xxi (1967), 97–147; Strohm, *The Rise of European Music*, chap.4.

[50] The fundamental work on the social contexts of British fifteenth-century music is F.Ll. Harrison, *Music in Medieval Britain* (London, 1958, 2/1963/R1980).

[51] R. Strohm, 'European Politics and the Distribution of Music in the Early Fifteenth Century', *EMH*, i (1981), 305–23.

[52] G. Curtis, 'Jean Pullois and the Cyclic Mass – or a Case of Mistaken Identity?', *ML*, lxii (1981), 41–59.

[53] Lionel Power, *Mass 'Alma redemptoris mater'*, ed. G. Curtis (Newton Abbot, 1982).

[54] *Four Anonymous Masses*, ed. M. Bent, EECM, xxii (1979).

[55] Formerly believed to be a work by Dufay and printed in his *opera omnia*; see Bukofzer, *Studies in Medieval and Renaissance Music*, chap.7. For the new position, see R. Strohm, 'Quellenkritische Untersuchungen an der Missa "Caput"', in *Quellenstudien zur Musik der Renaissance II*, ed. L. Finscher (Wolfenbüttel, 1984), 153–76.

[56] P. Gossett, 'Techniques of Unification in Early Cyclic Masses and Mass Pairs', *JAMS*, xix (1966), 205–31.

[57] Fallows, *Dufay*, 173–5.

[58] Strohm, 'The Ars Nova Fragments'.

[59] J. T. Igoe, 'Johannes Franchois de Gembloux', *NRMI*, iv (1970), 3–50.

[60] Johannes Ockeghem, *Collected Works*, ed. D. Plamenac (New York, 1947, 2/1966).

[61] D. Fallows, 'English Song Repertories of the Mid-Fifteenth Century', *PRMA*, ciii (1976–7), 61–79.

[62] According to a reconstruction by Brian Trowell; see Strohm, *Music in Late Medieval Bruges*, 125.

[63] L. Lockwood, *Music in Renaissance Ferrara 1400–1505* (Oxford, 1984), 115.

[64] Edited in *Sechs Trienter Codices, 2. Auswahl*, DTÖ, ix, Jg.xxii (1904).

[65] Reese, *Music in the Renaissance*.

[66] F. A. Mayer and H. Rietsch, *Die Mondsee-Wiener Liederhandschrift und der Mönch von Salzburg* (Berlin, 1896).

[67] The complete songs edited in *Die Lieder Oswalds von Wolkenstein*, ed. K. K. Klein and W. Salmen (Tübingen, 3/1987).

[68] For a facsimile edition of the later manuscript in Innsbruck, see *Oswald von Wolkenstein: Abbildungen zur Überlieferung*, i: *Die Innsbrucker Wolkenstein-Handschrift B*, ed. H. Moser and U. Müller (Göppingen, 1972).

[69] For a facsimile edition see *Das Buxheimer Orgelbuch*, ed. B. A. Wallner (Kassel etc, 1955).

[70] W. F. Prizer, *The Frottola and the Unwritten Tradition* (in preparation).

[71] Much of the music is edited in the following vols. of DTÖ: xiv–xv, Jg.vii; xxii, Jg.xi/1; xxxviii, Jg.xix/1; lxi, Jg.xxxi; lxxxvi, Jg.xl; and cxx; a complete facsimile is available from Bibliopola, Rome.

[72] A complete edition by T. Noblitt in the series EDM is in preparation.

[73] R. J. Snow, *The Manuscript Strahov D.G.IV.47* (diss., U. of Illinois, 1968).

[74] J. Černý, 'Zur Frage der Estehungs- und Verwandlungs-prozesse der mehrstimmigen Repertoires in Böhmen', in *IMSCR, xiv: Bologna 1987* (in preparation). See also the series *MMA* (1955–).

[75] For a facsimile edition with commentary, see *Die Hohenfurter Liederhandschrift (H 42) von 1410*, ed. H. Rothe (Cologne, 1984).

[76] M. Perz, (contribution to round-table discussion: 'Processes of Constitution and Conservation of Polyphonic Repertories'), *IMSCR, xiv Bologna 1987* (in preparation); *Sources of Polyphony up to c.1500*, ed. M. Perz, AMP, xiii–xiv (1973–6).

[77] Hungarian and Polish survivals of Western sources are described in C. E. Brewer, *The Introduction of the Ars Nova into East Central Europe: a Study of Late Mediaeval Polish Sources* (diss., City U. of New York, 1983).

[78] H. J. Moser, *Paul Hofhaimer: ein Lied- und Orgelmeister des deutschen Humanismus* (Stuttgart, 1929).

[79] P. M. Higgins, *Antoine Busnois and Musical Culture in Late Fifteenth-Century France and Burgundy* (diss., Princeton U., 1987).

[80] For a facsimile edition and commentary see *The Mellon Chansonnier*, ed. L. L. Perkins and H. Garey (New Haven, 1979).

[81] A. Smijers, *De Illustre Lieve Vrouwe Broederschap te 's-Hertogenbosch* (Amsterdam, 1932).

[82] Jacob Obrecht, *Werken*, ed. J. Wolf and A. Smijers (Amsterdam, 1921); *New Obrecht Edition*, ed. C. Maas (in preparation).

[83] Strohm, *Music in Late Medieval Bruges*, 87.

[84] See P. E. Carapezza, '*Regina angelorum in musica picta*: Walter Frye e il "Maître au feuillage brodé"', *RIM*, x (1975), 134–54; S. W. Kenney, *Walter Frye and the Contenance angloise* (New Haven, 1964).

BIBLIOGRAPHICAL NOTE

Historical background

J. Huizinga's *The Waning of the Middle Ages* (London, 1955) is a brilliant and pathbreaking work (first published in 1919) on fifteenth-century culture in France and the Low Countries, and owes its legendary fame to its slightly exaggerated main thesis, expressed in the title. Its real value lies in vivid and perceptive readings of all kinds of cultural phenomena, focussing on literary works but including music and music aesthetics. M. Vale, 'The Civilization of Courts and Cities in the North, 1200–1500', and P. Denley, 'The Mediterranean in the Age of the Renaissance, 1200–1500' in *The Oxford Illustrated History of Medieval Europe*, ed. G. Holmes (Oxford, 1988) are suggestive and well-illustrated surveys and are also strongly recommended. M. Aston, *The Fifteenth Century: the Prospect of Europe* (London, 1968/*R*1979) is a good popular book which surveys political and artistic tendencies in a concise manner. K. Fowler, *The Age of Plantagenet and Valois* (London, 1967) is a generously illustrated account, to which may be added R. Vaughan's *Valois Burgundy* (London, 1967). This is an amalgamated version of four books, each on one of the late medieval dukes of Burgundy. It is a reliable account concentrating on the political and economic development of the dynasty. D. Hay, *The Italian Renaissance in its Historical Background* (Cambridge, 1960) gives a good introduction to the context of the Renaissance, whilst a particularly enlightening treatment of artistic tendencies and attitudes is provided by M. Baxendall, *Painting and Experience in Fifteenth Century Italy* (Oxford, 1972/*R*1984).

Music and musical life

H. M. Brown, *Music in the Renaissance* (Engelwood Cliffs, 1976) is a very useful introduction to the understanding of musical styles, with musical examples and guidance for further reading. The major standard work on the period is G. Reese, *Music in the Renaissance* (New York, 1954/*R*1978), although it is in need of revision. A brief and skilful introduction for the non-specialist discussing selected problems of late medieval music is F.A. Gallo, *Music of the Middle Ages* (Cambridge, 1985). E. A. Bowles, *La pratique musicale au Moyen Age* (Geneva, 1983), contains an admirable collection of later fourteenth- and fifteenth-century pictures (mostly French or Franco-Flemish) showing aspects of musical life including processions, tournaments and banquets. See also I. Cazeaux, *French Music in the Fifteenth and Sixteenth Centuries* (Oxford, 1975), a useful compilation of secondary sources.

Still of value is J. Marix, *Histoire de la musique et des musiciens de la Cour de Bourgogne sous le règne de Philippe le Bon (1420–1467)* (Strasbourg, 1939/*R*1974), a documentary history which has not been superseded; it is instructive for the non-specialist and indispensable for students of Burgundian culture. To this may be added A. Pirro, *Histoire de la musique de la fin du XIVe siècle à la fin du XVIe* (Paris, 1940) and *La musique à Paris sous la règne de Charles VI (1380–1422)* (Strasbourg, 1930). The former is a masterly synthesis of musical styles and the role of music in social life and the latter is a brilliant and dense documentary account. The only reliable and detailed scholarly study of musical style of the period *c*1390–1420 is E. Dannemann, *Die spätgotische Musiktradition in Frankreich und Burgund vor dem Auftreten Dufays* (Strasbourg, 1936).

N. Pirrotta, *Music and Culture in Italy from the Middle Ages to the Baroque* (Cambridge, Mass., 1984), is an anthology of writings by the leading authority on Italian music; essays 5–11 concern the late medieval period, with emphasis on the relationship between written and oral traditions of music. S. Zak, *Musik als 'Ehr und Zier' im mittelalterlichen Reich* (Neuss, 1979) is the only up-to-date monograph on the use of music in medieval public life and its relationship with ceremonial and legal tradition. Though based on archival and narrative documents from Germany, the conclusions are of broader significance. *Ars Nova and the Renaissance 1300–1540*, ed. D. A. Hughes and G. Abraham, NOHM, iii (1960), comprehensive in coverage but uneven in value, this teamwork volume is most useful for the music student as an introduction to late medieval English music (chapters by Bukofzer and Harrison). The information is partly dated. M. M. Bukofzer, *Studies in Medieval and Renaissance Music* (New York, 1950), comprises seven research essays, pathbreaking in their time and still of great interest, on English polyphony *c*1350–1450, choral music, dance music and cantus firmus masses.

Two recent studies of fifteenth-century composers are D. Fallows, *Dufay* (London, 1982, rev. 1987), the best biography of a medieval composer; and M. Bent, *Dunstaple* (Oxford, 1981). Surveys of music in particular cities or countries include F. Ll Harrison, *Music in Medieval Britain* (London, 1958 rev.4/1980); R. Strohm, *Music in Late Medieval Bruges* (Oxford, 1985); C. Wright, *Music at the Court of Burgundy 1364–1419: a Documentary History* (Henryville, 1979); and L. Lockwood, *Music in Renaissance Ferrara* (Oxford, 1984). The last three volumes reflect the recent trend of musicological scholarship towards individual places, courts and institutions. Finally, R. Strohm, *The Rise of European Music, 1380–1500* (in preparation) is a broadly-based history of musical styles, composers, institutions and musical practices. It combines technical descriptions of works with discussions of musical life and general culture in many European countries.

Chronology

Antiquity and the Middle Ages

MUSIC AND MUSICIANS	POLITICS, WAR, RULERS
(BC)	**(BC)**
c970 Death of David, King of Judah; the earliest psalms may date from this time.	
c962–22 Worship in the Temple of Solomon organized involving musicians and a professional music school.	**776** First recorded Olympic Games, the first certain date in Greek history.
7th century Terpander is believed to have established the *nomos kitharōdikos*. Music of the Phrygians, influential in Greek music, reached its height.	**753** According to tradition, Romulus founded Rome. All subsequent Roman events are dated from this year.
c700 Olympus the Mysian, Phrygian aulos player and composer, is credited with the introduction of instumental music into Greece and the invention of the enharmonic genus and the Lydian mode.	**c724** The Spartan victory in the First Messenian War gives her control over the rich plains of Messenia.
	616 Date traditionally given for the Etruscan Tarquins becoming kings of Rome. The first was Tarquinius Priscus.
c600 Sappho and Alcaeus lead the Aeolian school of lyric poetry at Lesbos. The Dithyramb, a choral song of Dionysus, assumes its conventional form under Arion at Corinth.	**597** Fall of Jerusalem. Beginning of the Babylonian captivity (–538).
586 Sakadas wins at the Pythian games with his aulos solo depicting the victory of Apollo over the Dragon.	**594** Solon appointed archon of Athens. He reforms the Draconian laws and founds the Athenian democracy.
c530–497 Pythagoras active: he propounded the scientific basis of music and established a school of Greek music theory.	**510** Tarquinius Superbus expelled from Rome (*d*495); the Republic commences.
late 5th century Sophocles and Euripides admired for their music.	**509** Cleisthenes rises to power in Athens. In 507 he reforms the law and the constitution; ten new tribes replace the previous four and all citizens given a vote in the Assembly.
c450 Pindar excels in the choral lyric.	
c450–c360 Thimotheus, Greek composer and singer to the kithara, active.	**480** Xerxes, the son of Darius, crosses the Hellespont and advances to the pass of Thermopylae where the heroic Spartans under Leonidas fight to the death; Athens is taken, but then the Athenians defeat the Persian fleet in the Bay of Salamis.
406 Death of Euripides, who added solo monody to the musical resources of the Athenian tragedy.	
405 The *Frogs* of Aristophanes depicts a musical contest in Hades between Euripides and Aeschylus.	**442** Pericles becomes sole ruler of Athens until 429. During his reign Athens is dominant militarily, commercially and culturally.
c400 The heyday of Philoxenos and Timotheus, who marked the end of classical Greek music with their virtuosic innovations.	**431** The Peloponnesian war between Athens and Sparta (–404 BC) results in the loss of Athenian leadership in Greece and the end of her 'Golden Age'.

LITERATURE, PHILOSOPHY, RELIGION	SCIENCE, TECHNOLOGY, DISCOVERY	FINE AND DECORATIVE ARTS, ARCHITECTURE
(BC) *c*800 Composition of the great Homeric epics, the *Iliad* and the *Odyssey*. *c*733–701 Isaiah preaches the coming of a Messiah. **early 8th century** The Boeotian poet Hesiod writes his *Works and Days* and the *Theogony*. **641** Josiah, King of Judah, oversees the Deuteronomic reform and centralizes worship at the Temple in Jerusalem (–610 BC). *c*600 Jeremiah active, prophet of Jerusalem's destruction and purported author of the *Lamentations*. **600** Thales, 'The First Greek Philosopher', seeks the origin of all things in the element of water (–546 BC). *c*590 Zoroaster reforms the Persian religion from a form of polytheism to the worship of a single god. *c*534 Thespis is reputed to have developed Greek tragedy from the Dionysian dithyramb. **484** Aeschylus wins first prize in the Athenian Tragedy competition. **468** Sophocles defeats Aeschylus and wins the prize for Tragedy. **455** Euripides produces the first of *c*92 plays; 18 survive, including *Alcestis, Medea, The Trojan Women* and *Iphigenia in Tauris*. *c*450 Protagoras active, the first of the Sophists. *c*440 Herodotus travels to Babylon and Egypt to research his history of the Persian Wars. **424** Aristophanes begins writing comedies, 11 of which survive, including *The Clouds, The Wasps, The Birds, Lysistrata* and *The Frogs*.	(BC) **763** First record of an eclipse of the sun appears in Assyrian archives. **668** King Assur-bani-pal of Assyria accumulates a library at Nineveh with over 22,000 clay tablets recording Assyrian achievements in medicine, mathematics and astronomy (–631). **600** Chaldean astronomers invent the signs of the Zodiac, name many constellations, establish the seven-day week and the 24-hour day (–550). *c*590 Anaximander is said to have introduced the sundial (*gnomon*) to Greece and to have made the first map of the world (–*c*550). *c*530 Pythagoras and his followers are considered to have founded the mathematical study of acoustics and music, together with many early geometrical discoveries including the Pythagorean Theorem. *c*432 Meton, Athenian astronomer, announces the discovery of the *ennaedecateris*, a luni-solar calendar of 235 months or 19 years. It later became the model for the Persian, Chinese and Jewish calendars, and the method by which the date of Easter is calculated. *c*430 Hippocrates of Chios, Greek mathematician, active (–*c*400 BC). Euclid bases the third and fourth books of his *Elements* on Hippocrates' lost work.	(BC) **Late 8th century** End of the Geometric period of Greek art and beginning of the Archaic; anatomy of the human body becomes a preoccupation. *c*630 The Doric order of Greek architecture first recognizable at Thermon. *c*600–580 The earliest surviving large-scale architectural sculptures in stone on the west pediment of the temple of Artemis in Corfu. **mid-6th century** Earliest appearance of the Ionic order in the gigantic temples of Artemis at Ephesus and Hera at Samos in Asia Minor. The black-figure style of vase painting reaches its maturity whilst the red-figure technique is in its earliest stages. *c*480 Archaic period in art ends with the destruction of Athens by the Persians; the classical period begins. *c*470 Temple of Zeus at Olympia (–*c*455 BC), an early classical masterpiece of the Doric order. **447** Building of the Parthenon on the Acropolis at Athens (–432 BC). *c*435–30 The work of Phidias culminates in his great statues of Athena at the Parthenon and Zeus at Olympia. *c*420 The Temple of Apolla Epicurius at Bassae containing the first Corinthian columns.

MUSIC AND MUSICIANS	POLITICS, WAR, RULERS
*c*380 Plato proposes the ideal Greek musical education in his *Republic*.	336 Alexander the Great wins for himself the greatest empire ever.
?*c*350 The Books of Chronicles tell of instrumentally accompanied psalmody in the Temple of Jerusalem.	323 After the death of Alexander his empire is fragmented.
?*c*315 Aristoxenus, greatest of the Greek musical theorists, writes his *Harmonic Elements*.	264 First Punic War between Rome and Carthage, ending in victory for Rome's new navy at the Aegates in 241.
*c*300 Euclid, Greek mathematician, active in Alexandria; two musical works are attributed to him, *Introduction to Harmonics* (more likely by Cleonides) and *Division of the Monochord*.	219 Second Punic War (–201 BC). Hannibal invades Italy by crossing the Alps in 218 and defeats the Romans in 217.
	166 Judas Maccabee takes over the Jewish rebellion against Antiochus IV of Syria (–161 BC).
*c*240 Eratosthenes, Greek scholar, writes on the mathematical theory of music in his *Platonikos*.	149 Third Punic War (–146 BC). Carthage is besieged for two years and is finally taken by Scipio Africanus the Younger. The province of Africa established.
*c*220 Plautus incorporated features of Hellenistic song and Euripidean monody with Greek literary style in his Roman comedies. The introduction to *Stichus* names the musician Marcipor as the composer of the accompaniments.	146 Rome crushes a revolt in Macedonia which becomes a Roman province. Corinth is destroyed and Greece comes under Roman hegemony.
	60 Pompey, Crassus and Julius Caesar form the first Triumvirate.
*c*200 A setting of Euripides' *Orestes* survives on the papyrus, with music possibly by Euripides.	57 Caesar defeats the Gaulish and Belgian tribes. He invades Britain in 55.
*c*166 Terence's six *fabulae palliatae* include much recitative *cantica*, lines intoned to pipe accompaniment. In the prefaces he mentions four kinds of pipe and names the composer Flaccus.	52 Revolt of the Gauls under Vercingetorix. Crushed by Caesar at Alesia, his greatest military success.
	49 Caesar crosses the Rubicon initiating civil war with Pompey and his allies. Caesar triumphs and by 45 BC maintains dictatorial power.
*c*138 'First Delphic Hymn', in 'vocal' notation; one of two hymns in honour of Apollo engraved in stone in the Athenian treasury at Delphi.	44 After refusing a king's crown, offered by Mark Antony, Caesar is assassinated on the ides of March. Octavian, Caesar's grand-nephew, claims the succession.
*c*128–12 'Second Delphic Hymn', in 'instrumental' notation by Limenius of Athens, uniquely describing the place of music in sacrifice.	30 Octavian triumphs over Mark Antony and his bride Cleopatra at Actium; he is declared 'Augustus' in 28 BC, thus signalling the beginning of the Empire.
*c*30 Vitruvius, Latin writer, who described the hydraulis in some detail.	4 Death of Herod the Great after the execution of his eldest son. Jerusalem pacified by a Roman Legion after a revolt by the Pharisees; Herod Antipas succeeds to the Tetrarchy of Galilee.

LITERATURE, PHILOSOPHY, RELIGION	SCIENCE, TECHNOLOGY, DISCOVERY	FINE AND DECORATIVE ARTS, ARCHITECTURE
399 The death of Socrates, whose teachings are presented in Plato's dialogues. **c368** Plato's *Republic*, his central work. **343** Aristotle (384–22) becomes tutor to Philip of Macedon's son, Alexander. **306** Epicurus founds a school in Athens, teaching that freedom from pain and peace in body and mind is the highest good. **c300** Zeno of Cyprus founds the Stoic school of philosophy. **c250** The Septuagint translation of the Hebrew Bible into Greek. **c200** Plautus, Roman comic dramatist, active. **187** The Temple of Jerusalem plundered by Antiochus III of Syria. **166** Terence, Latin comic playwright, active. **165** Judas Maccabee rededicates the Temple at Jerusalem. **55** Cicero pulishes *De oratore*, and in 54 BC *De republica*; he was the most influential of all Latin stylists. **c30** Horace, perhaps the most influential Roman poet, active. Virgil writes the *Aeneid* (–19 BC). **19** Herod the Great begins the restoration of the Temple in Jerusalem. **4** Most probable date for the birth of Jesus Christ. **c2** Ovid (43 BC–AD 17) begins to write the *Metamorphoses*.	**c377** Death of Hippocrates, considered the founder of scientific medicine. **323** Death of Aristotle, influential exponent of empirical method and first great botanist and zoologist. Euclid, Greek mathematician and physicist, active at Alexandria (–c285 BC). **c283** The great lighthouse, one of the seven wonders of the ancient world, erected on the island of Pharos in the mouth of the Nile, opposite Alexandria. **280** Aristarchus of Samos active (–264 BC), astronomer and mathematician, the first to postulate the heliocentric universe. **c250** Ctesibius, Alexandrian physicist, active. He is said to have invented a *clepsydra* (water clock), a hydraulic organ and other mechanical devices. **211** Death of Archimedes of Syracuse, who developed the displacement theory known as Archimedes' principle, and invented the Archimedean screw and war machines. **c150** Hipparchus of Alexandria catalogues 850 or more stars, invents the planisphere, discovers the eccentricity of the solar orbit and the precession of the equinoxes (–c125 BC). **47** Sosigines, Alexandrian astronomer, devises at Caesar's command the Julian Calendar.	**336** The conquests of Alexander bring the classical period of Greek art to an end and introduce the fourth and final period, the Hellenistic (323 BC). **3rd century** The Etruscans build true arches with radiating voussoirs, a technique to be perfected by the Romans. **c280** The sculptor Chares of Lindos completes the Colossus of Rhodes, the celebrated bronze statue of Helios the sun-god, and one of the wonders of the ancient world. **c200** The Winged Victory of Samothrace sculpted from marble. **c100** The Venus de Milo, a marble statue of Aphrodite, created. End of the Hellenistic period in the arts and transition to Graeco-Roman, which sees many copies of famous Greek statues that are now lost. **20** The *Pont du Gard*, near Nîmes in southern France, built (–16 BC), its three storeys carrying the aqueduct across the gorge. **13** The *Ara Pacis* set up by Augustus on the Campus Martius in Rome (–9 BC), the first great Roman commemorative sculptured monument, combining documentary reliefs with scenes from Roman mythology.

MUSIC AND MUSICIANS	POLITICS, WAR, RULERS
(AD)	**(AD)**
	14 Death of Augustus, who is deified by the Roman state. He is succeeded as emperor by his stepson Tiberius.
30–35 Quintilian born, Roman orator and writer who included music among the arts boys should study before beginning rhetoric. *Institutio oratoria*, a eulogy of music, seeks to demonstrate its antiquity and power.	**37** Death of Tiberius; succeeded by Caligula, Claudius and Nero.
	43 Roman invasion of Britain; the conquest is consolidated by AD 47.
59 The first public appearance of Nero singing to his own accompaniment on the kithara.	**64** Burning of Rome, suspected by the Romans to have been started by Nero.
70–120 Plutarch (born *c*47), Greek philosopher and biographer, active. Frequent references to music in his philosophical works provide evidence of the musical information and vocabulary current among the educated.	**69** Election of Vespasian as emperor after suicide of Nero, restoring relative stability to Roman rule; Vespasian turns over the conduct of the Jewish war to his son Titus.
	70 Siege of Jerusalem. After a heroic defence of 139 days the city and Temple is destroyed and the population dispersed.
	79 Eruption of Mt Vesuvius, destroying Herculaneum and Pompeii.
?c85 The evangelist Luke records the *Magnificat*, *Benedictus* and *Nunc dimittis*.	**86** The Dacians advance across the Danube under their king Decebalus.
111–12 Pliny the Younger mentions hymn-singing at an early morning Christian service in Asia Minor.	**116** Trajan extends the eastern boundaries of the Roman Empire to the Persian Gulf.
c120–35 Mesomedes composes his kitharoedic lyrics at the court of Hadrian.	**122** Hadrian visits Britain and gives orders for the building of a wall.
	135 Jewish revolt under Simeon Bar-Cochba; end of Judea as a nation.
?c130 Claudius Ptolemy, the great Alexandrian scholar, constructs a complex theory of music in his *Harmonics*.	**138** Death of Hadrian. The reign of his adopted son Antoninus is peaceful.
	161 Antoninus Pius dies, to be succeeded by his adopted son Marcus Aurelius.
c198 Tertullian describes spontaneous singing at the Christian *agape*.	**180** Death of Marcus Aurelius, followed by instability and barbarian initiative.
c230 The Apostolic tradition describes the singing of Alleluia psalms at Rome during the *agape*.	**254** Valerian, seeing the Empire threatened on all sides, divides it; he rules in the East and his son, Gallienus, in the West.
?3rd century Aristides Quintilianus compiles a comprehensive survey of ancient music theory in his *De musica*.	**293** Diocletian creates the *Quattuor Principes Mundi*, a system of government with an Augustus and assisting Caesar for East and West. His reforms endure for the remaining century and a half of the Western empire.

LITERATURE, PHILOSOPHY, RELIGION	SCIENCE, TECHNOLOGY, DISCOVERY	FINE AND DECORATIVE ARTS, ARCHITECTURE
(AD)	**(AD)**	**(AD)** **1** The period of domestic landscapes murals such as those at Pompeii (–69).
*c***30** Arrest and Crucifixion of Jesus Christ at the time of the Passover.		
*c***35–6** Conversion of Saul of Tarsus (St Paul) on the road to Damascus.		
*c***50** Apostolic Council in Jerusalem, convened to discuss whether or not Gentile Christians should be circumcised and made to observe Mosaic law.		
64 According to tradition, Peter martyred at Rome during Neronian persecutions, with Paul suffering the same fate.		**72** Building of the great Roman Colosseum (–80).
73 Destruction of the Jewish community at Qumran, site of the Dead Sea Scrolls.	*c***77** Pliny the Elder writes the *Historia naturalis*, a scientific pharmacology and mineralogy, with material drawn from nearly 500 authors of antiquity.	**81** Reliefs on the triumphal Arch of Titus show the tumultuous events surrounding the sack of Jerusalem.
*c***98** Juvenal, Roman rhetorician and poet, begins to write his *Satires*.		**2nd century** The earliest examples of Christian art, frescoes appearing on the walls of catacombs.
*c***155** The *First Apology* of Justin Martyr, the first Christian thinker to seek to reconcile the claims of faith and reason.	*c***127** Ptolemy active, (–*c*151), great Alexandrian scholar, who establishes the geocentric system of the universe in his *Almagest*, and provides the most accurate ancient description of the earth's surface in his *Geographia*.	**106** Trajan's column in Rome decorated with a spiral frieze showing events in the Dacian wars (–113).
*c***240** Mani, a Persian prophet, begins to teach Manicheism, a belief based on a radical conflict between good and evil.		*c***130** The Pantheon in Rome rebuilt with the largest domed structure of the ancient world.
*c***250** Widespread persecution of Christians under Decius (–*c*258).	**163** Galen arrives in Rome as court physician; his work in physiology and medicine remained standard for more than 1000 years.	**211** The Baths of Caracalla built (–217), the best preserved of the monumental bath-complexes of the Imperial era.
270 Porphyrius publishes the philosophical treatises of Plotinus (–300).		
*c***285** St Anthony of Egypt retires into the desert where he becomes responsible for the birth of Christian monasticism.		

MUSIC AND MUSICIANS	POLITICS, WAR, RULERS
early 4th century Desert monks introduce the practice of continuous psalmody.	**312** Constantine, witnessing a vision of the Christian cross in the sky, defeats Maxentius at the Milvian Bridge, and subsequently grants freedom to Christians in the so-called Edict of Milan.
c375 Antiphonal psalmody becomes popular in the Christian East.	
c380 The *Apostolic Constitutions* mention the singing of the Sanctus and a communion psalm at the Eucharist.	**325** Constantine rebuilds Byzantium as Constantinople, and transfers the captial of the Empire there (330).
386 Ambrose introduces vigils and popular psalmody at Milan.	**361** Julian the Apostate rules both East and West from Constantinople (–363).
391 Augustine completes the sixth and final book of his *De musica*.	**403** Honorius leaves Milan for Ravenna which becomes the Western capital.
early 5th century An annual cycle of Alleluia psalms documented for Jerusalem.	**410** Alaric sacks Rome.
c410 Augustine describes the responsorial singing of a gradual psalm at Mass.	**429** The Vandals invade Africa from Spain (–430), besieging and capturing Hippo where St Augustine dies during the siege.
c420 The African scholar Martianus Capella establishes the standard order of the seven liberal arts in his *De nuptiis Philologiae et Mercurii*.	**452** Pope Leo I persuades Attila the Hun to retreat from Italy to Hungary.
c425 Pope Celestine I introduces the responsorial singing of a gradual psalm in the Roman Mass. Cassian adapts Egyptian monastic psalmody to Western usage.	**476** End of the Western Empire with the deposition of Romulus Augustulus by Odoacer, a Goth, who becomes King of Italy.
451 The Trisagion is mentioned first at the Council of Chalcedon, later to be introduced into the Byzantine liturgy.	**493** Theoderic murders Odoacer and rules Italy until 526.
c495 Boethius writes his *De institutione musica*, an influential digest of ancient music theory.	**533–4** Justinian's general Belisarius captures Carthage from the Vandals and begins to wrest Italy from Gothic control.
c530 Benedict arranges the weekly order of monastic psalmody in his *Rule*.	**568** The Lombards begin their conquest of Italy, weakened by decades of war.
?c570 The Cheroubikon established as a Byzantine offertory chant under Justin II.	**577** The Saxons win the battle of Deorham and become virtual masters of England.
?c650 The Roman *schola cantorum* founded.	**622** Mohammed flees from Mecca to Medina and establishes himself as a religious and political leader.
678 John the archcantor teaches the Roman chant in York.	**632** Death of Mohammed, followed by an extended period of Muslim conquest.
c700 Sergius I introduces the Agnus Dei into the Roman Mass.	**711** The Moors begin their conquest of Spain.
early 8th century *Ordo romanus I* describes the Roman Stational Mass.	**726** Pope Gregory II rejects Byzantine taxes; the Papal States ensue.
	723 Charles Martel checks the Moorish advance at Tours.

LITERATURE, PHILOSOPHY, RELIGION	SCIENCE, TECHNOLOGY, DISCOVERY	FINE AND DECORATIVE ARTS, ARCHITECTURE
325 Council of Nicea convened by Constantine to consider the Arian heresy which denied the divinity of Christ. **382** St Jerome produces the Vulgate translation of the Bible (–384). *c***400** St Augustine writes his spiritual autobiography, *The Confessions*. *c***431** St Patrick (*c*390–460) begins his Irish mission. **496** Conversion and baptism of Clovis, King of the Franks. *c***500** The *Celestial Hierarchy* of Dionysius the Pseudo-Areopagite written; its synthesis of Christian teaching and neo-platonism greatly influenced medieval thought. **523** Boethius (*c*480–524), imprisoned by Theoderic, writes *De consolatione philosophae*. *c***525** St Benedict founds his monastic community at Monte Cassino and writes his influential *Rule*. **597** Pope Gregory sends Augustine and some 40 companions on a mission of conversion to England. **610** Mohammed receives his vision from the Archangel Gabriel telling him he is the messenger of Allah. **726** The Emperor Leo II initiates the period of iconoclasm, which lasts intermittently until 842. **731** The Venerable Bede, a monk at Jarrow, completes his *Historia Ecclesiastica Gentis Anglorum*.	*c***305** Theon of Alexandria active. Ptolemy's astronomical tables were known to Islamic science and western Europe. *c***320** Pappus of Alexandria active, author of the *Collection*, a handbook of Greek mathematical sciences, invaluable for its citing of Greek achievements. **415** Theon's daughter, Hypatia, Alexandrian neo-platonist philosopher, murdered by Christian monks. *c***535** Cosmas Indicopleustes of Alexandria writes the *Topographia Christiana* (–*c*547), designed to prove the literal accuracy of the biblical picture of the universe. *c***636** Isidore of Seville's *Etymologiae*, preserving much ancient lore in a form palatable to the Middle Ages. *c***650** First definite reference to the Hindu numerical system which became known to Europe as arabic numerals is given. **673** Callinicus of Heliopolis, an architect, is credited with 'Greek Fire', a terrifying new weapon which enabled the Byzantines to defeat the Saracens. *c***725** Bede revises an earlier treatise *De temporum ratione* and becomes the first to tabulate a perpetual cycle of Easters on the basis of the 19-year lunar cycle.	**306** Maxentius begins to build the massive Basilica Nova in Rome, completed by Constantine. **337** Death of the Emperor Constantine, who initiated the great period of the Christian basilica; among those he commissioned himself were St Peter's at Rome and the monumental churches at Jerusalem and Bethlehem. *c***400–450** The Vatican Virgil illustrated, one of the very few surviving illustrated classical manuscripts. *c***450** Mausoleum of Galla Placidia at Ravenna, richly decorated with mosaics, including *The Good Shepherd*. **532** Hagia Sophia in Constantinople built by Justinian (–537). **540** Building of San Vitale in Ravenna with its magnificent mosaics (–547). *c***660** At Sutton Hoo in Suffolk a pagan king's boat and treasure are buried in a ceremonial funeral. *c***675** The Church of All Saints, Brixworth, Northamptonshire built, substantially surviving today in its Anglo-Saxon form. *c***696** The decoration of the Lindisfarne Gospels (–698), a masterpiece of intricate Celtic decorative art.

MUSIC AND MUSICIANS	POLITICS, WAR, RULERS
?8th century The Octoechos is first employed in Byzantine ecclesiastical music.	**751** The last Merovingian king is deposed; Pepin the Short becomes King of the Franks, founding the Carolingian dynasty.
c754 Pepin orders the Gallican chant to be replaced by the Roman.	**768** Death of Pepin the Short; succeeded by Charlemagne and Carloman who dies in 771, leaving the former sole king of the Frankish lands.
757 The emperor Constantine Copronymus makes the gift of a pipe organ to Pepin's court.	
c750 Death of St John Damascene, renowned at Constantinople as the author of ligurgical hymns.	**774** Charlemagne defeats the Lombards in Italy (–776) aiding the papacy.
c756 The Byzantine Emperor Constantine Copronymus sends an organ to Pepin III in France. It is the first seen there.	**793** The monastery at Lindisfarne is destroyed by the Vikings who will terrorize Europe for the next 200 years.
791 Death of Mansur Zalzal al-Darib, Arab musician who reformed the scale of the lute.	**800** On Christmas Day, Pope Leo III crowns Charlemagne as 'Augustus' in Rome. The Holy Roman Empire lasts for 1000 years.
c800 The earliest extant liturgical books with all the texts of the Mass chants.	**814** Death of Charlemagne; succeeded by his son Louis the Pious.
c802 Charlemagne hears Eastern singers perform antiphons for Epiphany, and orders that the chants be translated into Latin and adapted to the original melody.	**840** Death of Louis the Pious. The distribution of the Carolingian lands among his sons is regularized by the Treaty of Verdun in 843.
840–50 Aurelian of Réôme writes *Musica disciplina*.	**866** The Danes capture York and establish a kingdom there in 875 or 876.
c880 The anonymous *Musica enchiriadis* provides the earliest extant examples of polyphonic music.	**878** Alfred the Great, King of Wessex since 871, defeats the Danes at Edington.
c900 The earliest extant chant books with neumatic notation.	**962** Otto I is crowned Holy Roman Emperor by Pope John XII.
c970 The *Regularis concordia* of Winchester gives the text of the earliest extant liturgical drama.	**987** Hugh Capet, Duke of the Franks, is crowned King of France, founding the Capetian dynasty which lasts until 1328.
c994 A pipe organ is installed in the Old Minster at Winchester, one of several in contemporary English Benedictine churches.	**1060** Norman conquest of Sicily begins under Robert Guiscard and his brother Count Roger I.
c1000 'The Winchester Troper', a manuscript now at Cambridge, provides the earliest extant substantial repertory of ecclesiastical polyphony.	**1066** Invasion of England by William of Normandy and defeat and death of Harold at Hastings.
	1076 Pope Gregory VII excommunicates the emperor Henry IV.
c1020 Guido of Arezzo describes the musical staff.	**1095** Pope Urban II proclaims the First Crusade. In 1099 the Crusaders capture Jerusalem; the Latin kingdom of Jerusalem is founded.

LITERATURE, PHILOSOPHY, RELIGION	SCIENCE, TECHNOLOGY, DISCOVERY	FINE AND DECORATIVE ARTS, ARCHITECTURE
		*c*800 The Book of Kells; a surpassing example of Celtic manuscript illumination.
862 The Brothers Cyril and Methodius are sent by the Emperor Michael II to evangelize in Moravia; Cyril invented the Slavonic or 'Glagolitic' alphabet.	786 Haroun al-Raschid, Caliph of the newly-founded capital, Baghdad, supervises the translation of Greek treatises into Arabic and thus inspires the revival of ancient science and learning.	816 Decoration of the *Utrecht Psalter* (–835), its classical personifications reminiscent of murals in Roman villas.
*c*892 Alfred the Great translates into Anglo-Saxon a number of important books including those by Boethius and St Augustine of Hippo (–*c*899).	*c*790 The Vikings develop the longship, a slender boat with a keel to give it added rigidity, in which they were able to cross the North Sea.	822 Consecration of the (second) abbey church of Fulda, bringing the influence of the Roman basilica to the north.
909 William the Pious initiates the Benedictine order of Cluny with the foundation of a monastery at Cluny in Aquitaine.	874 Ingolfur Arnason, a chieftain from Norway, begins the settlement of Iceland with his family and dependants on the site of the capital Reykjavik.	*c*989 Novgorod Cathedral, the first Christian church in Russia, built in wood, with the first onion dome.
959 Dunstan becomes Archbishop of Canterbury and initiates the important English Benedictine reform of the later tenth century.	982 Eric the Red explores the south-west coast of Greenland and founds the first colony in 986.	1015 The bronze doors of Hildesheim, with their biblical reliefs.
1054 Final breach between the Eastern and Western Churches.	984 Earliest surviving astrolabe made by Ahmad and Mahmud of Isfahan.	1037 Building of Notre Dame of Jumièges (–1066), early Norman Romanesque church.
1073 Pontificate of Gregory VII, who worked for reform and moral revival within the Church (–1085).	1003 Voyage of Leif Ericsson to North America where he discovered 'Wineland'.	1051 Speyer Cathedral, finest German early Romanesque church.
1094 Anselm, Archbishop of Canterbury, completes his most important theological work, *Cur Deus Homo*.	1037 Death of Avicenna, great Persian philosopher and physician, whose synthesis of Greek learning had important influence in the West.	1067 The White Tower of the Tower of London begun, one of the earliest and largest towers in Europe.
1098 Foundation of the Cistercian order at Cîteaux by Robert of Molesme, a stricter form of the Benedictine order.		*c*1092 The Bayeux Tapestry completed; it pictures the Norman conquest of England.
		1094 Building of St Mark's, Venice completed, influenced by the Byzantine tradition.
		1095 Building of the new abbey church at Cluny (–1132), then the largest in Europe.

MUSIC AND MUSICIANS	POLITICS, WAR, RULERS
12th century The polyphonic *versus* is cultivated in Aquitanian monasteries like St Martial of Limoges. 'The Fleury Playbook', a collection of ten liturgical dramas possibly copied at St Benoit-sur-Loire.	**1138** Conrad, the first of the Hohenstaufen line, is elected King of the Romans.
***c*1135–95** Bernart de Ventadorn active. Widely regarded today as perhaps the finest of the troubadour poets and probably the most important musically.	**1147** Second Crusade preached by Bernard of Clairvaux, led by Louis VII of France and the emperor Conrad III.
***c*1150** The Codex Calixtinus: polyphonic music sung at Santiago de Compostela.	**1152** After the dissolution of the marriage between Louis VII of France and Eleanor of Aquitaine, she marries Henry of Anjou, future King of England (1154), bringing enormous lands in France to the English crown.
***c*1160–after 1213** Gace Brulé, most prolific of the early trouvères, and one of the best known.	
***c*1160–*c*1240** Conductus taken up by Parisian composers of the Notre Dame school.	**1189** Third Crusade begins, led by Frederick Barbarossa, Richard I of England and Philip II of France.
***c*1165–1200** The peak period of the German Minnesang.	**1198** Pontificate of Innocent III marks the climax of the political power of the medieval papacy (–1216). He is the first to employ the title 'Vicar of Christ'.
***c*1190–1200** Death of the troubadour Bernard de Ventadorn.	
late 12th century Léonin of Paris compiles his *Magnus liber*, a collection of two-voice polyphonic music for the entire Church year. The rhythmic modal system introduced into ecclesiastical polyphony.	**1206** Temujin, son of a Mongol chieftain, assumes the title 'Genghis Khan' and establishes the vast Mongol empire.
?*c*1180–90 Pérotin makes revisions to the *Magnus liber*.	**1215** King John of England agrees to the peace terms imposed by his barons in Magna Carta, including various curtailments of the king's powers.
1198–9 Pérotin composes four-voice organa for the feasts of Christmas and St Stephen.	
1200 Wolfram von Eschenbach active, (–1220), German Minnesinger and epic poet whose principal works were *Parzifal* and *Willehalm*.	**1244** Final expulsion of Christians from Jerusalem.
***c*1230** Death of Walther von der Vogelweide, most celebrated of the Minnesingers. Compilation of the *Carmina Burana*.	**1262** Kublai, grandson of Ghengis establishes his supremacy as Great Khan. He continues the conquest of China, rebuilding Peking as his winter capital.
***c*1240** Johannes de Garlandia writes *De mensurabili musica*.	**1270** Death of Louis IX (St Louis), King of France, whilst on crusade in Tunisia.
***c*1240–?88** Adam de la Halle active, composer of chansons, jeux-partis, motets and plays with musical inserts.	
***c*1250** The polytextual motet begins to supersede the conductus as the most important non-liturgical polyphonic genre.	**1273** Rudolf, the first Habsburg, elected King of the Romans.
***c*1280** Franco of Cologne describes a mensural notation in which individual notes have fixed rhythmic values.	**1279** Florence, Lucca, Siena and other cities form a Tuscan Guelf League with a customs union and jointly employ an army.
***c*1284** The late trouvère Adam de la Halle compiles the *Jeu de Robin et de Marion*.	

LITERATURE, PHILOSOPHY, RELIGION	SCIENCE, TECHNOLOGY, DISCOVERY	FINE AND DECORATIVE ARTS, ARCHITECTURE
c1115 St Bernard becomes first abbot at Clairvaux.		**c1125** Gislebertus sculpts the *Last Judgement* on the tympanum at Autun (–1135).
1142 Death of Peter Abelard, famous for his romance with Heloise.	**c1145** Death of Adelard of Bath, one of first Western scholars to translate Arabic scientific works into Latin.	
mid-12th century The *Poema del Cid*, a Spanish epic.		**1140** Abbot Suger's east end at St Denis marks the beginning of Gothic architecture.
1155 Peter Lombard writes his *Sentences* (–1158), a compilation of quotations that became a standard theological textbook.		**1153** Building of the Baptistery at Pisa, a large rotunda, designed by Diotisalvi.
1170 Murder of Thomas à Becket in Canterbury Cathedral by followers of Henry II.		**c1168** *Portico della Gloria* at the Cathedral of Santiago de Compostela sculptured by Mateo de Compostela, (–c1188).
1200 The Middle High German epic, the *Nibelungenlied*, written down around this time.	**1217** Death of Alexander Nequam, English scholar who first mentioned the compass.	**1174** William of Sens works on the new choir of Canterbury Cathedral (–1178), introducing French Gothic architecture into England.
1209 Beginning of the Albigensian Crusade, led by Simon de Montfort against the Manichean Cathars of southern France.	**1226** Lübeck, refounded in 1158 by Henry the Lion, becomes an Imperial Free City and a prime organizer of the Hanseatic League.	**1194** All of Chartres Cathedral, except the West Front, destroyed by fire, occasioning the building of the existing High Gothic masterpiece.
1210 St Francis of Assisi establishes his order. Gottfried von Strassburg working on his *Tristan und Isolde*.		**1212** Gothic cathedral at Rheims begun.
early 13th century Many universities founded including Oxford (by 1214), Salamanca (1220), Padua (1222), Cambridge (by 1226), Naples (1224), Toulouse (1230).	**1235** Robert Gosseteste, Bishop of Lincoln, writes on natural philosophy, including a commentary on Aristotle's *Physics* (–1253).	**1236** Building of the first truly Gothic church in Germany, St Elizabeth, Marburg (–1257).
1216 St Dominic (1170–1221) founds the order of Dominicans.	**1266** Roger Bacon (c1214–92) completes his *Opus maius*, a compendium of universal knowledge. He was an early advocate of experimentation and direct observation.	**1243** Building of the Sainte-Chapelle at Paris (–1248).
c1223 Inquisition begins.		**1265** Nicola Pisano carves the pulpit of Siena Cathedral (–1268).
c1230 The Aristotelian commentaries of Averroes become known in Europe.		
1274 Death of St Thomas Aquinas (*b* c1225).	**1298** Marco Polo, the first European to travel across all Asia, dictates his *Book of Travels to Tartary and China* (–1299).	
c1275 Jean de Meun completes *Roman de la Rose*.		

MUSIC AND MUSICIANS	POLITICS, WAR, RULERS
1316 An elaborately illuminated manuscript of the *Roman de Fauvel* provides the first isorhythmic motets.	**1305** Philip IV secures the election of Pope Clement V who in 1309 fixes his residence at Avignon, thus inaugurating the 70 years 'Captivity'.
1320 Philippe de Vitry describes the four rhythmic prolations in his treatise *Ars nova*.	
1325 John XXII cautions against elaborate polyphonic church music.	**1328** Death of Charles IV of France, last of the Capetians; succeeded by Philip VI who founds the Valois dynasty.
1340 Machaut takes up residence as a canon at Rheims.	
?c1360 Death of Jacopo da Bologna, most celebrated trecento composer before Landini.	**1337** Philip VI seizes Gascony, sparking the Hundred Years War between France and England (–1453).
?c1370 Machaut composes his *Messe de Notre Dame*, the first Mass Ordinary by a single composer.	**1348** The Black Death, bubonic plague, sweeps across Europe (–1349), killing an estimated one-third of the population.
1377 The death of Machaut.	**1356** The Golden Bull of the emperor Charles IV provides for the election of future Holy Roman Emperors by seven Electors.
late 14th century The height of the Ars Subtilior with the Avignon school.	
1397 Death of Landini, blind Florentine organist, who was the most prolific of trecento composers.	**1371** Accession of Robert II, who founds the Stewart dynasty in Britain.
early 15th century Squarcialupi Codex, lavishly illuminated Florentine manuscript with 352 trecento compositions.	**1413** Death of Henry IV of England; succeeded by his son Henry V who resumes the Hundred Years War with France, winning the battle of Agincourt in 1415.
1412 Death at Padua of Johannes Ciconia, first important northern composer to work in Italy.	**1419** Reign of Philip the Good, Duke of Burgundy (–1467); Burgundy, allied with England during the Hundred Years War, eventually becomes the dominant realm of French-speaking Europe.
c1420 The Old Hall Manuscript is compiled, a large collection of English ecclesiastical music.	
1427 Dunstable in the service of Queen Joan of Navarre, second wife of Henry IV (–1436).	**1422** John, Duke of Bedford, regent of English territories in France during the minority of Henry VI (–1436).
1428 Dufay joins the papal choir.	**1429** Joan of Arc relieves the siege of Orléans and persuades Charles VII to be crowned king at Rheims. Later she is burnt at the stake by the Anglo-Burgundian faction.
c1430 The first English cantus firmus masses.	
1434 Dufay meets Binchois when the Burgundian *chapelle* visits Savoy for the wedding of Louis of Savoy and Anne of Cyprus.	**1434** Cosimo de' Medici returns from exile and becomes the effective ruler of Florence until his death in 1464.

LITERATURE, PHILOSOPHY, RELIGION	SCIENCE, TECHNOLOGY, DISCOVERY	FINE AND DECORATIVE ARTS, ARCHITECTURE
*c*1314 Dante writes in the Italian vernacular, *La Divina Commedia*, the greatest poetical work of the Middle Ages (–*c*1321).	*c*1312 First eye-glasses thought to be introduced by Alessandro della Spina of Florence.	*c*1305–6 Giotto di Bondone, the first Western painter to make a decisive break with Byzantine stylization, paints his Padua frescoes.
1324 Marsilio of Padua completes his *Defensor Pacis*, challenging the temporal power of the Church.	1324 First indication of a cannon to be made in Europe, forged at Metz.	1308 Duccio de Buonin-segna, whose work points to the International Gothic style, paints the *Maestà* altarpiece (–1311).
1349 Death of William of Ockham, author of the doctrine of two truths, that of faith and of reason.		*c*1319 Ambrogio Lorenzetti of Siena paints the first great landscape of Italian art in the allegory of *Good and Bad Government*.
1349 Giovanni Boccaccio writes the *Decameron*.		1325 The Parisian illumi-nator Jean Pucelle paints the exquisite *Hours of Jeanne d'Evreux* (–1328).
1374 Death of Francesco Petrarch, who helped initiate the revival of Greek and Latin literature.		*c*1349 Completion at Gloucester Cathedral of the Great East Window, the Early Perpendicular choir, and the cloisters (the earliest surviving English fan vaulting).
1378 Start of the great schism (lasting until 1417) during which Western Christendom was split by the rival claims of two and sometimes three popes.		*c*1417 The *Très Riches Heures* of Jean de Berry, painted by the Limburg brothers.
*c*1380 Wycliffe's followers, Nicholas of Hereford and John Purvey, make the first complete translation of the Bible into English.		*c*1420 Donatello completes his *St George*, a celebrated early example of his work which revolutionized Renaissance sculpture. Filippo Brunelleschi builds the Florence cathedral dome (–1436).
1387 Geoffrey Chaucer writes *The Canterbury Tales*.		
1414 Council of Constance (–1418); the election of Pope Martin V ends the great schism.		
1415 John Huss burnt for heresy, becoming a Bohemian national hero.	1420 Prince Henry the Navigator of Portugal encourages the exploration of the African coastline and Atlantic islands (–1460).	1430 Brunelleschi, who influenced all subsequent Renaissance architecture, designs the Pazzi Chapel (–1443).
1425 The *De Imitatione Christi* of Thomas à Kempis, a popular manual of the Christian interior life.	1434 João Diaz, Portuguese explorer, rounds Cape Bojador.	1432 Completion of the *Adoration of the Lamb* in Ghent Cathedral by Jan van Eyck (*d* 1441).

MUSIC AND MUSICIANS	POLITICS, WAR, RULERS
1436 Dufay composes his isorhythmic motet *Nuper rosarum flores* for the dedication of Brunelleschi's dome at Florence.	**1450** Francesco Sforza accepted as Duke of Milan after besieging the city.
1438 Dunstable *serviteur et familier domestique* in the household of Henry, Duke of Gloucester.	**1451** Mohammed II becomes Emir of the Turks.
1439 Dufay returns to Cambrai as a cathedral canon, there to remain until his death, except for a last stay in Savoy (1452–8).	**1452** Frederick III crowned Holy Roman Emperor by Pope Nicholas V. **1453** Hundred Years War ends with England holding only Calais. Fall of Constantinople to Mohammed the Conqueror, marking the end of the Byzantine Empire.
c1440 MS Canonici misc.213, 'is copied at Venice; this manuscript, now at Oxford, contains 325 compositions of Dufay and his early Burgundian contemporaries.	
1450 Chair of music instituted at Bologna University.	**1455** Richard, Duke of York, defeats the forces of Henry VI at St Albans, beginning the Wars of the Roses. Death of Pope Nicholas V; election of Calixtus III.
1452 Conrad Paumann completes *Fundamentum organisandi*.	**1457** Emperor Frederick III inherits Upper and Lower Austria.
1452–8 Dufay composes his *Missa 'l 'homme armé'* for Savoy, the first to use that famous tune as cantus firmus.	**1458** Death of Pope Calixtus III; election of Pius II. Death of Alfonso V, 'the Magnanimous', King of Aragon, Naples and Sicily. Succeeded in Aragon and Naples by John II, and in Naples by Ferrante I.
1453 First record of Ockeghem in the service of the French court. The death of Dunstable.	
1456 Death of Nicolas Grenon.	**1461** Edward of York crowned Edward IV of England. Death of Charles VII of France; succeeded by Louis XI.
1457 Robert Morton a member of the Burgundian chapel choir (–1476).	**1463** War between Venice and the Turks over Mediterranean islands and coastal possessions (–1479).
1459 Josquin Desprez a singer at Milan Cathedral (–1472).	**1464** Death of Pope Pius II; election of Paul II. Death of Cosimo de' Medici; succeeded by Piero.
1460 Death of Gilles Binchois and Johannes Bedyngham. *Buxheimer Orgelbuch* compiled (–c1470).	**1465** Louis XI defeated by rebel French allied to Burgundy.
1462 Ockeghem visited Cambrai.	**1466** Death of Francesco Sforza; succeeded by Galeazzo Maria.
1463 Johanned Regis *magister puerorum* at Notre Dame, Antwerp.	**1467** Death of Philip II of Burgundy; succeeded by Charles the Bold.
1467 Antoine Busnois entered the Duke of Burgundy's chapel at Dijon (–1477).	**1469** Marriage of Ferdinand of Aragon to Isabella of Castile. Death of Piero de' Medici; succeeded by Lorenzo, 'il Magnifico'.
1469 Johannes Vincenet in the service of the royal court at Naples.	

LITERATURE, PHILOSOPHY, RELIGION	SCIENCE, TECHNOLOGY, DISCOVERY	FINE AND DECORATIVE ARTS, ARCHITECTURE
		1436 Leone Battista Alberti writes the *Della pittura* grounding painting in the laws of perspective.
		c1438 Rogier van der Weyden paints his expressive *Deposition from the Cross*. Fra Angelico paints his series of frescoes for the friary of S Marco in Florence, including the celebrated *Annunciation*.
1440 Lorenzo Valla, in his *De falso credita et ementita Constantini*, proves that the Donation of Constantine was a ninth-century forgery designed to bolster papal authority.	**1440s** The Guinea coast of Africa explored by Portuguese mariners, opening the way for the eventual rounding of the Cape of Good Hope by Bartholomew Diaz in 1488.	**1452** Lorenzo Ghiberti completes the 'Gates of Paradise', for the Baptistery, Florence. Filippo Lippi paints frescoes in Prato Cathedral (–1464). Piero della Francesca paints frescoes in S. Francesco, Arezzo (–1459).
1453 The Metropolitan of Moscow assumes leadership of the Orthodox Church.	**1456** Johann Gutenberg prints his Bible at Mainz, using the movable type he had devised several years earlier in Strasbourg.	
1457 Death of Italian humanist Lorenzo Valla.	**1454** Johann Gutenberg produces the Indulgences, the first document printed in Europe.	**1454** Paolo Ucello paints three episodes from the *Battle of S Romano* (–1457).
1458 Battista da Verona writes *De ordine docendi et studendi*, a manual on humanist education.	**1455** Alvise da Cádamosto explores the rivers Senegal and Gambia and discovers five Cape Verde Islands (–1456).	**1457** *Judith and Holofernes*, bronze sculpture by Donatello (–1460).
1459 Death of Poggio Bracciolini.		**1458** The Palazzo Pitti, Florence begun, possibly designed by Filippo Brunelleschi. Jean Fouquet completes illuminated manuscript of *Les Grands Chroniques de France*.
1463 Marsilio Ficino translates the dialogues of Plato into Latin (–1469).	**1465** First Italian printing press established at Subiaco, and first Swiss printing press at Basle.	
	1466 Louis XI of France establishes silk industry at Lyons, using experienced Italian workers.	**1463** Andrea della Robbia sculpts *Bambini*, on the façade of the Foundling Hospital, Florence.
1467 The first ballad about William Tell appears.		**1465** Giovanni Bellini paints *The Agony in the Garden*.
	1469 Fernão Gomez crosses the equator and explores the Gold Coast (–1471).	**1466** Giovanni Antonio Amadeo begins sculptural decorations for the Certosa near Pavia.

Index

Page numbers in *italics* refer to captions to illustrations.

The Publisher: Ghost House Books
Distributed by Lone Pine Publishing

10145 – 81 Avenue	1808 – B Street NW, Suite 140
Edmonton, AB T6E 1W9	Auburn, WA 98001
Canada	USA

Website: http://www.ghostbooks.net

Library and Archives Canada Cataloguing in Publication

Mott, A.S. (Allan S.), 1975–
     Gothic ghost stories / A.S. Mott; Jessica Casey Dean, illustrator.

     ISBN 1-894877-39-X

     1. Ghost stories, Canadian (English) I. Dean, Jessica Casey, 1974– II. Title.
PS8576.O88G68 2004   398.2'0971'05   C2004-904087-1

Editorial Director: Nancy Foulds
Project Editors: Shelagh Kubish, Lee Craig
Production Manager: Gene Longson
Cover Design: Gerry Dotto
Layout & Production: Jeff Fedorkiw
Illustrations: Jessica Dean

We acknowledge the financial support of the Government of Canada through the Book Publishing Industry Development Program (BPIDP) for our publishing activities.

PC: 05